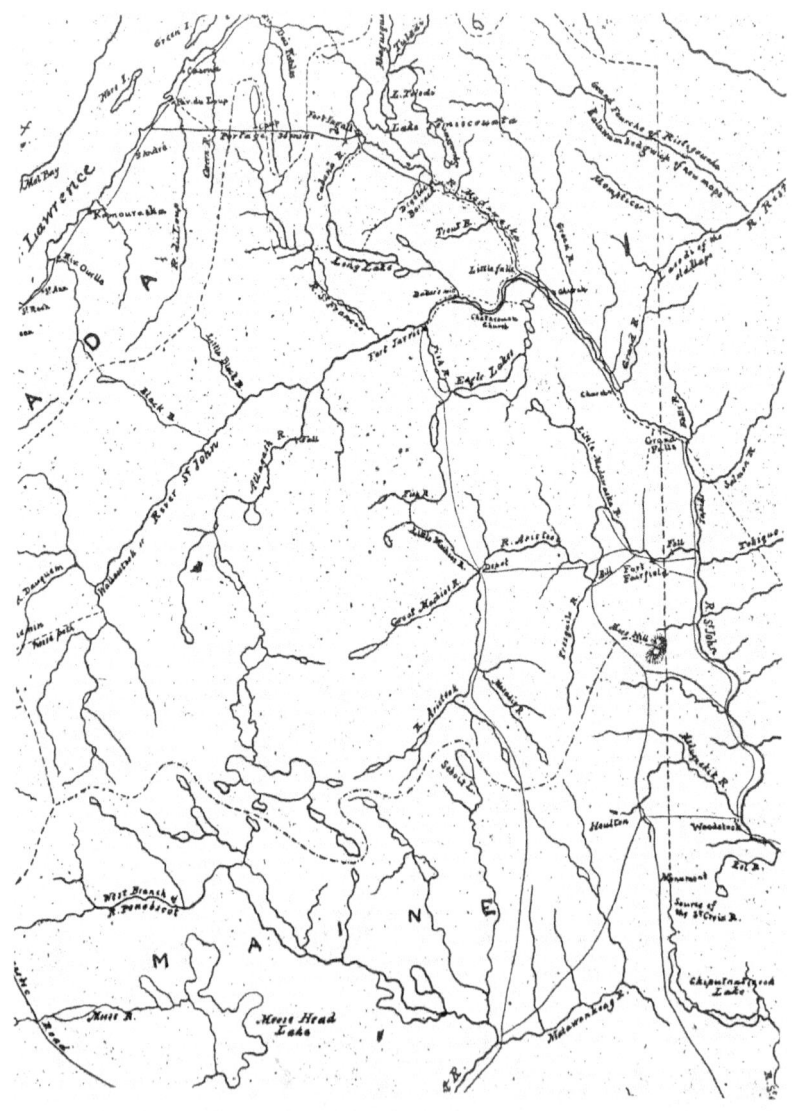

TIES OF COMMON BLOOD

A History of Maine's Northeast Boundary Dispute with Great Britain

1783–1842

Geraldine Tidd Scott

HERITAGE BOOKS
2014

HERITAGE BOOKS
AN IMPRINT OF HERITAGE BOOKS, INC.

Books, CDs, and more—Worldwide

For our listing of thousands of titles see our website at
www.HeritageBooks.com

Published 2014 by
HERITAGE BOOKS, INC.
Publishing Division
5810 Ruatan Street
Berwyn Heights, Md. 20740

Copyright © 1992 Geraldine Tidd Scott

All rights reserved. No part of this book may be reproduced or transmitted in any form or by any means, electronic or mechanical, including photocopying, recording or by any information storage and retrieval system without written permission from the author, except for the inclusion of brief quotations in a review.

International Standard Book Numbers
Paperbound: 978-1-55613-541-5
Clothbound: 978-0-7884-6062-3

ACKNOWLEDGMENTS

I wish to express my gratitude to all who have aided me in the research and writing of this book. I owe special thanks to the staff of the Maine Historical Society Library. I am grateful to my husband, Mahlon Scott, for his steadfast support; to Wilbur Harding Tidd, for his valuable contributions concerning Maine geography; to Greg Scott, Ph. D., for his inspiration and advice; to William David Barry, whose concern for many writers included me; to Robert Taylor, for giving a helping hand; to Elizabeth Ashby, Dr. and Mrs. Sidney Branson, Thomas Gaffney, Ph. D.; Arthur Gerrier, deceased; Lorraine Tidd Little, Elizabeth Miller, Courtney Scott, Jill MacKay Scott, Stephen Seames, Millard and Marguerite Simpson, James Swanson, Marian Tidd Swanson, Patricia Street, Joan Thibodeau Tidd, James Vickery and Margaret Lowell Weeks for their encouragement and cooperation.

This book is dedicated
to every descendant
of all residents of the Disputed Territory,
and especially to those who, like myself,
had grandparents from both sides of the Line,
and loved them all, despite their differences.

CONTENTS

List of Illustrations		xi-xii
Foreword		xiii
Preface		xv-xvi
Introduction	Silhouettes, Shadows and Smoke	xvii

PART ONE: EVOLUTION

Chapter I   The Evolution of Maine's Northeast
Boundary Dispute with Great Britain   1-17
The War of 1812; The War of 1812 in the District of Maine of Massachusetts

Chapter II   The Evolution of Claims in
The Disputed Territory   18-35
The American Claim; The British Claim; The Wulastegwiak; The Acadians; Massachusetts Land Sales and Grants in the District of Maine; The Kennebec-Madawaska Connection.

PART TWO: CONTENTION

Chapter III   Contention for Jurisdiction of the
Disputed Territory   36-58
Maine Statehood; Contention Begins; Governor Enoch Lincoln Contends for Jurisdiction; John Baker Charged with Sedition and Trespass on Crown Lands; The Madawaska Riot; The Arrest of John Baker; The First Trial of John Baker.

Chapter IV Contention During the First Negotiation
           for a Boundary Settlement   59-70
           The Second Trial of John Baker; John Baker is
           Released from Jail; John G. Deane's Investigation
           of the Location of the Original Northwest Corner
           Boundary Marker; Construction of Hancock Barracks
           and the Military Road.

Chapter V Contention During Arbitration of the
           Northeast Boundary Dispute   71-93
           Great Britain Moves to Strengthen her Claim by
           Instituting the Office of Warden of the Disputed
           Territory; Arbitration Begins; The Award of the
           Arbiter Received and Rejected; Meanwhile, on the
           Northeastern Frontier; Madawaska's First Town
           Meeting; Madawaska's Second Town Meeting; The
           Trial of Hunnewell, Wheeler and Savage.

Chapter VI The Second Negotiation for a
           Boundary Settlement   94-122
           A British Attempt at Sovereignty Over the Disputed
           Territory; Maine Contends for Jurisdiction Through
           Ebenezer Greely; Maine Prepares for a Confronta-
           tion; Maine Surveys the Northeast Boundary; British
           Troops Move Through the Disputed Territory on the
           Way to Quell Rebellion in Quebec.

PART THREE   CONFRONTATION

Chapter VII Civil Confrontation   123-147
           John Fairfield becomes Governor; A Civil Posse
           is Organized to Protect State Property; The
           Departure of the Civil Posse; The Capture of Maine
           Land Agent Rufus McIntire; Charles Jarvis Is
           Appointed Provisional Land Agent; Sir John Harvey
           Mobilizes the New Brunswick Militia; The Examin-
           ation of McIntire, Cushman, Webster and Bartlett;
           The Capture of James Maclauchlan, British Warden
           of the Disputed Territory; With the Civil Posse
           on the Disputed Territory.

Chapter VIII Military Confrontation   148-187
Governor Fairfield Mobilizes the Maine Militia;
With the Civil Posse on the Aroostook River as
Hodsdon's Troops Advance; The Bangor Rifle Corps;
Justification; General Winfield Scott Called to
Washington; Military Activities At Augusta; The
Civil Posse Moves Eastward along the Aroostook
River; Meanwhile, In New Brunswick and Nova
Scotia; Charles Jarvis Establishes Fort Fairfield;
Major General Hodsdon and Staff Arrive in Houlton;
British Troops Arrive in the Disputed Territory.

Chapter IX National Attention Is Focused
Upon Maine   188-220
Major General Winfield Scott, the Great Pacificator;
The Winfield Scott-John Harvey Relationship; Major
General Hodsdon with the Militia At Houlton; Political Intrigue Reaches the Frontier; Land Agent Rufus
McIntire and the Civil Force at Fort Fairfield;
Hodsdon Moves His Troops from Houlton to Fort Fairfield; Brigadier General George W. Bachelder Leads
Troops to Hodsdon's Western Flank; Military and
Political Affairs in New Brunswick, March, 1839.

PART FOUR: ARMISTICE
WITH CONFRONTATION AND NEGOTIATION

Chapter X Armistice   221-242
Armistice; Demilitarization in New Brunswick;
The Civil Posse Prepares to Cope with Maine
Militia Withdrawal; Plans are Laid for Blockhouses
At Fort Fairfield; Maine Militia Withdrawal Begins;
Colonel Jarvis and Captain Nye Lead Civil Volunteers in Aroostook; The Militia Units Return to
Bangor; Militia Units Are Inspected, Mustered
and Discharged.

Chapter XI Waiting for a Treaty   243-261
Return of the Bangor Rifles; Trespassing on the Disputed
Territory Continues; The Attack on Fort Fairfield; The Fish
River Expedition, Soldier Pond and Fort Jarvis.

Chapter XII Continued Friction
in the Disputed Territory 262-277
British Troops Are Stationed at Temiscouata; The
Mudge-Featherstonhaugh Fluff; British Troops are
Stationed at Madawaska; Edward Kent Wins Second
Term as Governor; U.S. Artillery Stationed at Fort
Jarvis -Fort Kent and at Fort Fairfield;
Tyler, Too! A Postscript to this Period.

PART FIVE: RESOLUTION

CHAPTER XIII Final Negotiation 278-292
The Influence of Francis Ormond Jonathan Smith;
Final Negotiations; The Treaty of Washington, 1842;
Repercussions.

CONCLUSION: Reflections 293-294

BIBLIOGRAPHY 295-306

APPENDICES:

Appendix I: Settlers in the Disputed Territory
and in Neighboring Aroostook
County Towns in 1820, 1830 and
1840. 307-322
Appendix II: Canadian Timber Harvesters on
the St. John and Aroostook Rivers
in 1825. 323-324
Appendix III: Federal Troops in Aroostook
County 325-341
Appendix IV: Settlers on the Disputed
Territory in 1831 342-350
Appendix V: The Land Agent's Civil Posse 351-356
Appendix VI: Muster Rolls: Maine Militia 357-365
Appendix VII: Commercial and Political
Establishments in New Brunswick 366-375

Appendix VIII: Commercial Establishments in
Northern Maine: Aroostook, Washington and Penobscot Counties   376-394

Appendix IX: Verified Land Claims of Aroostook
Land Holders, 1854 and 1857   395-404

INDEX   405-445

LIST OF ILLUSTRATIONS

Frontispiece: Detail from *Sketch of the Disputed Territory, showing the Military Posts occupied by the British and Americans in 1840*, compiled from the Reports and Sketches of Lieutenants Bainbridge and Simmons, Royal Engineers, and other sources, under the direction of Lieutenant Colonel Oldfield, K. H., commanding the Royal Engineers in Canada, Head Quarters at Montreal, 12 August 1840. National Archives, Washington, D. C.

Map: Plan of the Northeastern part of Maine, made to accompany *A Circular from the Land Office Descriptive of the Public Lands of Maine*, Noah Barker, Land Agent, 1858, page xiv.

Map: Maine: War of 1812, *Maine Bicentennial Atlas, An Historical Survey*, Gerald E. Morris, editor, Maine Historical Society, Portland, 1976, facing page 10.

Images of John Baker and Sophia Baker from "Barbara Frietchie of Aroostook," by Alice Lord, *Lewiston Journal*, November and December, 1917; images of Charles S. Daveis and Governor Enoch Lincoln from H. S. Burrage, *Maine in the Northeast Boundary Controversy*, printed for the State of Maine, Portland, 1919, facing page 66.

A *camera lucida* drawing: *Katahdin, bearing about south 30 East, and Tohudnahunk, bearing about South 20 East, as seen from the eastern shore of Lake Chamberlin*, by artist P. Harry, made for Talcott's Northeast Boundary Survey of 1842, National Archives Record Group No 76, Series 11, No. 1, facing page 67.

Lithograph: Sir John Harvey, 1778-1852, by James Henry Lynch (d 1868), after Stephen Pearce (1819-1904), Collection of the New Brunswick Museum, Webster Canadiana Collection; image of Daniel Webster from Charles W. March, *Reminiscences of Congress*, Baker and Scribner, NY 1850; image of General Winfield Scott, from *Memoirs of Lieutenant General Scott, LL. D.*, Sheldon and Company, NY, 1864; image of Francis Ormond Jonathan Smith from Maine Historical Society *Newsletter*, Vol. 10, No 2, November, 1970, facing page 192.

Images: Governor John Fairfield, Governor Edward Kent and Reuel Williams, from H. S. Burrage, *Maine in the Northeast Boundary Controversy*, Portland, 1919; image of Rufus McIntire from *Historical Collections of the Piscataquis County, Maine*, 1910, facing page 193.

Sketch of Fort Kent, December, 1842, from Collections of the Maine Historical Society; photograph: The Original Fort Jarvis-Fort Kent Block House, Marian Swanson, 1983, facing page 248.

Sketch: The Larger of two Blockhouses at Fort Fairfield, from H. S. Burrage, *Maine in the Northeast Boundary Controversy*, Portland, 1919; photograph: The Reproduction of the Smaller of Two Blockhouses at Fort Fairfield, Marian Swanson, 1983, facing page 249.

Map: Maine: Northeast Boundary Settlement, *Maine Bicentennial Atlas, An Historical Survey*, Gerald E. Morris, editor, Maine Historical Society, Portland, 1976, facing page 290.

Map: Detail of northeastern Maine, showing township designations, from Official Transportation Map, 1979-1980, Maine Department of Transportation, facing page 291.

FOREWORD

When the District of Maine of Massachusetts achieved statehood in 1820, the new state of Maine found that her most difficult problem was the location and marking of her boundaries. The history of the northeast boundary dispute, as it involved the actual participants at all levels of authority, both British and American, has not previously been written. One worthy volume, published in 1919, gives an overview of the dispute. Single chapters in several other dependable publications develop certain aspects of the problem. A doctoral thesis examines the tremendous influence of one particular individual. A scholarly article in the *New England Quarterly*, June, 1989, examines Maine and States' Rights in this period. Some newspaper accounts of small segments of the story are reliable; some depend on hearsay and bear little resemblance to documentary evidence. Fortunately, numerous institutions have preserved many journals, documents, speeches, letter books and collections of correspondence of the participants on both sides of the controversy. These sources have made possible a completely fresh look at Maine history from 1820 to 1842.

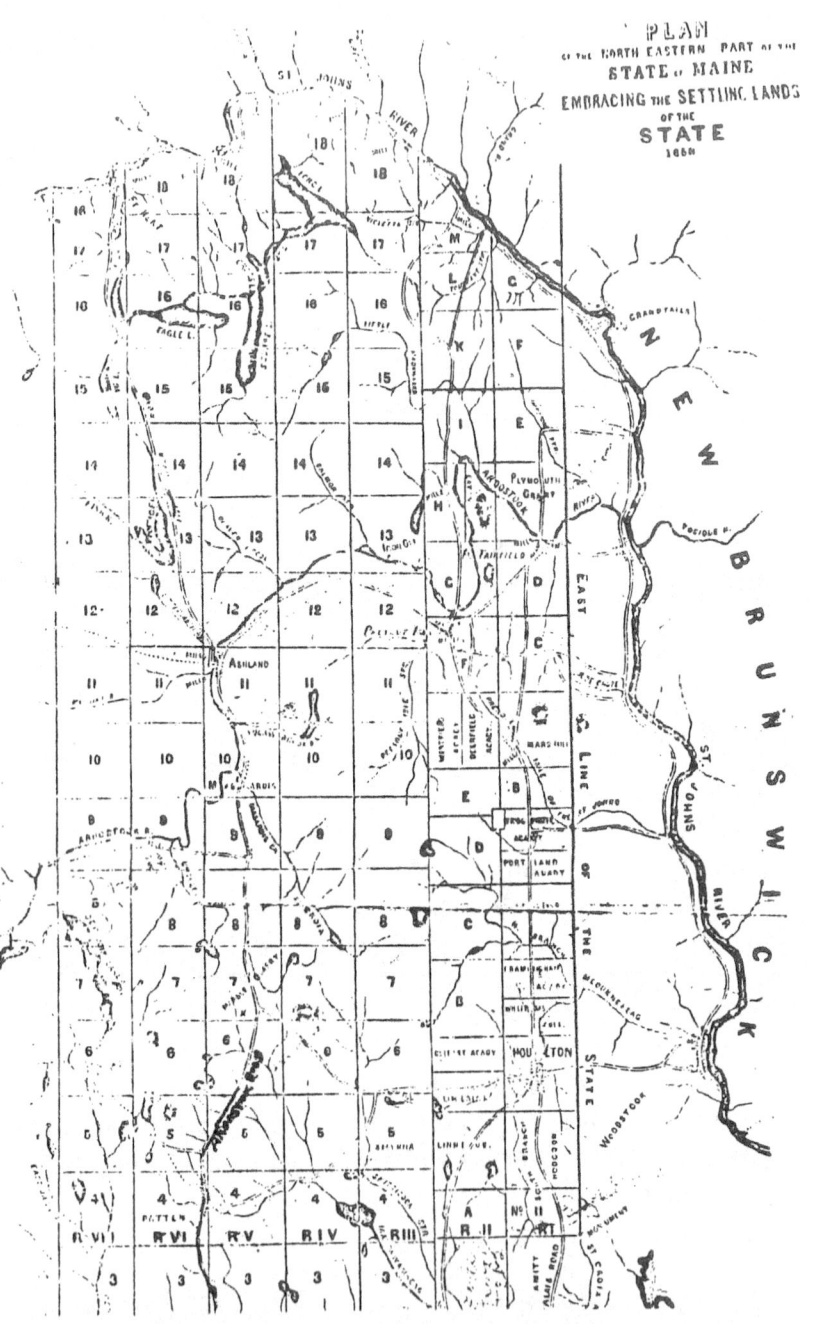

Plan of the Northeastern Part of Maine,
to accompany A Circular from the Land Office
Noah Barker, Land Agent, 1858.

PREFACE

In the 19th century, General Winfield Scott of the United States Army was looking far into the future when he wrote to Sir John Harvey, Lieutenant Governor of New Brunswick, on March 9, 1839, these prophetic words:

The ties of common blood, language, civil liberty, laws, customs, manners and interests must, in a reasonable period, that is, as soon as we can forget past wars, and they are almost forgotten, work out a strong compact for reciprocal feelings far more binding than written engagements, which the other nations of the world would be wholly unable to dissolve or resist. ... for who shall say what hostile combinations ... may not take place among other nations to require the united strength of England and America for the safety of their common principles and interests.

In the twentieth century, during World Wars I and II, the British and the Americans were unfailing allies in struggles that demanded their utmost cooperation. A feeling of comradeship had been developed that had been non-existent during the Revolutionary War, the War of 1812 and the twenty-two years of tension (1820-1842) that almost ended in a clash of arms. "Ties of common blood" counted for very little during those years, as will be demonstrated in the following chapters.

Early cartographers, both British and American, had delineated a northeast boundary for Maine that ran directly north from the Bay of Fundy to the highlands south of the St. Lawrence River. Royal commissions to Lieutenant Governors of Lower Canada, Nova Scotia and New Brunswick had verbally described their dominions as shown on the early maps. The Treaty of Paris of 1783 described that line and especially after the agreement on the location of the River St Croix, in 1798, there was a general understanding of the location of "the Line" even though it had not been officially surveyed and marked.

However, during the War of 1812, the British government became increasingly aware of the inconvenience of having their traditional land communication route between New Brunswick and their military headquarters at Quebec, via *Rivier du Loup*, on the St Lawrence River, pass through the northern portion of the hostile territory of the Commonwealth of Massachusetts. With this realization, diplomatic and economic struggles began which might, without the intervention of certain peacemakers, have ended in a third bloody confrontation.

New research in archival sources brings new understandings of those struggles. This chronology deals with the experiences of citizens and officials at the local, state and provincial levels, far removed from the diplomats at London and Washington. It reveals human strengths and weaknesses, which, when weighed in the balance, bring feelings of pride to the people of both Maine and New Brunswick. Their forebears, as instruments of their respective governments, tried their best to do "the right thing," as far as their knowledge and sense of duty allowed them to understand it.

INTRODUCTION

Silhouettes, Shadows and Smoke

It's the year 1839. The night is bitterly cold and dark. Part of the Aroostook Expedition has paused on its way to Maine's northeastern frontier. Shadowy sentries stand silhouetted against the snow at the edges of the encampment. Horses, tethered to a rope stretched between tree trunks, chomp hay and grain, toss their heads and whinny to each other. Men hover around blazing campfires, taking what warmth they can get, for the cold damp air portends a storm, and they have miles to go before they reach their posts along the Aroostook River.

A breeze runs through tall spruces and mast pines. Swishing branches scatter conversations: "Bloody British," "chase those Red Coats out of the territory," "those Bluenoses better watch out," "General Hodsdon's coming up," "when will the supply wagons catch up?" and "heard one feller's toes were so frozen that the surgeon had to amputate!" Regimental flags aflutter in the firelight identify these troops as Maine Militia. In the morning their drummer's beaten rhythms will shake them awake and urge them along, but smoke swirls up as the fires are fed and the darkness of fifteen decades hides their faces. Their names and deeds will be obscured by time.

Shapes in the smoke, sounds in the snow give us few clues, but archival sources will bring light into their encampment, meaning to their words, faces to their shadowy forms.

We begin as they began, with the evolution of the boundary dispute, and follow it to its peaceful solution.

PART ONE: EVOLUTION

CHAPTER I

THE EVOLUTION OF MAINE'S NORTHEAST BOUNDARY DISPUTE WITH GREAT BRITAIN

In order to understand the attitudes of the people of Maine, New Brunswick and Nova Scotia during the period of active boundary dispute, 1820 to 1842, it is necessary to review the struggles of the Revolutionary War and the War of 1812.

In the eighteenth century, British colonists in North America, simply by being far removed from their seat of government, had begun to experience new kinds of freedoms. They had organized their own institutions and had begun to resist oppressive measures, especially taxation without representation. Opposition came from the economic beneficiaries of the old society. The clash of opposing interests brought about the American Revolution, the most significant event in modern history.

As early as 1580, English explorers had discovered North America's vast treasure of masts and naval stores. Depletion of timber in England and the Baltic region had caused the British navy to obtain timber from Bermuda and Virginia as early as 1615. The amount of timber required to keep trade and war ships afloat, to protect Britain's very existence during long wars with nations on the continent, was tremendous. In the Colonies, magnificent white pines for ship masts were abundant. New England sent its first cargo of masts to England in 1634.[1]

Beginning with the reign of William and Mary, in 1688, to preserve the mast pines for exclusive British use, the old mark for naval property, a hack-mark shaped like a crow's track and called the "Broad Arrow" was used to reserve trees that measured twenty-four or more inches in diameter for the King's exclusive use. Mast ships were built or modified to carry from forty to one hundred masts, as well as many yards and spars. Masts were loaded through *le sabord*, special stern ports, cut close to the water's edge.[2]

By 1772, the District of Maine of Massachusetts had surpassed New Hampshire as the leading colonial exporter of masts. A few mast ships had sailed to England in the spring of 1775 with the last American pine masts the British would acquire for seven years. The British naval administration failed to replenish the stock from other sources. During the Revolution, many British ships were forced to put to sea with worn out masts and timbers infected with dry rot. In their last naval battle, hurricane-force winds that battered the King's ships did relatively little damage to the victorious French fleet.[3] On September 3, 1783, the final Treaty of Paris of 1783 was signed.

In 1793, and again in 1802 and 1803, Britain went to war with France over the area that is now Belgium. Admiral Nelson defeated the French fleet at Trafalgar in 1805, but this war continued until the Battle of Waterloo

---

1   Robert G. Albion, *Forests and Sea Power, 1652-1862*, Cambridge: Harvard University Press, 1926, 231-232.
2   Albion, loc. cit., 238-254; Lower, Arthur M., *Great Britain's Woodyard, British America and the Timber Trade, 1763-1867*, Montreal: McGill-Queens University Press, 204, 227-228, 346-355.
3   Richard G. Wood, *A History of Lumbering in Maine, 1820-1861*, Orono: University of Maine Press, 1961, 28-29. See Albion, loc. cit., Chapter VII, for detailed information on dry rot and worn masts.

in June, 1815. Concurrently, 1812 to 1815, Britain was at war with the United States.

In 1804, Britain's storehouse of masts on the St. John River, in what had been Nova Scotia but had become New Brunswick in 1784, was almost untouched. Her major source of ship building materials was in Upper Canada and Lower Canada, on the St. Lawrence River. The British were prevented, by trade embargos, from buying at American markets, but Vermonters' proximity to the timber market in Quebec encouraged them to ignore the law and sell vital supplies of oak. A constant procession of ships from Quebec and from the Mirimichi and St. John Rivers in New Brunswick carried timber to England. Part of these cargoes came from the upper St. John River Valley, in the northern part of the District of Maine, that would become known as the Disputed Territory.[4] When the United States declared war on Britain in 1812, the first land strike came in the region of Upper Canada, near the source of her timber supply.

The War of 1812

General Winfield Scott, one of the key figures in the settlement of the northeast boundary dispute, the man who would become a trouble-shooter for several future American presidents, commented in his *Memoirs* that he could not understand "how two kindred nations, the United States and Great Britain, could brutalize each other as they did in the War of 1812."[5] The unnatural attitude of the royal government in this supposed parent-child relationship is partly explained by its desperate need for ship building materials to carry on a life-and-death struggle with France and its desire to expand the British empire. Kinship succumbed to British needs and

---

4 Lower, loc. cit., 357-359.
5 Winfield Scott, *Memoirs of Lieutenant General Winfield Scott*, New York: Sheldon and Company, 1864, 176.

American determination that the United States would survive attempted British domination with their resources intact.

Other causes of the War of 1812 were interference with American shipping and the fact that President Madison believed that the British were inciting incidents among the Indians in the Northwest Territory. This large tract of land lay south and west of the Great Lakes. To the north was the former Province of Quebec, which had been divided into Upper Canada and Lower Canada in 1791. Upper Canada, with its capital at Newark, now Niagara on the Lake, bordered the Great Lakes. York, now Toronto, was capital of Lower Canada, which extended from the lower St. Lawrence River north to Labrador. Several famous fortifications stood at intervals along the St. Lawrence River. Sir George Prevost, Governor General of the Canadas, was in command of the British North American troops along their twelve hundred miles of frontier.[6]

1812

On the 19th of June, 1812, Congress obliged President Madison by declaring war against Great Britain. When Lieutenant Colonel Winfield Scott was ordered to Philadelphia to collect companies for his regiment, the States were not prepared for war on land and America's situation at sea was almost hopeless. The British navy had a thousand warships and the United States had less than twenty frigates and sloops of war.

The American Secretary of War believed that the Americans could take Upper and Lower Canada without soldiers; he had only to send in officers, and the people, disaffected toward their own government, would rally round the American flag. However, by August 3rd, General

---

6 Lady Edgar, *General Brock*, Toronto: Morang and Co. Ltd., 53-5, 157-158, 190-201.

William Hull's disastrous attempt to enter Canada on the Niagara frontier had failed.[7] American leadership had miscalculated the mood of the opposition. Especially strong was the resistance of the United Empire Loyalists. They were determined enemies, still suffering both the physical and psychological wounds of the American Revolution, and to offer those men and women "freedom" was to add insult to injury.[8]

Cannons roared, muskets spewed death and defeat for both sides at Sandwich, Fort Dearborn and Queenstown Heights. At the end of 1812, the Americans had only their sea victories to console them. The *Constitution* had defeated the *Guerriere* and Captain Isaac Hull was a hero. The *Wasp* had captured the British sloop *Frolic*, and Captain Stephen Decatur had captured His Majesty's frigate *Macedonian*. The *Constitution* sank the British frigate *Java*. Four American victories had damaged only a small proportion of the British fleet, but had caused consternation in Britain and raised the morale of the Americans.[9]

1813

American armed forces reorganized in 1813 and attempted to take back the Michigan territory surrendered by Hull. Pitched battles, slaughter, treachery and all of the horrors of Indian warfare characterized encounters at Raisin River, Malden, Fort Meigs, Fort Defiance, Fort George and Beaver Dam.[10]

The experience of the 104th New Brunswick Regiment exemplifies the devotion and determination of its men to the British cause. This unit had departed by

---

[7] Ibid., 27-28; 202-215.
[8] C. Prestwood Lucas, *The Canadian War of 1812*, Oxford: Clarendon Press, 1906, 7, 15.
[9] F. F. Bierne, *The War of 1812* New York: E. P. Dutton and Company, Inc., 1949, 34.-5..
[10] Beirne, loc. cit., 139-153; 162-65; C. P. Lucas, loc. cit., 17-18.

companies on successive days from Fredericton, beginning on the 16th of February, 1813, when the temperature stood at seventeen degrees below zero. They had travelled by companies, single file, on showshoes, six men to pull each toboggan-load of supplies. In the wilderness the men had taken turns breaking trail with their snowshoes. At night they had cut firewood and erected bough shelters. Sometimes the night temperature went down to twenty-seven degrees below zero. For seven days they travelled through towns along the St. John River. They moved on toward Temiscouata; and over the Grand Portage, where they were actually blown back by a fierce wind and were forced to spend three days in shelters. Their food consisted of biscuits and salt pork, which they cooked on sticks over their campfire. A month later, Sir George Prevost and the people of Quebec greeted them warmly and cheered them on to Kingston. After fifty-two days, seven hundred miles on foot, about five hundred and fifty men paraded at Kingston; some of them eventually died from the exertion of this trip. They suffered many casualties during their tour of duty. One of their valiant officers, Lieutenant James A. Maclauchlan, would later figure prominently in the boundary dispute, as British Warden of the Disputed Territory.[11]

At Stony Creek, in May, 1813, Lieutenant Colonel John Harvey, who would be Lieutenant Governor of New Brunswick during the height of the boundary dispute, personally led his troops into hand-to-hand combat against Winfield Scott's command. In a night attack, he approached Scott's encampment undiscovered. "The sentries at the outskirts of the camp were bayoneted in the quietest manner" and Harvey led his men into the center of the American camp. They fell upon the artillery and bayoneted the men at the guns. This attack saved the Niagara

---

[11] See W. S. MacNutt, *New Brunswick, A History: 1784-1867*, Toronto: Macmillan of Canada, 1963, 157-160. See also "The One Hundred and Fourth", Vol. I, *New Brunswick Magazine*, July, 1898, 305-315.

District and Kingston for the British, but the nature of the war changed "after that most manly affair."[12]

At sea, American Captain James Lawrence, aboard the *Chesapeake*, did battle with the *Shannon* near Boston Light and gained fame with his rallying cry, "Don't give up the ship!" Then, in September, the American brig *Enterprize* battled the brig *Boxer* at the mouth of the Kennebec River. Lieutenant William Burroughs of the *Enterprize* captured the British ship but both he and Commander William Blythe of the *Boxer* were killed in the battle.

Lieutenant Oliver Hazard Perry, on Lake Erie, with one hundred and fifty seamen and officers, in constant danger from British attack, had built and launched three gunboats and two twenty-ton brigs. His flagship was the *Lawrence*, and a large square motto flag of blue muslin flew from the mast with Lawrence's dying words emblazoned with white letters, *Don't give up the Ship!* Perry's nine vessels, with fifty-four guns[13] met the British fleet with six ships and sixty-three guns. After the battle, Perry wrote to William Henry Harrison, on the back of an old letter, "We have met the enemy and they are ours; 2 ships, 2 brigs, 1 schooner and one sloop. Yours with great esteem and respect, O. H. Perry." The victory placed Lake Erie in American control and raised the morale of the nation.

Encouraged by Perry's success, Harrison, supported by four thousand Kentuckians, including a thousand mounted riflemen and two hundred and sixty Indian warriors, met Colonel Procter at Fort Malden. Proctor, with one thousand regulars, had the aid of Tecumseh and three thousand five hundred warriors. Guns spoke and bodies broke; the Kentuckians engaged in hand-to-hand fighting

---

12 James Hannay, *The War of 1812*, *Nova Scotia Historical Society*, Vol. XI, 1901, 175; Lucas, loc. cit., 97; Henry J. Morgan, *Sketches of Celebrated Canadians*.

13 Bierne, loc. cit., 206-212.

with the Indians. Tecumseh bravely directed the fighting, but was killed and his men fled. Then the Battle of the Thames ended organized Indian opposition in the Northwest Territory and brought American control to Detroit and Lake Erie.[14]

In the second land campaign on the Niagara frontier, seven thousand Americans drove toward Montreal. On November 11th, the inconclusive Battle of Chrysler's Field was fought in a sea of slush. Then Americans devastated Canadian towns and the British retaliated in like destruction of American settlements.

1814

In 1814, Brigadier General Winfield Scott, in charge of a camp of instruction at Buffalo, instituted the first formal large-scale military drill in the United States Army. This inspired new confidence within the army units, but did not replace the lesson learned in the Revolution, the value of their own unique military style, patterned after Indian warfare.[15]

By April of 1814, Britain's war with Napoleon had ended, releasing sixteen thousand seasoned troops to the Canadian frontier. In May, with the Americans outnumbered ten to one, the British captured Fort Oswego.[16] On July 3rd, Winfield Scott's brigade captured Fort Erie. The battle of Chippewa ensued. Scott's men advanced, halted, fired and then moved on with deadly effect. In the final

---

14 Hannay, loc. cit. 213, 219. Harrison had Wyandottes under Chief Lewis, Sawnoese under Black Hoof, and Seneca under Black Snake.
15 Scott, loc. cit., 118.-19, 121.
16 Lucas, loc. cit., 165. One of the officers commanding a company at Oswego was Captain Rufus McIntire, who would become Maine's Land Agent in 1839. He had enlisted in the United States Army on June 6, 1812, five days after President Madison's declaration of war. *Register of Enlisted Men in the U. S. Army*, Vol. 76, p. 213, #5937, National Archives, Washington, D C; Hannay, loc. cit., 281-282; Beirne, loc. cit., 251-252.

charge "the men stopped firing, threw bayonets forward and advanced to the shock." The clash of bayonets left the field strewn with enemy dead and wounded. This victory raised American morale; bonfires blazed and bells rang, but yet another battle was to be fought at Lundy's Lane.[17]

During the battle of Chippewa, New England leaders had met at the Hartford Convention and had deliberated possible secession from the Union. In its report, on January 6, 1815, the Convention had severely scolded the administration for its conduct of the war. Nullification had been threatened if conscription were applied.[18]

On August 24th and 25th, 1814, a British fleet that had lain at anchor in the Potomac for a year, arrived at the United States capital at Washington, D. C., burned the Capitol, the Arsenal, the Treasury, the War Office and the White House. The capital was almost undefended, because General Armstrong and his military leaders had believed that nearby Baltimore, with its shipping, commerce and privateers, was a more logical target.

On the south side of Baltimore stood a modern fortress, Fort McHenry. On September 13, 1814, British fire bomb vessels attacked. The noise and glare of the missiles had a terrifying effect on troops, but did small damage to the fort. Francis Scott Key was sent, under a flag of truce, aboard a cartel ship, to obtain the release of a Dr. Beanes, a physician. Key, a virtual prisoner on the ship, watched the American flag, occasionally visible "in the rocket's red glare," and wrote what became the national anthem, *The Star-Spangled Banner*. The British, driven back, abandoned the attempt against Baltimore.[19]

During this time, General Andrew Jackson had been preparing for a British attempt at conquest of Louisiana, which had become the 18th state of the Union in 1812.

---

17 Beirne, loc. cit., 251-252, 130-131.
18 Samuel Eliot Morrison, *The Maritime History of Massachusetts*, Boston: Houghton Mifflin Co., 1941, 210-212,
19 Ibid., 309-316, 316-319.

Supported by six thousand Tennesseans, he manned fortifications, armed batteries at strategic locations and commanded a flotilla of gunboats. From their Jamaica rendezvous, British regular forces numbering at least ten thousand men aboard fifty ships arrived about December 9th, 1814, in the Gulf of Mexico. A naval engagement ensued. On December 24th, 1814, unknown to the combatants, the Treaty of Ghent was signed, ending all hostilities of the War of 1812. However, on December 22nd, British troops landed fifteen miles from New Orleans. Jackson led two thousand men to meet them. Attacks came intermittently until January 8th, when, at the Battle of New Orleans, the British were stunningly defeated. On February 16, 1815, when the Treaty of Ghent was ratified by the United States Senate, peace was publicly proclaimed.

The War of 1812 in the District of Maine of Massachusetts

The Embargo of 1807 had had a tragic effect upon the economy of the District of Maine of Massachusetts.[20] Exports had dropped, jobs for laborers and seamen had become scarce and merchants and shipowners had been driven into bankruptcy. An unemployment rate of about sixty percent had sent hundreds of Portlanders to soup kitchens. Vessels lay rotting at the wharves all along the

---

20 The District of Maine, formerly known as Yorkshire, extended to the western limit of North Yarmouth, being "That whole tract of land beyond the river of Piscataqua northerly, together with the Isle of Shoals, within our said bounds in 1652. By 1685, Massachusetts assumed jurisdiction of this District, Yorkshire's boundaries were reestablished in 1716, and in 1760, Yorkshire was divided into York, Cumberland and Lincoln Counties. In 1778 the Continental Congress made the three eastern counties a judicial district, called the District of Maine. By 1812, the District of Maine had eight organized counties. Stanley B. Atwood, *The Length and Breadth of Maine*, Orono: U. of Maine Press, 1971; H. W. Richardson, *York Deeds*, 1887, Portland, Vol. I, 74.

Maine coast, and perishable goods went to waste in the warehouses. Widespread smuggling between Maine and New Brunswick became a means of survival and profit.[21]

At the outbreak of hostilities, on July 25, 1812, the people of Eastport had met and laid the groundwork for continued trade with New Brunswick. British policy makers encouraged Maine coastal residents to break federal laws "without awakening any fresh vigilance or restraint on the part of the American government." To facilitate this, they designated Halifax, Shelbourne, St. John and St. Andrews as free ports. This economic warfare brought unknown prosperity to the provinces.[22]

Perhaps partly because of the cooperation of this unique trading community on and near the St. Croix River, the British had believed that "New England might be conquered with kindness," and until the summer of 1814, had deliberately spared the District the ravages of war. However, this policy had been tainted with the same error in judgment that had led the Americans to believe they could easily conquer the Canadas: underestimating the opposition. Republicans in Maine could not be coerced; the majority of the people of Maine were willing to trade but not to be conquered.

When news of the outbreak of war reached Boston, late in June, 1812, Governor Caleb Strong, a Federalist, in opposition to "Mr. Madison's War," defied the president's call for troops and forbade Massachusetts militia to leave the Commonwealth. He claimed that the law of 1797, that allowed the president to call up the militia in times of emergency, did not apply, since, in his view, no emergency existed.[23]

---

21 Harvey Strum, "Smuggling in Maine During the Embargo and the War of 1812", Colby Library *Quarterly*, Vol. XIX, No. 2, 90-97.
22 Herold A. Davis, *An International Community on the St. Croix, 1604-1930* Orono: U. of Maine, 1974, 103-8. MacNutt, loc. cit., 144-7.
23 Alden Bradford, *History of Massachusetts for 200 Years*, Boston: Hilliard, Gray and Co, 1835, 390; Ronald F. Banks, *Maine Becomes a State*, Portland: Maine Historical Society, 1973, 55-569.

William King, a man born to a leadership position on Massachusetts' District of Maine frontier, had made a fortune in shipbuilding, lumbering and world trade. A member of the General Court, in 1808 he had been commissioned as major general in command of the Eleventh Division of the Massachusetts militia, which consisted of four regiments stationed in the District of Maine. During the War of 1812, he directed the District's military defenses. Coastal towns were always alert to the approach of British ships and *shaving mills*, shallow Nova Scotia craft with open decks, carrying sails and sweeps, manned by six or eight armed men, whose mission was to capture coasting vessels and plunder seacoast towns. On September 15, 1813, coastal inhabitants from St. George to Rockland watched the battle between the *Boxer* and the *Enterprize*.[24]

In December of 1813, Congress passed an embargo act so severe as to interdict the coastal trade between ports in the same state. Yankee ingenuity went to work. A fleet of "mud clippers" named the "Horse Marine" operated on the roads of Maine from the Penobscot River to Boston, New York and south. Newspapers reported their arrivals and departures in the same way they reported ship arrivals.[25]

While, as previously mentioned, the British moved against Washington and Baltimore, and while Sir George Prevost, in Upper Canada, advanced into New York State, the British opened a third theatre of operations in the eastern part of the District of Maine. Their purpose was two-fold: occupation of that District would protect their communications between Halifax and Quebec, indispensable to Prevost for sending vital dispatches to London

---

[24] Marion Jacques Smith, *General William King* Camden: Down East Books, 1980, 143-4; Bradford, loc. cit., citing William D Williamson, *History of the State of Maine*, Hallowell: Glazer, Masters & Co, 1839, Vol II, 632; George Prince, "Scrapbook of George Prince Materials," Maine Historical Society, Portland, 32-33.
[25] Bradford, loc. cit., 394-395.

during the winter months; and the New Brunswick Council and the Halifax Committee of Trade, believing that eastern Maine was rightfully theirs, but had been ceded to the United States after the Revolution to appease the Americans, petitioned the British government for the occupation of eastern Maine.[26]

British warships began testing the strength of the resistance they might encounter from the District of Maine. In June, 1814, a British battleship made several attempts at the mouth of the Kennebec River and on the Sheepscot, but was beaten off. Major General King sent militia to defend the coast, and similar British attempts met resistance at Georgetown, Bath, New Harbor, Damariscotta, Friendship, Pemaquid Old Fort, Boothbay and Harpswell.[27]

The first part of a two-pronged British invasion of the District of Maine began July 9, 1814, when Admiral Cochrane dispatched an amphibious force to Eastport, on Moose Island. (The jurisdiction of this island had not been defined by the boundary commission of 1798 when they declared the Schoodic River to be the true St. Croix River and therefore the Maine-New Brunswick boundary.) The naval flotilla assumed attack positions around the island. A 74-gun "ship-of-the-line" opened her ports, ran out her guns, lighted her matches and with men at battle stations, stood ready to bombard the fort. Eastport's situation was hopeless. After the surrender, the enemy declared possession of "what was his due by the treaty of 1783 and no more." Forty or fifty cannon were mounted at the fort, a Deputy Collector of the Customs was appointed, and eight hundred troops were installed in the

---

[26] Barry J. Lohnes, "A New Look at the Invasion of Eastern Maine, 1814," Portland, 1975, Maine Historical Society *Quarterly* Vol. XV, No. 1, Summer, 9-10, citing "Memorial of the Halifax Committee of Trade to Bathurst", October 8, 1813, *Public Archives of Nova Scotia*, Vol. 304, Document 6, No. 66.

[27] U. S. Congress, *House of Representatives Document No. 3*, hereinafter referred to as HRD3, 17, 34, 39, 40., 68, 16..

fort. The squadron departed, but in passing threatened Robbinston, Camden and Thomaston.28

On August 26th, 1814, a second British fleet under Lieutenant General Sherbrooke and Rear Admiral Griffith had left Halifax to carry out the second prong of the invasion of the District of Maine. Their first objective had been to capture the town of Machias, but when they learned that the U. S. Corvette *John Adams* was at Hampden, near Bangor, they changed plans and on August 30th, 1814, began pursuit up the Penobscot River. Three British warships called "74's," two frigates, two sloops of war, an armed schooner as well as ten troop transports and a large tender made up this fleet. Aboard were two British regiments, two rifle companies from another regiment, a detachment of Royal Artillery and Engineers, in all about three thousand five hundred people, including crews and families of army officers. This flotilla paused in Castine long enough to capture the town, invest the fort and take temporary possession of Belfast.29

Sherbrooke secured both sides of Penobscot Bay and sent his expedition up the river. Nightfall found them as far up the river as Marsh Bay. Meanwhile, Captain Morris of the *Adams*, had called for and received the assistance of General Blake and his Bangor-Brewer militiamen. On the first two days of September, the combined force worked feverishly to remove the guns from the *Adams* and place them along the crest of Academy Hill. On the morning of the third day, the British arrived in Hampden. The militia opened fire, but when they saw such large numbers of scarlet uniforms advancing through the fog, they fled. When Morris learned of the militia's retreat, he ordered the guns spiked and the *Adams* burned.

Around noon, the fleet sailed into Bangor, met flags of truce, demanded unconditional surrender and obtained pledges of loyalty from many citizens. Looting

---

28 Williamson, loc. cit., 640-2.
29 Ibid., 651; HRD3, 44-5.

was widespread; seventeen vessels lying at anchor at Bangor and Brewer were burned; Bangor was left in danger of being consumed by flames. The invaders returned to Hampden, looted cargo ships, and on the 6th, proceeded down river to Frankfort, where they demanded oxen, sheep, geese, arms and ammunition. On the 10th of September they captured Machias, East Machias and the Point Battery.[30]

Later in September, Sherbrooke returned to Halifax taking all but two ships of his fleet. He left Eastport defended by six hundred men, including artillery. Upon arrival at Halifax on September 21, 1814, he proclaimed a provincial government established over a new province, which included the whole area between New Brunswick and the Penobscot River and all of the coastal islands.[31]

At Portland, at the beginning of August, in 1814, United States troops took up duty at Fort Scammel and Fort Preble. Residents hauled their vessels up above the bridge and prepared them to be sunk; all valuable property was conveyed from the town, and home owners removed their furniture. The Committee of Safety arranged "telegraphic communication" as far as fifty miles west of Portland and as far east as Pemaquid Point: signals by day, and beacons at night.[32]

General King, still taking precautions to protect against harassment and invasion west of the Penobscot

---

30 John E. Godfrey, *Annals of Bangor*, in *History of Penobscot County, Maine* Cleveland: William Chase and Company, 1882, passim.; Hanney, loc. cit., 349.

31 Williamson, loc. cit., 651-656; Donald B. Webster, Jr., "Penobscot Expedition of 1814," *Tradition*, Vol. IV, No. 1, [January 1961], 58. D. C. Harvey, "The Halifax-Castine Expedition" *Dalhousie Review*, July, 1938, 213. The government set up at Castine after the British occupation of the Penobscot-St Croix region in September, 1814, lasted until the British forces evacuated Castine on April 26, 1815, when Gosselin returned to Halifax with the profits of the customs house in his coffers, from which Dalhousie University was established.

32 HRD3, 59. Sumner to Brooks, September 19, 1814; HRD3, 119.

River, appealed to the Commonwealth for assistance in defense of its District of Maine. Governor Strong commended King for his able generalship, but explained that the federal government had refused to pay the costs of defending the District until such time as he, Strong, agreed to place the militia under federal direction. Determined to resist, in 1814, Strong convened a special session of the General Court. The Federalist-controlled Court authorized Strong to borrow as needed from Commonwealth banks, but most of the funds were used for the protection of Boston and vicinity, and the already occupied District of Maine was given second priority. *Niles Weekly Register* reported that in reality it was not the General Court but Strong himself, who was refusing to assist in rescuing part of his own state from the hands of a foreign enemy. President Madison again tried to nationalize a portion of the Massachusetts militia to form an expeditionary force to be sent against the British at Castine. The leader of the expedition was to be General King. However, Madison could supply no funds for this expedition because the Boston banks, which had liberally lent money to the British, now found themselves lacking funds for this purpose.[33]

On February 6, 1815, the British took formal possession of Bucksport, but on the 15th, news of peace, of the signing of the Treaty of Ghent, reached America. It was received with much joy, "illuminations," discharge of cannon and festive dinners.

In the Province of New Brunswick, disappointment and bitterness followed the signing of the Treaty at Ghent. They felt they had "won the war but lost the peace." The boundary New Brunswick desired, across territory which allowed communication with the Canadas, had been in the minds of the British ministry, but the Duke of Wellington declared that their military position did not warrant demands of this kind upon the United

---
[33] Banks, loc. cit., 60-62; Bradford, loc. cit., 400-40.

States. Renewed negotiation was their only alternative: the Fourth Article of the Treaty of Ghent provided for the appointment of a Commission to determine the ownership of Grand Manan and the islands in Passamaquoddy Bay and the Fifth Article provided for a second Commission to decide the remainder of the Maine-New Brunswick boundary.[34]

The British troops evacuated Castine on April 25, 1815, after an encampment of eight months. Eastport, however, was to remain under British control until Moose Island was restored to the United States under the Treaty of Ghent. The British departed that town on June 30, 1818, less than two years before Maine became a state, on March 15, 1820.[35]

The war of 1812 had intensified the dispute. The British conquest of eastern Maine had left a bitter legacy of Anglophobia downeast.[36]

---

34 MacNutt, loc. cit., 160-161.
35 Banks, loc. cit., 65-67.
36 J. Chris Arndt, "Maine in the Northeast Boundary Controversy: States' Rights in Antebellum New England", *The New England Quarterly*, June, 1989, 205-223, The Colonial Society of Massachusetts and Northeastern University; direct quote from page 205.

CHAPTER II

THE EVOLUTION OF LAND CLAIMS IN THE DISPUTED TERRITORY

The American Claim

The Disputed Territory had as its water-highway-system the upper St. John River and its tributaries.[1] Rich in mast pines and tall timber, it extended northward and

---

[1] The upper St. John River has its source in the five St. John ponds in Township 4, Range 17, Somerset County, Me. These ponds drain northward through Baker Lake, to form the Baker Branch, which is joined by the Southwest Branch that rises in the mountains along the Maine-Quebec border. It is then met by the Daaquam River and unites with the Big Black River, the Chimenticook and Pocwoc Streams and the Little Black River, before joining with the Allagash. The Allagash joins the St. John's northward flow to the Peecheenegamook, the St. Francis River of the St. John, and travelling eastward, picks up the waters of the Madawaska and the Fish Rivers. Gradually it takes a southerly course, collecting the waters of the Iriquois, Green, Quisibis and Grand Rivers, and pours it over the Grand Falls. Below Grand Falls, the St. John accepts the flow of the Salmon, Tobique and Aroostook Rivers. Meandering through east central terrain, it meets the Presque Isle of the St. John [Prestile] and the Meduxnekeag Stream, where the Disputed Territory ended. What is known as the lower St. John River collects much more flowage from other New Brunswick rivers before it empties into the Bay of Fundy at the city of St. John.

westward toward the St. Lawrence River and southward toward the Kennebec and Penobscot Rivers. The lower St. John River, generally spoken of as the the part below Grand Falls, was within the acknowledged territory of the Province of New Brunswick.

Americans documented their ownership of the Disputed Territory, (the northern portion of the District of Maine, Massachusetts,) from the signing of the Treaty of Paris of 1783. Article Two of that treaty defined the Colony of Massachusetts' northeast boundary as extending:

> From the northwest angle of Nova Scotia which is formed by a line drawn due north from the source of the St. Croix River to the highlands, along the said highlands which divide those rivers that empty themselves into the St. Lawrence from those which fall into the Atlantic Ocean; ... East by a line drawn along the middle of the River St. Croix, from its mouth in the Bay of Fundy to its source, and from its source directly north, to the aforesaid highlands, which divide the rivers that fall into the Atlantic Ocean from those which fall into the River St. Lawrence ...

This was the same boundary that had separated the British colony of Massachusetts from the British colony of Nova Scotia, (before and after the western part of Nova Scotia had been set off to be the Province of New Brunswick) and the British Colony of Quebec (before and after it had been divided into the colonies of Upper and Lower Canada.) Copies of the commissions of the several British Lieutenant Governors of the Provinces of Quebec, Nova Scotia and New Brunswick, from the year 1763 to 1786 inclusive, gave detailed descriptions of these boundaries, the same as claimed by Massachusetts (and after 1820 by the State of Maine) as the limit of her territory.[2]

The British Claim

There had been no formal British claim to the Disputed Territory (the portion of the District of Maine of Massachusetts, through which mail carriers, messengers, trappers, traders, settlers and soldiers had long been accustomed to travelling from Fredericton, up the St. John to the Madawaska River, to Temiscouata Lake and from hence to the St. Lawrence River and Quebec) until the War of 1812. However, the intent to somehow gain possession had early been made a priority. In 1784, a Boundary Commission had been established with Edward Winslow of Fredericton, New Brunswick, as its secretary. James Sullivan of Berwick, York County, Maine, conducted the American case before the Commissioners, and Ward Chipman, Loyalist jurist of St. John, New Brunswick, served as agent for the British interests. Explorations, archaeological excavations and negotiations had resulted, in 1798, in the formal declaration that the Schoodic River and its northern branch, the Cheputnaticook, comprised the true River St. Croix and that its source was the northernmost headspring of the Cheputnaticook. A monument had been erected at that spot. Amity is the present-day township in Aroostook County that is situated nearest to this monument. In the early part of 1799, Edward Winslow wrote:

... The decision may be considered favorable to Great Britain. Had the Americans established their claim on the Magaguadavic, the River St. John would have been intersected within a few miles of Fredericton. The whole of St. Andrews and other valuable settlements together with two military posts of some

---

2 ROSM II.

importance, would have been embraced within their limits. As it is, we lose not a single British settlement. A few miserable Frenchmen at Madawaska, on the route to Canada, fall within their territory. I presume that some future negotiations will remove even this difficulty, and give us a free communication with Canada.[3]

In 1802, Rufus King, United States Minister in London, had received instructions to negotiate on the areas north of the St. Croix, on the northeastern border of Massachusetts and through the Bay of Fundy. The United States had been on firm ground in establishing claim to several of the islands at the rim of Passamaquoddy Bay, but Secretary of State James Madison had jeopardized his country's position by erroneously defining the highlands above the St. Croix as "elevated ground dividing the rivers falling into the Atlantic," and that the highlands of the treaty of 1783 were "found to have no definite existence." This bungling brought infinite complications.[4]

In 1806, James Monroe, American minister in London and William Pinckney, special envoy, had arranged and signed a treaty, but President Jefferson would not submit it to the Senate for ratification because the British Government would not renounce impressment of sailors. The Tory party had gained ascendency in Britain and stopped all agreements with the United States.[5] Boundary affairs worsened.

---

[3] Edward Winslow to E. G. Lutwyche, *Winslow Papers*, W. O. Raymond, editor, 1901, St. John, New Brunswick.
[4] Howard Jones, *To the Webster-Ashburton Treaty: A Study in Anglo-American Relations, 1783-1843*, Chapel Hill: University of North Carolina Press, 1977, 7-8. Jones cites Madison to King, July 28, 1801, June 8, 1802, and King to Madison, February 28, 1803, *American State Papers, Foreign Relations*, Washington, 1831-1859, Vol. II, 585, 590.
[5] Jones, loc. cit., 8-10.

During the War of 1812, John Quincy Adams, Albert Gallatin, Henry Clay, and others, new American commissioners to form a peace treaty, had met their British counterparts at Ghent, in British-occupied Netherlands. Impressment had been the major obstacle to agreement, but on June 24, 1814, President Monroe, facing British troops landing for the invasion of Washington, had directed the commissioners to omit any stipulation on the subject of impressment, if such were found indipensable to the termination of the war. The British agents had been advised not to yield on the subject of impressment, to have the boundary line dropped down to the navigable portion of the Mississippi in order to allow joint navigation of that river, to have America *cede* a part of northern Maine in order to provide for an all-British route from Montreal and Quebec to St. John and Halifax, and to not restore American fishing privileges to their former status. The British had also demanded complete military control of the Great Lakes and an agreement that the United States would not construct fortifications within a specified distance of the border. Their weakest specification had been the establishment of a neutral Indian state as a barrier between America and the western territories.[6] Since the issue of impressment had been the only one on which the British were adamant, they had backed down on the Indian barrier state. Time had passed, their armies had been repulsed from Baltimore, Prevost's army in Upper Canada had retreated after Commodore McDonnough's decisive victory on Lake Champlain, and there had been new trouble with France. Also, Parliament had become reluctant to vote more taxes to carry on the war in America. General Wellington had frankly told his government that after the loss of naval control on the Great Lakes, there was no ground for demanding territorial concessions. He had advised a peace

---

[6] Samuel F. Bemis, *A Diplomatic History of the United States*, 1955, New York, Henry Holt and Company, 159-163.

on the basis of *status quo ante bellum*.[7] The issue of impressment had not been mentioned in the Treaty of Ghent, but after 1815 Britain had ceased this practice.

The Treaty of Ghent, December 24, 1814, had provided for the mutual restoration of all territories, places and possessions that had been taken during the war or after signing of the treaty, etc. Mixed commissions had been established to settle portions of the old boundary of 1783: Moose Island, Dudley Island and Frederick Island had been awarded to the United States; Grand Manan, and all other islands in the Passamaquoddy Bay had gone to Great Britain. The river-and-lake boundary had been only partially worked out, and they had failed to resolve Article V, the establishment of the northeast boundary of the District of Maine.[8]

British diplomats continued their demands that Massachusetts *cede* the northern portion of the District of Maine. Massachusetts had no inclination to do so. Formalized diplomatic disdain met further American attempts at marking the boundary.[9]

It has been theorized that a factor contributing to the delay in marking the boundary was that British control of the seas was only as lasting as the strength of their ships' timbers and masts: their timber supply was even more critical than America's current dependency on foreign oil. After the need for warships had diminished, merchant ships had become a priority. Queen Victoria [1837-1901] guided her country through its period of greatest power. The demand for naval stores did not cease until the advent of iron steamships. Even though, in 1838, one year before the military confrontation on

---

7 Ibid., 164-166.
8 Ibid., 168-169.
9 Jones, loc. cit, 3-6. Technicalities, such as errors in the *Map of the British and French Dominions in North America*, made in 1755 by John Mitchell, served as a stumbling block. Lack of actual surveys had not prevented Mitchell from guessing at names and locations of rivers and mountains.

Maine's frontier, the British steamship *Sirius* became the first ship to cross the Atlantic entirely under steam power, sails were kept for emergencies on trans-Atlantic liners as late as 1884. To have settled the boundary would have been to draw a dividing line through one of the last important stands of mast pine.

The Wulastegwiak, the Original Inhabitants of the Disputed Territority

The Maliseets had lived in the St. John River Valley since before tribal memory. British and French monarchs had coveted their timber and their furs. In 1765, a Maliseet Indian leader had petitioned the British government that his tribe had been reduced to misery by the encroachments of Canadian beaver hunters. Catholic missionaries to the Indians had visited on the river intermittently since the French had arrived in Quebec. French traders, Pierre Lizotte and his half-brother, Pierre Duperre, had traded for fur in St. Anne des Payes Bas. About 1784, they moved up the St. John with the Acadians and set up a trading post on the south bank near the Indian village.[10]

The St. John River had always served the native tribes as a water highway through the region. Military expeditions and shippers of supplies often used this route to avoid encounters with their enemies at the mouth of the St. Lawrence River. Inter-provincial mailmen, Joseph Dufour, brothers Michael and Louis Mercure, and John Baptiste Martin, *coureur des bois*, in leather and

---

10 *Statement on the part of the United States, of the case referred, in pursuance of the Convention of 29th September, 1827, Between the said States and Great Britain, to his Majesty, the King of Netherlands, for his Decision thereon,* printed but not published, Washington, 1829, Appendix 49, 442-431; hereinafter referred to as SUSCAp49; Thomas Albert, *The History of Madawaska*, Madawaska: Northern Graphics, English translation by Sister Therese Doucette and Dr. Francis Doucette, quoting J. G. Deane's *Report to the Maine Legislature, 1825,* 18-19.

homespun garments and rawhide shoes, had carried messages and mail from St. John to Quebec, including the news of Cornwallis' surrender to the Americans at Yorktown.[11]

The Acadians of Madawaska, Inhabitants of the Disputed Territory

There is an old Dutch saying, "Never transplant an old tree!" Jean Baptiste Cyr would have agreed with this wisdom. Cyr, who had been evicted by the Loyalists who had arrived on the St. John River in New Brunswick after the American Revolution, was by this time an old man who had suffered through many of the Acadians' misfortunes. He is reported to have walked through his farm one last time, and there, bowed with age, discouraged, in his grief cried out, "My God! Can it be true that there is no place left on earth for a Cayen?"[12] He died shortly thereafter.

The history of Jean Baptist Cyr and his remarkably brave and durable companions who settled at the mouth of the Madawaska River in the Disputed Territory had begun in France with Sieur De Monts in 1603. Given permission by King Henry IV of France to plant a settlement and establish a fur trade in the New World, De Mont's first ship sailed on April 7, 1603, explored the area and spent the winter on an island at the mouth of the St. Croix River. Because of the location of the island, it was subject to rigorous winter weather; half of this group died.[13]

In the spring of 1605, Du Pont-Grave arrived with another shipload of supplies and De Monts transferred his

---
11 Albert, loc. cit., 17-18.
12 "Cayen" meaning Acadian. Albert, loc. cit., 39.
13 *The Habitation, Port Royal National Historic Park*, a brochure published by the Minister of Environment, Ministry of Supply and Services, Canada, 1981, n.p.

colony to the Annapolis Basin. There Champlain and Du Pont-Grave constructed the *Habitation*, a group of buildings surrounding a courtyard in the Normandy fashion. De Monts lost his trading monopoly in 1607, and the whole colony returned to France. In 1610 he came back with colonists and a grant to Port Royal.[14]

In 1613, Samuel Argall, at Jamestown, was ordered by the British to destroy all French settlements on the Atlantic coast. He plundered and burned the *Habitation*, but the Acadians survived among the Micmacs.[15]

Pierre Menlason had begun another settlement at the Basin of Minas, named Grand Pre. By 1700 it was the richest settlement in Acadia, but the British had sent raiding troops from New England in 1704. In reprisal for French and Indian attacks on the New England frontier, they had smashed the dikes, burned houses and killed cattle. By 1710, the British had captured Port Royal, renamed it Annapolis Royal and stipulated that the colonists might stay or leave their land, now renamed Nova Scotia. If they stayed they would be required to take an oath of allegiance to the British Crown, but their religious practices would not be interfered with. The Micmac Indians, early converts to Catholicism and strong allies of the French at Quebec, were thought likely to turn against the Acadians if they took the oath. For that reason, as well as their French patriotism, five years later most had still not taken the oath. However, in 1730, Governor Phillips induced them to take the oath with the understanding that they would never be forced to take up arms against their French relatives in Canada. Nevertheless, in 1744, despite the oath taking, Acadians had made French troops, which had just failed in another attempt to capture Annapolis Royal, welcome in their homes.

---

14 Ibid.
15 Ibid. The *Habitation* was reconstructed by the Canadian Government in 1938-1939.

By 1746, the British had strengthened their settlement at Halifax and felt that they could bring in settlers from New England to occupy Acadian farms. To clear the way for their arrival, in the spring of 1755, the new British Governor, Charles Lawrence, seized all Acadian boats and confiscated all firearms, leaving them without guns for hunting or self-defense.[16] Lieutenant Colonel John Winslow built a palisade around the Catholic church at Grand Pre, established his headquarters in the church and encamped his forces within the palisade. Then Lawrence sent special orders to his British commanders for the *Grand Derangement*. On September 2, 1755, Winslow ordered all men and boys over ten years of age to assemble at the church in three days' time. On September 5th, four hundred and eighteen Acadians had assembled. With the church doors locked Winslow announced that the Acadians were now His Majesty's prisoners, that their possessions were confiscated to the Crown, and that all Acadians would be transported to foreign lands. They and their families were forced at gunpoint aboard waiting ships that took them to numerous places of exile in the American colonies.[17]

    A few years before the tragedy of 1755, at the insistence of the missionary La Loutre, many families that eventually came to Madawaska left Grand Pre for Beausejour. When Lawrence's forces captured Fort Beausejour in June, 1755, these Acadians refused to take the unqualified oath of alleigance. Some of them went to the St. John River Valley.[18]

---

16 Ibid.
17 Ibid.; Albert, loc. cit., 24-25.
18 Albert, loc. cit., 24. See W. S. MacNutt, *The Atlantic Provinces*, McClelland and Stewart, Ltd., 1965, Chapter II; in April, Lawrence burnt the village of Beaubassin, and drove the inhabitants and cattle before him. Among the families who left Grand Pre for Beausejour were Jean Cyr, Jean Baptiste Cormier, Joseph Daigle, Simon Hebert, Joseph Theriault, Jean Baptiste Thibodeau, Zachary Ayotte, Joseph Mauzerole and a family by the name of Potier.

The *Grand Derangement* of 1755 was not the end of the British effort to rid Nova Scotia of the Acadians. Colonel Moncton went into the St. John Valley with twelve hundred Rangers. In two months' time, southern St. John River towns were laid in smoking ruins. Most of the inhabitants escaped up river to St. Anne, now Fredericton. Then, on the night of January 28-29, 1759, Moses Hazen, with another group of Rangers, made a surprise attack at St. Anne, burning homes, killing those who resisted and taking twenty-three prisoners. Many refugees went into the forest or north to Lower Canada.[19]

In 1759, after the fall of Quebec to the English, two hundred Acadians who had fled to the Quebec area decided to take the oath of allegiance before Judge Cramache. He gave them signed papers and a statement by Brigadier General Moncton that permitted them to return to their homes on the St. John River. In October, 1759 they arrived at Fort Frederick. They presented their papers to Colonel Arbuthnot, who referred the matter to Governor Lawrence at Halifax, who ordered their arrest. He sent them to Halifax as prisoners of war. When the Treaty of Paris of 1763 left Britain in control of all Canada, Acadia and Newfoundland, the future founders of Madawaska were either prisoners of the British or were in hiding in the forest.[20]

The victory of the Rebel colonists in the American Revolution and the expulsion of over thirty thousand Loyalists from the United States to Nova Scotia in 1783 caused the final uprooting of the Acadian population. The Loyalists had so much political influence that the partitioning of Nova Scotia and the establishment of a new province, New Brunswick, was accomplished by June 18, 1784. Under Governor Carleton, most government offices were held by Loyalists. At first the capital was at Parrtown, at the mouth of the St. John, but it was soon moved

---

19 Albert, loc. cit., 31-32.
20 Ibid., 32.

to Fredericton, and Parrtown took again its historic name of St. John. The new arrivals showed little sympathy for the Acadians. Hostilities developed, and the eviction of the "French squatters" followed.[21]

On February 24, 1785, Louis Mercure petitioned for himself, his half-brother Pierre Duperre and twenty-four heads of families lands located a mile and a half below the falls on the Madawaska River, a tributary of the St. John. Even though this land was west of the understood but as yet unmarked "Line" between New Brunswick and the District of Maine, permission was given for the petitioners to sell their lands and settle there upon grants of 200 acres for each head of household.[22]

In June of 1785, the Acadians boated up the St. John, portaged a mile around Grand Falls, and moved into the wide expanse of rolling hills of the upper St. John Valley. Joseph Daigle erected a cross, the sign of salvation and hope for the future, two and a half miles below the Maliseet village. The Acadians sent two men to Chief Francois Xavier at the Indian village to say that the elders of the group would call upon the chief the next day. At first the Indians were not pleased to have the new arrivals in their tribal lands. Grand-Pierre, Portis, Mielle Miselle, Sarrisin Shaougenet and Joseph Louis St. Aubin were present in the crowded council hall to meet with the Acadians. It is unlikely that they were strangers to each other, having lived and hunted in the St. John Valley for many years. Soon the meeting became cordial; Chief Francois Xavier made them welcome. Five years later the settlers received title of ownership to their lands from the Province of New Brunswick.[23]

---

21 Ibid., 34.
22 Ibid., 36. About half of the colony moved to Madawaska; others went to Memramcook, Miramichi, Tracadie, Caraquet, and Pisiquit.
23 Ibid., 43-49. On June 11, 1790, Pierre Duperre received the first British grant to land in the Madawaska Territory. On October 1, 1790, other settlers also received their grants.

Massachusetts Land Sales and Grants in the District of Maine

Land sales and grants were of particular interest to negotiators, for they demonstrated an early exercise of jurisdiction in the disputed territory by the Commonwealth of Massachusetts. As early as April 18, 1792, Massachusetts had sold to Henry Jackson and Royal Flint lands that encompassed a large part of the disputed territory. Through complicated negotiations involving General Henry Knox, William Duer, Henry Jackson and Royal Flint, William Bingham, eighteenth-century magnate, became the owner of immense tracts of Maine land. On June 1, 1797, Alexander Baring, later to become Lord Ashburton, purchased half of Bingham's holdings. The Commonwealth had, by 1795, sold or granted 150 townships, totaling three and one half million acres.[24]

Early grants in the District of Maine, in what was then Washington County, Massachusetts, (to be designated Aroostook County, Maine, in 1839) were initiated by a Resolve of the Massachusetts Legislature in 1793:

1801 Mars Hill (Soldiers Township)
1802 Hodgdon (Groton and Westford Academy Grants)
1802 Cary (Westford Academy Grant)
1802 Littleton (Williams College and Framingham

---

[24] SUSC Ap49; 355-369; Park Holland surveyed, in 1794, what he denoted on maps as "Bingham's Option," land "beginning at the northwest corner of Bingham's purchase, then run east on the line north of the said Purchase, to the northeast corner, thence north to the highlands that divide the water which fall into the St. Lawrence from those that run into the Atlantic, then westerly on the said highlands so far that a south line will strike the first mentioned corner." This tract was estimated to contain one million acres. F. S. Allis, Jr., Ed., *William Bingham's Maine Lands, 1790-1820* The Colonial Society of Massachusetts, 1954, Volume XXXVII, 217; Chapters II and III; 674-676; Wood, loc. cit., 48. During the period 1783-1820, five and one half million acres were sold for a total of $924,000.

Academy Grants)
1803 Bridgewater (Portland and Bridgewater Academy Grants)
1804 Haynesville and Forkstown (Grant to Benjamin Talmadge)
1805 Mars Hill (Grant to Revolutionary Soldiers)
1805 Houlton (New Salem Academy Grant)
1805 Weston (Hampden Academy Grant)
1806 Caribou (Eaton Grant)
1806 Westfield (Westfield Academy and Deerfield Academy Grants)
1807 Fort Fairfield (Town of Plymouth Grant)
1808 Linneus (Massachusetts Agricultural Society Grant)
1808 Caribou (General William Eaton's Grant)
1810 New Limerick (Limerick Academy Grant)
1810 Ludlow (Belfast Academy Grant)[25]

The Commonwealth of Massachusetts, from 1792 to 1810, "considering her right of sovereignty and jurisdiction co-extensive with her title, not expecting any intrusion, did not cultivate her whole territory or protect it by military force, relying upon the good faith of the British."[26]

A survey was carried out, in 1817-1818, under the provisions of the Treaty of Ghent. Colonel Joseph Bouchette represented Great Britain, and Colonel John Johnson, Surveyor General of Vermont from 1812-1822, represented the United States. They had received instructions dated June 11, 1817, to survey the northeast boundary of

---

[25] Harriett W. Marr, "Grants of Land to Academies in Massachusetts and Maine," *Historical Collections of the Essex Institute*, Vol. 88, 1952. On March 4, 1806, William Eaton, of Brimfield, MA, was rewarded for heroic service contributing to the release of many American prisoners held in slavery in Tripoli. He was granted a ten thousand-acre tract with part of the Aroostook River running through it.
[26] State of Maine, *Report of the Joint Select Committee*, House of Representatives, 1828.

Maine, as described in Article 2 of the Treaty of 1783. They proceeded up the St. John River in bateaux to the mouth of the Meduxnekeag Creek, established a base camp and went by way of the Houlton Road to the old post (at Amity) erected by the survey party of 1797. On July 31, 1817, they erected a new monument. After measurements and calculations, they extended the line, "opening the same 16 feet wide and planting posts or stone boundaries every mile, marking the number of miles thereon with NBJB on the east side and USJJ on the west."

Colonel Bouchette had hoped to prove that the line should extend from Mars Hill west across what is today the State of Maine to Mount Katahdin. He and Johnson continued their exploring survey northward until they had reached the Great Wagansis, the first branch of the Restigouche River. Detailed reports and maps were submitted to the commissioners by both parties. Some showed the British claim of a line running west from Mars Hill, while others showed the American Claim went farther north, to the Restigouche River, and then west and south to join the British claim lines at the western boundary of Maine. The Commissioners studied the survey results for nearly five years, but could not even agree upon a general map exhibiting the boundaries claimed by each party. They made separate reports to their governments. [27]

The Kennebec-Madawaska Connection

It was after the erection of the boundary markers between District of Maine of Massachusetts and New

---

[27] Donald A. Wise, "Surveying and Mapping the International Border of Northeast Maine, 1817-18," from *Surveying and Mapping*, Volume XL, No. 4, 1980, 419-427; "The Map of the Country Explored in the Years 1817-18, By Order of the Commissioners under the 5th Article of the Treaty of Ghent," by John Johnson, U. S. Surveyor, National Archives Record Group No. 76, Series 3, Map 1. See Bouchette-Johnson Survey Maps, Collection of the Maine Historical Society Archives, Portland.

Brunswick, in 1817-18, that men from the Kennebec River planned to move northward, west of that line. On Carleton's map of the District of Maine, 1795, a segment of land east of the Penobscot River, north of the Lottery Lands, northward to the highlands above the St. John River is delineated, dated and labeled: "This Tract of land, except for Townships numbered 1-5, sold to Wm. Bingham, Esq." Settlers residing on the tract of land on the Kennebec River known as The Million Acres, belonging to William Bingham, were aware that the gentleman who owned so much land in their area also had an option on or owned lands to the northward, even as far north as the highlands above the St. John River.[28] Not long after that date, a small migration of settlers from this community began.

By 1815, John Harford and his son Phineas were clearing lots west of the Acadian settlement at Madawaska.[29] By the summer of 1818, John and his son George had brought their families to live in houses they had built in what was referred to by Pierre Duperre as the Upper Settlement of Madawaska.[30]

Nathan Baker had visited the Madawaska community in February, 1818, in company with a Massachusetts

---

28 In 1810, U. S. Census listed, at Million Acres, north of Solon, among others, Aaron Rice, Barnabas Baker, Nathan Baker, Asa Fletcher, Reu-ben Baker, Abner Baker, Joseph Baker, John Harford and Asa Baker.

29 Deane and Kavanagh located Harford at Madawaska Point in 1815, six miles below the mouth of the St. Francis River in 1816, and at the west point of the Madawaska River in 1817. *The Deane-Kavanagh Report*, Ed. W. O. Raymond, *Collections of the New Brunswick Historical Society*, Vol. 2, No. 9, 1914.

30 Duperre to Wetmore, February 20, 1819, U.S. Congress, Senate document no. 130, 20th Congress, 1st Session, in the United States Congressional Serials Set, Vol.. 166, March 3, 1828; *Statements relat-ing to alleged aggressions on the rights of citizens of the United States by the authorities of New Brunswick on the territory in dispute between the United States and Great Britain*, 43 pages, commonly known as the "Barrel Report," hereinafter referred to as SD 130.

magistrate and had talked with Francis Duperre, captain of militia, about the possibility of forming a town government. Duperre declined to discuss the matter until the line was settled. In August, Baker moved to the Madawaska Settlement with his wife and family, and his brother John. At the mouth of the Maryumpticook River, he had built a house and had begun lumbering in partnership with a Captain Fletcher.[31]

On September 5, 1818, Francis Duperre, at Grand Falls, requested of New Brunswick authorities that British jurisdiction be enforced as usual in Madawaska, because several Americans, recently arrived from the Kennebec River, were trying to convince the Acadians that the jurisdiction of the United States was in force. He reported that Nathan Baker had cut about ten or twelve hundred tons of timber on the north bank of the River St. John and that "he appeared to be a man who took much upon himself."[32]

By December, 1818, the presence of Kennebec settlers west of Madawaska had caused a stir at the international level. Charles Bagot, His Majesty's Envoy to the United States, was assured by John Quincy Adams, American Secretary of State, that his government would take proper measures. Adams appeared to think that these

---

31 Nathan Baker was the son of Joseph and Dorcas (Smith) Baker. *Makers of Moscow*, compiled by the Moscow, Maine, History Committee, 1966, records that Joseph Baker came from Readfield. Joseph and Dorcas Baker had eight children: Elizabeth, Mary, Lemuel, Joseph Jr., Asa, Nathan, Dorcas and John. Elizabeth Baker married Amos Fletcher; Nathan Baker married Sophia Rice, and their children were Amanda, Lovinda, Sophronia and Enoch. Nathan died about 1821. Then John Baker married Sophia Rice Baker, his brother's widow, and had at least two daughters. John Baker was born at Moscow, January 17, 1796 and died in 1864; SD 130, Duperre to Wetmore, February 20, 1819. It is possible that the magistrate referred to was James Bacon, SD 130.
32 Pierre Duperre to J. Murray Bliss, September 5, 1818; Duperre to Wetmore, in response to Attorney General Wetmore's Inquiry on the 8th of January, 1819, SD 130.

persons were squatters and should be dealt with accordingly. Bagot advised the Lieutenant Governor of New Brunswick, G. S. Smyth, that he "need not scruple to displace them."[33]

Accordingly, Attorney General Wetmore directed Pierre Duperre to inform him of the names of any American citizens who had taken up residence in the Madawaska settlement or near it, to the westward of the line of experiment lately run across the River St. John, "for until it was otherwise decided by the commissioners of boundary, the whole of the St. John and of course the Madawaska river must be considered as belonging to His Majesty."[34]

---

33 Charles Bagot to Colonel Barclay, December 18, 1818, SD 130.
34 Wetmore to Duperre, January 8, 1819; Duperre to Wetmore, February 20, 1819, SD 130.

PART TWO: CONTENTION

CHAPTER III

CONTENTION FOR JURISDICTION OF THE DISPUTED TERRITORY

Maine Statehood

The first movement for the separation of the District of Maine from the Commonwealth of Massachusetts began about two years after the Treaty of 1783. Citizens of the District felt disadvantaged because the Supreme Judicial Court and all official record keeping was located in Boston; because of fixed fees on deed transfers; because of lumber trade regulations that favored Boston; and because of poor representation in the Legislature. The Democratic Republican Party,[1] organized in 1803 by William King, John Chandler and William Widgery, worked for separation. They led their supporters through a series of defeats in state elections but finally, in 1819, King found the way to victory. He promised, in a new state, to appoint members of the opposing Federalist faction to public office in proportion to their numbers. By June, 1819, one hundred and twenty-five towns had petitioned the General Court for the separation from Massachusetts. During the presidency of James Monroe, on March 15, 1820, Maine became the twenty-third state to join the

---

[1] The Democratic-Republican Party, now the Democratic Party.

Union.[2] William King became Maine's first elected governor on June 1, 1820. The seat of government was at Portland.

In 1820, ninety percent of Maine's timberland was untouched. Massachusetts still owned more than four million acres in Maine and held as deep an interest in the boundary settlement as did Maine.

Contention Begins

Before King officially began his first term, an overt act of jurisdiction in the contest for possession of the Disputed Territory took place. On May 20, 1820, New Brunswick's Attorney General Thomas Wetmore issued a subpoena for trespass and intrusion on Crown lands to John Harford:[3]:

> Subpoena and Respondendum
> George the Fourth, by the Grace of God, of the United Kingdom of Great Britain and Ireland, King, Defender of the Faith and Etc., to John Harford; Greeting:
> We command you that, laying aside all excuses whatsoever, you be and appear in your proper person, before our justices of our Supreme Court of our Province of New Brunswick, at Fredericton, on Saturday after the second Tuesday of July next, to answer to us of and concerning certain matters which on your behalf shall be then and there objected against you; And this you are by no means to omit, under the penalty of one hundred pounds, which we will cause to be levied on your goods and chattels, lands and tenements, to our use, if you neglect to obey our present command.

By this document a Maine citizen residing on the St. John River, west of a line (as yet unsurveyed and un-

---

[2] Banks, loc. cit., Chapters I-VIII, passim.
[3] SD 130.

marked) running due north from the Monument at the source of the St. Croix River to the northwest angle of Nova Scotia, had been called to account by New Brunswick Courts. In the absence of a boundary settlement, an ongoing practice developed, by which officials at the province and state levels, through repeated acts of jurisdiction in the disputed territory, tried to reinforce their claims.

It became the first priority of the new state of Maine to define its own boundaries. On June 26th, the Legislature voted funds and Governor King appointed General James Irish of Gorham to be land agent. Irish inspected the territory and the Marshal of Maine took a census of the inhabitants settled on the St. John River and its tributary streams west of the meridian line from the Monument at the source of the St. Croix and the south line of Lower Canada.[4]

At the beginning of his second term, in 1821, King reported that all reasonable hope for a speedy action by the boundary commission had vanished and it rested with the Legislature to devise means to protect the State from a systematic pillage by claimants of pretended title. Dr. Benjamin Porter, land agent, was given power to arrest trespassers cutting timber in the Schoodic and Aroostook region and detain them and their teams at Houlton for due process. British subjects met Porter's terms and gave their assurances that they would withdraw across the line and desist.[5]

Governor King resigned to accept an appointment to the Spanish Claims Commission. While William D. Williamson was acting Governor, the boundary commissioners, had, as previously mentioned, on October 21, 1821,

---

[4] State of Maine, *Report of the Joint Select Committee of the Senate and House of Representatives of the State of Maine, 1828*, hereinafter referred to as RJSCSHRM 1828. See APPENDIX I for 1820 settlers.

[5] Burrage, loc. cit., 121-122, quoting *American State Papers*; George W. Coffin, "The Journal of George W. Coffin, Massachusetts Land Agent, September and October, 1825," Maine State Archives, Augusta.

delivered precisely opposite opinions. This ended the first attempt to settle the location of the northwest angle of Nova Scotia by the agency of a commission.[6] When Albion Keith Parris, Republican, became Governor of Maine on January 5, 1822, he cited the disagreement of the commissioners as the reason that the final division of lands owned in common by Maine and Massachusetts had not been accomplished. Massachusetts shared expenses, but relied upon Maine to prevent depredations by British provincials. Land Agent James Irish was given full power to prevent trespassing in the valleys of the Aroostook, Meduxnekeag and Presquile Rivers and their branches west of the meridian line from the monument.[7] During Parris' third term, 1824, a proposition was made by the government of the United States and accepted by the British government, to try for a second time to establish the boundary by negotiation rather than by arbitration by a foreign power, as provided by the Treaty.

In the spring of 1824, Maine and Massachusetts Land Agents seized all logs cut on the Aroostook and Madawaska Rivers that could be identified as belonging to either or both. In July, 1824, New Brunswick authorities organized Madawaska Settlement into a militia district under the command of Colonel Peter Frazier of Fredericton, and opened a land office, with authority to give grants of lands located fifty or sixty miles west of the line north from the Monument. It was rumored that Douglas had intentions to plant one hundred and fifty settlers there and grant them lands. Samuel Cook, Land Agent at Houlton, concluded, "They mean to get all the timber up the Aroostook and at Madawaska, unless measures are taken to prevent it; they do not expect to hold

---

6 William Frances Ganong, "A Monograph of the Evolution of the Boundaries of the Province of New Brunswick," *Transactions of the Royal Society of Canada*, [Series II, Vol. 7,] 317, 320-328.

7 RJSCSHRM 1828; Resolve, February 11, 1823, *Resolves of the State of Maine*, Vol. I, hereinafter referred to as ROSM I, 255. Mark Trafton, William Vance; Ephriam Whitney assisted them.

the territory, but pretended that they do; they are very abusive." By December, 1824, great depredations were under way on the Aroostook River by British subjects, under British permits, with at least one hundred teams of six oxen each. The firm of Cruickshank and Johnson, of St. John, had furnished $30,000 worth of supplies for timber men on the Aroostook, and Plymouth Township and Eaton half-township were in danger of being stripped. Sir Howard Douglas, New Brunswick's newly appointed Lieutenant Governor, gave orders for the seizure of all of the timber cut in 1824. James Irish, acting under the Resolve of the Legislature of January 24, 1825, published notices of his intent to bring trespassers to justice.[8]

John Baker (1796-1866), a younger brother of Nathan Baker, had come to Madawaska in 1817, but had continued on to the Bay of Chaleur. Two years later he had returned to Madawaska and engaged in business with his brother. Nathan had died about 1822; John had married Nathan's widow, Sophia (Rice) Baker, and had continued his brother's business. In 1823, John Baker had accepted from the New Brunswick government, four pounds five shillings and three pence, a bounty paid to settlers as a reward for growing ninety bushels of wheat on new land.[9] Also, in 1824, Custom House officer George West had seized three hundred logs from Baker, judging they had been cut on Crown lands without a license. But West said that Baker had spoken as if he considered himself a resident within the province, so Baker had been allowed to redeem his logs at a rate of two shillings, six pence, per

---

8 James Irish, *Report of the Land Agent, 1825-1826* James Irish to Albion Parris, July 14, 1824, U. S. Congress, *House of Representatives Document 90*, hereinafter referred to HRD90. Samuel Cook to James Irish, March 25, 1824, HRD90; Big Machias River and Little Machias River empty into the Aroostook River in Ashland.; Cook to [James Irish?] March 25, 1824; Asa Wyman, Judge of the Court of Sessions, Calais, to Parris, October, 1824; Anson G. Chandler, Assistant Land Agent, to James Irish, December 25, 1825, HRD90. See Appendix II.
9 SD 130.

one thousand feet, counting three logs to a thousand. This had given New Brunswick authorities cause to assume that he had accepted their jurisdiction. In contradiction to this, the *Portland Argus* maintained that, without a permit from the land agents of Maine and Massachusetts to cut timber, John Baker's mill at the mouth of the Meriumpticook would have been useless; that the government of New Brunswick had been informed that Maine agents had been appointed to grant permits to cut pine timber on the territory of the State.

Albion K. Parris, in his fourth term, 1825, was still watching the dilatory diplomatic negotiations. Strong affirmations as to the strength of the British claim were being made. Sir Howard Douglas had taken a belligerent stand, stating that "the British Government contends that the northern boundary line of the United States, running from the source of the St. Croix to the highlands, is terminated at Mars Hill, which lies southward of the Aroostook [River.]" His claim was vehemently contradicted by Maine authorities. While "they felt Sir Howard to be an honorable man, who did not intend to misrepresent the facts, they felt that he must have lacked proper research and was thus ignorant on the subject." The Committee on Public Lands considered but decided against employing a military force to expel the depredators from Maine's territory because of the expense and the danger of involving the national government and Maine citizens near the Line in serious difficulties.[10]

Land Agents James Irish and George W. Coffin, in October, 1825, were sent to investigate depredations, to execute deeds to settlers with permits from their Land

---

10 H. U. Addington to Henry Clay, May 23, 1825, HRD90; RJSCSHRM 1828; State of Maine, *Report of the Committee on Public Lands*, Joseph Parlin Jr., Chairman, January 18, 1825. ROSM I, 395-396.
See APPENDIX II for Canadian Timber Harvesters on the St. John and Aroostook Rivers in 1825.

Office and to sell timber in the undivided public lands lying contiguous to the waters of the St. John. They posted notices at Baker's mills and at the Catholic Church stating that for a fee of ten dollars, the Maine land agent was authorized to survey and deed one hundred acres of land to settlers in actual possession for more than thirty years on the undivided public lands on the St. John and Madawaska Rivers. Coffin and Irish surveyed and conveyed to John Baker one hundred acres at the mouth of the Maryumpticook. They recorded the number of houses and their occupants on the St. John River.

On October 2, 1825, Baker told Coffin and Irish that most of the two thousand inhabitants of Madawaska desired to unite their destiny with the United States, and would be pleased to have magistrates appointed among them and be represented in the Legislature of Maine. Coffin observed that the eastern boundary line crossed the St. John River about two miles above the Grand Falls, almost fifty miles from the Maryumpticook River.[11]

When Coffin and Irish arrived at the mouth of the Aroostook River, the water was so low that they were forced to give up their visit to settlers in the Aroostook Valley. At Fredericton, they were informed that the government of New Brunswick had received instructions from England not to grant any more permits to cut timber upon the Aroostook or Madawaska Rivers until the line was permanently defined. At Portland, Coffin took tea with Governor Parris and gave him an account of his trip. When New Brunswick officials protested their trip, Henry Clay replied that it appeared that the measures adopted by Massachusetts and Maine were "precautionary, and occasioned by previous acts of asserted authority over the disputed territory, which, if unopposed by counter-

---

[11] Coffin, loc. cit.; Resolves of the Legislature of the Commonwealth of Massachusetts, February 16 and June 11, 1825; Resolves of the Maine Legislature, February 25 and 26, 1825, ROSM Vol. I, 430-431, 440.

vailing acts, might have been relied on, at some future day, as strengthening the British and weakening the American claim."12

By the beginning of Governor Parris' last term, in 1826, President John Quincy Adams had been elected. The northeast boundary dispute was still under negotiation and the Committee on State Lands submitted resolves to the effect that the Governor be requested to take measures to procure for the use of the State, copies of all maps, documents and publications and surveys, relating to the Northeastern Boundary of the United States, as described in the Treaty of 1783.13

Governor Enoch Lincoln Contends For Jurisdiction

In the seventh year after the Separation, on the 4th of January, 1827, Enoch Lincoln took the oath of office as the third elected Governor of Maine. During his three terms, tensions concerning the northeast boundary of Maine reached alarming dimensions. A scholar and statesman with vision and determination, he defended Maine's rights against British denials and took a strong stand on state sovereignty, but concluded that the settlement of the boundary line was the rightful business of the national government to effect. He began the move toward extensive internal improvements to provide access to, and to facilitate the defense of, Maine's six million

---

12   Coffin; loc. cit., Henry Clay to Charles R. Vaughan and Governor Levi Lincoln of Massachusetts to Clay, January 15, 1826, HRD90.

13   State of Maine, *The Report of the Joint Standing Committee on State Lands*, ROSM Vol. I, 480-482. During the summer of 1826, Land Agent Irish reported that much less strip and waste has been made on the Aroostook and St. John in the Disputed Territory. Assistant Agents with deputy sheriffs had tried to arrest trespassers, who often escaped, but some were captured and prosecuted by Mr. Godfrey. James Irish, *Report of the Land Agent*, January 5, 1827, *Maine Documents*, Vol. II, 1825-1828, hereinafter referred to as MDII.

acres of largely unsettled territory.[14] He repeated Governor Parris' request for documents relating to the boundary dispute. Commissioner Albert Gallatin was in negotiation concerning the boundary, but it appeared that there would be no alternative to referring the problem to arbitration. Lincoln feared that states rights would not be served if an arbitrator were chosen.[15]

John Baker is Charged with Sedition and Trespass on Crown Lands.

On July 4, 1827, John Baker and about fourteen of his neighbors celebrated Independence Day. At the confluence of the Meriumpticook and St. John Rivers, on land conveyed to Baker by Maine and Massachusetts, Baker erected a flag staff. Two of the French settlers assisted him in a traditional flag-raising ceremony. A flag made by Sophia Baker, bearing a representation of the national eagle partially surrounded by stars, was raised. An ad-

---

14 Lincoln was the sixth governor of Maine if you count William D. Williamson, Benjamin Ames and Daniel Rose, Acting Governors to complete the term of Governor King. His father, Levi Lincoln, had served in Jefferson's cabinet. His elder brother, Levi Lincoln, Jr., was governor of Massachusetts in 1825. Enoch, born 1788 in Worcester, attended Harvard, received an MA from Bowdoin, studied law in Worcester, was a member of the Massachusetts bar. He moved to Fryeburg in 1812 and then to Paris in 1818. He served eight terms in Congress, was Maine's Governor in 1827-29 and died October 8, 1829. Edward H. Elwell, "Enoch Lincoln," in *Collections of the Maine Historical Society*, [Ser. II, Vol. I] 137-147; ROSM I.

15 Documents requested on February 23, 1827, ROSM Vol. I, 255; Lincoln to Clay, March 20, 1827, JSCSHRM1828. President John Q. Adams refused to furnish the reports and arguments of the commissioners. Henry Clay sent, on October 30th, 1827, by William Prentiss, twenty-four manuscript volumes on the subject of the northeast boundary lines, and forty-two copies of maps to Governor Lincoln for his exclusive use; Ganong, loc. cit., 330-331; Clay to Lincoln, March 27, and May 7, 1828, RJSCSHRM1828, Appendix, 25.

dress was followed by a feast. A French fiddler, Bellony Terrio, had been hired for the occasion and some of the Acadians from Madawaska were guests. In the evening, a ball at the home of James Bacon, at which by invitation many of the French settlers were present, concluded the festivities of the day.[16]

While it was normal to celebrate the Fourth of July in this fashion in the States, there is no doubt that this particular gathering had also as its purpose the exercising of jurisdiction. The flag thus raised, though it was not the stars and stripes, but more like a regimental ensign, was offensive to the Provincial authorities; it advertised the Americans' disregard for foreign authority. Shortly after the celebration, a paper drawn up by Stephen Grover was signed by most of the Americans. It was a compact by which they agreed to adjust all disputes among themselves, through referees, without appealing to British authority, for a period of one year. In the meantime, application was to be made to the government of Maine, to obtain state instituted authorities. Under the agreement, John Baker, James Bacon and Daniel Savage constituted a tribunal for the enforcement of law, with power to seize and sell property to settle debts. A constable was appointed.[17]

---

16 State of Maine, Legislature Document 18: *Report of Charles S. Davels, Esq. Agent appointed by Gov. Enoch Lincoln of Maine to enquire into certain facts relating to agggressions upon the rights of the State of Maine and of individuals citizens thereof, by inhabitants of the Province of New Brunswick* Charles Stewart Davels, Esq., hereinafter referred to as MLD18; SD130; *Historical Collections of Piscataquis County, ME, 1910*, hereinafter referred to as PCHS.

17 Charles Smart and Charles Stetson, in depositions of December 29, 1827, named Grover as the author. Baker signed it first and then thirteen others, but he was not present when the paper was presented to Peter Markee, a member of the French community. This paper was destroyed about a month after its signing. Charles Stetson's deposition, PCHS; MLD18; SD130.

On July 18, 1827, John Baker heard rumors that the route of the mail would be changed from its usual passage by canoe up the St. John River and on to Quebec. This would have been an inconvenience to the Americans. Baker, in a canoe upon the St. John, a short distance below the mouth of the Madawaska River, and above where the Line crosses the St. John, met Peter Sileste the mail carrier, who was poling his canoe up river and inquired if this were true. (Sileste later reported that Baker had forbade the passage of mail.) Upon finding that the mail actually would be passing on its usual route, on his return to Madawaska, Baker paid two dollars to the mail contractor for a subscription to a Quebec newspaper.[18]

George Morehouse, Justice of the Peace, County of York, received a report from Francis Rice, Adjutant of the Madawaska Militia, about the compact signed by the Americans; the report also said that Baker had tried to stop the passage of mail. Rice mentioned the "liberty pole" Baker had raised, and expressed concern that he would corrupt a great part of the Madawaska Militia.[19] Morehouse passed Rice's missive up the chain of command to Provincial Secretary William F. Odell, with the comment that the American subjects residing in that settlement were disposed to acts and aggressions which Lieutenant Governor Douglas might think proper to put a stop to. Thomas Wetmore, Attorney General, ordered Morehouse to investigate. As soon as it was known that Morehouse was in the American settlement, Baker and others hoisted the flag as a token of defiance. When ordered to pull it down, Baker declared that they had entered into a written agreement to keep the flag there; that nothing but a superior force would take it down; that they considered themselves on the territory of the United States; that they had bound themselves to resist the

---
18 This is John Baker's own version of his encounter with the mail carrier, in Davels to Fairfield, December [15?] 1827, PCHS, 391-394.
19 Rice to Morehouse, July 25, 1827, SD 130.

execution of the laws of Great Britain amongst them; and that they had a right to expect, and would receive the protection of their Government. Morehouse tried to get possession of the agreement, but was refused. He recommended to Wetmore that His Majesty's Government take measures to convince the French settlers that the Americans had no right to act as they had, and to "crush those banditti"; otherwise, the French would probably shortly consider New Brunswick officials to be intruders.[20]

Because of the incidents concerning the mailman and the flag raising, and the circumstances surrounding the written agreement and the supposed offering of it to Peter Markee, a Frenchman, John Baker would be charged with sedition. For his presence in the territory, his building of a home and mills and cutting timber, he would be charged with trespass and intrusion on Crown lands. A warrant was issued for his arrest.[21]

The Madawaska Riot

On August 9, 1827, an American, Phineas Hafford, (Harford) complicated matters by having a complaint sworn out, through the New Brunswick courts, against James Bacon. Joseph Sansfacon, Constable, Parish of Kent, with a warrant, set out to arrest Bacon. On the morning of August 11th, he took Bacon prisoner at his residence in the American colony, and demanded bail. Bacon declared he would not submit to the authority of that writ, and called for help. In the group that responded, John Baker came armed with a sword, John Schoedder

---

[20] George Morehouse to Wm O'dell, July 26, 1827, *Diplomatic Correspondence of the United States. Canadian Relations, 1784-1860*, Vol. II, Washington: Carnegie Endowment For International Peace, 1942, 658, hereinafter referred to as DCUSCR II. T. Wetmore to G. Morehouse, July 31, 1827, SD130. From August 7th to 9th, Morehouse took depositions from Peter Markee, Abraham Chamberland and Wm. Feirio. Report of Morehouse to Wetmore, August 11, 1827, HRD90.
[21] MLD18.

with a musket and Walter Powers, Nathaniel Bartlett, Daniel Savage, and Isaac Jones with clubs. Baker, Bartlett and Savage led the group that surrounded Bacon and declared they had bound themselves not to submit to the laws of England. The constable desisted and went away. Morehouse, because of this "flagrant conduct" announced that he would not attempt to issue any more writs; that sending constables among the Americans would be risking their lives. Attorney General Wetmore and Solicitor General Peters concluded that these men had committed high misdemeanors, punishable by fine and imprisonment. Morehouse and the high sheriff were ordered to arrest and jail the offenders unless they provided bail for their trials at the next term of the supreme court.[22]

Being fully aware that some reaction must come as a result of their defiance of New Brunswick authority, late in August, the inhabitants appointed John Baker and James Bacon to a two-fold mission to the Maine seat of government at Portland: to request that their case be laid before the Legislature and to inquire whether the governor recognized them as citizens entitled to the State's protection. Traveling by canoe, by way of the Allegash River, through Moosehead Lake to the Kennebec River, on September 1, 1827, they presented a petition to Governor Lincoln. It pointed out that they were situated far from the seat of government, exposed to oppression from New Brunswick; that even though they held title to their lands by virtue of deeds from Massachusetts and Maine, New Brunswick officials denied their right to hold their lands, assessed upon them the alien tax, refused them the right to export their produce as Americans, had seized such, and manifested a disposition to harrass and drive them by force out of the country. They had been ordered to pull down their flag. English agents required Americans to train in militia, imposed fines for failure

---
22 G. Morehouse to T. Wetmore, August 22, 1827, SD 130; HRD90.

to do so, and seized and sold their property to pay the fines. They had even sent civil writs and precepts requiring Americans to attend their courts at Fredericton. Furthermore, James Bacon, though duly authorized by Maine, had been forbidden on threat of imprisonment to issue licenses to cut timber. In conclusion, Baker and Bacon emphasized that the territory contained a large body of valuable white pine timber, that the quality of three fourths of the land was very fine for settlement and that their constituents were very uneasy about the long delay in settling the boundary line. They pleaded that the guardian care of the state and federal governments be extended over them, that they be provided with their own officers and magistrates, and be represented in the Legislature.

Baker and Bacon received affirmation and reassurance from Lincoln, along with injunctions to observe the utmost caution in their conduct. They left their application to be laid before the Legislature.[23]

By September 3, 1827, Governor Lincoln had informed Secretary of State Clay of the visit from Baker and Bacon. He urged Clay to "look at the exciting cause of the cupidity of Great Britain and the anxiety of Maine in this profligate claim. The material for ship building on the disputed territory may be calculated to be inexhaustible and the soil so fertile that the Madawaska Settlement exports many thousands of bushels of grain. The towns near the Bay of Fundy, both on the Schoodic and the St. John, under the exclusive policy of Great Britain, derives immense annual profits from ship building and they look with unholy interest and intent on the extensive

---

23 MLD18; Petition of the Inhabitants of the American Settlers on the St. John River to the Government of Maine, September 1, 1827, notarized by C. S. Davels, J. P.. Every American citizen was required to report himself, within two months after his arrival, to a regimental quarter-master, and is subjected to an annual assessment for the maintaince of the provincial militia. MLD 18.

forests of Maine." Lincoln warned that Maine would never assent to arbitration unfavorable to her interests.[24]

Henry Clay sent copies of Lincoln's missive to the President and to his Britannic Majesty's envoy, Charles R. Vaughan, who reiterated his former stand that the inhabitants westward of the Madawaska River were considered by the government of New Brunswick as aliens, therefore not entitled to hold real estate, must pay an alien tax, and could not transmit their produce as Americans.[25]

The Arrest of John Baker

On September 7, 1827, New Brunswick's Edward Winslow Miller, Esq., High Sheriff of York County, bearing charges against John Baker and others of violently opposing and resisting His Majesty's authority and attempting to seduce His Majesty's subjects to depart from their allegiance, departed Fredericton for Madawaska. He had been cautioned to use no more force than necessary for the execution of the warrant, two or three attendants at the most, that the service should be performed quietly, with the least possible parade.[26] Possibly intimidated by probable resistance from the Americans, against orders, he gathered a *posse* of sixteen armed men at Fredericton, and was proceeding to the Disputed Territory when the size of his *posse* was discovered and he was ordered back. Later he was allowed to proceed with only two men on horseback. Apparently, upon his arrival in Madawaska he enlisted the aid of others, for early in the morning of the 25th of September, while John Baker and

---

[24] Enoch Lincoln to Henry Clay, September 3, 1827, DCUSCR II, 136-7.
[25] Clay to Lincoln and Clay to Vaughan, September 14, 1827, C. S. Davels, *North East Boundary Collection* Maine Historical Society, hereinafter referred to as NEBCSDMHS 1827; HRD90.
[26] Wetmore to Miller, September 7, 1827, SD 130.

his family were asleep, he and about a dozen men, armed with *fusees*, etc., surrounded and entered Baker's home.[27] Asahel Baker, awakened by the entry, dashed into his Uncle John's bedroom. He was followed by Francis Rice, Adjutant of the Militia, who carried a pistol. Cyrus Cannon and a man with a musket followed Rice. They first took hold of Mrs. Baker, who was frightened and cried out to them not to kill her or her young child that was with her in the room. Sheriff Miller told her to be civil and he would not hurt her nor her husband. Baker, being awakened, before he got out of bed, was scolded by Sheriff Miller for causing him so much trouble, making him come two hundred miles to arrest him.

Baker arose and they were hurrying him from the room, when his wife asked them to let him dress. They agreed. Asahel Baker attempted to escape, but the door was guarded. Walter Powers came from upstairs, took up a chair and struck one of the *fusees* Battis Michaud held, and broke the breech. Michaud called out for help, and the Deputy Surveyor of Crown Lands drew a pistol and told Powers he had better be civil or he would be obliged to put the law in force.

One of Mrs. Baker's daughters had gotten out of a window; another had gotten out of the door, but was carried back into the house by two men. One of the girls was crying, asking what they were going to do to her father. She was told that they were not going to hurt him.

---

[27] SD130, Wetmore to Miller, September 13, 1827 and Wetmore to Douglas, Sept 18, 1828. John Baker's family consisted of his wife, four daughters and one son of hers by her former husband, and John's two daughters, the youngest being about a year old. Baker had a saw mill with two saws, and a gristmill. He was building a two-story house, while living in his older habitation. He had engaged two carpenters to finish the house, and a bricklayer to complete the chimney this season. Asahel Baker, nephew of John, Walter Powers and John Scudder worked for Baker and lived in his house. In the Sheriff's party were William Diblee, one Sansfacon, one Tibbetts of Tobique, Joseph Deba, Wezew Nadeau and his brother, and John Battis D'Aigle.

Baker tried to show his captors the legal papers he held from the State of Maine, etc., but they answered that that was nothing to them, that "he must submit, that he had better be as easy as possible, as he did not know which side he would fall upon." He proposed to take breakfast and requested time to get some money, but Miller refused and hurried him away, telling him he would fare as well as he himself did. The arrest had taken about ten minutes. Miller and his party hustled Baker down to the river and quickly conveyed him out of the territory. The other offenders, James Bacon and Charles Stetson, had escaped.28

The American community was alarmed. James Bacon, disheartened, thought the English would come up and take them all away. Charles Stetson said he was almost scared to death, and did not know what to do. Asahel Baker travelled to the Kennebec River to deposit in the nearest post office a report to the governor. When Asahel returned, he found that Stetson, Jacob Goldthrite, and Charles Smart had fled to Houlton.29

The First Trial of John Baker

The legal process of bringing John Baker to trial on two charges began with the statement of evidence for his arrest for trespass and intrusion on Crown lands and also for sedition, both dated September 17, 1827:

> John Baker, "being a person greatly disaffected to our said lord the King and his Government and contriving,

---

28 Asahel Baker's deposition, MLD18, 25.; SD130. The new Baker house remained unfinished. It had been boarded in and the window cases and one door case was in. One side of the roof had been shingled after Baker's arrest. His family remained together in the old house. His business was at a standstill. His wife and family were left in a lonesome situation and Mrs. Baker was at times exceedingly distressed and agitated. MLD18.
29 MLD18, 25; PCHS.

endeavouring and unlawfully, maliciously, factiously and seditiously intending to vex, molest and disturb the peace and common tranquillity of this Province, and to bring into hatred and contempt our most Serene Lord, the now King and his Government, and for creating false opinions and suspicions in the people and subjects of our said lord the King and of the Royal power and undisputed prerogative of our said lord the King, within this Province ... attempted to persuade and seduce the said Peter Markee to depart from and violate the allegiance which he owed to our said Lord the King, and did then and there present to the said Peter Markee a written paper to subscribe his name thereto, ... declaring that the government of our said lord the King, had no right to exercise any authority over the Inhabitants of the said settlement, and that the government of the United States of America would protect him, ... and endeavoured to oppose and obstruct the postman, then and there having the custody and carriage of His Majesty's Mail to Canada, in the prosecution of his journey with the same mail ...

Baker was tried on the charge of trespass and intrusion on Crown Lands, found guilty, fined £250 and sentenced to six months in jail. He would not come to trial on the charge of sedition until May 28, 1828.[30]

Troubles in the Aroostook River Valley Settlements

By 1827, the settlers in the Aroostook River Valley numbered about forty, nine of whom were American. None had a grant of land from either government. Lewis and Charles Johnson, born in Nova Scotia, and William McCrea, born in Ireland, were the earliest settlers. George Fields and William Pyles arrived in 1825. There were two settlements, the Upper Settlement, being about

---

30 SD130.

thirty miles from the mouth of the river, and the Lower, nearer the mouth of the Aroostook River.[31]

General James Irish, Maine Land Agent, was informed by the mail carrier from Houlton that John Baker had been committed to the Fredericton prison and that a British officer, who had tried to attach some property belonging to settlers on the Aroostook River, was resisted by force of arms and driven out of the settlement.

William Dalton, of China, Maine, had settled on the Aroostook. During September and October, he and other inhabitants of the Aroostook settlement had been afraid to sleep in their homes, had gone to the lower part of the settlement and spent the nights on the banks of the river and kept watch as in an Indian War. Dalton had been pursued by a British creditor. A New Brunswick constable and five armed men had taken Dalton's cow by force. The constable had said he did not care that he was outside the parish of Kent. Dalton had told him he had better not come again, but he said, "When I come again I shall not be obliged to show my authority to a parcel of damned Yankee settlers of Aroostook," and that he would "bring five hundred armed men and take every soul, men, women and children, to Fredericton jail." Dalton returned to China, Maine.[32]

The dwelling of Ferdinand Armstrong was entered in November, 1827, by a small party from down the St. John River that claimed to have authority to compel payment of a debt and costs. They seized his brother James and conveyed him in a canoe, out of the territory. He was obliged to give up articles of clothing, and what

---

[31] Deposition of George Fields, taken December, 1827, by James Houlton, J. P., at Houlton: In March, 1827, George Morehouse came to the settlement with John Davidson to mark timber to be seized, and forbad people from working, and Fields moved to Houlton. PCSH.

[32] SD 130; Sworn Deposition of William Dalton, October 27, 1827, DSCUSCRII. The constable was probably Richard Inman, who had been employed by Morehouse, and of whom the settlers were most afraid, since he and his party were armed. MLD 18.

money he had, in order to obtain his release. In consequence, Aroostook Valley residents were afraid to go down the St. John to mill their grain or to obtain their supplies. In December, they had tried to cut out a road completely within American territory. After more than thirty working days, suffering the most severe hardships, they found their way out at Foxcroft (Settlement) just north of Houlton.[33]

Jonathan Wilson, of Fairfield, Maine, reported to General Irish that John Baker was being held in a jail, "a place extremely loathsome, filthy and dangerous to the health." Irish informed Governor Lincoln, who asked Sir Howard Douglas for the facts in the case, "in order to allay the anxiety produced by the impression that the privileges of an American citizen and the jurisdiction of a sovereign power have been invaded."[34] Lincoln also sent Charles S. Daveis,[35] as a special agent in behalf of Maine, to investigate and to demand Baker's release. Douglas replied that his instructions did not allow him to explain

---

[33] MLD18. While "Foxcroft" has been interpreted to mean the community which became part of Dover-Foxcroft, in Piscataquis County, it is more reasonable to assume that in this writing it referred to the Foxcroft settlement, a part of Houlton, almost directly south of their settlements, near the Canadian border.

[34] Deposition of Jonathan Wilson, October 27, 1827, DSCUSCRII; Enoch Lincoln to Howard Douglas, October 22, 1827, *Mss Lincoln Family Papers*, Octavo Volume 35, American Antiquarian Society. Used by written permission from The American Antiquarian Society, Worcester, Massachusetts, hereinafter referred to as AASMssLFPOV35.

[35] Daveis' appointment dated November 5, 1827; many excerpts from his MLD18 are included in this text. Charles S. Daveis, born Portland, May 10, 1788, son of Captain Ebenezer and Mehitable [Griffin] Davis of Haverhill, MA. He married Elizabeth Gilman, daughter of Governor Gilman of N H. He was employed in the law office of his brother-in-law, Nicholas Emery, at Parsonsfield. Daveis pioneered equity practice in Maine. William Willis, *Law Courts and Lawyers of Maine*, 1863, Portland, Bailey and Noyes, 577-590, NEBCCSDMHS.

Baker's arrest. This lack of response brought the following proclamation:

> STATE OF MAINE
> BY THE GOVERNOR OF THE STATE OF MAINE
> A PROCLAMATION
>
> Whereas it has been made known to this State that one of its citizens has been conveyed from it, by a Foreign Power, to a gaol in the Province of New Brunswick; and that many trespasses have been committed by inhabitants of the same Province on the sovereignty of Maine and the rights of those she is bound to protect. Be it also known, that, relying upon the government and people of the Union, the proper exertion will be applied to obtain reparation and security. Those, therefore, suffering wrong, or threatened with it, and those interested by sympathy and principle, on account of the violation of our territory and immunities, are exhorted to forbearance and peace, so that preparations for preventing the removal of our land marks, and guarding the sacred and inestimable rights of American citizens may not be embarrassed by unauthorized acts.
> BY THE GOVERNOR: ENOCH LINCOLN
> Council Chambers, Portland, November 9, 1827 [36]

Governor Lincoln's protest to Henry Clay, against submitting the dispute to arbitration by the King of the Netherlands, read in part: "At last we learn that our strength and security and wealth are to be subjected to the mercy of a foreign individual, who, it has been said by your minister, 'rarely decides upon strict principles of law' and 'has always a bias to try, if possible, to split the difference.' I cannot but yield to the impulse of

---
[36] ROSM I.

saying, most respectfully, that *Maine has not been treated as she has endeavoured to deserve.*"37

President John Quincy Adams expressed regret and dismay at Lincoln's statement. He professed a full recognition of the validity of Maine's title to the territory contended for, but explained that it was his duty as president to submit the matter to arbitration.38

The State Department of the United States, on November 19, 1827, commissioned Samuel B. Barrel, Esq. as Special Agent to investigate every facet of previous jurisdictions and to inquire into all aspects of the incarceration of John Baker. 39

Charles S. Daveis, because he was an emissary of Governor Lincoln and not of President Adams, was kept awaiting the pleasure of Lieutenant Governor Douglas at Fredericton, but Barrel's arrival in New Brunswick opened doors and both he and Barrel were permitted to see Baker in prison. Baker appeared to be in tolerable health, and though he had to content himself with rigid confinement, he awaited his deliverance by the States. He said there had been "a great many suggestions to his disparagement, and injurious to his fame and family."40 (Baker

---

37 Enoch Lincoln to Henry Clay, October 30, 1827, U. S. Congress, Senate document No. 171, hereinafter referred to as SD171, ROSM I,1827.

38 Henry Clay to Enoch Lincoln, November 27, 1827, ROSM I, 1827.

39 The Commission of S. B. Barrel, SD130. His commission was acknowledged and sanctioned by Vaughan in Vaughan to Clay, November 20 1827, HD90, and in Vaughan to Douglas, same date, Vaughan directed Douglas to give Barrel every assistance. Douglas, however, never personally received Barrel. Barrel's report is in SD 130.

40 SD130; PCSH, 378-391. S B Barrel wrote: The prison ... precludes the possibility of rendering its tenants comfortable ... described by the grand jury of the county as a public nuisance. SD130: In C. S. Daveis to E. Lincoln, November, 26, 1827, Daveis wrote, "He [Baker] is accused of living with his brother's widow without being married. He assures me he was legally married and that his wife has the certificate. Daveis to Fairfield, about December 15, 1827, PCHS, 391-394; SD130.

was also imprisoned on civil process, at the suit of Robert Shear, residing in Lower Canada. He had confessed a judgment to Shear at Quebec, for £230 in 1821.) Daveis reported to Governor Lincoln that a new practice was taking place, that of removing people from their homes west of the supposed boundary and carrying them into New Brunswick; that the government of New Brunswick had extended the laws of the Province over the disputed territory, that their plan was publicly announced that "no persons are considered legally residing there except by the authority and sufferance of the Provincial government. Part of the territory was reserved as Crown Lands. ... A portion of Maine was thus actually incorporated into the adjoining province."41

---

41 MLD18.

CHAPTER IV

CONTENTION DURING THE FIRST NEGOTIATION FOR A BOUNDARY SETTLEMENT

Enoch Lincoln began his second term as governor in 1828 by reminding the Legislature that there was a perfect harmony of sentiment between the state and federal administrations in a most essential particular, in the words of Henry Clay, "the right to the territory is with us and not with Great Britain; this conviction is held by the President." Lincoln sought the advice of the Legislature as to what measures would be proper, if such acts as that of the arrest and incarceration of John Baker were repeated. He noted that Maine had forty thousand men in its militia, and it appeared proper to request of the general government the erection of some strong fortresses on our interior frontier.[1]

The Joint Select Committee of the Senate and House of Representatives in Relation to the Northeastern Boundary completely supported the President's and Governor's opinion that there was nothing uncertain about Maine's claim arising out of any obscurity in the Treaty of 1783, and further, neither the government of Great Britain, nor any of their negotiators had ever claimed the

---

1 Governor Enoch Lincoln's address to the Legislature, January 3, 1828, ROSM Vol. I, 617-629.

northern part of the State as a *right*, but had requested it as a *condition*. "Their claim, translated into plain language, rests on this proposition: the country lies between two of our provinces, it will be useful to us for facilitating communication and it is also important in a military point of view; we could not obtain it by cession, though we were willing to give an equivalent, but we *want* it and we *will* have it."[2]

The Maine Legislature, by February 9th, had resolved that a crisis existed, that the people of this State had good cause to look to the federal government for protection and that if new aggressions were made and seasonable protection was not given by the United States, the Governor was requested to use all proper means to protect Maine citizens.

On February 20th, 1828, President John Quincy Adams, through Secretary of State Clay, demanded of the British government, through Ambassador Vaughan, the immediate liberation of John Baker, and a full indemnity for his losses due to trial and imprisonment.[3] He again protested against any exercise of exclusive jurisdiction by British authority on the Madawaska, Aroostook, or within any other part of the disputed territory. Vaughan

---

2 John G. Deane, *The Report of the Joint Select Committee of the Senate and House of Representatives of the State of Maine, In Relation to the Northeastern Boundary of the State*, January 26, 1828, "the Deane Report," hereinafter referred to as DR1828. Deane, as an attorney in the Court of Common Pleas for Hancock County, was held in high esteem by the Court and Bar. During the war of 1812, in the militia, he became a Lieutenant Colonel. A Federalist, he represented the District of Maine in the General Court of Massachusetts from 1816-1819. He was a representative to the Maine Legislature from 1825-1828 and again in 1831. Llewellyn Deane, *John G. Deane, A Sketch of his Life*, Collections of the Maine Historical Society, Series II, Vol. I, 179-190.
3 On February 28, 1828, Sophia Rice Baker, at Madawaska, received notice of financial support from Maine's Secretary of State, Amos Nichols. Amos Nichols to Mrs. John Baker, February 28, 1828, AASMss-LFPOV35.

adamantly dissented on all points and commented that all Maine newspapers labored under misconceptions; that the disputed territory was invariably represented as a part of that State, unjustly withheld from it.[4]

Federal support for Maine's interests was demonstrated in the notification of General Chandler and Senator Parris of Maine, by Secretary of War James Barbour, at Washington, on March 22, 1828, that four companies of United States Infantry, under the command of Major N. S. Clark, would be stationed at Houlton Plantation. Samuel Cook and Joseph Houlton of Houlton Plantation were notified that a Senate bill had provided $15,000 for the making of a military road from the mouth of the Mattawamkeag River to Mars Hill. Federal troops to be stationed on that frontier were to be employed thereon.[5]

The Second Trial of John Baker

The second trial of John Baker was carried out in order to "establish in evidence that an actual practical sovereignty has been exercised by Great Britain, on that part of the territory in which those subversive acts have been committed, for upwards of thirty years."[6]

In the Hilary term of the Supreme Court, the grand jury for the county of York, New Brunswick, had found a true bill of indictment against John Baker. The defendant, being in custody, was arraigned, pleaded not guilty, protested against the proceedings and maintained that he

---

4 DCUSCR II, Document 998, 684-687.
5 Secretary of War James Barbour to General Chandler and Albion K. Parris, March 22, 1828, AASMssLFPOV35. Joseph Treat to Samuel Cook, April 28, 182 and Parris to Joseph Houlton, March 31, 1828, Mss, Cary Public Library, Houlton Maine. Used by permission of Joseph Inman, Librarian. An Act of the 20th U. S. Congress in its First Session provided for the opening of the Military Road in the State of Maine.
6 See: Douglas to Vaughan, May 12, 1828, U. S. 25th Congress, House of Representatives, 2nd Session, Executive Document 126, hereinafter referred to as ED 126.

was not amenable to the jurisdiction of their court. He was afterward admitted to bail, and entered into recognizance, himself, in £100, and two sureties of £50 each, for his appearance at the next term. In the meantime, he was to keep the peace and be of good behavior. Thursday, May 8, 1828, was appointed by the court for the trial.

The honorable Chief Justice Sanders, Mr. Justice Bliss, and Mr. Justice Chipman were seated. The defendant, John Baker, appeared, and declared he was ready for his trial. The clerk of the court read the indictment; the Attorney General stated the nature of the offence and set forth the evidence he believed substantiated the charge. The Attorney General called as witnesses: George Morehouse, Francis Rice, Abraham Chamberlain, Peter Marque, (Markee) Peter Sileste, Joseph Sansfason, Edward Miller, Peter Fraser, Henry Clopper, Simon Hebert and George West. The prosecution closed. The defendant was called upon for his defence; Baker addressed the court nearly as follows:

I am a citizen of the United States, and owe allegiance to that country. I have lately received my deed from the States of Maine and Massachusetts. I hold myself bound to their courts. I live in American territory, and hold myself only liable to the courts of that place, being the county of Penobscot in the State of Maine. I enter no defense, and call no evidence. I do decline the jurisdiction of this court.

Mr. Justice Chipman's charge to the jury claimed that the body of the offense was conspiracy to bring into contempt the King's authority, to spread false opinions among his subjects as to his power and prerogative over them, and in fact completely to unsettle their minds as to their allegiance to the Government under which they lived. He considered the overt act of hoisting the flag of the United States, with the express intention of subverting British authority, as full proof. Also, he had sufficient proof as to the written agreement by which they bound themselves to resist the British laws. He felt the court had presented a chain of evidence of clear possession and undisturbed jurisdiction on the part of New Brunswick from the period of its first erection down to the present time, a period of more than forty years.

On the following Monday, Mr. Justice passed sentence and John Baker was taken into custody by the sheriff.[7] The next day John Baker wrote to Governor Lincoln about his sentence:

> I have, respectfully, to inform your honor that the Government of this Province has proven against me, as a citizen of their community, for treasonable conspiracy without proving any act of violence and have sentenced me to two months of imprisonment and to pay twenty five pounds currency and stand committed until the penalty is paid. I provided no evidence in my favor, nor made any defense, but denied their rightful jurisdiction over me, which strengthened the proof that I do not consider myself under their jurisdiction and was not at enmity to their laws. There was much inquiry and incorrect testimony, which I shall make manifest at the correct time. In consequence of British invasion and oppression, my family is in want and distress, and entitled to protection. Being a citizen of the State of Maine, I petition and request that your honor would send relief to my family and take such measures as will effect my release from prison. I remain your most obedient servant, John Baker[8]

---

7 SD130. The jury consisted of Michael Fisher, William Miller, Edward Cambridge, John Bain, Joseph Sutherland, Donald McLeod, Joseph Estabrooks, Jr., John Collins, Samuel Curry, Thomas W. Peters, William S. Esty and Anthony Stewart.

8 Baker to Lincoln, May 13, 1828, AASMssLFPOV35.

Lord Aberdeen analyzed the results of Baker's May 12th conviction, asserted that justice had been done, and commented that Great Britain had never yet been practically divested of her ancient right of jurisdiction. American Ambassador Lawrence rejected Aberdeen's application of the "rule of law" and his erroneous suppositions and pointed out that Mr. Gallatin had stated in a despatch to the Secretary of State that Britain's Mr. Canning had suggested that both sides abstain from jurisdiction, pending suit, from any act of sovereignty over the contested territory.9

John G. Deane visited John Baker in jail in Fredericton. Baker had received a copy of the resolutions of the Legislature and Mr. Barrell's report, and had seen a newspaper account of the President's communication. His term of imprisonment was to expire the twelfth day of July, but he had decided not to pay his fine. On September 27, Baker was:

> still without any experience of release unless I pay the fine. It is very difficult for me to stop [stay] much longer, so much so that I would not for all the gold in Peru, if it is not *beneficial to my country.* I think that I have been here long enough for every purpose and as long as *duty requires.* [Emphasis added.] If I pay the fine, it is, in essence, force, for I must, or stop [stay] in prison.10

Charles Davels sympathized with Baker's impoverishment due to the repeated seizures of his property and his long imprisonment. His family was in distress for funds and without sufficient shelter, as the house he had

---

9 Douglas to Vaughan, May 12, 1828, ED126; Aberdeen to Lawrence, August 14th, 1828; Lawrence to Aberdeen, August 22, 1828, HRD90, 330-344.
10 J. G. Deane to Enoch Lincoln, July 2, 1828; and John Baker to Samuel Cook, September 27, 1828, ASSMssLFPOV35.

been erecting at the time of his arrest was unfinished. Also he was obliged to pay for his own maintenance in prison. Daveis intervened on Baker's behalf and Governor Lincoln referred Daveis' request to Henry Clay, noting that Baker's family, numerous and respectable, had been reduced to want by the absence of a husband's and parent's care and his property was falling fast to ruin. He was a solitary American in a foreign jail. In his conduct he had exhibited the utmost discreetness; and while, with the firmness of a freeman, and the dignity of a patriot, he has denied the jurisdiction of New Brunswick over his person and property, he has submitted with patience to the power which it belonged only to Maine and his country to resist. Lincoln concluded, "If he shall persevere, he will deserve to be called truly great."11

John Baker is Released From Jail

John Baker left Fredericton on the 25th of October, 1828. He had given his bond to pay his fine on the 25th of December. John Deane paid over to him monies he had received from the State Treasurer. There appears to have been about three hundred and sixty-five days of separation from his family when he was released.12

John G. Deane, after having had some time to reflect upon the character and personality of John Baker, wrote to Governor Lincoln that, soon after his arrival in Fredericton in June, the Sheriff of York County had allowed him to visit Baker in jail. To his astonishment, he had found Baker not confined by bars, bolts and locks, but allowed to leave them at his pleasure because merchants of Fredericton with whom he had done business had

---

11 C. S. Daveis to Enoch Lincoln, October 13, and Lincoln to Clay, October 23, 1828, ED 126.

12 John G. Deane to Enoch Lincoln, October 26, 1828, AASMss-LFPOV35. By November 6, 1828, Henry Clay had been authorized by the President to say that the State of Maine would be reimbursed the sum advanced to Baker. Clay to Lincoln, October 25, 1828, ED 126.

applied to Provincial authorities and had given security for £100 for a more lenient imprisonment. During several interviews with Baker, Deane had found that he possessed uncommon knowledge about the upper part of the St. John River and the Restigouche River. Deane wrote that in August he had learned that Baker had been liberated from prison through the intervention of some French people at Madawaska, who had given a note, payable on the 25th of December, which had directly or indirectly produced his discharge. He had visited with Baker for nearly five days and had seen a practical illustration of his knowledge of the country and that he was generally respected by the inhabitants of New Brunswick. He noted that in Madawaska Settlement Baker was greeted with a great deal of cordiality, attachment and respect. All had seemed willing to give him any credit he needed to carry on his business. Furthermore, Deane wrote, he had found Baker to be very devoted to Maine, doing all he could, in a prudent and cautious manner, to promote its interest. He noted that he was aware that there had been circumstances of a prior date against his character but was convinced he had sustained a good one since he had been settled in Madawaska. Therefore he recommended making Baker a Magistrate for the County of Penobscot.[13]

---

13   Deane to Lincoln, February 23, 1828. AASMssLFPOV35. The reference to Baker's character may be what is referred to in *The Makers of Moscow*, loc. cit., page 20: "Another of our natives, John Baker, son of Joseph Baker, and his brother Nathan, were found to be dishonest in trading with the Indians. Upon notice of their coming trial they migrated to Madawaska and started farming." John, having been born in 1796 would have been about twenty years old when he migrated northward. The author has been unable to prove or disprove these allegations.

John Baker

Sophia Baker

Charles S. Daveis

Governor Enoch Lincoln

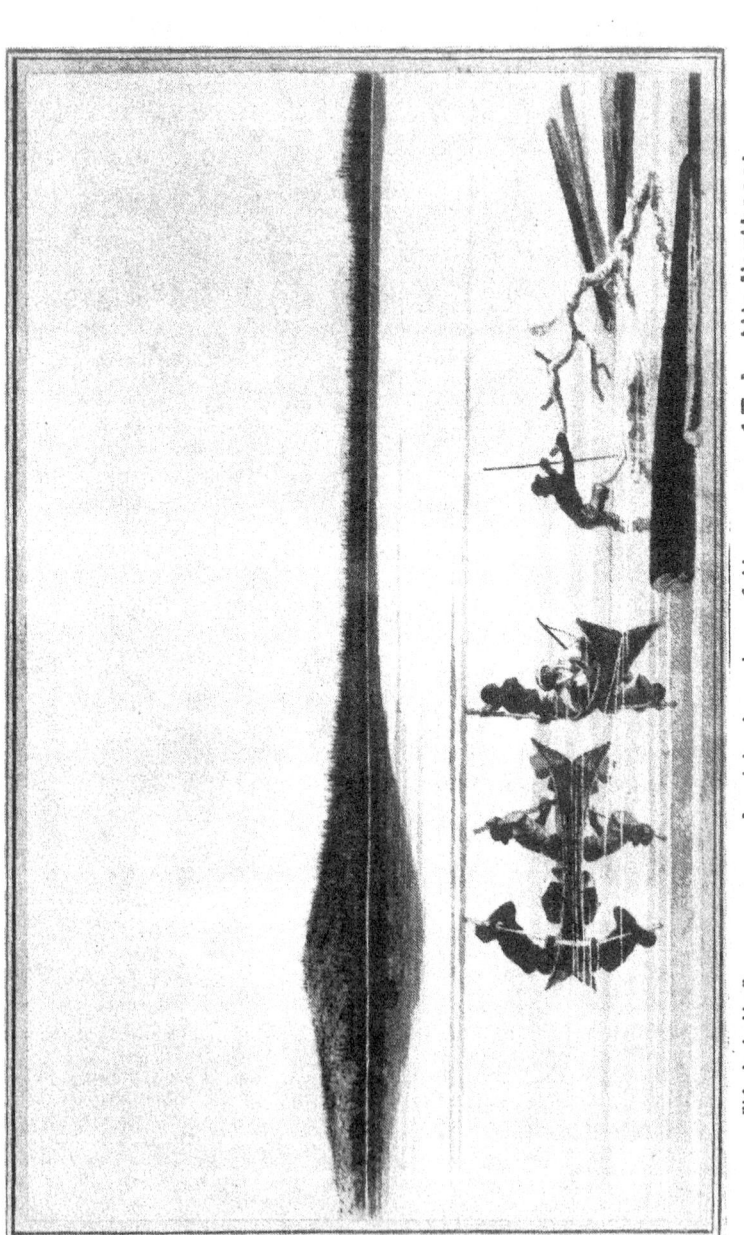

"Katahdin", a *camera lucida* drawing of the crew of Talcott's Northeast Boundary Survey of 1842, by artist P. Harry.

John G. Deane's Investigation of the Location of the Original Northwest Corner Boundary Marker

John G. Deane, late in 1828, investigated and documented the location of the old original boundary marker between Nova Scotia and Quebec. Pursuant to instructions from the Honorable William P. Preble, an Agent of the United States for settling the north-eastern boundary of the United States, he held conversations with many of the oldest and most prominent inhabitants of Madawaska Settlement.[14] When he asked where the boundary of Canada had always been considered to be, uniformly the answer was "St. Francis." When he asked whether they meant St. Francis River or Mountain, the explanation was, "the Mountain or some place upon it, at the head of the streams." When he asked what mountain they meant by St. Francis, they said "the mountain between the Grand Fourche and St. Francis Rivers". When he asked where these rivers empty themselves, the answers were "The Grand Fourche runs into Trois Pistoles, and the St. Francis into the River St. John." Some were more definite and pointed

---

14 SUSC Ap49, 345; Deane's report was based on depositions of Raphael Michaud and Jean Baptiste Long taken on November 8, 1828. Jean Baptiste Long, of Madawaska, Parish of St. Emilie, swore that he perfectly recollected the cedar post which he was always told was the line of (Lower) Canada; it was six feet high, hewed on four sides; the side next to the Portage Road and the side next to Canada were marked or written over from top to bottom. He said that the post stood on the southwesterly side of the portage road, between the Grand Fourch stream and the peak of Mount St. Francis. Four years ago last August, when going from the Lake Temiscouata to Canada, he saw this post had been cut down and put on a fire. He took it from the fire, and set it by the side of the road. About one month later the post was gone. Paulite Marchee, Michael Cire, Joseph Cire, Simon Baulier, Fearmer Herbert, Jeremiah Duble and Captain Fearmer Thibideau of Madawaska and Colonel Alexander Frazer who resided at Grand Portage supported their testimony. SUSC Ap 49, 339-347.

out the exact spot upon the St. Francis Mountain where a post formerly stood on the portage, which they understood to be the boundary of Canada. This spot he visited in company with Michael and Joseph Cire. The place where the post had stood was exactly upon the ridge or highland which separates the waters which flow into the Grand Fourche and the waters which flow into the St. Francis; and, as near as he could judge, the waters of the respective streams were not more than half a mile asunder. At the place where the post was described to have stood, there was a rock, peculiar for its size and appearance, differing from any other elsewhere on the Grand Portage. They further stated that fugitives from Canada had been considered free from arrest when they had passed the St. Francis.

Federal Troops Construct Hancock Barracks and the Military Road

During John Baker's internment in Fredericton, Federal troops had arrived at Houlton Plantation. Brevet Major N. S. Clark led the first Aroostook expedition. His unit of the 2nd United States Infantry had been en route to Houlton from Madison Barracks, Sackett's Harbor, New York, since April 17th, 1828. On June 27th, the first of the four Companies of his Regiment, Company C, arrived at Houlton Plantation and began building the Hancock Barracks.[15] The larger part of Clark's regiment, Companies E, F, and K, totaling 151 men under the command of Captain Thomas Staniford, would be assigned to build-

---

15 *Monthly Returns of the Commanding Officers of the 2nd Infantry at Hancock Barracks, Houlton, Maine from 1828 to 1839*, National Archives, Record Group 94, Muster Roll, Regular Army Companies, Records of the Adjutant General's Office, 1780-1917. National Archives Microfilm Publications, Microcopy 617, Roll 448, Hancock Barracks, Houlton, Maine, hereinafter referred to as NARG94.
See APPENDIX III for federal troop records.

ing the Military Road, already surveyed and located under the superintendance of J. B. F. Russell, A. Q. M., U. S. Army. In July 1828, Major Clark had 68 men at Hancock Barracks, in Companies C, H and part of Company K. The building of Hancock Barracks was in the style favored by United States Army engineers in other areas of the nation, a quadrangle of quarters and offices surrounding a parade ground, the whole being enclosed by a thick stockade. It was constructed upon an eminence of ground east of Houlton Village, on the north side of the Woodstock Road. The construction was difficult; ledge had to be blasted, the hollows filled, and gravel hauled in to make the surface of the parade ground smooth. Some soldiers cut and shaped trees and used their horses to bring them to the site and set them into the ground to form a stockade. A flagstaff was erected at the entrance on the south side. Other soldiers, aided by as many local workmen as could be employed, built the officers' quarters on the east side of the quadrangle. Barracks for the troopers were to be constructed on two sides, and space was planned for the offices, hospital, storage of supplies, and for a powder magazine. So enormous was the task and so small were the numbers of workmen, that it was not surprising that quarters for all of the troops were not completed in time, and many of the enlisted men spent the first winter in army tents.[16]

While work went on at Hancock Barracks, Captain Staniford and 151 soldiers were encamped at Beaver Brook,[17] twenty-two miles south of Houlton. Company F was under his personal command; 2nd Lieutenant William

---

16 NARG94; Francis Barnes, *The Story of Houlton*, Houlton, Maine, Will H. Smith, 1889, np. See "'A Class of Men': United States Army Recruits in Maine, 1822-1860", by Dale R Steinhaurer, pp. 92-119, Maine Historical Society *Quarterly*, Vol. 30, No. 2, Fall, 1990, for information about the life of army recruits at Hancock Barracks.

17 This Beaver Brook has its source in Linneus, and is a tributary of the East branch of the Mattawamkeag River; it is not be confused with the Beaver Brook of the Aroostook River.

Bloodgood commanded Company E; while 1st Lieutenant Charles F. Morton, in the absence of Captain Greenlief Dearborn, was in command of Company K. They spent the summer building what would be variously known as the Beaver Brook Road, the Soldier Road, the Military Road and eventually the Bangor Road. Staniford, in his July, 1828 Report, noted that Hiram T. Smith, Company F, had died July 1st, 1828.[18]

The road builders arrived at Hancock Barracks on the 29th of September. However, the road was not completed to Major Clark's satisfaction. On December 7, he sent Sergeant Pike, with fourteen men, under the direction of Samuel Cook, to determine how to improve the route and to instruct Pike in the mode of making winter roads. On January 14, 1829, Clarke informed Head Quarters at New York that the task of constructing the road in the manner of a turnpike was beyond the capabilities of his soldiers; besides, they were needed to complete and guard the post. He suggested that hired laborers complete the work. Future road building contracts were given to civilians.[19]

Sir Howard Douglas heard rumors that a military road was to be opened to Mars Hill and a military post established there. Martin Van Buren, assured Douglas that the President had no plan to occupy Mars Hill. Furthermore, in a spirit of conciliation, he had decided to postpone the building of a military road from Mars Hill to the mouth of the Madawaska River.[20]

---

[18] NARG94., Stanifords records show that Smith had enlisted at Sackett's Harbor on October 7, 1825. For many years his grave was marked by a a small white cross at the head of a heap of boulders, but in 1938 the Lydia Putnam Chapter, D.A.R., placed a granite marker on his grave. It is located on the east side of Route 2A, which wends its way north through Haynesville.

[19] Barnes, loc. cit. Note: "Head Quarters," as it appears in official documents, rather than "Headquarters", will be used throughout text.

[20] Douglas to Vaughan, December 11, 1828; Martin Van Buren to Charles R. Vaughan, May 11, 1829, HRD I 26, 17-19.

CHAPTER V

CONTENTION DURING ARBITRATION OF THE NORTHEAST BOUNDARY DISPUTE

President John Quincy Adams announced, at the end of 1828, that the last friendly expedient for a boundary settlement had been resorted to and in order to carry into effect the provisions of the fifth article of the Treaty of Ghent and the convention of the 29th September, 1827, His Majesty, the King of Netherlands had, by common consent, been selected to arbitrate the dispute.[1]

Andrew Jackson,[2] a Democrat, began his two terms as president in 1829. Governor Enoch Lincoln merely alluded to Jackson's election in his third and last Governor's address on January 8th, but he expressed alarm that the United States Army Engineers had failed to place fortifications to protect the security of Maine's principal river, the Penobscot. He feared, in case of war, the enemy might easily advance to Bangor and control what would become Maine's commercial capital, and beyond that, a

---

1 President J. Q. Adams, Fourth Annual Address to Congress, 1828, *A Compilation of the Messages and Papers of the Presidents*, the Joint Committee on Printing of the House and Senate, Fifty Second Congress, 1897, Bureau of National Literature, Inc., New York, Vol. II, 974, hereinafter referred to as MPP.

2 Andrew Jackson was born March 15, 1767, in South Carolina; he died at age 78 and was buried at Hermitage, Tennessee.

most valuable and extensive territory. He applauded the liberality of the United States Government in its appropriation for a Military Road.³

Great Britain Moves to Strengthen Her Claim by Instituting the Office of Warden of the Disputed Territory

Lumber mills were being erected in the disputed territory, on the Eton grant on the Aroostook River (now part of Caribou) with the avowed purpose of the owners of getting their supply of timber from Massachusetts owned forests. One proprietor, Dennis Fairbanks, had assurances from the New Brunswick authorities that he might cut timber without hindrance, provided he agreed to pay them for it if they succeeded in obtaining their right to the territory. Other mills were being built at Fish River, and inhabitants of the St. John River Valley had obtained permits from the Province. Much trespass timber was being cut in spite of the understanding that during arbitration neither party would perform any act on the disputed territory to strengthen his own claims or to effect the property in issue.⁴

Thomas Baillie, Commissioner of Crown Lands and Forests for New Brunswick, denied giving any person authority to cut timber on the disputed territory.⁵ Sir Howard Douglas despatched his new Deputy Commissioner of Crown Lands, James Maclauchlan, with instructions to inspect all lumber camps and mills and to seize any timber brought into the acknowledged boundaries of his

---

3 Speech of Governor Enoch Lincoln to the Maine Legislature, January 8, 1829, ROSM II, 2-30.
4 George Coffin, *Report of the Land Agent of Massachusetts*, Boston, December 8, 1828. Clay to Vaughan, January 9, 1829, HRD 126.
5 Thomas Baillie to H. Douglas, February 11, 1819, HRD 126, 13. The mills on the Fish River had been built by Wilmot and Peters, of Frederickton, without New Brunswick authority or grant and were in possession of two Americans, Savage and Bartlett.

province from the disputed territory. The proceeds would be held in trust for the eventual owner of the territory. This appointment of James Maclauchlan as Warden of the Disputed Territory, had, in effect, asserted British jurisdiction of that territory.[6]

In response, on February 23rd, the Maine Legislature recommended the passage of a bill to prevent foreigners from exercising acts of jurisdiction within the State through the serving of civil or criminal processes. On March 3, by Resolve, the land agent was empowered to serve precepts on trespassers.[7] Daniel Rose, Maine Land Agent, at Hawk Island, Penobscot River, on September 29, 1829, commissioned General John Webber, as Assistant Land Agent, to proceed to the St. John River and inspect all lands and trespasses within the state, north of the line run due west from the Monument.[8]

Enoch Lincoln, a Republican, whose re-election had gone uncontested for three successive years, had tried to act as a moderating influence by re-nominating incumbent office holders regardless of their politics. Unfortunately the National Republicans defeated his bipartisan efforts through their control of the Executive Council, by failing to approve his Democratic Republican nominations. Lincoln refused renomination by the Democratic

---

[6] Douglas to Vaughan, February 11, 1829., HRD 126, 13; Report of James A. Maclauchlan, Deputy Commissioner of Crown Lands and Forests for New Brunswick, April 4, 1829, ED 126. Machlauchlan traced the exploring line between Woodstock and Houlton, found that this line, intersected the St. John three miles above the Grand Falls and had it reblazed.

[7] ROSM II, 45-46.

[8] Daniel Rose, *Report of the Land Agent*, 1829, dated January 1, 1830. MD IV. Dr. Daniel Rose of Boothbay, born in Connecticut and graduated from Yale in 1791, settled in present-day Alna, Maine. He practiced medicine at Boothbay and Wiscasset. Member of the Maine Senate 1820-24, he became Warden of the Maine State Prison at Thomaston. He was Land Agent from 1828 to 1831. He died at Thomaston, October 25, 1833. Mundy, op. cit.

Republican caucus. His withdrawal caught party leaders unprepared, so they left the nomination to a state convention. In the meantime, the National Republicans had nominated Jonathan Glidden Hunton of Readfield. Hunton undoubtedly owed his nomination to the refusal of more prominent colleagues to risk their reputations in what was sure to be a hard-fought contest with Samuel Emerson Smith. The campaign quickly developed into one of the most vicious in the state's political history. Hunton's single term as Governor of Maine was characterized by such aggressive infighting that little room was left for progress. Moses Greenleaf's *Maps and Statistical Views of the State* was completed and copies of the commissions of the several Governors of the Provinces of Quebec, Nova Scotia and New Brunswick were deposited in the office of Maine's Secretary of State. These commissions gave detailed descriptions of the boundaries of the Provinces adjoining the District of Maine of Massachusetts, and described the same lines claimed by Maine as the limits of her territory.[9]

    M. P. Norton, Land Agent under Hunton, directed General Webber to visit the St. John River, to take the census and to check on depredations. Webber reported large quantities of timber cut on the Restigouche by British subjects; on the St. John and Aroostook, thefts were on a smaller scale. Sawmills were being erected on most of the streams that run out of Maine's territory into the St. John. The Provincial government was encouraging

---

[9] Thomas Gaffney, *Maine's Mr. Smith, A Study of the Career of Francis O. J. Smith, Politician and Entrepreneur*, Doctoral thesis, University of Maine, Orono, May, 1979, 50-60; citing (Portland) *Eastern Argus*, February 17, 1829, and Hatch, *Maine, A History* 197-198 Governor Enoch Lincoln died suddenly on October 8, 1829, at age forty. His decisive handling of the boundary controversy had won him great respect. Nathan Cutler served as Acting Governor from October 12, 1829, to February 10, 1830. Henry Sweetser Burrage, *Maine in the Northeastern Boundary Controversy* Portland: printed for the State of Maine, 1919, 157-158; ROSMII, 11.

settlement of the territory by emigrants from New Brunswick and the Canadas, so settlements on the St. John river extended almost to the mouth of the St. Francis.[10]

Arbitration Begins

After the Commission had failed, during the years 1814 to 1821, to agree on the location of the Northwest Angle of Nova Scotia, nine years had been spent in preparing statements to be presented to the arbiter, William, by the Grace of God, King of the Netherlands, Prince of Orange, Nassau, Grand Duke of Luxembourg, and etc. Henry U. Addington and William Huskisson, with the aid of Ward Chipman, Jr. and Sir Howard Douglas, prepared the British Statement. (Douglas had resigned his position as New Brunswick's Lieutenant Governor, while in England, for this purpose, leaving New Brunswick in an *inter-regnum* government under William Black.) Albert Gallatin, jurist and diplomat, aided by William Pitt Preble, Minister of the United States to the Hague, with the assistance of Charles S Daveis, prepared the American statement.[11] Dr. Tiarks and William Pitt Adams delivered the British statement to the Hague. Sir Howard Douglas went to the Hague, got an audience with the King and "slyly dropped into the royal ear a few well chosen words as to Gallatin's supposed readiness to split the difference." Adams, too "was wondering aloud" if the King could not give to Britain half of the St. John valley.[12]

The United States replied to the British statement with a four hundred and seventy-seven page *Definitive Statement*, which included the commissions of the governors of Nova Scotia, in full, from 1719 to 1782, and

---

10 M. P. Norton, *Report of the Land Agent*, 1830. See APPENDIX I for 1830 census information.
11 Ganong, loc. cit.
12 H. George Classen, *Thrust and Counterthrust, the Genesis of the Canada-UnitedStatesBoundary*, 1965, Longmans, Canada Ltd., 26-27.

also of Governor Carleton of August 16, 1784. This was the first time these documents had appeared in print. The British replied with a forty-one page document and the statements of the two nations were submitted to the King of Netherlands in April, 1830. But, on August 24th, the King's birthday, the Belgian populace rebelled and by the end of 1830, he ruled only Holland.[13]

The Award of the Arbiter Is Received and Rejected

On January 8, 1831, Governor Samuel Smith, reported a delay in the arbitration brought about by the revolt. Deprived of the greater portion of his kingdom, the King was made dependent upon Great Britain for support.[14] His weakened political situation would cause the American Commissioners to lose faith in his ability to be non-partisan. The Decision of the Arbiter was handed down on January 10, 1831. He had concluded, in fairness to both nations, that

...a line drawn due north from the source of the River St. Croix to the point where it intersects the middle of the channel of that River, ascending it to a point where the River St. Francis empties itself into the River St. John; thence through the middle of the channel of the River St. Francis, ascending it to the source of its southernmost branch, ... thence a line drawn due west, to the point where it unites with the line claimed by the United States of America and delineated on Map A; thence said line to the point at which, according to said map, it coincides with that claimed by Great Britain; thence the line traced on the map of the two

---
13 Ganong, loc. cit. 333-335; Classen, loc.cit., 27.
14 Governor Samuel E. Smith, Democratic Republican, born in Hollis, New Hampshire, 1788, graduated from Harvard College in 1808. H. S. Burrage, loc. cit., 161. Governor Smith's Speech to the Legislature, January 8, 1831.

powers, to the northwestern most source of the Connecticut River.[15]

The King of the Netherlands had simply expressed an opinion and not a final decision, and had merely split the difference between the two claims, even though he had given to the United States more territory than to Great Britain.[16] On January 12th, William P. Preble protested that the King had abandoned the boundaries of the Treaty, and substituted for them a different line of demarkation and this constituted a departure from the powers delegated to him.[17]

Lord Palmerston, on February 9, 1831, notified the British Minister in Washington that Britain had accepted the arbiter's award.[18]

The Decision was received by the U. S. Department of State on March 16, 1831. Martin Van Buren, by direction of President Jackson, transmitted to Governor Smith a copy and translation of the award. Smith sent copies to the Legislature. The Joint Select Committee approved Preble's protest, concluded that the adoption of the decision of the arbiter would violate the constitutional rights of the State of Maine, and put forth a strong statement of Maine's rights as a state of the Union:

... Among the rights and powers not delegated to the union as a whole, are the rights and powers of the States respectively to retain their entire territories and of exercising sovereign power over them; and the implication is as strong as the implication can be, that each State is bound to guarantee to the other the integrity of its territory. There is no power given to

---

15 Ganong, loc. cit., 336.
16 From Ganong's evaluation of the decision of the arbitrator, Ganong, loc. cit. 336.
17 State of Maine, *Report of the Joint Select Committee of the House of Representatives*, John G. Deane, March 30, 1831, ROSM II, 257-260.
18 Classen, loc. cit., 28-29.

Congress by the constitution to dismember a State. Such power cannot be exercised without the agreement and consent of the State, [without] altering the Constitution.[19]

At the beginning of 1832, the acceptance or rejection of the Award was still pending before the Senate and in the hands of the Committee of Foreign Relations. Governor Smith appointed Judge William P. Preble as Maine's special agent to Washington.[20]

On February 17, 1832, it was proposed that Maine should cede to the United States her claim and jurisdiction over that portion of the territory which lay northerly and easterly of the line recommended by the Arbiter, for an indemnity in land. Preble was authorized to enter into negotiation with persons designated by the President. The agreement could then be subject to ratification. The delegation from Maine agreed that it saved the honor of the State, would be immensely advantageous to the State and relieved the United States of pecuniary problems. Preble stressed that these propositions were to be made *confidentially*, and to be laid before the Legislature of Maine, confidentially, and their action would be kept *confidential*. Preble said there was unanimity in the delegation on this subject.

However, there had been *one dissenter*, George Evans. Maine's delegation had consisted of Evans, John Anderson and Edward Kavanagh (Kavanagh would later become Governor of Maine); Rufus McIntire (fated to become Maine's Land Agent during the confrontation of 1839); Leonard Jarvis (prominent merchant and politician, brother of Charles Jarvis, Assistant Land Agent to be, in 1839); Cornelius Holland, and James Bates. Evans ex-

---

19 Van Buren to Samuel E. Smith, March 18, 1831, ROSM II, 247-248; Governor Smith to the Legislature, March 25, 1831, ROSM II; Deane, loc. cit., ROSM II, 265-66: and 242-6.
20 Preble to Smith, February 3, 1832, ROSM II, 450.

plained his opinion as to the proper course to be pursued in response to the Governments "informal" proposition:

> If the General Government finds itself embarrassed in its proceedings on this subject, and desires the assent of Maine to enable it to act freely, the proper step to be taken is that the General Government should signify *formally and officially* to the Government of Maine, its wishes, accompanied by a proposition on its part, which the Legislature of Maine may deliberate upon, for the accommodation of the embarrassing question.[21]

On February 23rd, the press in Augusta revealed that the Senate and House of Representatives were holding *secret* sessions to discuss the matter. On March 3, 1832, the Maine Legislature, still in secret session, resolved that upon the appointment by the President of persons to enter into negotiation with Maine for the *relinquishment* of her claim to the territory lying north and east of the Rivers St. John and St. Francis, and for the *cession* of its *jurisdiction*, for an ample indemnity, the Governor, with the advice of Council was authorized to appoint three Commissioners in behalf of the State, to discuss the subject. Any agreement or treaty was to be *submitted to the Legislature* of Maine for approval or rejection.[22]

On the day that the House of Representatives approved the above resolve, an article was published in the *Maine Daily Journal*, entitled "TRUTH." The Editor claimed to have found it in his letterbox, in a handwriting unknown to him. It began with these words:

> Suppose the Legislature of Maine, in secret sessions, being bound by the solemnity of an oath, should

---

21 Evans to Preble, February 16, 1832, ROSM II, 459-461.
22 ROSM II, 466-467.

vote to sell the whole or any part of the State to the British Government and thereby become British subjects, would that oath be binding on those who do not agree with the bargain or sale; or ought they to speak and warn the people of their danger before it is too late? ... Suppose in secret session the whole number of votes to have been 149, 80 of whom were in favor of selling part of the State to Great Britain and 69 against, ought not the 69 to take aholdst and make the plot known to their constituents or are they bound by their oath to be gagged on such a momentous question?[23]

The Legislature continued in secret sessions until March 9, 1832. William P. Preble, Reuel Williams and Nicholas Emery formed the commission to meet with President Jackson's appointees, who were Secretary of Navy Levi Woodbury, Secretary of Treasury Louis McLane and Secretary of State Edward Livingston. On March 21, the Senate Foreign Relations Committee recommended the acceptance of the Dutch award. However, on June 12th, 1832, after the injunction of secrecy had been removed, Congress began to debate the issue. Henry Clay held the strong opinion that the British claim had no validity. There was resentment that on the previous March 21, 1832, in secret session, the United States Senate had adopted a *secret resolution* to the effect that the Senate would advise the President to inform the King of Netherlands that the United States *would* accept his decision as arbiter. Clay forcefully demanded that the Senate's proper task was to determine the validity of the award of the King of Netherlands. He propounded the view that the King's decision should be declined, and that negotiations should be reopened with Great Britain. He and his

---

23 One newspaper after another took up the discussion of the contents of this note. For a discussion see Burrage, loc. cit., 199-204.

supporters held forth until June 23rd, when the Senate rejected the award of the King of Netherlands.[24]

Meanwhile, On the Northeastern Frontier

Just after the injunction of secrecy was removed, the Maine Legislature incorporated the town of Madawaska,[25] set Madawaska off from Washington County, annexed it to Penobscot County, and declared that the town must hold an election. The Act to Incorporate, approved

---

[24] Burrage, loc. cit., 204-215.

[25] Section I: Be it enacted by the Senate and House of Representatives in Legislature Assembled, that territory called and known by the name of Madawaska Settlement, in the Counties of Washington and Penobscot, bounded as follows; beginning on the boundary line of this State and the province of New Brunswick, at the northeast corner of Township F on Greenleaf's map, near to and south of the River St. John; thence west by the north line of Township F and Township K to the east line of township numbered 16 in the third range of townships west of the east line of the State; thence north by the east line of said township No. 16, to the northeast Corner thereof; thence west to the north line of townships No 16 in the third, fourth, fifth, sixth and seventh ranges, west of the east line of the State; thence continuing the same course until it intersects the River St John; thence north until it intersects the River St. Francois; thence by the center of said river to the Grand Portage; thence by the Grand Portage to the line of Canada and this State; thence by the line of Canada and this State, as established by the commissions of Governor's Murray, 1763; Carleton and Haldimand, 1763-178; the Act of the British Parliament 1774; and the Treaty of Peace in 1783, to the northwest Angle of Nova Scotia, now the northwest angle of New Brunswick; thence south by the line established by the commissions of Governors Wilmot, Campbell, Legge, Hughes, Hammond and Parr, from 1763-1782, by the treaty of peace of 1783, and by the commissions to Sir Thomas Carleton, first Governor of New Brunswick in 1784, to the first mentioned bounds, being the east line of the State, on the true meridian north from the Monument at the head of the River St Croix; be, and the same is incorporated into a town by the name of Madawaska. *Private and Special Laws of the State of Maine,* Vol. II, 1829-1835, 243-244.

on March 15, 1831, was part of an effort to revitalize Maine's jurisdiction in the disputed territory. It described boundaries and stipulated that its inhabitants were subject to the same duties and liabilities, and vested with the same privileges and immunities as other incorporated towns.

A second effort was to ascertain the number of persons settled on the public lands north of the line running west from the Monument, and the manner in which they held their lands, to enable the State to adopt some mode of quieting these settlers in their possessions. On April 2, 1831, John G. Deane, Esq., of Ellsworth and Edward Kavanagh of New Castle, were assigned this duty.[26]

A warrant for a town meeting at Madawaska was issued by William D. Williamson, Justice of the Peace for Penobsot County:

> State of Maine to Walter Powers of Madawaska,
> Greeting: You are hereby required, in the name of the State of Maine, to notify and warn the inhabitants of said Madawaska, qualified to vote in town affairs, to meet at Mr. Peter Lizott's dwelling house, in said town, on Saturday, the 20th day of August, 1831, and there to transact such business as may come before them.
> 1st: To choose a Moderator to govern the meeting. 2nd: To choose a Town Clerk. 3rd: To choose Select Men. 4th: To choose Constables, and all other Town officers, and you are hereby required, in the name of the State of Maine, to make a return of this warrant, with your doings therein, at the said meeting at which you will preside until the moderator is chosen. Given under

---

[26] Resolve of the Legislature, Chapter 76, March 21, 1831 ROSM Vol. II, 240; Edward Kavanagh, [1795-1844], Maine statesman and diplomat, Governor of Maine and the first Catholic Governor of a New England State; see W. L. Lucey, S. J., *Edward Kavanagh*, Francestown, NH: Marshall Jones, n. d., preface.

my hand and seal at Bangor, in said County, 11th July, 1831. Signed: William D. Williamson, J. P.27

On July 11, 1831, the same day that the warrant was issued for the Madawaska town meeting, Deane and Kavanagh[28] began their tour, by way of Moosehead Lake to the Penobscot River, down that river to Chesuncook Lake, thence to Umbazookskus and Allagash Stream to the St. John and Aroostook Rivers. They visited all residences on both sides of the St. John River. Pierre Lisotte, a Captain of the Militia, who commanded nine companies of fifty privates each, lived on the south side of the river. On July 29th they lodged with him, advised him that he was now a citizen of Maine and urged him to seek election as representative from the District of Madawaska to the Legislature. Lisotte, fearful of acting in opposition to his allegiance to New Brunswick, refused.

On August 2nd, Deane and Kavanagh, six miles down river, dined with Leonard R. Coombs, Captain of the Mada-

---

27 HRD 126; William Durkee Williamson, a politician, lawyer and eminent historian, of Bangor and later Hancock County. Born in Canterbury, Connecticut, in 1779, graduated Brown University, studied law, county attorney for Hancock County; 1816-1820, Massachusetts Senator, President of the Maine Senate, and Judge of Probate, Penobscot County, until 840. He died on May 27, 1846. He wrote *The History of Maine from Its First Discovery in 1602 to the Separation, A D 1820* Willis, loc. cit., 517-521.

28 Edward Kavanagh, "Wilderness Journal," *Maine History News*, Maine League of Historical Societies and Museums, Vol. XVI No. 2 and No. 4, hereinafter referred to as WKJ. See *State of the Madawaska and Aroostook Settlements in 1831, Report of John G. Deane and Edward Kavanagh to Samuel E. Smith, Governor of the State of Maine*, (the Deane-Kavanagh Report) with editorial comments by W. O. Raymond, in *Collections of the New Brunswick Historical Society*, Vol. III, No. 9, 1914, hereinafter referred to as WORDK, for enumeration of residents on both sides of the St. John River and Peter Lizotte's Deposition, September 23rd, 1831. See APPENDIX IV for settlers in disputed territory in 1831.

waska Militia. James Maclauchlan landed from a birch bark canoe and asked them by what authority they were exploring territory under the jurisdiction of Great Britain. They responded that they were officers of the State of Maine, exercising their duties. He asked to see their commissions. Deane asked him for his authority to make such a demand. He answered that he was Warden of the Disputed Territory in behalf of the British Government, that his Government was in possession of the soil and in full exercise of jurisdiction over it; that he did not feel bound to show his authorization. After a few minutes, Deane showed him his commission. Maclauchlan made a copy.[29]

Maclauchlan had come from Fredericton to protest against their counting the inhabitants on the south side of the River. He warned them that if they proceeded to do so on the north side of the River, he had orders to arrest them. He asked what course they would then adopt. Deane and Kavanagh replied that they would waive no right given them by their commissions, that Maine had full sovereignty over all the land within her limits and had not agreed to any act which would bar her right to extend

---

29 WJK; WORDK; James A. Maclauchlan, Warden of the Disputed Territory, was the son of Captain James Maclauchlan, of Britain's Royal Engineers. Born in Scotland, educated at a military school, he was recruited into the 104th Regiment as an ensign. Machlauchlan shared his regiment's hardships and adventures en route to Upper Canada and during the battles of 1814. During this time he was promoted to Lieutenant and praised for his valor in the assault on Fort Erie. During that action, while leading the grenadier company into action, he was severely wounded. At the close of hostilities the 104th returned to New Brunswick, and in May, 1817 it was disbanded. Maclauchlan received a land grant on the portage between Lake Temiscouata and the St. Lawrence, but returned to Fredericton, where he married Sarah L. Plant and lived in Kingswood. He was appointed Deputy Surveyor-general, and Supervisor of Great Roads. By 1822 he was a magistrate for York County. Later he was commissioned Lieutenant Colonel in the New Brunswick militia. WORDK

her jurisdiction to the utmost extent to which she had ever made claim. Maclauchlan mentioned the decision of the King of the Netherlands, and said that Great Britain, being in sole possession of the soil, had a right by the law of nations to retain sole and exclusive jurisdiction until she was divested of that right by proper means. He remarked that it was his duty to accompany them while in the settlement unless they promised not to make inquiries of the settlers on the north side of the River. They refused, and he accompanied them for four days.

Deane and Kavanagh returned south by way of Fish River, across the portage of the Fish River, to Little Machias River, to the first settlement on the Aroostook River and found I. F. Currier living on the south bank on land owned by Mr. Black,[30] the interim Governor of New Brunswick. They dined with Mr. Goss, visited Mr. Hooper and Dennis Fairbanks and descended the St. John to Woodstock. They went overland to Hancock Barracks and arrived in Bangor on August 23rd.[31]

Madawaska's First Town Meeting

On August 19th, while Edward Kavanagh had been visiting with Major Clark at Hancock Barracks, Walter Powers, at Madawaska, had been following the directions given in the warrant:

---

30 William Black, shipper, merchant and politician, b 1771 in Aberdeen, Scotland. Brother of John Black, the prosperous timber exporter of John Black and Company, the principal New Brunswick supplier of masts to the British Admiralty. By 1812, they possessed one of the largest business enterprises in British North America. In 1817 William Black was mayor of St. John, then president of the Council, and served as interim governor when Douglas went to England and until the arrival of Sir Archibald Campbell. *Dictionary of Canadian Biography*, Vol. IX, 1976, University of Toronto Press, 53.
31 WJK

NOTICE   Madawaska, August 19, 1831
By a warrant to me directed, from William D Williamson, Esq., one of the justices of the peace for the County of Penobscot and State of Maine, this to notify and warn the inhabitants of the town of Madawaska, qualified to vote in town affairs, to assemble at the dwelling house of Mr. Peter Lizotte, on Saturday, the 20th August, 1831, at one o'clock in the afternoon, to act on the following articles, viz: 1st, to choose a moderator; 2nd, to choose a town clerk; 3rd, to choose select men; 4th, to choose constables. Walter Powers[32]

Fifty or sixty inhabitants assembled at the dwelling house of Peter Lizotte. Walter Powers called the meeting to order and began the choice of officers. John Baker was present. Captain Coombs and Francis Rice, a Justice of the Peace of New Brunswick, protested against all proceedings and threatened the inhabitants with imprisonment if they voted. Powers brought the meeting to order. Twelve or fifteen persons elected Barnabas Hunnewell, Moderator; Jesse Wheelock, Town Clerk and Daniel Savage, John Harford and Amos Maddocks, Selectmen. The town meeting was adjourned.[33]

Madawaska's Second Town Meeting

On September 12, 1831, eighty inhabitants attended a second town meeting at the dwelling of Raphael

---

[32] HRD126
[33] ROSM II, 478-479. Jesse Wheelock, born Northborough, MA, October 15, 1782, died June 28, 1873. He married Sophronia Baker, daughter of Nathan and Sophia (Rice) Baker, who was born at Moscow, ME, May 20, 1816. From the genealogical information of Nora Baker Branson, courtesy of Sidney and Alice Branson of Windham, ME.; Deposition of John Baker, taken at Portland, Maine, on October 12, 1831, by Francis OJ Smith, Justice of the Peace. ROSM II, 478-9.

Martin, on the south side of the St. John. Francis Rice again present, opposed the proceedings and "again used menacing language toward them." The Selectmen called him to order, proceeded, and elected Peter Lezart (Pierre Lizotte), resident of the south side of the River, state representative. Rice noted the names of all voters.[34]

When Major General Sir Archibald Campbell, New Brunswick's newly arrived Lieutenant Governor, received Rice's report, he wrote to Governor Smith of his surprise and regret that some people from Maine had crossed the Boundary Line actually existing between the two countries and taken possession of a part of the territory still in dispute. He demanded that the Governor recall the aggressors and subject their conduct to judicial inquiry. Campbell threatened: "Your Excellency is well aware of the undoubted right vested in me by the Law of Nations, to seize the offenders and deal with them according to the Laws of this Province."[35]

Campbell followed up on his threat by arriving in Madawaska Settlement with a Colonel, a Captain of Militia, his Attorney General, the Warden of the Disputed Territory, and the Sheriff of York County. On September 24, 1831, warrants were issued against all those who had voted at the town meetings.[36] On Sunday, the 25th, John Baker received information that a military force was collecting at the Madawaska Chapel, on the north side of the St. John River, about 18 miles below his residence. In the afternoon, he heard that Lieutenant Governor Campbell was at Simon Hebert's house fifteen miles below, on the south side of the river. Hebert was a Cap-

---

[34] Deposition of John Baker, taken at Portland, October 12, 1831, by Francis O. J. Smith, J. P., ROSM II, 479

[35] Archibald Campbell to Samuel Smith, September 4, 1831, ROSM II, 468; Smith to Campbell, September 29, 1831, ROSM II, 469 Campbell to Smith, September 13, 1831, ROSM II, 469-470. Smith to Campbell, October 10, 1831, ROSM II, 470-1.

[36] Wheelock and Savage to Roscoe Green, September 28, 1831, *Maine Documents* 1831-32, hereinafter referred to as MD 1831-2.

tain of the Provincial Militia of New Brunswick and reportedly had one hundred and fifty fire arms stored at his house.

The next morning, news came that the armed force at Hebert's house had arrested Selectman Daniel Savage and Town Clerk Jesse Wheelock.[37] At noon, John Baker discovered about twenty-five canoes coming up the St. John, in great haste. As they landed north of his mills, he retreated to a distance and watched. They searched his mills and dwelling and posted sentinels armed with muskets. They searched other homes. While Baker watched, his wife came to him and told him that Barnabas Hunnewell, Daniel Bean and several French settlers were being held as prisoner, by the soldiers, at his house; that Sheriff Miller had told her to advise him to surrender; that if he would go to Simon Hebert's house, where the Lieutenant Governor was, and give bail for his appearance at Court in Fredericton, he would be released; that it was in vain for him to think of keeping out of the way, as they intended to keep up a garrison and force him into compliance.

While Baker was receiving this message, he discovered a horse-boat with fifty armed men on board coming up the river and landing at his house. He learned that some of them were to proceed up river. About sunset, as he set off to the northward, he heard musket fire below and supposed the soldiers to be drilling. About three o'clock Tuesday morning, he raised the alarm in the upper settlement and all but six of the men fled into the woods with him.[38]

In the afternoon, finding the pursuers searching both banks of the River, Baker's party retreated farther into the woods. On Wednesday morning they saw the armed force returning down the river. Fearing ambush, they spent that night even deeper in the forest, and on Thurs-

---
37 Deposition of John Baker, September 12, 1831, ROSM II, 479-80.
38 Ibid.

day, ventured back to the River. They were met by Mrs. Bartlett, who had been at Baker's house. The soldiers had declared their determination to garrison the settlements and capture Baker and his party. The inhabitants were afraid to return to their ordinary labors. Harvesting was left unfinished, and several families were in a distressed condition.

Fearing that he would be imprisoned if captured, and without seeing his family, Baker with Phineas Harford spent twelve days travelling to Portland to convey a statement of affairs at Madawaska to Governor Smith.[39] They arrived on the 12th of October, 1831.[40] Smith learned that John Harford, Amos Maddocks, Nathaniel Bartlett, Walter Powers, Joseph Wiley, Augustin Webster and Charles McPherson, as of September 29th, had been pursued to the head of the Settlement, into the woods, and had slept in the woods three nights without fire or covering, and by stratagem had obtained potatoes from the fields for subsistence.[41]

Meanwhile, on September 28th, Jesse Wheelock and Daniel Savage notified Roscoe Green, Maine's Secretary of the State, by mail, that they had been taken prisoner, and were being sent to Fredericton Jail. Sheriff Miller and Captain Coombs had also taken Barnabas Hunnewell and Daniel Bean and about thirty French prisoners. The

---

39 Deposition of Phineas Harford, October 10, 1831, MD 1831-2. John Harford, to escape capture, fled to the woods and hid for about sixty days. His crops were damaged by loose cattle. He abandoned his land. On March 7th and March 9th, 1836, the Legislature voted sums of $100 each to Phineas Harford and John Harford. Chapters 38 and 41, ROSM III, 40, 41; Maine was reimbursed by federal government. ED I 26
40 Deposition of John Baker, ROSM II, 481.
41 MD 1831-32. Chapter 46, March 19, 1838, provided compensation of $350 to John Baker, $125 to Walter Powers, and $50 each to Nathaniel Bartlett, Augustine Webster, Isaac Yearington and John Harford, Jr., for sufferings and losses in consequence of organizing the town of Madawaska in 1831. The federal government reimbursed the State, ROSM III, 290-291.

French had all given bonds, some for trial and some for good behavior.[42]

On October 1st, 1831, Charles Bankhead, his Brittanic Majesty's Charge d'Affaires at Washington, and Edward Livingston, U. S. Secretary of State, exchanged notes, complaints and documents and Livingston conveyed the President's request to Governor Smith for information on the town meeting. Smith explained that the Act to incorporate the town of Madawaska had been intended to assert the claim of Maine to jurisdiction over that portion of the territory which they knew to be within the limits of Maine, but it was *not* to be carried into effect until circumstances should render it proper and expedient. The measure adopted by the inhabitants of the territory, "of voluntarily organizing themselves into a corporation, *was unexpected by me, and done without my knowledge.*" Smith appealed to the President to adopt the necessary measures to procure the release of Maine citizens from imprisonment, and to protect the State from invasion.[43] Livingston informed Bankhead that, as actions in the disputed territory had been disavowed by Governor Smith, and no exercise of jurisdiction had followed the election, he suggested that Bankhead recommend to Campbell that the prisoners be released.[44]

The Trial of Hunnewell, Wheelock and Savage

The *Royal Gazette*, of Fredericton, New Brunswick, reported on the trial of Barnabas Hunnewell, Jesse Wheelock and Daniel Savage before the Supreme Court of

---

42 Wheelock and Savage to Roscoe Green, September 28, 1831, MD 1831-2.
43 Bankhead to Livingston, October 1, 1831, ROSM II, 495-6; Livingston to Smith, October 5, 1831, ROSM II, 472-3; Smith to Livingston, October 12, 1831, ROSM III, 473-6; Smith to Livingston, October 13, 1831, MD 1831-2.
44 Livingston to Bankhead, October 17, 1831, HRD 126

the Province of New Brunswick at Fredericton on Saturday, the 15th of October: A long indictment by the Grand Jury of the County of York cited Barnabas Hunnewell, John Baker, Walter Powers, Jesse Wheelock, Daniel Savage, Randal Harford, Nathaniel Bartlett, Augustin Webster and Amos Mattocks (Maddocks), the men elected to and sworn in to town offices in Madawaska, "as being pernicious and seditious, and greatly disaffected to our Lord the now King and his Government, ... devising and practising and falsely, unlawfully, unjustly, maliciously and seditiously to disturb, molest and disquiet the peace ... to move, stir up and procure sedition and to subvert His Majesty's authority and to set up and establish a foreign power and dominion in place."45

At the trial, on the motion of the Attorney General, Barnabas Hunnewell, Jesse Wheelock, and Daniel Savage, the only defendants who had been arrested and jailed, were arraigned, pleaded not guilty and said they were ready for trial.

Saturday, October 15, 1831, Chief Justice, Mr. Justice Bliss, Mr. Justice Botsford and Mr. Justice Chipman were present. The Attorney General announced that the defendants were being indicted for a misdemeanor only, and moved for trial. The jurors were called. The Attorney General called the witnesses: Leonard R. Coombs, Francis Rice, Romaine Micheau, Edward Miller, John Roberts, Peter Fraser, Michael Tight, Henry G. Clopper and James A. Maclauchlan were called. The prosecution closed its case and the defendants were informed that they were at liberty to address the Court or Jury and produce evidence. Defendant Wheelock told the Court that they had been misled by the acts of the two officers, Maclauchlan and Coombs; they had concluded that they were not doing wrong so long as they confined themselves to the *west*

---

45 *Royal Gazette*, Fredericton, N B, on microfilm at Harriet Irving Library, University of New Brunswick, Fredericton, October 19, 1831, hereinafter referred to as RG 183 IHIL.

side of the River. He called witness Coombs to verify that Maclauchlan had told him that he had told Deane and Kavanagh that so long as they confined themselves to the west side of the River, in taking their account of the inhabitants, he would not interfere with them, further than to protest. Coombs had mentioned this to Savage and Wheeler before the first Town Meeting. The defendants then put in evidence the Act of the State of Maine and the original warrant for the town meeting.

The jury found the three defendants guilty. Each was sentenced to pay a fine to the King of £50, and to be imprisoned for three months and remain committed until the fines were paid.[46]

President Andrew Jackson's reaction to the jailing of Madawaska town officers was to state that he had made it understood that there would be no exertion of the State authority in the parts of the disputed territory which were actually held by the British; that he could not consider the continuation of the occupation by civil or military officers of the British Province as an invasion. He would, however, take all proper measures to procure the release of the ill-advised persons who have been the cause of the disturbance.[47]

Discountenance, by the President, of the proceedings at Madawaska, was received by British authorities with such great satisfaction that Campbell did not lose a moment in releasing the prisoners, Barnabas Hunnewell, Jesse Wheelock and Daniel Savage, and remitting their fines.[48]

---

46 RG1831HIL; Jurors were: George Nevers, James Tibbets, James Cameron, William Miller, John Russell, Holland Esty, Asa Coy, Thomas Gardiner, Robert Gowan, William J Esty, Thomas Stewart and John Payson.RG1831HIL.

47 Secretary of State Livingston to Governor Smith, October 21, 1831, ROSMII.

48 Charles Bankhead to Livingston, October 17, 1831, HRD126, 26; Campbell to Bankhead, November 8, 1831, HRD126, 29.

On December 6th, in a presidential address, Jackson again reinforced the British claim to jurisdiction west of the Treaty line of 1783 by stating:

> It affords me satisfaction to inform you that my suggestions have produced the release of certain American citizens who were imprisoned for setting up the authority of the State of Maine *at a place in the disputed territory under the actual jurisdiction of his Britannic Majesty* ... I have the best hopes that a good understanding will be kept up until it is confirmed in the final disposition of the subject.

[Note: For insight into the amount and complexity of commercial ventures in both New Brunswick and Maine, see Appendices VII and VIII.]

CHAPTER VI

THE SECOND NEGOTIATION
FOR A BOUNDARY SETTLEMENT

When the Senate of the United States, on 23 June, 1832, advised President Jackson that the award of the Arbiter had been considered not obligatory, he was required to open a second negotiation with his Britannic Majesty for a boundary settlement. This effort would require almost ten years to conclude.

On March 4, 1833, the Maine Legislature repealed the Resolve of March 3, 1832, that had provided that a boundary agreement must be submitted to the Legislature, and instead resolved that no arrangement should have any binding force until it had been submitted *to the people* of Maine in their primary assemblies and approved by a majority of their votes.

Diplomatic exchanges continued. On April 14, the British envoy concurred with the American minister in the principle of continuing to abstain, during negotiation, from extending the exercise of jurisdiction within the

Disputed Territory, beyond the limits which it had been exercised by the authorities of either party.[1]

While a temporary peace reigned on the St. John River, at the international level, negotiations, with the usual diplomatic posturings and verbal duelling continued between Sir Charles Vaughan and the Honorable Louis McLane, Secretary of State.[2] On March 21, 1834, McLane concluded a long letter to Vaughan by stating that two choices remained: "to discard the line called for by the Treaty of 1783 and adopt a new conventional line, or to make a further effort to discover the true line of the Treaty of 1783. Since the United States has no power to adopt the former alternative without the assent of Maine, ... his Britannic Majesty was invited to consider the latter." Vaughan responded, that he would seize the earliest opportunity to lay this invitation before His Majesty's Government. In 1835, the British proposed that the Americans accept the St. John, from the termination of the line due north, to its source. This was declined, but the United States offered to try to obtain the consent of Maine to accept as a boundary the St. John from its source to its mouth. Great Britain would not assent.[3]

President Van Buren watched "land fever," overspeculation in lands, take place on all American frontiers. Maine, with its rich pine forests, was severely affected. Land changed hands with great rapidity. Dishonest

---

1 Chapter 96, ROSM II, 580-581; U. S. Congress, *Senate Document No. 414*, 5-7; hereinafter referred to as SD414. This passage, and another in a letter of July 2, 1832, formed Britain's stated basis for her claim to exclusive jurisdiction.

2 Alfred DeCelles, In *Papineau* Makers of Canada Series, Morang and Company Ltd. 1906, p 78, wrote of British diplomacy: "the rule of action of the English system, which is averse to the absolute, and proceeds only from compromise and mutual concession, however small it may be, must be accepted and ... made the basis for further demands."

3 McLane to Vaughan, March 21, 1834, SD414, 35-40; Vaughan to McLane, March 24, 1834, SD414, 41; Ganong, loc. cit, cites *Blue Book 29*.

surveys were prevalent.[4] This was followed by the Panic of 1837, a crisis caused by unstable currency issued by banks whose assets could not justify their issue. Van Buren, like Thomas Jefferson, believed that federal regulations should not interfere with business. He would not recommend legislation to aid those who suffered economically. As to the boundary dispute, he told Congress, on December 3, 1837, that the sole result of the negotiations appeared to be a conviction that a conventional line must be adopted.[5]

A British Attempt at Sovereignty
Over the Disputed Territory

The year 1837 brought changes in Great Britain. The death of his Britannic Majesty, William IV, on June 20, 1837, brought his niece, Victoria, to the throne. At the age of 18, on June 28, 1838, she was crowned at Westminster Abbey. England's government was a constitutional monarchy, and as Queen, Victoria would have immense influence over her prime ministers.[6]

In Maine, during his second term, Governor Robert P. Dunlap, had appointed two individuals to visit the City of Quebec and consult with the civil authorities and merchants of the Canadas as to the feasability of constructing a railroad from the City of Quebec to some point on Maine's Atlantic seaboard.[7] The suggested route had been from Belfast through Unity to Solon or Bingham and then to the northwestern line of the State.[8] The Maine Legislature's Joint Committee on the Northeastern Boundary had discovered that the British, too, had had plans for a

---

4 Wood, loc. cit., 1820-1861, 74-81.
5 HRD3, 3-4.
6 ROSM III, 135-145.
7 ROSM II, 689-95; Chapter 31, March 10, 1835, ROSM II; Chapter 50, March 16, 1836; Chapter 60, March 22, 1836, ROSM III, 1836, 45, 52.
8 *Private and Special Acts*, loc. cit., Chapter 97, March 9, 1836.

railroad. They had reported, on February 27th, 1837, before the King's death:

> ... His Britannic Majesty's pretensions are growing every day! ... The Legislature of New Brunswick, sanctioned by the government at home, has enacted legislation incorporating the St. Andrews and Quebec Rail Road Company and the King has granted £10,000 to aid the enterprise. ... To give a railroad corporation powers over our rights and property is the strongest act of sovereignty. ... This railroad must not only cross the disputed territory, but it crosses it fifty miles south of the St. John and almost to the southerly extremity of the British claim. ... It is, then, a deliberate act of power, palpable and direct, claiming and exercising sovereignty far south even of the line recommended by the King of the Netherlands. ...[9]

Governor Dunlap once more called on the President to have the northeastern boundary of Maine explored, surveyed and marked according to the Treaty of 1783.[10] President Van Buren warned British Ambassador H. S. Fox that this undertaking, if persevered in, would lead to disaster. By August 24, 1837, her Majesty's Government had ordered Lower Canada and New Brunswick to cease all operations of the railroad project within the disputed territory.[11]

Maine Contends for Jurisdiction Through Ebenezer Greely

Lieutenant Governor Archibald Campbell, in the years 1836 to 1837 had had his problems with the elected Legislature of New Brunswick over the disposition of

---
[9] State of Maine, *Report of the Joint Select Committee of the Maine Legislature on the Northeast Boundary*, February 2, 1837.
[10] Chapter 54, March 25, 1837, ROSM III, 184-185.
[11] HRD31, 29-31; H. S. Fox to Forsyth, August 24, 1837, HRD31, 32.

public revenues and insufficient funding for the militia. He had felt hobbled by the military command at Halifax, and believed that the regular troops in his province were utterly insufficient. On the other hand, the Legislators found their problems with Campbell to be insurmountable, and requested his recall by the British Government.

Sir John Harvey was chosen by the Colonial Secretary to replace Campbell and came to New Brunswick from a similar post at Prince Edward Island. He looked upon his appointment to the larger colony and the greater responsibilities, in the face of Maine's resistance to British demands, as eminently suited to his talents and accomplishments. His only regret was his lack of military authority, which rested in the hands of the Lieutenant Governor of Nova Scotia, Sir Colin Campbell, a friend and protege of the Duke of Wellington. Harvey's letter to the Colonial Secretary resulted in his being given control of the New Brunswick militia, so that he might "discourage measures of petty aggression which otherwise might be attempted." On June 6th, he notified Maine officials that he had assumed the administration of the Government of New Brunswick.[12]

President Jackson reported a surplus of public money in the United States Treasury. Governor Dunlap and the Legislature planned for the disposal of their share of the excess revenues deposited in Maine. Ebenezer Greely, a partner with Colonel Joshua Carpenter in a saw mill in Dover, Penobscot County, was employed by the Commissioners of that County to take the census of Madawaska for the purpose of distribution of surplus funds.[13]

---

12 Classen, loc. cit., 42-43. Born in 1777, Harvey was a veteran of several military campaigns, including the War of 1812; Harvey to Dunlap, June 12, 1837, U. S. Congress, *House of Representatives document No. 31,* hereinafter referred to as HRD31, 16-17.

13 President Jackson's eighth annual message, December 5, 1836, MPP III, op. cit., 1458-1465; Act of the Maine Legislature, March 29, 1837: Sections 11, 12, and 13, HRD 31, 21; Ebenezer Greely to Robert Dunlap, June 12, 1837, HRD31, 18.

On Tuesday, May 23rd, Greely began his duties in the Disputed Territory by hiring Daniel Michaud, of Grand Falls, as an interpreter. Upon reaching the different houses in the Madawaska Settlement, under the authority of the County of Penobscot, State of Maine, he asked for their names and the number of the people in the family. He told the inhabitants that they would shortly receive two or three dollars per head of family from the surplus revenue of the United States. He continued this duty until the 27th, when he arrived at the home of Magistrate Francis Rice who refused to give him this information. Rice and Leonard Coombes warned Greely not to proceed with the census or they would arrest him. He replied that he would "not stop but go straight ahead," that his orders were to go on until he was arrested. They issued a warrant for his arrest and Michaud, now his captor, conveyed him to Woodstock Gaol. John Winslow, Sheriff of Carleton County, declined to act, and told Greely he might go about his business. Winslow considered his behavior a "mere speculative attempt, since he had seemed extremely disappointed at not being imprisoned." He felt the duty of the Magistrates had been fulfilled by having the offender removed from the scene of his mischief; that his twelve-year-old son could bring Greely back if he again defied authority.[14]

On the 5th of June, Greely again hired Michaud and proceeded with taking the census. A. K. Wetmore, Clerk of

---

14 Rice and Coombs to Wetmore, May 29, 1837 and Warrant for the arrest of Ebenezer Greely, May 29, 1837, Carleton County, NB. *Public Archives of Canada Microfilm COP 188 B 12*, hereinafter referred to as PACCOP 188B12; John Winslow to authorities at Fredericton, June 6, 1837; Warrant of Commitment, May 29, 1837; Deposition of Daniel Michaud, June 8, 1837. PACCOP 188 B 12. Ebenezer S. Greeley, born at Hallowell, Maine, 1797; married Esther Moore, born Norridgewock, ME, 1800. Children, born Dover, Maine, were Council; Anna, Sarah and Lucinda. Greely was a first selectman of Dover in 1822. *The Geneology of the Greely-Greeley Family*, by George Hiram Greeley, Boston, 1905, 528.

the Peace, Carleton County, reported Greely's behavior to Charles Peters, Attorney General, who advised the Lieutenant Governor that Greely's offence was of a serious nature. This prompted Harvey to ask Lord Glenelg for a force "by which the upper St. John Valley could be defended by a system of moveable columns acting under his own command." Glenelg directed him to employ her Majesty's troops in preference to the Provincial Militia if any military movement became necessary.[15]

James Maclauchlin left Woodstock in pursuit of Greeley, whom he overtook a short distance above Green River, and told him that if he would not desist, action would be taken. Greely stated that he intended to complete the census if he were not prevented. Maclauchlan arrested him on the 7th of June and committed him to York County Gaol on June 10, 1837. From his cell Greely wrote to Governor Dunlap[16] that since he was employed in business of the State, he expected his government to intercede and liberate him from prison. Dunlap sent Greely's letter to President Van Buren, urging Greely's early release. The President said he lacked enough detailed information concerning this outrage to warrant the interference of the government, but in the meantime, Mr. Fox, the British minister at Washington, would communicate with Harvey, requesting, unless there were

---

15 A. K. Wetmore, to the Government at Fredericton, May 31. 1837; Peters to Harvey, June 5, 1837. PACCOP 188 B12; W. S. MacNutt, "New Brunswick's Age of Harmony," *Canadian Historical Review*, Vol. XXXII, No. 2, [June, 1951], 117. MacNutt, "Age of Harmony", cites Public Archives of Canada, film CO 88/199, Harvey to Glenelg, June 6, 1837; Lord Glenelg's Despatch No. 24, August 12, 1837, PACCOP 188 B12.

16 John Winslow to authorities at Fredericton, June 6, 1837, PACCOP 188 B12; Maclauchlan to Harvey, June 10, 1837, HRD31, 17-18. Maclauchlan's order to the keeper of the Gaol at Fredericton to receive the prisoner, Ebenezer Greely, dated June 10, 1837. PACCOP 188 B12; Ebenezer Greely to Governor Dunlap, June 12, 1837, HRD31, 18.

very extraordinary reasons against it, that Mr. Greely be set at liberty.[17]

On June 12th, Sir John Harvey wrote to Governor Dunlap that upon receiving his assurance that he would exert his authority in restraining Greely or any other citizen of Maine in similar pursuits within the British limits, Greely would be set free. Three days later, Harvey advised Glenelg that "the time had come to force the United States to a settlement."

Governor Dunlap, on June 26th, demanded Harvey's retraction of the wrong done to the United States and the State of Maine.[18] Then a Canadian newspaper announced that Governor Dunlap had put the Maine Militia on alert:

> We copy the following General Order from an "extra sheet" of the "AGE", said to be the official paper published in Augusta, State of Maine. We vouch not for its authenticity, though we have no reason except its absurdity, to doubt its being a genuine document:
>
> STATE OF MAINE   Augusta, June 27, 1837
> HEADQUARTERS   General Order No. 57
> Fellow Soldiers: The soil of our State has been invaded! One of our citizens, while in the performance of duty required by law, was arrested within the territory of Maine, and carried to an adjacent foreign Province, where he now remains incarcerated within the walls of a prison. This is but a repetition of former acts of injustice committed against our border inhabitants, by

---

17 Governor Dunlap to President Van Buren, June 19, 1837, HRD31, 18; Forsyth to Dunlap, June 26, 1837, HRD31, 19. On June 27, Governor Dunlap sent copies of the letters of Sir John Harvey and James A. MacLauchlan, concerning the arrest of E. Greely, to the President, HRD31, 16; Dunlap to Forsyth, July 3, 1837, HRD31, 19-20.

18 John Harvey to Governor Dunlap, June 12, 1837, HRD31, 16-17; MacNutt, loc.cit.; Macnutt, "Age of Harmony," cites CO 188/199, John Harvey to Lord Glenelg, July 15, 1837 Dunlap to Harvey, June 26, 1837, PACCOP188B12.

officers acting under the authority of the British Province of New Brunswick. The integrity of the State must be served. Maine looks to the General Government for redress. Our citizens must be secure within our limits, and it may be found necessary to bring forth military power to give that protection to which they are entitled. The Commander-in-Chief therefore calls upon the Militia to hold themselves in readiness to obey such orders as the security of our citizens and the honor of the State may require. By the Commander-in-Chief A. B. Thompson, Adjutant General.[19]

From the British Consulate, Maine and New Hampshire, at Portland, June 29, 1837, His Majesty's Consul, Joseph S. Sherwood sent a copy of this order to Sir John Harvey and to Mr. Fox at Washington.[20] Andrew Stevenson, Esq., American envoy, Legation of the United States, London, demanded the release of Mr. Greely, and a suitable indemnity for his imprisonment.[21] On July 28, 1837, an irate Governor Dunlap remonstrated to President Martin Van Buren:

Sir ... British authorities have for many years been indulged, the rightful jurisdiction of Maine has been subverted, her lands ravaged and her citizens dragged to a foreign jail. These outrages have been the subject of repeated remonstrances by the State. ... *What relief has been brought to us by the Federal Government?* The invaders have not been expelled. ... Grave discussions have resulted in supplying new encouragements to the aggressors. Diplomatic ingenuity,

---

19 General Order No. 57, PACCOP 188 B12
20 Sherwood to Harvey, June 29, 1937, PACCOP 188 B12.
21 Forsyth to Stevenson, July 12, 1837, HRD126, 4. Stevenson to Forsyth, August 21, 1837, HRD126, 5-7. Mr. Forsyth to Dunlap, July 14, 1837, and Forsyth to Dunlap, July 14, 1837, HRD31, 22-23.

the only foundation of the British claim, has been arrayed against the perfect right. Now, under the negotiation process, a writ of protection appears to have been spread by our own Government, over the whole mass of British aggressions. ... I will not attempt to conceal the mortification I have realized, that no reply has been made [to my request of April 22nd] nor any measures taken. ... I have therefore the honor again to request that the President will cause the treaty line upon the northeastern limits of Maine to be run and marked ...[22]

Van Buren's response came through John Forsyth on August 17, 1837:

... The present President of the United States, upon taking office, found that a distinct proposition had been made by his predecessor for settling this long-disputed controversy; no answer has yet been received.

... However unbounded may be the confidence of the Legislature and people of Maine in the justice of their claim, the President's is not less so; no exertions have been or shall be spared to bring a favorable and speedy termination.[23]

Mr. Fox informed Sir John Harvey that the Secretary of State and the President had confidentially expressed their anxiety that Greely be set free, lest his continued detention irritate Maine and add to the difficulty of a settlement. ... He advised Harvey that the liberation of Greely, if it could be done without any relinquishment of British rights, would be productive of good consequences; there was no benefit to be obtained by bringing Greely to trial. If Harvey felt justified in releasing Greely it would be best if his release took place in sufficient time for the news to reach Washington

---

22 Dunlap to Van Buren, July 28, 1837, HRD31, 24-26.
23 Dunlap to Forsyth, August 17, 1837, HRD31, 26-29

before the opening of Congress on the 4th of September. At that time, Greely's arrest would be referred to in the President's message and if Greely should still be in custody the case would probably be referred to in an angry tone. This Fox desired to prevent. He concluded by stating that "whatever terms the President of the United States may be finally brought to agree to, it would be his business and that of his Government, either to persuade or compel the subordinate governments of the Frontier States to acquiesce. We are not called upon nor is it of any use for us to trouble ourselves with the unauthorized language or assertions of the State Governments or to resist any proceeding that does not assume the form of overt action."[24]

Ebenezer Greeley, on August 8th, presented himself at Government House in Fredericton to express his thanks for attentions to his comfort. Sir John Harvey received him civilly, stated that "he regretted his arrest and detention, that he had been happy to grant Gorham Parks' request that he have free liberty to walk about town; that the necessity of his arrest was imposed by his duty to maintain British jurisdiction and possession of the Disputed Territory." He considered enough had been done for that purpose, especially as Greely's commission has expired." Greely was released on the 10th of August.[25]

Sixteen days after his release from Fredericton Gaol, Ebenezer Greely informed Harvey of his return to the Madawaska area and of his intention of proceeding "to close up the census which he had commenced in May." Harvey sought advice from Fox, reminding him that if Greely persisted he would subject himself to immediate

---
24 H. S. Fox to John Harvey, July 24, 1837, PACCOP 188 B12.
25 Harvey to Fox, August 10, 1837, PACCOP 188 B12; Gorham Parks, Democrat, of Bangor, was U. S. Senator from 1833-1837, and lacked only five hundred votes to defeat Governor Edward Kent in 1837. W H Robinson's Report of Meeting between Harvey and Greely, August 8, 1837, PACCOP 188 B12.

arrest by the local authorities, and a collision might be produced, as he had heard rumors of an intended mustering of the militia volunteers on the frontiers of Maine.26

Frederick Street, Solicitor General of New Brunswick, at Woodstock, on the Thursday preceding September 5th, encountered Greely, and inquired of him as to his objective and asked him if he meant to tell these inhabitants that they were citizens and inhabitants of the State of Maine. Greely replied that if they asked him that question he would certainly tell them so. Street forbad him to proceed and gave him notice that if he did so he would be imprisoned. Greeley replied that he understood all that, he expected to be taken prisoner and would proceed until he was stopped and that New Brunswick authorities might depend upon it that as soon as he was taken prisoner his Government would appoint another person to succeed him, with a sufficient force to support him in the act. Street asked him if it would answer his purpose equally well if he were to go back and inform his Government that he was met by the Provincial Authorities at Woodstock and stopped in his proceedings; he offered to give Greely a written certificate to that effect and this would prevent the necessity of taking him prisoner. Greely declined.

Street made arrangements for the coming arrest, and recommended that since Greely had come under the direction of the Government of the State of Maine, he be treated as a State Prisoner. As such, he should be detained as a prisoner until the pleasure of her Majesty's Government was known. His conduct could not be looked on as an offense of a private individual, but rather as the act of one of the subordinate States of the United States Government, and Greely the mere instrument for carrying that act into effect. It was, consequently, an offense of one foreign state against another, to be adjusted be-

---

26 Street to Harvey, September 5, 1837 and Harvey to Fox, August 29, 1837, PACCOP 188 B 13

tween the Supreme Governments to which each of those States belonged.[27]

On September 5th, Harvey apprised Mr. Fox and Lord Glenelg of the situation and planned that in the event of the arrival a second person, supported by an armed force, such an act should be promptly met by a corresponding military demonstration.[28]

A message from Harvey, on September 10th, informed Governor Dunlap that Greely had again come into New Brunswick and assumed the exercise of jurisdiction within it. He stressed that he possessed no discretionary power upon the subject, and if the whole military force of British America should be necessary to enable him to give effect to those instructions, that force would be placed at his disposal. By September 11th, Greely had been arrested a third time and conveyed to jail at Fredericton a second time.[29]

On the same day, Sir John Harvey ordered up two companies of the 43rd Light Infantry, one to be stationed at Woodstock and the other at the Grand Falls, to be in readiness to support the civil authorities. He also sent up a few hundred stand of Militia Arms to be distributed to such volunteers of the Militia of the Madawaska Settlement upon whom reliance could be placed. He planned to go to the Grand Falls to prevent any indiscreet application of this force.[30]

Governor Dunlap again appealed to President Van Buren to facilitate the release of Mr. Greely.[31]

In London, on November 22, 1837, American envoy Andrew Stevenson, protested to Lord Palmerston:

---

27 Report of Street to Harvey, September 5, 1837, PACCOP 188 B 13
28 Harvey to Fox and Glenelg, September 5, 1837, PACCOP 188 B 13.
29 Warrant for arrest of Greely, September 6, 1837; Harvey to Dunlap, Sept. 10, 1837; Harvey to Glenelg, Sept. 11, 1837, PACCOP 188B 13.
30 Harvey to Glenelg, September 11, 1837, PACCOP 188 B 13.
31 Dunlap to Van Buren, September 9, 1837, 25CR 2; Forsyth to Dunlap, September 26, 1837, HRD 126, 3. Forsyth to Stevenson, September 28, 1837, HRD 126, 8.

... By what authority the provincial government of New Brunswick felt itself justified in exercising such acts of sovereign power, the undersigned is at a loss to conceive, unless, indeed, upon the ground that the jurisdiction and sovereignty over the disputed territory, pending in the controversy, rests *exclusively* with Great Britain. If such should turn out to be the fact, it can hardly be necessary again to repeat that, in any such claim of power, the Government of the United States cannot acquiesce.[32]

Sir John Harvey had departed from Fredericton on September 22nd, to be with his troops at Woodstock and Grand Falls. All was quiet. A week later Governor Dunlap notified Harvey that he was precluded from any actions in relation to Greely, whose authority to take the census was derived from an act of the Maine Legislature and from the Commissioners of Penobscot County. Therefore, it was beyond his power to interdict the proceedings of Greely. He then needled Harvey:

... May there not be something peculiar in the character of that claim which can thus incite its advocate to anticipate, from a peaceful people, such measures as to justify the military preparations referred to? Might it not be fairly deduced from these arrangements that there exists some conscious *uneasiness* as to the foundation on which that claim is made to rest?[33]

---

[32] Stevenson to Palmerston, November 22, 1837, HRD126, 8-10. Chapter 182, approved April 16, 1841, Resolved: That there be paid to Isaac Hodsdon, the sum of $78.78 in full for money expended by him in traveling into the Province of New Brunswick, in 1837 to obtain information relative to liberating Greely from jail. RDSM IV, 561.

[33] Harvey to Glenelg and Dunlap to Harvey, September 28, 1837; PACCOP188B13.

From Grand Falls, on October 1st, Harvey had informed Lord Glenelg that his "little military demonstration" had infused confidence in the inhabitants ... and had checked "a meditated invasion into the Disputed Territory"; that as soon as he had received Dunlap's letter, "disavowing the mission of Greely as an agent of the Executive Government of Maine," he had permitted a Company of the 85th Regiment to return to Nova Scotia. He then proposed building forts along the St. John River.[34]

The Maine election of 1837 gave Edward Kent 34,385 votes to Gorham Parks' 33,879, and brought him to the governorship for his first non-consecutive term on January 19, 1838. Along with the nation's unstable currency, the distribution of the surplus money from the Federal Treasury remained a concern. A month later, Kent received a letter from Ebenezer Greely, who had been discharged from Fredericton Gaol on February 2nd. He enclosed a copy of his discharge, which contained a phrase to which Governor Kent objected: he told the Legislature that no communication nor any action of the Executive Department had authorized the words: "that the offenses for which the said Ebenezer S. Greely so committed will no longer be persisted in."[35]

---

34 Harvey to Glenelg, October 1, 1837, and Harvey to Glenelg, October 7, 1837, PACCOP188B13. Dunlap's letter of September 28th, 1837, did not disavow the mission of Greely, but pointed out that Greely was as an agent of the Legislative Department, not the Executive Department of Maine; Harvey to Glenelg, October 7, 1837 and Harvey to Glenelg, October 10, 1837, PACCOP188B13.

35 Ebenezer S. Greely to Governor Edward Kent, February 2, 1838, *MS Correspondence and Documents Relating to the North East Boundary Dispute*, Maine State Library, Augusta, Maine, hereinafter referred to as CDRNEBMSL; Order for release of Greely, February 2, 1838; Special message of Kent to Legislature, February 15, 1839, ROSM. II. The Legislature paid Ebenezer Greeley $500 for all sufferings and losses from arrest and imprisonment at Fredericton. Maine was reimbursed by the federal government. Chapter 37, March 12, 1836, ROSM Vol. III, 287.

Maine Prepares for a Confrontation

President Van Buren invited Governor Kent to ascertain the sense of the State of Maine with respect to the expediency of attempting to establish a conventional line of boundary ... and whether the State of Maine would agree, and upon what conditions, to abide by such a settlement. Nine days later the Legislature passed resolves to the effect that Maine would not assent to treat for a conventional line, but would insist on the line established by the treaty of 1783. Neither would Maine agree to the appointment of a new arbiter. Her Congressional delegation was urged to fight for the passage of the Bill for the Survey of the Northeastern Boundary of the United States, then pending. Then the Legislature delivered an ultimatum: If the above bill should not become law during the present session of Congress, and if the government of the United States, either alone or in conjunction with Great Britain or the State of Maine shall not, on or before September 1st, establish and appoint a commission for a survey of the boundary line, Maine's Governor must appoint commissioners and surveyors for ascertaining, running and locating the northeastern boundary line of this State, and to cause the same to be carried into operation.[36]

March 28, 1838, brought forth another set of resolutions, including one to extend protection of Maine laws to the people of Madawaska and vicinity by constructing a winter road from the Aroostook River to the mouth of the Madawaska River. The cooperation of Massachusetts was requested and that commonwealth responded that if the general government remained silent, or by repeated

---

36 Forsyth to Kent, March 1, 1838, SD319, 14-33. Resolves of the Maine Legislature, March 23, 1838, MD1838, 343-344. Edward Kent was born on January 8, 1802, at Concord, N H, graduated Harvard in 1821, settled at Bangor, ME, became a prominent attorney and expert on the northeast boundary dispute. MD1838, 243-272.

concessions strengthened the claims of a foreign government, Massachusetts would take the subject into her own hands, and proclaim the grievances of an injured people in the ears of the nation.[37] Governor Kent admonished Maine's delegation in Congress, John Ruggles, Reuel Williams, John Fairfield, J. C. Noyes, George Evans, F. O. J. Smith, Thomas Davee, H. J. Anderson, and Edward Robinson, that the question was a national one and action thereon ought to be national, but "it becomes us to do all that we can to urge our claims upon the General Government, so that if we resort, in self-defense, to independent action, there may be no imputation upon our State of neglect in setting forth her claims or declaring her ultimate determination."[38]

Because of their great concern for the passage of the bill and the urgency of setting up fortifications, the Governor and Council commissioned Charles S. Daveis, Esq. of Portland as Special Messenger and Agent to Washington. Kent instructed Daveis that he was to use strong and decided language to express Maine's determination. Governor Kent explained in a letter to President Van Buren, that the people of Maine were not desirous of a border warfare, they had no anxiety to gain territory by conquest, but they knew their rights and dared to maintain them. Daveis' efforts were not effectual, but a Congres-

---

37 Commonwealth of Massachusetts, *The Report of the Joint Committee on Public Lands for the Commonwealth of Massachusetts*, February 7, 1838, MD 1838.
38 Kent to Congressional Delegation, April 16, 1838, State of Maine, Executive Department Records, hereinafter referred to as SMED, 25-7.

sional Report on the question of right, resulted in Resolves unanimously asserting the validity of Maine's title.[39]

Maine Surveys the Northeast Boundary

Because of the Congressional postponement of the bill providing for the survey, Governor Kent appointed as a commission of survey, John G. Deane, Milford P. Norton and James Irish, Esquires, Commissioners, and Captain William P. Parrott, Esq., Surveyor. During the progress of their survey, in June, 1838, James A. Maclauchlan, Warden of the Disputed Territory delivered to S. S. Whipple, Surveyor General of Maine, a written protest, warning Whipple "forthwith to desist from proceeding further with your proceedings." Whipple denied Maclauchlan's right, and asserted that he would acknowledge no government but that of the State under which he acted.[40]

The Survey Commission reported that the exploring line was found and marked near the northwest angle; that the base of country rose constantly and regularly from

---

[39] SMED, 38-39; MD 1838.; Kent to Van Buren, April 28, 1838. Kent noted, in a speech to the Legislature on January 2, 1839, that no reply had been received from Van Buren to this letter, but Van Buren had responded to it by sending it, with a message, to the U. S. Senate: on May 19, 1828. U. S. Congress, *Senate Document 451*, hereinafter referred to as SD451, 1; Kent's speech to the Maine Legislature, January 2, 1839. The Senate Bill under consideration may be found in U. S. Congress, *Senate Document 502*, 1-16.

[40] Ganong, loc. cit., 340-1. Chapter 34, ROSM III, 42: On February 22, 1839, Legislative Resolve paid John G. Deane, James Irish, Milford P. Norton, and their assistants. Joseph Polis, Sampson S Powers, Alfred Nelson, M. G. Deane, Francis Enees, Alfred Hunter, Daniel D. Dudley, Samuel Leadbetter, James Campbell, Jr. and William Bryant, for their services in running and locating the North Eastern Boundary line of the State, by virtue of a Resolve approved March 23rd, 1838; Maclauchlan to Whipple, June 27, 1838, and Whipple to Maclauchlan, June 30, 1838, State of Maine, Executive Department Records, hereinafter referred to as SMED, 89.

tion, with muskets that had no flints. However, new Hall's Rifles had been received. Orders had been issued for eight 6-pound brass cannon with carriages and apparatus.[42]
Adjutant General A. B. Thompson reported to Governor Kent on April 5, 1838, on Maine's military defences, pointing out that Maine's thousand-mile frontier was vulnerable to invasion as it had practically no fortifications. The seacoast had been partially examined, and works projected but no military works had been erected on the inland frontier except the small post at Houlton. Should there be war with Great Britain, the whole military force of that empire in North America might concentrate at Quebec, and an invading army might reach our towns on the Kennebec and Penobscot. A thorough examination of our inland frontier was requested of the federal government. Joel R. Poinsett, Secretary of War, designated Brigadier General John E. Wool to a make a reconnaissance and to report a plan of defence.[43]

Beginning on the 3rd of July, Wool, with topographical engineers Major Graham and Lieutenant Johnston, explored Moosehead Lake, as far as the highlands dividing Maine from Lower Canada. Wool selected a position for a military post for the protection of the northwestern frontier of Maine. Then he and Governor Kent examined the military position at Houlton and found it to be well calculated for the defence of that region. Wool requested of Kent a return of the number of militia that could be concentrated, in ten to twenty days at the Kennebec Forks, Mattawamkeag and Calais. Kent replied from Augusta, that Maine could muster:

---

42 RAGRV1838.
43 Thompson to Kent, April 5, 1838, MD 1838; Kent to Poinsette, April 5, 1838, MD 1838; Cooper to Kent, May 1, 1838, MD 1838.; Macomb to Wool, May 12, 1838, MD 1838; John E. Wool, Brigadier General, "The Wool Report," U. S. Congress, *Senate Document 35* submitted to the J. R. Poinsett, Secretary of War, October 30, 1838, and found in hereinafter referred to as WRSD35.

situated somewhere between Hilton's and the frontier line, was the advanced post.⁴⁵

The fourth position, at Houlton, is extremely interesting because of its proximity to the strong military garrisons at St. John and Fredericton, and to Halifax, the great depot and arsenal from whence all maritime operations would be conducted against us. This frontier, one hundred and sixty miles from the source of the St. Croix to Mars Hill, is undefended except by the garrison of Hancock Barracks, at Houlton. The position at Houlton occupies a commanding eminence upon the Meduxnekeag Stream, within one mile of our eastern boundary line, and about ten miles north of the source of the St. Croix. Thirteen miles east of Houlton is Woodstock, on the St. John River, in New Brunswick, which, it is said, has been selected and determined upon as a site for a British Garrison. It guards the military road along the St. John Valley, Madawaska River, Temisconta Lake, etc, between the military posts of New Brunswick and Quebec on the St. Lawrence.

The value of Houlton as a military position is evident, as the means of checking any hostile movement. It is important that the Hancock garrison be augmented. In lieu of the stockade, a proper field work should be constructed of earthen parapets and ditches, of sufficient dimensions to contain a full garrison of regular troops, besides such number of militia as would have to be concentrated here. There is an excellent military road between Houlton and Bangor, on the Penobscot, a distance of one hundred and seventeen miles, by which supplies are easily conveyed.⁴⁶

---

45 Wool to Poinsette, November 10, 1838, 4-5, WRSD3; "The Graham Report," submitted November 16, 1838, in U. S. Congress, Senate Document 35, hereinafter referred to as GRSD35; Graham's survey mentions Tachevan's house, on the high ridge, on the Quebec Road. Graham to Wool, November 1, 1838, GWSD35.

46 GWSD35. Graham's survey took measurements at Hasey's Tavern at Houlton.

The fifth position is at Calais, at the head of ship navigation on the southern margin of the St. Croix River, with posts of observation at or near Weston post office upon Grand Lake, distance thirty two miles from Houlton, and at the Amity Post office, two and a half miles west of the Monument erected to designate the headwaters of the St. Croix, and fourteen miles from Houlton. There should be a field work at Calais, constructed in the same manner as recommended for Houlton, and a road of communication with Bangor should be opened by the most direct practicable route. The defenses at Eastport consist of a stockade enclosure for the accommodation of one hundred troops, and a small artillery battery, now in a state of dilapidation, overlooking the roadstead, near the wharves where vessels usually are moored. Proper defences of this port, have been recommended. The sixth position at Butterfield's and the seventh at Dunn's on the road leading to Houlton, are for posts of observation.[47]

The establishment of an armory at Bangor and a fortification opposite Bucksport, near the mouth of the Penobscot River, were urged.[48]

**British Troops Move Through the Disputed Territory
On Their Way to Quell Rebellion in Quebec**

The news of a rebellion in Lower Canada appeared in American newspapers in 1837. Coastal city editors called for "no overt acts of intervention" in behalf of those in revolt. Neutrality, based upon the Act of 1818, was recommended, with comments such as "the Canadians must fight their own battles," and "we shall not

---

47 Ibid. Graham's survey took measurements at Thompson's Hotel in Calais; at the "Western" (Weston[)] post office; at the Amity Post office at Dunn's, GWSD35.
48 WRSD35; GRSD35.

depart from our neutrality in this contest or have our Government compromitted by any act or measure which may sustain or aid this family quarrel."⁴⁹

The Lieutenant Governor of New Brunswick focused much of his attention, during the winter of 1837-1838, on the open rebellion in Lower Canada and Upper Canada. His military means were ready to support British troops in those areas at any time.

Louis Joseph Papineau (1786-1871) had been active in the movement of the *Patriotes*, French Canadians for reform in the British Government of Lower Canada, since 1815. His counterpart in Upper Canada, where the population was largely English, Scots, and American Loyalists, was William Lyon Mackenzie. These two fiery leaders headed bloody uprisings against the British government in 1837 and 1838.⁵⁰

When conflict seemed probable, Sir John Harvey was alerted to hold the 43rd Light Infantry in readiness to proceed to Lower Canada by way of the Grand Falls and Madawaska Settlement, as soon as the season was sufficiently advanced to make the winter roads practicable. This necessitated that the British troops pass through a part of the disputed territory. He asked British Ambassador Fox to ascertain whether the United States Government or Maine had any objection. He suggested that it might be possible to get the President's permission to allow passage of British reinforcements through the acknowledged territory of the United States, by way of Houlton, through the "Kennebec" or "Craigs" Road, straight

---

49 Albert B. Corey, *The Crisis of 1830-1842 in Canadian-American Relations*, 27-28, New Haven, Yale University Press; Toronto.
50 During this period of conflict and unrest, in Feb., 1838, Lord Durham, British High Commissioner, came to the Canadas to study the causes of the rebellion and to gather information. His *Report* eventually brought about a new order under a more responsible government. The union of Upper and Lower Canadas would take place in 1840 and the united colony would have limited self-government in 1846.

to Point Levi (Quebec).⁵¹ This route was never used. On December 16, 1837, Harvey, from Fredericton, wrote to Sir John Colborne:

> I have the satisfacion of acquainting your Excellency that the last Division of the 43rd Light Infantry [Regiment] left Fredericton this morning, the leading Company ... being this day at the entrance of the Temisquata Lake. The 85th follows by grand divisions, and will have passed through Fredericton on the 20th. These two Regiments, accompanied by three pieces of light ordnance, viz, two twelve pound cannonades and a cohorn, which I have caused to be mounted on sleighs, ... may be expected to reach Quebec about the 1st of January. I am instructed by Sir Colin Campbell to hold the 34th in readiness to follow. ... J. Harvey ⁵²

The Maine Legislature protested that the use made of the disputed territory by the British Government, as a thoroughfare for its troops and a place on which they encamped without authority, was a palpable outrage upon the sovereignty of Maine, and of the United States, and a fresh cause for complaint.⁵³

Colborne's forces crushed the *Patriotes* at St. Eustache. On December 5, 1837, Lord Gosford proclaimed martial law in the District of Montreal. With a price on his head, Papineau escaped to the United States.⁵⁴

On the night of the 4th of December, 1837, rebels were abroad in the city of Toronto, under the leadership of newspaper editor William Mackenzie. Chaos prevailed. Volunteers loyal to the government were called in and armed. After some sharp skirmishes, Mackenzie rallied

---
51 Harvey to Fox, November 10, 1837, PAC COP 188 B 13.
52 Harvey to Colborne, December 16, 1837, PAC COP 188 B 13.
53 Resolves of the Maine Legislature, March 28, 1838, MD 1838.
54 Alfred DeCelles, *Papineau*, 1906, The Makers of Canada Series, Morang and Company, Ltd., 137-138. Note: Papineau, exiled in France, returned to Canada in 1845.

his men and seized Navy Island, just above Niagara Falls, where he was joined by large numbers of American sympathizers.

The next day a mass meeting was held in Buffalo, New York. Patriotic music, speeches and general excitement prevailed. Resolutions were passed, approving the episodes of rebellion. Oswego, Ogdensburg, and Troy in New York and Montpelier in Vermont held similar meetings. Mackenzie, in Buffalo on December 11, 1837, began recruiting an armed force to aid the rebellion in Upper Canada. On December 15, 1837, Mackenzie ran up a flag, formed a provisional government, and offered one hundred dollars in silver and three hundred acres of Canadian land for each volunteer who joined them before the first day of May. This "Patriot Army," by January, 1838, was drilling in Detroit, and two more groups were organizing.

To meet the transportation needs of the force on Navy Island, December 28, 1837, the owners of the American steamboat *Caroline* were cutting it out of the ice at its dock. Colonel Allan MacNab, commander of the Upper Canadian Militia, sent Commander Andrew Drew, Royal Navy, on a night mission to destroy it. In Schlosser, New York, Drew and fifty men found the *Caroline*, docked, with a crew and about twenty passengers aboard. Drew led his men in a small battle on deck. Amos Durfree was killed and several people were wounded. The ship was set on fire and towed out into the current of the Niagara River where it sank before it reached the falls.[55]

The news about the *Caroline* reached Washington on January 4, 1838. President Van Buren summoned Major General Winfield Scott to protect American interests on the New York and Vermont frontiers. The following day, Van Buren issued a proclamation warning Americans not

---

55 Corey, loc. cit., 34-37. [In 1841, so strong was British sentiment against an American trial, conviction and possible execution in New York, of Alexander McLeod, a Canadian, for his alleged part in the murder and in the destruction of the *Caroline*, that it almost led to war.]

to compromise the neutrality of their government by interfering in an unlawful manner with the affairs of the neighboring Provinces. He was determined to maintain the peace of that frontier without use of force. Scott was on the Canadian Frontier by January 6, 1838, with about four hundred regulars under his command. On into the early part of 1839, Scott was busy exercising his influence for peace and enforcing the Neutrality Act of 1818.[56]

Since the Act of 1818 had been chiefly penal and not preventive, it was replaced by The Neutrality Act of 1838. The President was required by this Act to officially disapprove of all activities by Americans to aid those in rebellion against the British Government in Upper and Lower Canada.[57] The Rebellion in Lower Canada was put down, but the spirit of the movement still lived in upper Vermont, where the *Patriotes* were gathering arsenals, food and money. They worked so quietly that Brigadier General John E. Wool, the United States Army Commander in Vermont, did not even call out the militia.

In direct opposition to the Neutrality Act, recruiting stations were opened.[58] One fiery recruiter was Charles Grandison Bryant, noted Bangor architect, confidant and friend of Governor Edward Kent and Major General Isaac Hodsdon of Bangor.

The *Waldo Patriot* of Belfast, Maine, published an appeal from Bryant, Grand Eagle of the Hunter's Lodge, from Patriot Camp, Cotwell's Manor, November 5, 1838, for volunteers to go to the aid of "oppressed inhabitants of Lower Canada, who, having suffered for more than half a century the iron yoke of despotism from their cruel and haughty conquerors, have determined to make one more effort to rid themselves of their bloody and vindictive taskmasters, and to change their form of government

---

56 Ibid., 47-48, 63.
57 Ibid., 44-47.
58 Ibid., 41-42.

from a miserable colonial vassalage to a free and independent Republic."59

In Maine there were said to be ninety nine lodges of Hunters. A network of lodges had spread over the northern part of the United States, as well as into some southern states and the Canadas. Estimated to have as high as two hundred thousand members, perhaps a figure of forty to fifty thousand during 1838 and 1839, was more realistic. The invasion of Prescott, in Upper Canada was their objective. The Hunters, for lack of funds and because of the sharp opposition encountered on both sides of the border, gave up, for the time being, their plans for the invasion of the Canadas and occasionally sent over small marauding parties to burn and destroy property, in hope of producing retaliation.60

Bryant's activities, as the Grand Eagle of the Hunter Lodge, took place in areas where Winfield Scott was doing his best to suppress the movement. Dr. Jean Baptiste-Henri Brien, an active Patriot leader, who was captured and sentenced to hang, was said to have confessed that Bryant claimed to be an instrument of Governor Kent, whose aim was to embarrass the English Government in Lower Canada. Bryant was arrested in Bangor on June 7, 1838. Governor Kent was mentioned as having offered bail money for Bryant and "public rumor had it that Kent and his supporters were squarely behind

---

59 James H. Mundy and Earle G. Shettleworth, *The Flight of the Grand Eagle: Charles G. Bryant, Maine Architect and Adventurer*, Maine Historic Preservation Commission, Augusta, Maine, 1977, Appendix V, 143, quoting article from the *Waldo Patriot*, November 23, 1838.

60 Corey loc. cit., 76, 113; Corey quotes the *London Morning Chronicle's* November 15th list of lodges in the United States and British North America: Maine 99; Vermont 107, New York 283; New Hampshire 78; Wisconsin 7; Illinois 21; Indiana 14; Ohio 86; Pennsylvania 49; Kentucky 11; Virginia 21; Maryland 16; Delaware 2; New Jersey 17; Missouri 39; Iowa 2; Louisiana 11; Upper Canada 81; Lower Canada nearly the whole population; New Brunswick, a few; British North America, elsewhere, scattered; United States, elsewhere, 100.

Charles G. Bryant, the Canadian Patriot."[61] Bryant would reappear on Maine's northeast boundary in 1839. The rebels and their associates were defeated. During 1837 and 1838, many American citizens were in Canadian jails, held on charges of felony. President Van Buren sent investigator Aaron Vail, who failed to secure their release, but by February and March, 1839, when Maine militia troops were on the New Brunswick frontier, many were released. In May, July and August, most of the prisoners had been unconditionally pardoned. Seventeen executions and seventy-eight sentences of transportation for life to Tasmania had been the lot of the unreleased. After a few years, pardons were extended to almost all. Later, both Mackenzie and Papineau were allowed to return to their homes in Canada and both men were elected to seats in the Canadian Assembly.[62]

---

61 Mundy and Shettleworth, loc. cit,. 75-89, 83. Mundy and Shettleworth bring to light Bryant's brilliant career as a Bangor architect. Charles Grandison Bryant's grandfather and grandmother, Charles and Jerusha Bryant, had come to the Newcastle-Thomaston, ME area from Marshfield, MA, before the Revolution. They had seven children, of whom Charles, Jr., a shipwright, was the oldest. Charles Jr. married Elizabeth Hatch Lowden and they had six children: Eliza, Jerusha, Charles Grandison, Caroline, Louvisa and Wealthea. Preface. Note: Jerusha Bryant, sister of the architect-adventurer, married Reverend Royal Crafts Spaulding. See: *Spauldingania, Autobiographical Sketch of Reverend Royal Crafts Spaulding, and Extracts from Letters of Himself and His Wife, Jerusha Bryant Spaulding,* Francis Barnes, Editor, Houlton, ME, Press of William H. Smith, 1891.

62 Larned, *History for Ready Reference and Topical Reading* Vol.. I, MDCCCXCV, 126-29, citing W. P. Greswell, *History of the Dominion of Canada,*.Chapter 16, Section 15, and Rude, *Protest and Punishment,* for information on the fate of many of those arrested in the revolt.

PART THREE: CONFRONTATION

CHAPTER VII

CIVIL CONFRONTATION

At the beginning of 1838, John Fairfield,[1] a Democrat, from Saco, was being talked about as Maine's next governor. He had been serving in the United States House of Representatives since 1835. In February, the Cilley-Graves duel brought him national fame, when his personal friend, Jonathan Cilley, of Thomaston, also a Maine delegate to the House, was shot in a duel. Fairfield announced Cilley's death in the House, and moved resolutions of inquiry into the cause of his death. A bill to prevent

---

1 John Fairfield, born January 20, 1797, in Saco, Maine, attended Thornton and Limerick Academies. During the War of 1812, he had some experience on a privateer. He married Anna Paine Thornton in 1825. He studied law in Saco with Judge Ether Shepley, was admitted to the bar in 1826, and was a law partner of George Thatcher, Jr., son of Judge Thatcher of the U.S. Supreme Court. In 1835 he was elected to the U.S. House of Representatives. Washington was familiar to him; his wife's uncle, Richard Cutts of Saco, who had served seven terms in Congress from 1800 to 1813, resided in Washington. Cutt's son Madison was a friend of Fairfield's, as were his daughters, Mary Cutts and Dolley Cutts Madison. Arthur G. Staples, Ed., *The Letters of John Fairfield*, Lewiston Maine: Lewiston Journal Company, 1922, ix-xxii.

duelling was introduced.[2] Also, Fairfield had assumed leadership in the matter of the boundary dispute, when, in the midst of the uproar about Cilley's death, on March 8th, he had delivered the major speech in favor of a bill to provide that the President cause the northeastern boundary line to be surveyed.[3]

When the Democratic State Convention met at Augusta on June 20, 1838, John Fairfield was nominated for Governor. Free from party in-fighting, and respected as a man and a politician, he brought a healing influence to the party.[4] The gubernatorial election of 1838 gave incumbent Governor Edward Kent, Whig candidate, 42,879 votes, while John Fairfield, Democrat, captured the governorship with 46,216 votes.

Maine's preparations for a possible crisis had been going on all through the 1830's. The state had strengthened her ability to defend her territory through extensive internal improvements such as roads and bridges, and through diligent efforts in behalf of the Militia. The Land Agents had supervised the road building, and tried to guard the timber belonging to Maine and Massachusetts.

---

2 Fairfield to his wife, January 27, 1838, Staples, Ed., loc. cit. 192; James H. Mundy, *Speakers of the Maine House of Representatives from 1820.* Clerk of the House, printed by J. S. Mc Carthy, Augusta, 1981. Cilley, prominent in Maine politics, had served six terms in the Maine House of Representatives, and during the last two of these terms he had served as Speaker of the House. Born in Nottingham, NH, July 2, 1802, a graduate of Bowdoin College, he was well connected, having an uncle who served in Congress and a brother who would become a U. S. Senator. Many Democrats labelled his death political murder. Fairfield to his wife, February 26, 1838; Fairfield to his wife, February 28, 1838; John Fairfield's fearless fight to outlaw duelling made him a national figure. Staples, Ed., loc. cit., 204-208, 183.

3 Fairfield to wife, March 7, 1838, Staples, Ed., loc. cit., 248-250.

4 Gaffney, loc. cit. 223.

John Fairfield began the first of four non-consecutive terms as Governor of Maine on January 4, 1839.[5] On the 11th, as Commander-in-Chief of the Maine Militia, he appointed as his Aides-de-Camp, Hannibal Hamlin, Esq., of Hampden, Frederick Cogswell, Esq. of Berwick, Bion Bradbury, Esq., of Calais, and Joseph H. Williams, Esq., of Augusta. Each received the rank of Lieutenant Colonel. Abner B. Thompson replaced Rufus Vose as Adjutant General.[6] Fairfield found the condition of the "Independent Companies" truly gratifying; they were "animated by a right spirit and exhibited a degree of military skill and discipline highly creditable to them and to the State."

In his first address as Governor, Fairfield commented that he wondered how much longer the pacific temper of Maine could be taxed by the continual assertion of a preposterous claim to her territory. He reasoned:

A struggle of arms is but a poor arbiter of right between contending parties, and is a calamity too dreadful to be lightly hazarded. But there is a point beyond which forbearance would be more than pusillanimity. It would be dishonoring our noble ancestry, and committing treason against those who are to succeed us. ... We are not remediless. If Maine should take possession of her territory, up to the line of the treaty of 1783, resolved to maintain it with all the force she is capable of exerting, any attempt on the part of the British government to wrest that possession from her must bring the general government to her aid and defence ... This step, however, is only to be taken after

---

5 Fairfield's Governor's Council for 1839 included Henry Hobbs, John Webb, John Walker, Alpheus Lyon, Nathan C. Fletcher, Nathaniel Milliken and Samuel Cony. Asaph R. Nichols was Secretary of State, Jeremiah Goodwin was Treasurer, Abner B. Thompson was Adjutant General and Rufus McIntire was Land Agent. Job Prince was President of the Maine Senate and Hannibal Hamlin was Speaker of the Maine House.
6 General Order No. 1, signed by Adj. Gen. Rufus C. Vose, *General Order Book, Maine Militia*, Vol. III, Maine State Archives.

mature deliberation. Once taken, it can never be abandoned![7]

Elijah Hamlin, Esq., Land Agent under former Governor Kent, presented Fairfield with the report of the mission of his Deputy, George W. Buckmore, Esq., on January 22, 1839. In December, Buckmore, after travelling for ten days, had found the amount of depredations to be much larger than had been anticipated. He was unable to arrest the trespassers or to take off their teams and supplies. He had found, a short distance above the Grand Falls, at Grand River from forty to fifty men at work making timber, and from twenty to thirty persons cutting timber on Green River. At the Madawaska Settlement, the Governor of New Brunswick had given permission to each settler to cut one hundred pine logs on his lot, and most were cutting logs for Sir John Caldwell's mills at the Grand Falls. Magistrates Francis Rice and Leonard R. Coombs informed Buckmore that they had been authorized to *arrest* all persons attempting to exercise jurisdiction on the part of the American Government. Several crews were at work cutting timber on the Madawaska, St. Francis, and Restigouche Rivers. On the Fish River, he had found Mr. Whalen, with eight men and a team of six oxen, supplied by Francis Rice; C. Fernandee and S. Herbert, with six men and one team; a crew of fourteen men and one team supplied by Mr. Carle of Madawaska; Joseph Dominkee, with nine men and a team supplied by Mr. Brunsieu of Canada; Mr. Woobert and R. Martin, with fourteen men, one team of horses and one team of oxen; and several small crews, making about ten pair of horses, sixteen yoke of oxen and from fifty to seventy-five men. Most of these trespassers were located on Township No. 16, Range 7, (Eagle Lake) belonging to Maine.

---

[7] Speech of John Fairfield to the Legislature, January 4, 1839 ROSM Vol. III, 17-28.

On the main St. John River, between the St. Francis and Madawaska Rivers, he had found two crews under Leonard R. Coombs; one under Messrs. Wheelock and Caton, supplied by Sir John Caldwell; and one crew each under S. Herbert, William Gardner, Mr. Hunnewell, Messrs. Makay and Decenado, Mr. Canada, and D. Dagel, nine crews in all. They would probably cut on the St. John and its tributaries above the Grand Falls at least seventy-five thousand tons, about one third of which would be cut on Fish River.

Buckmore had explored the Aroostook River, a one hundred mile long tributary of the St. John River. (Its source is at the confluence of Munsungun Stream and Millinocket Stream in 8R8 WELS, and it flows from there through 9R8, 9R7, Oxbow, 10R6, to 10R5 or Masardis where it is joined by the St. Croix Stream, then on to Ashland, where it is joined by the Big Machias River and the Little Machias River; to Castle Hill, where it is joined by Beaver Brook; to Wade; to Washburn, where it is joined by Salmon Brook; to Mapleton; to Presque Isle, where it is joined by the Presque Isle of the Aroostook; to Caribou, where it is joined by the Little Madawaska River; to Fort Fairfield, and on to empty into the St. John. The Little Madawaska of the Aroostook is not to be confused with the Madawaska of the St. John which flows from Temiscouata Lake.)

On the Aroostook River, on its tributary Beaver Brook, Buckmore found crews supplied by Peter Bull who informed Buckmore that since there was trespassing below, he would not stop and would resist any attempt to take away his teams. On Salmon Stream, another tributary, Wilder Stratton, James Swetor, David Swetor, Michael Keeley, John Coffee and John Smiley, all from New Brunswick, were at work, did not intend to quit, would defend themselves and resist all authority from Maine.

On Township Letter H, belonging to Maine, (part of present day Caribou) Mr. Johnson, with a crew of ten men, six oxen and one pair of horses, refused to quit, would continue to cut timber in spite of both Governments, and used much threatening language. At the mouth of the Little Madawaska, there were about seventy-five trespassers with twenty yoke of oxen and ten pair of horses, well supplied with provisions from the Province. In Buckmore's opinion they were violent and lawless men, determined to resist arrest. At the Aroostook Falls, he found thirty men with six yoke of oxen cutting timber within the American line and hauling it into the river below the Falls. Fifteen to twenty thousand tons of timber would be taken off the townships on the Little Madawaska River that winter.[8]

Land Agent Hamlin's opinion, based upon Buckmore's report was that nothing short of an armed force of at least fifty men could effectively break up the trespassing. In a matter of that magnitude the Land Agent did not feel authorized to proceed without directions from the Governor and Council, or from the Legislature then in session.

A Civil *Posse* is Organized to Protect State Property

Governor Fairfield took Buckmore's report to a secret joint session of the Legislature on January 23, 1839. He pointed out that the trespassers not only refused to desist, but defied the power of Maine's government to prevent them from cutting timber estimated at one hundred thousand dollars during that season. He concluded that the supremacy of law, as well as the sanctity of right, could not be set aside with impunity, without weakening Maine's authority and inviting renewed aggression. He declared that such outrageous conduct called for the most prompt and vigorous action. He then set forth a course of action which all previous governors had avoided, the use of arms to protect State property:

---

8   George W. Buckmore, *Report of the Land Agent*, submitted on January 22, 1839, for an inspection done in December, 1838.

Under these circumstances I would recommend that the Land Agent be instructed to proceed to the place of operation on the Aroostook, and also upon the Fish River, if practicable, with a sufficient number of men, suitably equipped, to seize the teams and provisions, break up the camps, and disperse those who are engaged in this work of devastation and pillage.

Fairfield cautioned that this extraordinary measure would involve considerable expense, and the sanction of the Legislature was necessary. He reminded them that he had communicated this information in secret session in order that the trespassers might not learn of it and join forces to resist a Land Agent's *posse.* [9]

The Maine House and Senate then passed the Resolve of February 24, 1839:

Resolved, That the Land Agent be, and is hereby authorized and required to employ forthwith sufficient force to arrest, detain and imprison all persons found trespassing on the territory of this State, as bounded and established by the Treaty of 1783; and that the Land Agent be, and is hereby empowered to dispose of all the teams, lumber, and other materials in the hands and possession of the trespassers ... and that the sum of ten thousand dollars be, and hereby is appropriated for the purpose of carrying this resolve into effect ...
Signed: Hannibal Hamlin, Speaker of the House of Representatives; Job Prince, President of the Senate.[10]

---

9 State of Maine, *House of Representatives, document 222,* 6-7, hereinafter referred to as HRD222.
10 HRD222, 7.

The Departure of the Civil *Posse*

Rufus McIntyre, Governor Fairfield's newly appointed Land Agent, in response to the Resolve of January 24th, preferring to use the ordinary civil authority, engaged Hastings Strickland, Esq., Sheriff of Penobscot County, to collect an armed *posse*.

Three groups of men were organized, one at Bangor, one at Oldtown, and one at Lincoln. The first group was to move from Lincoln, via Sebois to be on the Aroostook River on February 6th. Messrs. Stover Rines, William P. Parrot and (Ward?) Witham, the commanders of the different sections, were judged to be men well fitted to their situations.[11] Despite the Governor's plan for secrecy, the *Bangor Daily Whig and Courier* announced, on February 5th, that the Sheriff, with a strong *posse*, had left that morning for the disputed territory, to serve writs on trespassers. McIntire and Strickland, with about two hundred chosen men, travelled in bitterly cold weather (the temperature at Bangor on the 7th was twenty four degrees below zero) to Township No.10, R5 (Masardis) west of the area of trespass operations.

Prior to the *posse's* arrival at No. 10, about three hundred trespassers, forewarned and well armed, had combined to resist every effort to break them up. Finding that the Land Agent had mounted a brass six-pounder, they retired from the ground, and went down the river.[12]

Asa Dow, who resided near Woodstock, New Brunswick, and was said to have had fifteen hundred dollars invested in supplies for his crews, had been at the Aroostook River when he heard of the arrival of an armed

---

11 Barnes, loc. cit., quoting from the *Letterbook of Major R.M.Kirby*; *Bangor Daily Whig and Courier,* February 15, 1839.
12 *Bangor Daily Whig and Courier,* February 5, 1839 and February 8, 1839. Governor Fairfield's message to Legislature, February 15, 1839, HRD222, 8-9. See Appendix V, LAND AGENT'S CIVIL FORCE.

force of Americans. He believed they had no right to exercise authority over the Territory. He and other settlers planned to oppose them. They met and waited, but the *posse* did not arrive, so they dispersed.[13]

McIntire and the *posse* descended the Aroostook River on the ice as far as the mouth of Beaver Brook.[14] They found several lumber operations abandoned by trespassers, but met no resistance. Having heard that there was much alarm and misapprehension among the inhabitants on the River concerning his objectives, McIntire went, in advance of the *posse*, to Mr. Hooper's on Letter G, Range 2, WELS, (Maysville) to explain that he had come to serve precepts upon the trespassers, and hoped that they would not join the trespassers or aid them if they resisted. He encountered no hostility on the river. But the next morning, Sheriff Strickland, with a driver, was going down the river in a sleigh, when, near Peter Bull's property, a mile above Hooper's, fifteen or sixteen armed men paraded in single file along the river, guarding two teams of horses and their drivers, who were trying to escape down river to New Brunswick. Strickland pursued the teams. When he passed through the file of armed men, some of them fired and slightly wounded his horse. The teams failed to escape, for that "excellent and energetic man" left the armed men to be dealt with by his *posse*, pursued the teams for six or seven miles, overtook, captured and brought them back.[15]

The Sheriff's *posse* had captured about 20 armed men, and since he had come prepared to issue and execute writs, court was held on the ice of the Aroostook River.

---

13 Rufus McIntire, *Report of the Land Agent*, 1839, hereinafter referred to as RLAMI 1839; *The Queen versus McIntire, Cushman, Bartlett and Webster*, February 18, 1839, PAC COP188 B16, herein-after referred to as QVMPAC.
14 This Beaver Brook is a tributary to the Aroostook River. Its source is in 13 R 5 WELS, and its course is through that township, through northern Ashland to where it joins the Aroostook in Castle Hill.
15 RLAMI 1839; WELS means "west of the east line of the State."

Sheriff Strickland was there; Gustavus G Cushman, and Thomas Bartlett, lawyers, acted as magistrates. About ten British subjects were held prisoner on a legal process of the State of Maine referring to the trespassing of Foreigners on the Public Lands of Maine and also for felonious assaults on the Sheriff of Penobscot County by the snapping of a firearm at him and firing off a musket. These men would remain prisoners until they could procure sufficient bail. Peter Bull was held for bail but Dennis Fairbanks and Colonel Webster served as security for his bail rather than see him taken away. Charles Johnson and another man had been arrested, but were dismissed after two hours.[16]

The *posse* moved on to the mouth of the Little Madawaska River,[17] to intercept trespassers reported to be up that stream. Land Agent McIntire had, in going to Hooper's, crossed the portage at a bend in the river, and gone to the house of James Fitzherbert, Letter D Range 1, (present day Fort Fairfield,) six miles below the Little Madawaska, where it had been reported that many of the Aroostook River settlers were assembled. He found none and believed they had fled into the Province. He returned

---

16 Governor Fairfield's message to Legislature,February 15, 1839, HRD222, 8-9; Mr. Fairbanks lived on the northwest corner of Letter F, Range 2, had a good sawmill, a grain mill, two dwellings,one of which was a fine farmhouse, two large barns, and about one hundred acres of cleared land under neat cultivation. *Bangor Daily Whig and Courier*, July 7, 1838. Hooper lived about a mile and a half from Fairbanks, and a Mr. Goss lived about half a mile above the mouth of the River Presque Isle. Report, Deane and Kavanagh, 1831, loc. cit.. Memorandum of Captain Hawkshaw, and deposition of Punderson Beardsley, QVCMPAC; *The Age*, February 19, 1839, reporting events of February 15th, 1839, reported that the ringleaders, five in number were, by February 17th, lodged in the Penobscot jail.

17 The Little Madawaska River, a tributary of the Aroostook River, has its source in Bog Lake and its course is through 14 R 5 WELS, Perham, Westmanland, 16R4 WELS, Stockholm, New Sweden, Connor and empties into the Aroostook River at Caribou.

to Sheriff Strickland and *posse*. Not expecting any more resistance, he made arrangements for some of the men to guard the timber left by the trespassers, and planned for the return to Bangor of as many of the *posse* as could be spared.[18]

Warden Maclauchlan was known to be returning to the Aroostook River from a visit to Madawaska. McIntire had written to him, informing him that he was going to Tibbett's at Andover, New Brunswick the following day, and wished to confer with him.[19] On the evening of the 11th, in company with four others, McIntire returned to the house of James Fitzherbert, intending to pass the night there. George Raymond of New Brunswick was present in the kitchen with Fitzherbert when Colonel Ebenezer Webster came in. Fitzherbert remarked to Webster, "You got along without any trouble, Colonel."

Webster replied that they had met with no opposition as yet and the people residing in the territory would soon be all American citizens; that those of the settlers who behaved civilly would be well treated and those who did not would be taken prisoner and punished. He said he was happy to have found that many of the settlers were willing to come under their jurisdiction.[20]

Meanwhile, the group of trespassers that had confronted the Land Agent at Masardis had retired to the Province, where they had gotten arms from the stores of A. Carman, Esq., Charles Connell, Esq., and Mr. James

---

18 RLAMI 1839
19 QVMPAC; A typescript at the Public Archives of New Brunswick gives biographical information on the Tibbets family: James Tibbets, b 1804, located at Andover, N B, where he engaged extensively in the lumber business as operator and shipper, being among the first operators on the Upper St John.
20 Deposition of George Raymond, dated February 15, 1839, given before John Diblee and J M Connell, Justices of the Peace, QVCMPAC.

Segee, in Woodstock, all places of safekeeping for arms belonging to Her Majesty.[21]

Asa Dow had left Fitzherbert's and gone over to Tibbetts' where he found many men together for the purpose of surprising the American force and capturing their teams and men. While Dow and his group were at Tobique, Penderson Beardsley a lumberman and farmer from Woodstock, had been watching the movements of the Americans. He had been at the house of James Fitzherbert at about dusk when the five American citizens arrived. He shook hands with Colonel Webster, who invited him to go into the parlour where he was introduced to Rufus McIntire, Gustavus G. Cushman, his lawyer and legal advisor, Squire Thomas Bartlett and Captain J. H. Pilsbury, also from Maine. They had a long conversation in relation to the present difficulties on the Aroostook. Beardsley referred to the trials of prisoners taken by the *posse*, and remarked to Webster that he thought "it was a summary way, their exercise of trying people on the ice of the river." He said he thought his Government would not be disposed to submit to it. Webster replied that they had come prepared to enforce Maine's laws there. Beardsley commented that he had understood there were five hundred Red Coats coming up. Webster replied that he did not care, that the American party could have two thousand men there in ten days. McIntire and Webster both stated to Beardsley that they expected to see Maclauchlan, and intended to make him an offer to let what timber had been cut go down the St. John River upon the payment of their Land Agent of five shillings per ton.[22]

---

21 Major Kirby to The Adjutant General of the U.S. Army at Washington, DC, Feb 15, 1839, Barnes, loc. cit. Ketchum and Winslow to Harvey, February 12, 1839, *Letterbook of Governor Harvey*. Public Archives of New Brunswick, hereinafter referred to as LGHPANB. The recovery of the arms and ammunition was announced on February 15th. Letter from Ketchum, Diblee, Buell, DeMill, and Connell, Justices of the peace, to Harvey, February, 15, 1839. LGHPANB.
22 QVMPAC

The Capture of Maine Land Agent Rufus McIntire

Penderson Beardsley had assigned several persons to different locations to "look out" and send the earliest information to Tibbet's so that they might know what the Americans were doing. His brother, Lieutenant Paul Beardsley, reported to Dow on the Tobique River that there were five Americans spending the night at Fitzherbert's; that they were the leaders of the *posse*, and that the remainder of the armed force was encamped a few miles back up the Aroostook.[23]

After receiving this information, Dow ordered two spans of horses to be harnessed and took fifteen or eighteen men on two sleds to Fitzherbert's,[24] and surrounded the house. At about midnight Dow, Paul Beardsley and party awakened the lodgers by rushing into the house and ordering them at gunpoint to get up and dress and go with them. Beardsley arrested them. Colonel Webster asked by what authority he was taken, and Beardsley, with his gun standing on the floor, referred to it and said "that is my authority." Webster said he would not go as he was pursuing his private business. Beardsley said he must go with them, he could make no distinctions. They took all five prisoners, Gustavus Cushman, Thomas Bartlett, Colonel Webster, Captain Pilsbury and Rufus McIntire, to Tibbetts' on the St. John River. McIntire inquired whether the letter he had sent to Colonel Maclauchlan had arrived and enquired as to his whereabouts. The captors searched

---

23 Ibid.
24 *The Bangor Daily Whig and Courier*, March 9, 1839, reported that James Fitzherbert, the man at whose house McIntire was arrested, was brought to Bangor on March 8th, and was examined on the 9th on charges of having aided and abetted sundry of her Majesty's subjects in the high misdemeanor of arresting McIntire. He was bound over in a sum of $500, to appear at the Court of Common Pleas to be held next May in Bangor.

their prisoners for arms. Dow took Cushman's pocket pistol and McIntire's pocket carbine.[25] From Tibbetts' at Andover, the captives were taken down river to James Jones' place at Wakefield, twelve miles above Woodstock. Dow left them and went on to Woodstock to alert the authorities of what had been done. McIntire sent a note to Governor Fairfield from Wakefield stating that he had left his force at the mouth of the Little Madawaska of the Aroostook and stressed that "those concerned in the trespassing have done this!"[26]

Dow met Captain William Hawkshaw, of Her Majesty's Corps of Royal Engineers and Acting Adjutant Quarter Master General of troops in New Brunswick, who, in the absence of James Maclauchlan, had been sent to investigate. Dow told him he had taken some prisoners, so Hawkshaw returned with him to Jones' and met with the captives. He asked McIntire if there were armed men on the Disputed Territory from the State of Maine. McIntire replied in the affirmative, and produced the papers stating the authority under which he acted. McIntire told the Captain that Cushman and Bartlett were magistrates; that with the Sheriff of Penobscot County they had all arrived in the Disputed Territory with armed men, but not Militia; that their sole instruction was to prevent trespassing on the Territory; that they did not intend to remain longer than the 15th, but would probably leave a few men to mark the lumber the trespassers had made; that it was not his intention to send an armed force to Madawaska, since Maclauchlan was there and would put a stop to the lumbering in that quarter. Hawkshaw remarked that it was a pity that the Governor of Maine had kept this proceeding so secret as even to stop the newspapers

---

25 QVMPAC.
26 RLAMI 1839; McIntire to Fairfield, February 13, 1839, JFPC 145B 3/7, MHS; Kirby to Fairfield, February 14, 1839, *The Papers of John Fairfield,* Mss 19264, microfilmed by the Library of Congress, used by courtesy of Sally Huot and the Dyer Library, Saco, Maine; hereinafter referred to as PJFDL; QVMPAC.

during the secret session of the Legislature. He said that if any blood were shed, it might ultimately lead to a war between the two nations.27

The five Americans were brought to Woodstock where Dow's proceedings were sanctioned by a consultation of Magistrates. Webster and Pilsbury were released, judged not attached to the expedition of the Land Agent. A company of the New Brunswick Militia paraded before the inn where the prisoners were quartered. The doors were guarded by armed sentinels, and no American citizens, including Major Kirby from Hancock Barracks, were permitted to see them. Richard Ketchum and John Diblee, Justices of the Peace at Woodstock, charged McIntire, Cushman and Bartlett with overt acts of jurisdiction over the Disputed Territory. That afternoon, the prisoners were sent on a horse sled guarded by four armed men and Militia Captain Cunliffe, to Fredericton Gaol to await the pleasure of the Lieutenant Governor.28

The next day, Penderson Beardsley and George L. Raymond arrived in Woodstock and deposed that Colonel Webster was a principal in the American Armed Party; he was again taken into custody.29

Charles Jarvis is Appointed Provisional Land Agent

On the 12th of February, Hastings Strickland began his famous ride to Bangor to inform State authorities of the capture of McIntire and the threat of armed opposition. He travelled 160 miles, arriving in Bangor at four

---

27 Report of Captain Hawkshaw, LGHPANB.
28 McIntire to Fairfield on February 14, 1839, *John Fairfield Papers*, Collection 145, file B3/7, Maine Historical Society Archives, Portland, hereinafter referred to as JFPC 145 plus file number. Ketchum and Diblee to Harvey, February 14, 1839, LGHPANB; RLAMI 1839; H. W. Judkins and Isaac Tabor to Governor Fairfield, February 14, 1839, JFPC 145-B3/6 MHS; McIntire to Fairfield, February 14, 1839, JFPC 145B3/7;
29 Ketchum, Diblee, Buell, De Mill and Connell to Harvey, February 15, 1839; William F. Odell to Harvey, February 15, 1839, LBGHPANB

o'clock P M, on February 13th.[30] Then he went to Augusta, where he reported all events verbally to Governor Fairfield, including the information that the Land Agent's force was then fortified at No. 10, on the Aroostook, and expected to be attacked. Naturally, news of the capture of McIntire caused great excitement in Maine. Public opinion in Bangor held that because the State had commenced on just grounds, and was being opposed by only a lawless mob, it was Maine's duty to quell that mob at once, with strong forcible measures, even to the death.[31]

On February 15th, Fairfield reported Strickland's information to the Legislature, recommended sending reinforcements to the *posse*, and the appointment of a temporary Land Agent to lead the expedition. He had dispatched Jonathan P. Rogers, Esq., as special messenger to Sir John Harvey, to "ascertain whether the high-handed proceedings of the trespassers were authorized, or in any

---

30 Sheriff Strickland's courage had been held up to ridicule by part of the Maine press. The *Bangor Daily Whig and Courier*, February 13, 1839, sarcastically reported: "Mr. Strickland arrived in this city about four o'clock yesterday PM, having travelled 160 miles between that time and the day before. This is certainly extraordinary speed, considering the flight was in the woods, but there is no calculating a man's velocity when he's skeert!" Editors of the *Bangor Daily Whig and Courier* were repeatedly accused by the *The Age* (at Augusta) of bias in reporting, to which they responded on February 24, 1839: "The assertion of the *Age* that we wished to cast ridicule on the Aroostook Expedition is wholly false." Again, on March 1, 1839 the *Bangor Whig and Courier* defended itself against similar charges from the *Bangor Democrat*. "It is bald falsehood, charging us with an attempt to sneer down the Aroostook Expedition." Deny it though they might, the owner of the *Bangor Daily Whig and Courier*, John Edwards of Portland, allowed his paper to carry sarcasm and innuendos which amounted to yellow journalism. Documentary evidence does not support this attitude. Land Agent McIntire reported Strickland's action as courageous and Strickland received the approbation of Governor Fairfield.
31 Fairfield's message to Legislature, Feb. 15, 1839, HRD222, 8-9; Benamin Wiggin, Jr., to Fairfield, February 14, 1839, JFPC 145B 3/6.

way countenanced by the Provincial government," and to procure the release of the Land Agent and party.
Fairfield experienced no difficulty in procuring men for the reinforcement to the *posse*; "indeed, it was hard work to hold volunteers back, for thousands and thousands would have gone if permitted."[32] Charles Jarvis of Ellsworth was appointed as Provisional Land Agent. He was on his way to Bangor within an hour of receipt of the Governor's request. He met with Major Strickland, and it was agreed that Jarvis would maintain the present posts until reinforcements could be sent.[33]

Sir John Harvey Mobilizes the New Brunswick Militia

Sir John Harvey heard from Lieutenant Colonel Richard Ketchum and Sheriff John Winslow of Woodstock that Maine's civil *posse* was in the Disputed Territory to drive off persons cutting timber on the Aroostook, and then to proceed to Madawaska for the same purpose.[34]
Harvey mobilized units of the New Brunswick Militia to confront the American *posse*.

A PROCLAMATION
Whereas I have received information that a party of armed persons to the number of two hundred or more have invaded a portion of this province under the jurisdiction of Her Majesty's Government, from the neighboring State of Maine, for the professed object of

---
32   Fairfield to Jonathan P. Rogers, Esq., February 15, 1839, *Collection of Official Papers, Northeast Boundary Dispute*, Maine Historical Society, Portland, hereinafter referred to as COPMHS; HRD222, 8-9. Fairfield to his wife, February 16, 1839, Staples, Ed., loc.cit.
33   Resolve of February 16, 1839, HRD222, 9; Fairfield to Jarvis, February 15, 1839, COPMHS; Jarvis to Fairfield, February 15, 1839, JFPC145 B3/7, MHS; Jarvis to Fairfield, from No. 4, Aroostook Road, undated, probably February 16, 1839, JFPC145B 3/8, MHS.
34   Ketchum and Winslow to Harvey, February 12, 1839, QVMPAC.

exercising authority, and driving off persons stated to be cutting timber therein;

And that divers other persons have, without any legal authority, taken up arms with the intention of resisting such invasion and outrage, and have broken open certain stores in Woodstock, in which arms and ammunition belonging to Her Majesty were deposited, and have taken the same away for that purpose, I do hereby charge and command all persons concerned in such illegal acts forthwith to return the arms and ammunition illegally taken, to their place of deposite; as the Government of the province will take care to adopt all necessary measures from resisting any hostile invasion or outrage that may be attempted upon any part of Her Majesty's territories or subjects. ...

I command the officers commanding the first, and second battalions of the militia of the County of Carleton, to proceed, as the law directs, to the draughting of a body of men, to consist of one-fourth of the strength of each of those battalions, to be in readiness for actual service, should occasion require. ... [35]

In a spirited address, Colonel Maxwell of the 36th Regiment, told the First Battalion, Carleton Militia, under command of Major Diblee, that the promptness with which the Militia volunteered their services to protect their country from hostile invasion convinced him that he had come amongst the right stuff, for they were famed as good woodsmen, good marksmen and gallant warriors; and their devotion and loyalty to their queen and Mother Country and Fatherland was unequalled.

A rather heated correspondence between Harvey and Fairfield ensued. On February 13th, Harvey informed Fairfield of his surprise and regret that without the courtesy of any previous intimation, an armed force from the State of Maine had entered the Territory; that his

---

35 RGHIL 1839.

instructions did not permit him to suffer any interference with that possession and jurisdiction. He requested the immediate recall of that force and gave notice that he had directed a strong force of Her Majesty's troops to be in readiness to support Her Majesty's authority in the event that his request was not immediately complied with. Also, he had given directions for a boom to be placed across the mouth of the Aroostook River, where the seizing officer, protected by a sufficient guard, would be able to prevent passage of any timber into the St. John in the spring, to seize it and expose it to public sale for the benefit of the "disputed territory fund." Similar precautions would be adopted in regard to any timber cut upon the upper St. John, or the tributary streams falling into it.[36]

In response, on the 19th, Fairfield notified Harvey that the proceedings of the Land Agent were in execution of a Resolve of the Maine Legislature, adopted in a secret session, and that no notice of their proceedings could have been given without an unqualified breach of faith and duty. ... Furthermore, the territory bordering upon the Aroostook River had always been in the possession and under the jurisdiction of Massachusetts and Maine, and Maine had exercised her exclusive jurisdiction over this territory. When a body of armed men had gone into this territory and begun cutting vast quantities of timber, defying the power of this State to prevent them, the Legislature directed the Land Agent's forces to protect the State from plunderers, and if Harvey chose to send an armed force to attempt their expulsion, Maine would endeavour to meet any such attempt as it deserved.[37]

---

36 Harvey to Fairfield, February 13, 1839, JFPC 145B 3/8, MHS.
37 Fairfield to Harvey, February 19, 1839, HRD222, 15-16.

The Examination of McIntire, Cushman,
Webster and Bartlett

McIntire, Cushman, Webster and Bartlett had been lodged in Fredericton Gaol, but after Jonathan Rogers arrived they had been at large, by the indulgence of the Sheriff, had comfortable accommodations and were kindly treated. They had been informed that they would be brought before the examining magistrates the next morning on the charge of Committing Overt Acts of Jurisdiction and Interference with the Disputed Territory. Affadavits of the witnesses would be taken in their presence; they would not be called upon to plead or make any defense, but they might cross-examine the witnesses. Unacquainted with these proceedings, they hired council.[38]

On Saturday, the 16th, they were present at the examination of the witnesses. Then the Americans moved counsel, but he was not permitted to put questions or make remarks except through the prisoners.[39] They cross-examined Asa Dow. He admitted that he was not a magistrate or a peace officer of any kind, that he had no authority to lumber upon the Disputed Territory; that it had been of no use to apply to New Brunswick for permits; he had not applied to the State of Maine as he considered they had no right to give such authority. He admitted that most of the persons involved in the capture of Maine's land agent were trespassers on the Disputed Territory; that there was not a peace officer in the group; that there were about thirty-eight or forty men who volunteered to go to surprise the Americans; that two or three Indians "were shaken" to go and spy on the Americans but they would not go; that the force that went from Tibbitts' was armed with muskets and rifles and loaded with powder and ball and if the whole Amer-

---

[38] McIntire to Fairfield, February 18, 1839, JFPC 145, 3/8, MHS.
[39] Ibid.

ican force had been at Fitzherbert's they would have made an attack on them that night.[40]

On Sunday morning, the 17th, before their next court appearance, by request, McIntire, Cushman, Webster and Bartlett called upon Lieutenant Governor Harvey and had a short conversation with him. He told them he regretted much of what his legal advisers thought necessary, and assured them that he would, as early as possible, relieve them from their situation. McIntire felt sure that they would be released so as to take the stage home on Monday.[41]

The decision from the Attorney General's Office was handed down on Monday, February 18th. The prisoners were to be allowed to sign a parole of honor:

> Whereas the offense wherewith you stand charged has been pronounced by the Law Officer of this Province as one against the Law of Nations and of Treaties rather than against the Municipal Laws of the Country, and as such must be referred for the opinion of Her Majesty's Government, you are hereby required to pledge your Parole of Honor to present yourself at Fredericton in the Province of New Brunswick whenever such decision shall be communicated, or you shall otherwise be required by or on the part of this Government, and for this purpose you shall make known the place or places requisition shall be sent.
> signed: J. Harvey
> We have no hesitation in giving and hereby do give the parole of honor above referred to: Signed: Rufus McIntire Parsonsfield, Maine; Gustavus Cushman, Bangor, Maine; Thomas Bartlett, Orono, Maine; Ebenezer Webster, Orono, Maine.[42]

---

40 QVMPAC
41 McIntire to Fairfield, February 18, 1839, JFPC 145, 3/8, MHS.Ibid.
42 PACCOP188B16.

Rufus McIntire arrived in Houlton on the evening of February 19th. That same day, Sir John Harvey heard a rumor relative to the arrest and detention of Warden James Maclauchlan by the American *posse*, and demanded of Fairfield that "this being correct, the officer be enlarged and the grounds of his detention explained."[43]

The Capture of James Maclauchlan, British Warden of the Disputed Territory

Captain Stover Rines and the *posse* had stationed themselves at the termination of the Aroostook Road, in Township No. 10 (Masardis). Warden Maclauchlan had heard, on his return from Madawaska, that the Maine Land Agent had a force on the Disputed Territory. Doubting it, and determined to know the facts, he had proceeded to within two miles of Rines' encampment with his horses, and walked in. The first object that met his eyes was a cannon pointed directly at him. He presented himself, and in the name of Her Majesty, warned the *posse* to disperse. Maclauchlan and his two assistants were taken into custody, and Maclauchlan and one assistant, Mr. Tibbetts, were immediately sent to Bangor and detained. A third man remained in custody at the Camp.[44]

Maclauchlan and Tibbetts arrived in Bangor on February 17th, under the charge of Mr. Haines, and were quartered at the Bangor House. A large crowd of Bangor citizens, "on the approach of Her Majesty's Warden, opened to the right and left, all extremely pleased to see him captive, but made no expression of their sentiments."[45]

On February 17th, the day after the capture of Maclauchlan and Tibbets, and the day of arrival of Colonel

---

43 HRD222, 34-35.
44 Governor Fairfield's report to the Legislature, February 18, 1839, ROSM III, 152-155. Samuel Smith to Fairfield, February 17, 1839, JFPC I 45 3/8 MHS.
45 Samuel Smith to Fairfield, February 17, 1839, JFPC I 45 3/8 MHS.

Jarvis to assume command of the *posse*, the Solicitor General of the Province of New Brunswick, George Frederick Street, from the Mouth of the Aroostook, under a flag of truce, sent an ultimatum to the commander of American civil force. He expressed surprise that such a force would attempt jurisdiction there, that they would seize upon and maltreat and imprison British subjects. He had been directed by Harvey to give notice that unless they immediately removed themselves from any part of the Disputed Territory, discharged all British prisoners, and ceased attempting to exercise authority not authorized by the British Government, every person of that party that could be found would be taken and detained as prisoners, to answer for this offence. Further, a large military force was then assembling in New Brunswick, part of which had already arrived to carry out these orders. His Excellency was desirous to avoid collision that might lead to bloodshed, so if they departed peaceably, His Excellency would not think it necessary to move the British troops farther. If they did not, he would take military possession of the territory.[46]

Colonel Charles Jarvis replied, on the 19th, that he, Street, must have been misinformed as to the place where his force was located, or he would have been spared the impropriety of addressing such a communication to a citizen of Maine, one of the North American confederacy of the United States. Jarvis stressed that his location had been under the jurisdiction of Maine since she took her rank among the independent states. Therefore, as a citizen of Maine, in official capacity, he had but one answer to the threat conveyed. He was there under the direction of the Executive of the State, and must remain until otherwise ordered by the same; and deeply as he would regret a conflict, he would consider the approach

---

46 HRD222, 25-26.

to his station by an armed force as an act of hostility, to be met by him to the best of his ability.[47]

With the Civil *Posse* on the Disputed Territory

When Colonel Jarvis first arrived at No. 10 from Bangor, on the 17th, he had found the men in good spirits making temporary but effectual defenses of logs and brush. A "4-pounder," a brass field cannon, had been well planted, so as to command a reach of about eighty rods in the river. The felled trees had been arranged so that a force of one hundred men could stand against five hundred. Retreat was out of the question.

When Jarvis found two or three applications for discharge, he had the men paraded and explained the importance of making good their stand. After appealing to their pride, he ordered those who wished to withdraw to ground arms. He was mortified when first one musket came down, and then another, until twenty-two were on the ground. These were discharged. Twelve supply teams were just starting for Bangor, lightly loaded. The discharged men wished to ride. He refused, told them "their blood was too cold, they had better walk, the progress of the teams should not be impeded by their lubberweight."

At this time Jarvis had only one hundred muskets, but he wrote to the Governor that a finer looking lot of men he had never seen, that the honor of the State was in safe keeping. Ira Fish of Lincoln arrived at No. 10 at midnight, bringing cheering news: sixty good men would reinforce the *posse* by evening of the next day and four hundred more were on the way. Jarvis advised Fairfield that when all had arrived, he would take a position about twenty miles below, at Beaver Brook, "unless previously occupied by Sir John." He had had reports that an English

---

[47] HRD222, 26-27.

officer in uniform had been looking out a place for an encampment.[48]

Previous to February 18th, Mr. Pollard, of the civil *posse* had requested and been refused loan of an American flag from Hancock Barracks. Major Kirby wrote to Jarvis, that it was his duty not to compromise the General Government on the question of jurisdiction until otherwise ordered by his superiors. On the 20th, when Kirby informed Headquarters of the Army of the request he explained that he had declined to commit any act which would be in furtherance of the measures adopted by the Government of Maine.[49]

Major Hastings Strickland, on the 19th, had despatched about six hundred men, in good spirits, with provisions, equipment and ammunition, to support Jarvis at No. 10. He expected to join them there by the next evening. He had had a little trouble with General Hodsdon and Captain Lambert of the Maine Militia, in obtaining guns, but it had been amicably settled.[50]

---

[48] Jarvis to Fairfield, February 19, 1839, JFPC 145B 3/8, MHS.
[49] Kirby to the Land Agent, February 18, 1839, Barnes, loc. cit.
[50] Strickland to Fairfield, February 19, 1839, JFPC 145,3/8, MHS.

CHAPTER VIII

MILITARY CONFRONTATION

Governor Fairfield Mobilizes the Maine Militia

Considering Lieutenant Governor Harvey's proclamation to be a declaration of war, John Fairfield, as Commander-in-Chief of the Maine Militia, on February 16, 1839, ordered Major General Isaac Hodsdon, Commander of the Third Division, to detach one thousand men, properly officered and equipped, with three days' provisions, to rendezvous at Bangor. He was then to proceed to the place occupied by the Land Agent's force on or near the Aroostook River, and give such aid as necessary to enable him to carry out the Resolve of January 24, 1839. General Order No. 6 clarified the call-up: eight hundred and fifty Infantry, Light Infantry and Riflemen, and one hundred and fifty Artillery. Companies were to be organized with sixty-four privates, four sergeants and two musicians each. The men were to report themselves to Bangor on Thursday, the 21st. Hodsdon was to command the detachment in person, with one Colonel, one Lieutenant Colonel, one Major of Infantry, and one Major of Artillery, with the appropriate Staff. Their term of service would be three months unless sooner discharged.[1] Major General Hodsdon availed himself of "such troops as would seem best adapted to what might prove to be the nature of the service required."[2] He was concerned about moving so large a detachment of troops, wholly unacquainted with camp duty, in the winter. He requisitioned tents for the men but planned that if they marched in separate companies, at some distance from each other, they might be able to obtain quarters during their march through settled areas. He reminded A. B. Thompson, Acting Quarter Master General that the hardship to his troops, on foot, encumbered with their arms, knapsacks, rations, etc., would be very great, and as the civil force had had transportation furnished for themselves and their baggage, he expected suitable provisions to be made for the Militia. Thompson, at Augusta, sent George Stanley to Bangor, to procure supplies, take charge of the conveyance of baggage and the distribution and storage of supplies.[3]

Governor Fairfield informed the Legislature, on February 18th, of Harvey's Proclamation, of the gathering of four to five hundred reinforcements for the Land Agent

---

[1] Abner B. Thompson, *Report of the Adjutant General, 1839* hereinafter referred to as RAGABT 1839; General Orders No. 5 and 6, in *Aroostook War, Historical Sketch and Roster of Commissioned Officers and Enlisted Men Called into Service for the Protection of the Northeastern Frontier of Maine From February to May, 1839*, Augusta, Kennebec Journal Print, 1904, hereinafter referred to as AWKJ.

[2] Hodsdon to Fairfield, February 17, 1839, JFPC 145 3/8 MHS. By "troops as would seem best adapted, etc." he may be indicating that he sought the services of at least some of the Independent Companies, for several of these served in his force. See Appendix VI, MAINE MILITIA.

[3] Ibid.; General Order No. 6, February 17, 1839; Thompson to Stanley, February 18, 1839, *Official Hodsdon Papers*, Maine Historical Society Archives, Portland, hereinafter referred to as OHPMHS. On February 20, 1838, Lt. George G. Green was appointed Assistant Commissary of Subsistence, salary $15.00 per month. OHPMHS.

and of the progress in mobilization. He had requested the cooperation of Major Kirby at Hancock Barracks. Then the Governor requested funds for a further draft of at least ten thousand men, to be held in instant readiness. He noted that he had not yet called upon the President for aid, having postponed that step until the arrival of information from Colonel Rogers. He asked for the consensus of the Legislature as to whether the President should be notified before that time. He reported the contents of Harvey's letter of the 13th, concerning jurisdiction. McIntire and party were still being detained at Fredericton. The affront to Maine's honor was great, but Fairfield was gratified that on this subject the din of party warfare was hushed, that unanimity prevailed.[4]

By the Resolve of the 18th of February the Legislature appropriated $800,000 militia expense. At the request of the Legislature, Fairfield apprised the President of all events, and again asked for "that aid and assistance which the whole States have guaranteed to each other in such an emergency."[5]

Major Kirby's response, from Hancock Barracks, was that the three Companies at that Garrison barely

---

[4] Governor Fairfield's report to the Legislature, February 18, 1839, ROSM III, 152-5.; The British statment of their supposed claim is stated in Stevenson to Forsyth, April 5, 1839: The ground and nature of the claim of jurisdiction were explained, he said, by Sir Charles Vaughan, in his note to the Secretary of State of the 16th of Sept., 1827, and the qualified and limited manner in which the right had been exercised was also clearly stated by Sir Howard Douglass, in his despatch to Sir Charles Vaughan of the 4th of October, 1827, which was communicated to the Secretary of State on the 26th of the same month. The nature and grounds of the British Claim, his lordship said, were further explained by their Minister in February, 1828, and in the note of Lord Aberdeen on the 14th of August, 1828. *Documents Relating to the Public Lands in Maine*, Maine Historical Society, Portland, hereinafter referred to as DRPLM.

[5] HRD222, 12; Chapter 33, February 20, 1839, ROSM III, 42; Chapter 35, February 22, 1839, ROSM III, 43; DRPLM.

sufficed to protect that position and guard the Government supplies. While he was fully impressed with the obligation imposed upon him to aid the civil and military authorities of the State in repelling invasion, the limitations of those means must necessarily confine his operations to that immediate neighborhood. It would be his duty not to compromise the General Government in the question of jurisdiction upon that portion of the territory of Maine by any act of occupation by troops of the United States until ordered to do so by his superiors. However, Kirby suggested the establishment of a line of expresses to Houlton, under the direction of a confidential agent, in order that he might send intelligence reports to the Governor as quickly as possible. He noted that the 36th Regiment from the West India Station had arrived in the Province; that on the 16th, one company of that Regiment passed from Woodstock to the area north of the Aroostook, and that morning another company had followed, under the command of Lieutenant Colonel Maxwell. He expected a post to be established at Woodstock of two companies of the same Regiment. It was rumored that one of the Regiments that recently passed through to Canada was ordered back, and that two more Regiments were daily expected from the West Indies.[6]

Fairfield's General Order No. 7, February 19, 1839, alerted ten thousand three hundred and forty-three officers, non-commissioned officers and privates of the militia to hold themselves in readiness for an immediate call into the service of the State. He sent information of British troop movements to the President, asked that as many regiments of United States troops as could possibly be spared from other service be ordered to the Maine frontier, and that Major Kirby might receive orders to cooperate with Maine's forces in repelling an invasion.[7]

---

6 Kirby to Fairfield, February 18, 1839, PJFDL.
7 AWKJ, 8; Fairfield to Van Buren, February 19, 1839, COPMHS.

By February 21st, the Governor conferred with Land Agent McIntire and Colonel Rogers in Augusta. Fairfield wrote to his wife that it appeared that collision was inevitable, that Harvey's insolent demands would never be complied with "while we have a sword to draw and arm to wield it," and that "one spirit animates our whole people. Our house was thronged last night, after McIntire returned. McIntire and Rogers had to address the people; they were cheered with great enthusiasm."[8]

Words of encouragement came from Boston, where volunteer companies were voting with perfect unanimity to go to Fairfield's assistance as soon as a wish might be expressed.[9] In Maine, Fairfield was praised by Stephen Emery, of Paris, for his "firmness, decision and patriotism. The honor and interests of the state could not be committed to better hands." Emery commented: "One spirit pervades our whole community; one spontaneous burst of approbation from the whole people. The parties in Maine are one, indivisible, at this trying time. Let this strengthen your hands and encourage your heart." Overwhelming support of his policies caused Fairfield to conclude that "this was the time to strike a blow for our rights. If we let this golden opportunity pass without improvement, we shall deserve to lose our territory and win the contempt of the world."[10]

A. G. Jewett, Esq., shared Fairfield's enthusiasm, but warned of an undercurrent of political opposition:

The people are united and will sustain you in all reasonable measures to maintain possession of the territory or to run the line and mark the boundary. But

---

8 Fairfield to his wife, February 21, 1839, Staples, Ed., loc. cit.
9 Barnes to Fairfield, February 21, 1839, PJFDL.
10 Emery to Fairfield, February 22, 1839, PJFDL; Fairfield to his wife, February 24, 1839, Staples, Ed., loc. cit.

some of the leading Federalists and conservatives [11] in this city manifest a feeling at war with every feeling of patriotism, and stand ready to take advantage of every real or imaginary error that may be committed by the executive or any subordinates. As the appearances of real danger dissipate, they begin to exhibit feelings, and indulge in expressions that truly surprise me, showing that the last wish of their hearts is that Maine should now maintain the noble stand she has taken. ... But they cannot carry their own party with them, so long as the action of the State manifests a determination to hold that soil and property until the question shall have been settled. ...[12]

On February 19th, 1839, Brigadier General George W. Bachelder, with the detachment made from the First Brigade, Second Division, pursuant to General Order No. 7, was ordered into the service of the State. Assembly was to be at the Court House in Augusta on Monday, the 25th, with equipments and three days' provisions. His staff was to include one Brigade Major, one Aid-de-camp, and one Brigade Quarter Master.[13] Major General Ezekiel Fos-

---

[11] Maine's leading Conservative at this time was F. O. J. Smith, of Portland. Gaffney, loc. cit., p 224, wrote: Under the leadership of Samuel Veazie, John Hodgdon and others, the Conservatives held their own convention in Bangor on July 19, 1838. Attended by sixty or seventy delegates, including ... bank presidents, directors, and cashiers, the convention severly condemned the supporters of the Clifford resolution for having made it impossible for the Conservatives to support Fairfield without abandoning their opposition to the Independent Treasury ... and nominated F. O. J. Smith as their gubernatorial candidate. ... While the Conservatives realized they had no chance of electing Smith, they hoped to poll enough votes to prevent the popular election of either Fairfield or his Whig opponent, Edward Kent.
[12] Jewett to Fairfield, February 25, 1839, JFPC 145B 3/10, MHS.
[13] General Order No. 10, AWKJ.

ter and men of the Seventh Division were ordered into the service at Calais, under the same order.[14]

The draft of one thousand men from the Third Division had been made with great dispatch. The troops arrived promptly at the place of rendezvous in good spirits and anxious for the order to march for the frontier.[15]

Colonel Rogers had delivered a letter from Harvey to Fairfield demanding the discharge of the men arrested by the the civil *posse*. Fairfield replied that he had neither the disposition nor the authority to interfere. However, he had recommended that James McLaughlin and Mr. Tibbets be released upon a parole of honor.[16]

On February 22nd, Governor Fairfield again sent copies of recent documents to President Van Buren with the plea that "since an attack upon the citizens of this State by a British armed force is in all human probability inevitable, the interposition of the General Government at this momentous crisis should be promptly afforded."[17]

With the Civil *Posse* on the Aroostook River as Hodsdon's Troops Advance

Charles Jarvis was a prompt and decisive commander. His civil force of three hundred men was pleased to be under his command and was well acquainted with fortifications. He sent about one hundred of his *posse* to Fish River, to break up the gang of trespassers there. Alvin Nye, who had been in charge, executed it perfectly.

---

14 General Order No. 11, February 22, 1839, AWKJ, included four Captains, four Lieutenants, four Ensigns, sixteen sergeants, two musicans and sixty-four privates of the Light Infantry. The Detatchment will be immediately organized into Companies of sixty-four privates, four sergeants and two musicians, Requisition for supplies, including military stores, will be presented to Randall Whidden of Calais, Captain of the Calais Artillery.
15 HRD222, 22-23.
16 Fairfield to Harvey, February 21, 1839, HRD222, 24-5.
17 MPP, 521-522.

George W. Buckmore, who had been with Nye, said that so difficult were the obstacles encountered, in ascending the streams and clearing over five miles of road to avoid places where the streams were open, that he would have turned back, but Nye had been determined to proceed at all events. Nye and his men brought out with them four settlers from Madawaska and let five others go home. They drove out two horses and four yokes of oxen. At the request of Buckmore, Nye and party, Jarvis released the settlers, on their promise never to cut westward of the North Line. Because of their obvious poverty, men of the posse contributed twelve dollars to pay them for damage sustained by their forced and toilsome march. Jarvis believed that the men were sufficiently punished to be deterred from trespassing again. He also considered it very important to ingratiate the feeling of the population.[18]

Major General Isaac Hodsdon's Third Division of Militia had assembled at Bangor and Lincoln. On the 21st day of February, they took up their march for the Aroostook. Albion Frost, Aid-de-Camp to Hodsdon, was one of an advanced party who arrived at Township No. 4 (Patten) on the Aroostook Road. There he found about two hundred and fifty reinforcements for Jarvis' *posse* without a commander, refusing to advance until furnished with arms and blankets. When Frost arrived at No. 10, the next day, he most certainly reported this condition to Jarvis. He consulted with Jarvis about troop movements. On the 23rd, Jarvis sent Captain Fairbanks to meet the advance unit of militia and deliver a letter saying that he was pleased that Hodsdon had been ordered on to sustain him in his movements. He suggested that Hodsdon might more effectively contribute to his aid by making his advance by way of Houlton. Reliable information had it that there was a good road from Houlton to within about

---

18 B. Wiggin Jr., to Fairfield, February 22, 1839, JFPC 145, 3/9, MHS; Fairfield to his wife, February 24, 1839, LJF; Jarvis to Fairfield, date indistinct, probably February 27, 1839, JFPC 145 4/1.

six miles of the confluence of the Aroostook and Presque Isle Rivers. There was a portage of six miles across a large bend in the Aroostook, saving a distance of eighteen miles by the river. Those six miles had been partially cleared, so as to be practicable for sleds. It would be necessary to have this road cleared; it was the only way that could be depended on for their return, because the ice-covered Aroostook river would soon be too weak to be relied upon as a highway. Jarvis explained his strategy to Hodsdon: he had at that time a post on the Aroostook River twelve miles below No. 10 and within four miles of the confluence of the Presque Isle. Unless prevented by English authorities, he would soon take possession of both ends of the portage, which would give him the command of the Aroostook River as far down as a place below the Little Madawaska, the principal seat of the trespassers. Therefore, Hodsdon's movement, by way of Houlton, would greatly facilitate this object, not only because it was the shortest and best route to the most important station on the Aroostook River, but it would also distract the English authorities, as it was on the direct route to Woodstock, until the point of divergence was met at Houlton. He submitted his plan to Hodsdon's judgment, adding that Captain Fairbanks, well acquainted with the route, could give him reliable details.[19]

Major General Hodsdon, still in Bangor, countermanded his order for the militia to march by way of the Aroostook Road and ordered them to proceed by way of Houlton. The change in orders overtook the troops at the beginning of the Aroostook Road. Half of Hodsdon's force had already entered that road, and two companies had marched as far as No. 4, (Patten) but all turned around

---

19 RAGABT 1839; Frost to Hodsdon, February 22, 1839, OHPMHS Collection 8, 1/6. The *Bangor Daily Whig and Courier* in a report on February 25, 1839, referred to No. 4 as Fish's Mills, now known as Patten. Frost to Hodsdon, February 22, 1839, OHPMHS Collection 8, 1/6; Jarvis to Hodsdon, February 23, 1839, OHPMHS.

and were back on the Military Road to Houlton by the 26th.[20]

Elijah L. Hamlin, Superintendent, Cavalry Corps of Videttes, was establishing a line of videttes between Bangor and Houlton, with two men stationed every ten miles, to link Bangor and Augusta with the Aroostook. Cavalrymen were to complete their line on Wednesday, the 27th. Abner Thompson was moving supplies and new Hall's Patent Rifles up to Hodsdon, who departed Bangor for Houlton on the 25th, in the same Stage, with the British Warden of the Disputed Territory, Maclauchlan.[21]

The Bangor Rifle Corps

One militia unit that went north under Hodsdon was the Bangor Rifle Corps. Bangor had become the military center of eastern Maine. The people of Bangor, "ever prompt to resent an insult and redress a wrong," saw them off with shouted sentiments such as, "Sir John Harvey says, 'If you put troops on the Line, I'll put them off!' Lets see him do it! Guess he forgot Bunker Hill and Lexington and Yorktown! We'll give him a second edition, revised and corrected!"[22]

---

20 Samuel E. Smith to Hodsdon, February 24, 1839; and Smith to Fairfield, February 26, 1839, JFPC 145B 3/10, MHS.
21 Smith to Fairfield, February 26, 1839, JFPC 145B 3/10, MHS; *The Bangor Daily Whig and Courier*, Feb. 25, 1839; Thompson to Hodsdon, February 24, 1839, OHPMHS. Charles W. Miller, David Page, Elijah Pike, George W. Stanley, George G. Green and Charles Stetson, Esquires, were appointed as assistant Commissaries, Quartermasters and Paymasters. Thompson to Hodsdon, Feb. 28, 1839, OHPMHS On Feb. 23, 1839, Col. Charles Stetson was appointed to assist Paymaster Albert G. Bodfish. OHPMHS; Jewett to Fairfield, Feb. 25, 1839, JFPC 145B 3/10, MHS
22 Elijah M. Lowe Jr., to Francis Barnes, February 14, 1890, used by permission of Cary Public Library, Houlton, Maine, hereinafter referred to as ELL.

The Bangor Rifle Corps[23], an elite group of young men, had tendered their services to Major General Isaac Hodsdon and received orders on February 17th, to be ready to meet on the 20th, at the Bangor House, armed and equipped with rifles, twenty-four rounds, balls and cartridges, three days' rations and blankets. Three days before Hodsdon departed Bangor, on February 22nd, the Corps joined the Aroostook Expedition. They marched to the Railway Depot, boarded cars, and arrived at Oldtown at eleven thirty. After a noon stop at the residence of Jefferson Sinclair, Esq., they marched to Greenbush (23 miles) and made camp. The next day, after roll call and easy marches they arrived at Lincoln (25 miles) On February 24th, with their baggage and provision teams, they marched until one thirty and camped at Mattawamkeag Point (13 miles). Roll Call was at six A M; at eight they resumed their march, with teams, having there been directed to proceed to Houlton instead of the Aroostook River. Part of this unit had gone ahead three or four miles, and finding their mistake, returned and reported they had found a piano at a home three or four miles in the woods, and a civilized family and a young lady who could play on the piano, a Miss McNamarra. On their way to Molunkus, they saw a log house with a cat-and-clay chimney and a fireplace made of three large flat rocks, sides and back, and a log fire. At twelve thirty they camped at Molunkus (9 miles). That bitterly cold day had necessitated the first service of the Surgeon. A Corpsman had had his toes frozen. Anesthetics were unknown, so "they had to get the poor fellow drunk with New England rum. He stood the operation hardily until the instrument touched the quick. Then he stretched himself and uttered a long A A A A A A H H H h h h h h h!"[24]

---

23 *Bangor Rifle Corps, Records from its Organization in 1835 to June 20, 1840, including the Aroostook War*, Maine State Library, Augusta, Maine, and hereinafter referred to as BRCR.
24 BRCR, ELL.

From Molunkus, on February 26th, at nine thirty AM, with their baggage and provisions teams, they resumed marching on the Houlton Road. At five thirty P M, they stopped at the Forks of the Mattawamkeag (22 miles) made an improvised bush camp, "and found their heads, in the morning, on the snowbanks." The next day, they proceeded as far as Letter A, but because of a heavy snowstorm, made their encampment at noon (9 miles). But at about four P M, they resumed marching and arrived in good order at Linneus at six P M, and camped for the night, (5 miles).[25]

On February 28th, at noon, they arrived in Houlton and took up quarters at the Judkin's House, half way up the hill, on the left side of the street leading to Hancock Barracks (9 miles). Divided into messes, they began drawing rations, had morning parades, target practice and the regular detail of camp duty. Nine other companies of the Third Regiment also took up quarters in different parts of town, but at morning parades they assembled in the lower part of town.[26]

The Dexter Rifle Corps was one of the first militia groups to appear at Houlton. They wore black velvet caps decorated with ostrich plumes, drab (brownish yellow) coats faced and trimmed with black velvet, drab pantaloons with inch-wide velvet stripes up and down the outside leg seams, drab knapsacks with black painted border and the letters D R C in the middle. The uniforms had cost $30, and their rifles $11 each. Quarters were assigned to them at the house of Aaron Putnam. Other units were quartered at Shephard Cary's, in an empty house on the Bradford farm, at the Ingersoll place and at the Washburn place. James Drew had the contract to supply these

---

25 Ibid.
26 Ibid.

troops and had employed many men and teams to transport them.[27]

Most rigid discipline was enforced at encampment Houlton. Regular guard mounting at quarters was strictly maintained. None could enter, even superior officers, without the countersign and without permission from the superior officer. At Reveille beating, at dawn, all officers, non-commissioned officers, musicians and privates turned out, washed, prepared for duty, and attended the sunrise roll call. Morning reports were completed and delivered to the Colonel Commandant. The officer of the day inspected the new guard, the state of their arms and equipments, their ammunition, the cleanliness of their persons and their clothing. Commanding officers mustered and drilled their companies at least four hours each day, from nine to eleven A M and from one to three P M. Musicians of the Regimental Band practiced regularly. The troops turned in to quarters for the night at Tattoo beating and observed profound silence until Reveille beating.[28]

Signs of scouts of invasion had been seen for many days near Hancock Barracks. One snowy night when the snow was two feet deep, Elijah Low, Jr., of the Bangor Rifles, was ordered to a post on the Line, the first belligerent guard in the State of Maine. As there was no challenge from the other side of the Line, the guard was relieved in the morning.[29]

---

27 Barnes, loc. cit.; Stanley Plummer, *History of Dexter*, Bicentennial Issue, Dexter, Maine: Dexter Historical Society, 1976, 50. Barnes loc. cit., says twelve companies arrived.
28 ELL. Elijah Lowe Jr. summed up the attitude of the militia units at Houlton: "We were called out to defend the honor and integrity of the State of Maine; it was of little consequence to us whether Hancock Barracks existed or not. Whatever criticism or burlesque may be made of the Aroostook War, no part will apply to the military. We found the New England Boundary like an old, frayed-out dishcloth and we left it a clear, well-defined border"; BRCR Regimental Orders No. 2 and No. 3.
29 ELL

Justification

Meanwhile, at Washington, Senator Reuel Williams, of Augusta, Democrat, was in constant correspondence with Governor Fairfield at Augusta. A week or more was required for delivery of mail. On February 17th, Williams wrote that he had been trying to get the Military Committee to provide funds for the fortification and protection of Maine as recommended by General Wool. He told Fairfield about the attitude of President Van Buren:

> It seems to me that he has a feeling that we are attempting to thwart his plans. At one time I was conversing freely with him about introducing, again, the bill to run the line. He said, "very well, if you and the Congress think you can manage the question better than the Executive, I can have no objection, but if it be left to me, you will find the course I shall pursue very distinctly shadowed forth in my letter to Governor Kent." I now fear that the President will not do anything that can be construed into an approval of any course tending to bring on hostilities, and he thinks the people of Maine are inclined to take steps which they and the nation may regret.[30]

Again, on the 20th, the discouraged Senator wrote to Fairfield:

> On Sunday evening I went to the President with your communication. He will confer with the Secretary of War, and do what he can for the defense of the frontier, but doubts if any force can be spared at present, from other duties; that in the event of invasion the militia must be principally relied upon, that it will require your utmost caution not to be carried along by

---

30 R. Williams to Fairfield, February 17, 1839, JFPC 145 3/8 MHS.

local feeling faster than the nation will sanction, and that he relies much upon your good sense and prudence to keep within constitutional power and duty.[31]

On February 22nd, Williams was trying to persuade the President and Secretary of War to send an experienced military officer to Maine, and to authorize Fairfield's requisitions for ammunition, etc.[32] Williams wrote to Fairfield, on the 23rd:

> Mr. McCrate (Fairfield's special emissary to the President) arrived last night and delivered his charge to the President, and this morning we had a meeting of our delegation.[33] Mr. McCrate has seen the President and cabinet today, and has been questioned pretty closely. He says Mr. Fox has demanded that our force be withdrawn from the disputed territory.[34] I am glad of this, as it may open the case to the Executive in a

---

[31] Williams to Fairfield, February 20, 1839, JFPC 145 3/8 MHS.
[32] Williams to Fairfield, February 22, 1839. JFPC 458 3/9, MHS.
[33] The Maine Congressional Delegation in 1839 included Senator Reuel Williams, Senator John Ruggles of Thomaston, Representatives F. O. J. Smith of Portland, Moses Mason of Bethel, Thomas Davee of Blanchard, H. J. Anderson of Belfast, Tomothy J. Carter of Paris, Albert Smith of Portland, Virgil D. Parris of Buckfield, Nathan Clifford of New Field, Joshua A. Lowell of Machias, Democrats, and Joseph C. Noyes of Eastport and Benjamin Randall of Machias, Whigs. Jim Brunelle, *Maine Almanac*, Portland: Guy Gannett, 1978, 334-335.
[34] To: The Honorable John Forsyth: Sir: ... all of the Disputed Territory is placed under the exclusive jurisdiction of her Majesty's authority ... bound to remain so by explicit agreement between the Governments ... until the final settlement of the question of the north Eastern Boundary. ... it will become the bounden duty of the Lt. Governor of New Brunswick to resist the attempt, and to expel by force the Militia of Maine, if the present incursion be persisted in. ... I invoke the immediate interference of the General Government of the United States, to prevent the threatened collision, by causing the authorities of Maine to withdraw voluntarily their Militia Force, and to desist, ... from their present unwarrantable proceeding. ... H. S. FOX, HRD222, 18-19.

better light than we have been able to make him see it. The fact is that *the President is exceedingly averse to war,* the cabinet knows that we are unprepared, and nothing but necessity will bring the general government to our side. There seems to be a prevailing opinion that Maine has been hasty and is going faster than public opinion will sustain. Of this opinion, I understand, are Mr. Clay, Mr. Webster and Mr. Davis. Mr. Calhoun thinks we cannot have war without previous preparation; others think we have suffered long enough and that the question should now be settled. ... We shall probably have a message from the President on Monday, and I hope it will sustain the honor and rights of Maine.

The feeling that Great Britain has abused us on the boundary question, as well as others, is growing strong, and it will not require much to make Congress willing to meet a crisis. All the *commercial interests will be most active to prevent a war,* [Emphasis added.] but how far that interest can control a sense of national honor and the protection of our rights remains to be seen.[35]

General Winfield Scott Is Called to Washington

By the evening of February 23rd, General Winfield Scott had arrived in Washington. Williams and McCrate called upon him. They found that he understood the situation and were reassured that the justice of Maine's claim would influence the course to be pursued.[36]

The eagerly awaited Message from the President, to Congress came on February 26th, 1839. After giving a brief review of events in the Disputed Territory, Van Buren upheld Maine's right to jurisdiction:

---

35 Williams to Fairfield, February 24, 1839, JFPC 145, 3/9, MHS.
36 Ibid.

The Lieutenant Governor of New Brunswick, in demanding the recall of the Land Agent and his party from the Disputed Territory, and the British Minister, in making a similar demand, proceed upon the assumption that an agreement exists between the two nations conceding to Great Britain, until the final settlement of the boundary question, exclusive possession of and jurisdiction over the territory in dispute. ... Instead of sustaining the assumption of the British functionaries, all correspondence disproves the existence of any such agreement. ... The State of Maine has a right to arrest the depredations complained of. ... If it shall be found that there is ... a difference not to be reconciled, I shall not hesitate to propose to her Britannic Majesty's Government a distinct arrangement for the temporary and mutual exercise of jurisdiction, by means of which future difficulties may be prevented.

Van Buren explained, however, that between an effort on the part of Maine to preserve the property in dispute from destruction, and a military occupation by that State of the territory with a view to hold it by force, there was an essential difference. He still felt that it was his duty to submit another proposition to the Government of Great Britain to refer the decision of the question to a third power. If, however, the authorities of New Brunswick should attempt to enforce their claim of jurisdiction by means of a military occupation, he would consider the contingency provided by the Constitution as having occurred, on the happening of which a State has the right to call for the aid of the Federal Government to repel invasion.

As the session of Congress was about to terminate, and the intervention of the President might become necessary during the recess, the President asked that body to consider such measures as would obviate the necessity for a call for an extra session.[37]

The "distinct arrangement for the temporary and mutual exercise of jurisdiction" suggested by the President in his message, came in the form of *The Memorandum of February 27, 1839,* signed by John Forsyth, Secretary of State of the United States, and H. S. Fox, Her Britannic Majesty's Envoy Extraordinary and Minister Plenipotentiary, which read in part:

> In the meantime, the Government of the Province of New Brunswick and the Government of the State of Maine will act as follows: Her Majesty's officers will not seek to expel, by military force, the armed party which has been sent by Maine into the district bordering on the Aroostook River; but the Government of Maine will, voluntarily, and without needless delay, withdraw beyond the bounds of the disputed territory, any armed force now within them; and if future necessity shall arise from dispersing notorious trespassers, or protecting public property from depredation, by armed force, the operations shall be conducted by concert, jointly or separately, according to agreement between the Governments of Maine and New Brunswick. The civil officers .. of New Brunswick and Maine, who have been taken into custody by the opposite parties, shall be released. Nothing in this memorandum shall be construed to fortify or to weaken in any respect whatsoever the claim of either party to the ultimate possession of the disputed territory.

H. S. Fox, upon the signing of *The Memorandum,* wrote to Harvey:

---

[37] James D. Richardson, *A Compilation of Messages and Papers of the Presidents* Washington, D. C.: Government Printing Office, 1896, Vol. III, 516-520.

... In this state of affairs it becomes us, as servants of a Sovereign whose generous forbearance is unequalled in the history of nations, to refrain from further action until the time shall have been afforded to Her Majesty's Government to attempt the adjustment of the differences by friendly means.[38]

Reuel Williams sent *The Memorandum* to Fairfield on February 27th, commenting:

... The Message and documents are referred to the Committee on Foreign Relations. I expect a report in the morning. ... I am not without hope that Congress may yet do something that may secure our rights ... The Administration is too anxious to get rid of present difficulties without securing the great object. Sick and exhausted, I am very truly yours, R. Williams.[39]

Major General Winfield Scott was called before the Committee on Foreign Relations of both Houses of Congress, where he urged and succeeded in securing the passage of two bills, one authorizing the President to call out the militia for six months, and to accept the service of fifty thousand volunteers, and the other to place to his credit ten million dollars.[40] Senator H. J. Anderson of Belfast wrote to Fairfield, about Scott's efforts:

Washington, February 28, 1839

---

38 Fox to Harvey, February 27, 1839, *Royal Gazette*, 1839, from microfilm at the Harriet Irving Library, University of New Brunswick, Fredericton, hereinafter referred to as RG 1839HIL.
39 Williams to Fairfield, February 27, 1839, JFPC145 B3/10 MHS; SD222, 39-40.
40 Scott, loc., cit., 333; Marcus J. Wright, *General Scott*, in Great Commanders Series, James Grant Wilson, Ed., 1897, New York: D. Appleton and Company, 1897, passim.

Dear Sir, We have a most glorious report[41] and bill presented to the House this morning by the Foreign Affairs Committee. It seems to me to be unquestionably assuming the quarrel of Maine, and to pledge the National Government to bear out and sustain our cause, and consequently to relieve our State from the position she now occupies, of standing alone. But to the particulars: the Bill[42] authorizes the President to raise twenty thousand men, infantry, artillery and dragoons; to increase the naval force to its full capacity, and to meet the extraordinary expenses of such an array, appropriates [___] millions of dollars to be raised by loan. This "blank" the Committee proposes to fill with ten million dollars. ... The best spirit seems to pervade the House, and I have no doubt that we shall be fully sustained in both branches. ...
PS I forgot to say that the Bill appropriates eighteen thousand dollars for a special embassy to London, to aid in terminating the controversy by a settlement of the question, provided no war intervenes or grows out of the present difficulty. H.J.A.[43]

---

41 *House of Representatives Report no. 314, Disturbance in Maine,* hereinafter referred to as HRD314, excerpt: The riotous and desperate character of the marauders upon the Aroostook is manifested by their breaking open an arsenal upon the British territory, to supply themselves with an additional quantity of arms to resist and repel the party approaching under a civil officer to require submission to the laws. The proclamation of the Lieutenant Governor was issued before any steps were taken by Maine to sustain the civil force by military power, and was directed against the interference of the ministerial officers of the law. The first appeal to military force was made by him, and the subsequent proceedings of Maine are defensive.
42 A Bill, giving to the President of the United States additional powers for the defence of the United States, in certain cases, against invasion and for other purposes. HRD314.
43 Anderson to Fairfield, February 28, 1839, JFPC 145B 3/10.

On March 2nd, Reuel Williams reported to Fairfield that the bill had just passed the Senate from the House, without amendment, unanimously.[44]

Military Activities at Augusta

While in Washington *The Memorandum* was being signed and the legislation was being passed for Federal support for Maine's cause, war preparations went on at Augusta and Fredericton, and maneuverings were taking place in the Disputed Territory.

On the 26th of February, at 3:00 P M, about six hundred of Brigadier General George W. Bachelder's Second Regiment assembled in Winthrop Street, Augusta. Governor Fairfield, riding a fine saddle horse loaned by Thomas W. Smith, reviewed the troops. Thousands of spectators were on hand in windows, on rooftops and in the streets. Trees were full of boys. The Governor took his station in front of the troops, in the center of his aides, advanced a few steps and took off his hat. During a flourish of music the whole regiment saluted him by presenting arms. He then walked his horse down the lines of troopers, inspecting the men and their arms. Then the troops marched by him while he stood, hat off, receiving the salute of the officers as they passed. He found the appearance of the troops to be highly creditable. Then they were drawn into a hollow square, and he addressed them:

Fellow Soldiers: It is with feelings of the utmost satisfaction that I witness the promptitude with which you have responded to the call of your state, and taken up arms in her defense. This is no ordinary crisis. ... The time has arrived when we must make a vigorous and manly defense of our soil or ignobly permit it to be wrested from us by a foreign power. At such an

---

44 Williams to Fairfield, March 2, 1839, JFPC 145, 4/1, MHS

alternative can a freeman hesitate? NO! - is the response and simultaneous shout of this whole people. ... Fellow Soldiers: An unfounded, unjust and insulting claim of title has been made by the British Government to more than one third of the whole territory of your State. More than this, it insists on having exclusive jurisdiction and possession until its claims of title is settled, while in the meantime its subjects are stripping this territory of its valuable growth of timber, in defiance of your authority and power. A few days since, you sent a civil force under your Land Agent, to drive off these bands of armed plunderers and protect your property from their work of devastation, but the Agent, while employed in the performance of this duty, with two of his assistants, was seized, transported beyond the bounds of the State, and incarcerated in a foreign jail under British authorities. Those who remain are threatened with a forcible expulsion by British troops. ... And perhaps before this moment, your soil has not only been polluted by the invaders' footsteps, but the blood of our citizens may have been shed by British Myrmidons.

This, fellow soldiers, briefly is the case now made up. Are you prepared to act? I know you are. I know you will not tamely submit to such indignities - to such arrogant pretensions- that you will not quail under British threats. Two wars have already taught our aggressors the force there is in a freeman's arm when weilded in a just and holy cause. More than once we have seen their self-styled Invincibles overpowered and prostrated by the prowess of an American Militia. More than once have we seen their proud St. George struck down by one arm of a citizen soldiery, the other bearing aloft the stars and stripes of their country. What has been done may be done again. And it is to you, fellow soldiers - and you, armed citizens of Maine, we look for such a bearing of yourselves in this crisis as shall sustain your well-earned reputation, and answer the high expectations of your State. I have no fear of the result. Go - and may he who holds the destinies of nations in his hand, in due time return you to the bosom of your families, crowned not only with the laurels of victory but with the more enduring wreath worn by DUTY PERFORMED

His speech was responded to by shouts and claps of the whole multitude. The troops were in excellent spirits and anxious to march for the Aroostook. After services by the chaplin the troops were dismissed to their quarters for the night. About half of the detachments, including Artillery and Rifle companies, took up their line of march for the frontier on the 27th, and the remainder on the 28th.[45] Immediately, General Orders No. 12 and No. 13 called up more troops from the Fourth, Fifth, Sixth, and Eighth Maine Militia Divisions.

The Civil *Posse* Moves Eastward Along the Aroostook River

The Aroostook River Valley was a most beautiful country, definitely the best part of Maine for farming. There were over two hundred thousand acres of land equal to any in the world, and the timber was decidedly better than any other in our country, with high pine trees making five tons of timber each.[46] There were no forces of the Provincial Government nearer than the confluence of the Tobique and the St. John Rivers, about eight miles distant, their whole force being less than one hundred regular troops, when, on the night of February 25th, seventy-one men of the civil *posse*, under the command

---

45 Fairfield to his wife, Fairfield 27, 1839, PJFDL; *The Age*, February 28, 1839; Reverend Charles Blanchard of Augusta accompanied the detachment as Chaplain, Dr. Cony of Augusta as Surgeon, and D.r Frost of Sidney as Surgeon's Mate; AWJK, 14.
46 Benjamin Wiggin, Jr., to Fairfield, February 27, 1839, JFPC 145 B 3/10 MHS.

of Lieutenant Towle, went from Post Machias down the Aroostook River to take possession of the upper end of the portage below the Little Madawaska River, at its confluence with the Aroostook, three and a half miles from the east line of the State. Then, on the 26th, Colonel Jarvis and Towle's group moved to the lower end of the Portage, one mile from the Meridional Line, and built a slight fortification of hewn timber and some camps and set twenty-two men to guard duty during the night. At about dark they were joined by fifty men under Captains Chamberlain and Doughty,[47] who had reached there by forced march, and brought their total number to one hundred and thirty-one men. Jarvis expected to have his whole force concentrated there by the night of the 27th. He concluded that all that remained to be done to carry into effect the Resolve of the Legislature for the security and preservation of the public timber, would be to build a boom below the mouth of the Little Madawaska, and another strong boom below the portage where he was then located. It would be no use to do this unless a Post was established, but he had decided to proceed to build a boom without waiting further instructions. It would be for the Governor to decide the kind of forces to be stationed there. He surmised that one hundred Militia would be sufficient to overawe a mob, and not less than five hundred or a thousand to secure it against the Provincial authorities. He had already chosen the location of the Post, near to the boom in question. In so doing, Jarvis had discharged his temporarily assigned duties and desired to return home, but awaited word from the Governor.[48]

---

47 The names of Lt. Col. Joshua Chamberlain Jr., Lt. Luther Chamberlain of Foxcroft, and Capt. Calvin S. Doughty of Sangerville, appear in Joseph Porter's list of officers in the civil force, found in the *Bangor Historical Magazine*, Joseph Porter, Ed.
48 B Wiggin to Fairfield, February 27, 1839, JFPC 145 B3/10 MHS.

Meanwhile, in New Brunswick and Nova Scotia

The *Royal Gazette* published a Report submitted on February 27th, signed by James A Maclauchlan, Warden of the Disputed Territory, but written by someone else, as revealed in a letter from Sir John Harvey to Sir John Caldwell, marked "Private," and dated March 6, 1839, which stated in part:

> A most triumphant vindication of the conduct of the Government and indeed of the proceedings of the Warden has been prepared by a very able person and signed by McLaughlan [Maclauchlan] as his report. It embraces the whole period since his appointment in 1829, and shall be made public. It distinctly reposes all the late troubles to the conduct of Massachusetts and Maine, in granting licenses to cut timber on the Disputed Territory.[49]

The report:

> EXTRA SUPPLEMENT TO THE ROYAL GAZETTE
> FREDERICTON, N B, 6TH MARCH, 1839
> Fredericton, 27th February, 1839
> May it please your Excellency,
> The Government of the State of Maine, having recently dispatched an armed force to enter upon a part of the Territory now in dispute between the Governments of Great Britain and the United States, on the plea of protecting the same against trespassers, I consider it due myself, as the Warden of this Territory, to repel any idea or insinuation that such trespassers have in the slightest degree been encouraged or countenanced by the British Government or the Provincial authorities of this Province. Your Excellency is prob-

---
[49] Sir John Harvey to Sir John Caldwell, LBJHPANB.

ably aware that, since the year 1829, I have been employed ... to watch over, and as far as possible, guard against all depredations on these lands, whether committed by British or American citizens. That in pursuance of this duty, ... I have every year seized all the timber which could be ascertained or even suspected as coming from this Territory, the moment it was brought within the acknowledged limits of this Province, and thereupon either proceeding to the condemnation there of, or exacting heavy prohibitory duties, the proceeds of which being scrupulously paid over to the Receiver General of the Province, as a Special Deposit, with the known and understood purpose of being hereafter paid over to the Government in whose favor the right thereof might ultimately be decided. ...

Notwithstanding these measures, during the present year, a large number of American citizens most of whom, under pretense, and indeed many of them under actual authority and permission from the States of Massachusetts and Maine, entered upon this territory, with large lumbering parties, and have cut and made large quantities of timber thereon, with the intention of driving the same down the River St. John in the spring, in which they were no doubt joined by many British subjects, all animated by a common desire of plundering the timber off these lands; with this difference, however, that British subjects were expressly forbidden by their Government to enter and cut timber thereon. The authority thus given by the States of Massachusetts and Maine to cut timber on this Territory, not only furnished their citizens with a pretext to continue their depredations, but also induced many British subjects to join them. ... This statement, confirmed as it is by official documents, will, I trust, be conclusive to show that every possible exertion, without recourse to an armed force actually entering upon and expelling trespassers from the Territory, was made by the Provincial authorities, to prevent, as far as possible, trespassers on these lands; and if any violation of this principle or duty is anywhere to be found, it is in the American Authorities granting permission to their citizens to cut timber on the Territory in dispute.

Last fall I was directed by your Excellency to make it generally known that no timber whatever which came from this Territory would, in future, be allowed on any terms or conditions to pass down the River St. John, but that the same should be seized and destroyed, and for this purpose, arrangements were directed and in progress for the erection of the boom at the mouth of the Restook [Aroostook] River, for securing all timber that might be brought down the River in the Spring of 1839; the assurance was given by your Excellency, that an armed force could be stationed at the mouth of the Restook, if necessary, to support me in the seizure and detention of such timber. ...[50]

On the same date, Maclauchlan was ordered back to duty on the the Disputed Territory. To prevent collision with the American citizens, he was told to check in with military authorities at Houlton, exhibit his instructions, explain the object of his mission, and request such directions to persons under their authority as might be requisite to prevention of any opposition. He was at liberty to take with him such armed assistance as he found necessary.[51]

Nova Scotia staunchly supported New Brunswick verbally, militarily and monetarily. Her Legislative Council declared, on February 28, 1839:

> Whereas it appears to this House that under the the pretense of removing trespassers, a forcible inroad

---

50 RGHIL 1839.
51 Copy of Maclauchlan's orders made by Hodsdon's ADC. March 2, 1839, OHPMHS, Collection 8, Box 1/6, MHS.

has been made by the authority of the State of Maine upon that part of the Province of New Brunswick which is claimed by the United States, but of which the exclusive possession and jurisdiction have ever been in Great Britain; and that the Government of the said State has adopted measures to levy an armed force, and to raise a large sum of money with the avowed object of committing further outrages upon the Sovereignty and Dominion of Her Majesty: ...

The House of Assembly resolved that one third of the Militia force of the Province between the ages of eighteen and forty five, be drafted, to the extent of eight thousand men, to be funded by a sum of one hundred thousand pounds, for the protection of Nova Scotia and New Brunswick from invasion. Three hearty cheers were given; never before had such cheers been heard in their House of Assembly.[52]

HMS Crocodile had sailed for St. John with a division of the 69th Regiment; the *Eliza*, transport, with another detachment, followed, along with the *Numa*, with the remainder of the Corps from Barbados.[53]

Charles Jarvis Establishes Fort Fairfield

Provisional Land Agent Jarvis had been persuaded to stay on, under McIntire, as Assistant Land Agent. He wrote from a place he had designated as Fort Fairfield, on March 1, 1839:

I have now reached the extreme of my route; from where I am now stationed I can cast my eye over a portion of the territory of "Her Majesty." I hope that taking this liberty occasionally will not be considered an infringement on "Her Majesty's" territorial rights,

---

52 A supplement to the *Royal Gazette*, March 6, 1839, RG1839HIL.
53 RG1839HIL.

for the line runs over an elegant ridge which is pleasant to the eye, a gratification I should be sorry to relinquish. I have ordered a party of twenty men, well armed, and fifteen of them equipped with good axes, to the meridional line on the Tobique Road, to fall the last tree on our side, which, if it should happen to incline toward "Her Majesty's" territory, it will inevitably fall thereon; this cannot be considered as the act of man but to the power that gave the inclination to the tree and disposed it to a preference of Monarchial Government. May all bipeds share the same fate. About one mile of the Tobique Road passes over our territory; that will be so obstructed as to be impassable.

Fitzherbert, the keeper of the house where Mr. McIntire was arrested, may be put to some inconvenience, if more is deemed to be necessary.[54] His situation is far from pleasant; his house is in the direct line of our guns and the aforesaid road, and in case of an attack upon our position must be riddled. ... The position now occupied by me is naturally strong; no exertions will be spared to add to its natural strength. Should an attack be made, the Governor may rely that the name of our Post shall not be disgraced, that the honor of Maine shall not be tarnished. My force here, when all parties are called in, will not vary much from six hundred picked men, equivalent to twelve hundred drafted Militia; whether we do well or ill, estimation may be made on that criterion. ... [55]

---

54 Jarvis wrote to Fairfield again, on the 3rd of March, about Fitzherbert: "Yesterday afternoon, having obtained direct and positive testimony that Fitzherbert sent a man and horse to Tobique to give notice that Mr. McIntire was at his house and that he asked a man to take part in the taking of him, I caused him to be arrested and shall send him to Lincoln for trial per committnent." Jarvis to Fairfield, March 3, 1839, JFPC 145, 4/1 MHS.

55 Jarvis to Fairfield, March 1, 1839, JFPC 145, 4/1, MHS.

A Mr. Smith, of Houlton, had agreed to clear the road between Houlton and Fort Fairfield of snow and break it out with a four-horse team, for two hundred dollars. On the evening of March 2nd, Smith came to Jarvis' encampment to inform him that the work had been done. The next morning, Sunday, at nine, the *posse* paraded on the river ice, opposite Fort Fairfield, under the command of Colonel Joseph Porter, Esq.[56]

The Honorable Rufus McIntire, upon returning to his duties as Land Agent, advised Governor Fairfield that he did not think there was much danger in marching the Militia and transporting supplies by the road to the Aroostook River area via the Presque Isle River, but it would be necessary to keep a showing, if not the main force at Fairbanks on the Presque Isle. Also, a road from the mouth of the Presque Isle to the mouth of the St. Croix should be opened soon, as the mouth of the Machias was beginning to be unsafe due to softening ice.[57]

Major General Hodsdon and Staff Arrive in Houlton

Major General Hodsdon set up his Head Quarters at Houlton on the February 28, 1839.[58] His Division Staff included: John L. Hodsdon, Aide de Camp; Oliver Frost, Aide de Camp; Joseph C. Stevens, Division Inspector;

---

[56] Jarvis to Fairfield, February 24, 1839, JFPC 145, 3/10; Jarvis to Fairfield, March 3, 1839 JFPC 145 4/1, MHS; *Bangor Historical Magazine*, Vol. II, 123-124.

[57] McIntire to Fairfield, March 3, 1839, JFPC 145 4/1, MHS

[58] Assistant Quarter Master Ebenezer Gilman Rawson, from Bangor, on March 6, 1839, by Express to Hodsdon, informed him that in the last *Bangor Democrat*, in an article headed "Compulsion," the Editor had abused him, to the effect that he had not arrived in Houlton until some time after his troops had arrived. Rawson had informed Mr. Haynes that Hodsdon had, in fact, arrived at their place of destination in advance of the whole detachment. Haynes was perfectly willing to have the correction made in his next paper. Rawson to Hodsdon, March 6, 1839, OHPMHS.

Joseph Gilman, Division Quarter Master; Ebenezer G. Rawson, Paul Varney, Henry Warren, Daniel Wood, and Shepard Cary, Assistant Quarter Masters: Elijah L. Hamlin, Esq., Superintendent of Videttes; William H. McCrillis,[59] Aide de Camp Pro Tem; and George W. Bachelder, Brigadier General, in command of a separate detachment.[60] Hodsdon sent advance militia, under Captain Maxfield, to prepare the way, north of Houlton, for the main

---

59 OHPMHS; John Littlefield Hodsdon was the adopted son of Isaac Hodsdon; Joseph Gilman was a leading lawyer and first mayor of Bangor; Ebenezer G Rawson was a Bangor attorney and a Penobscot County Commissioner; Shepard Cary, a member of the House of Representatives from Houlton, was engaged in large scale lumbering and trading. William McCrillis, b. Georgetown, 1813, Bangor attorney, was one of the leading lawyers of the State; a member of the House of Representatives in 1838, he was Penobscot County Attorney. H C Williams, *Biographical Encyclopedia of Maine of the 19th Century*, Boston: Metropolitan Publishing and Engraving Co., 1885.

60 The Roster of Officers of the Third Division in actual service under Major General Isaac Hodsdon, at Houlton, were: Col. David Walker, Lt. Col. Lysander Cutler, Lt. Col. G. W. Cummings; Adj't Pro tem, Maj. James Smith, Capt. Enoch R. Lumbert, Lt. John Quimby, Lt. Fifield Lyford, Capt. Eliphalet Maxfield, Lt. Jabez Bradbury, Ens. Goodrich Cummings, Capt. Charles H. Wing, Lt. Abraham Morris, Ens. Jacob P. Landers, Capt. Daniel Dority, Ens. Joseph Eaton, Lt. Ames Pickard, Capt. Wm. H. Mills, Lt. James Carlton, Ens. Henry L Stewart, Ens. Jeremiah Burnham Jr, Ens. James Dunning, Capt. James Huxford, Lt. Andrew D. Beal, Lt. Francis Thorndike, Ens. Benjamin Rowe, Capt. Samuel Fish, Lt. F. I. Cummings, Capt. Moses H. Young, Capt. David Dow, Ens. Simeon P. Atkins, Capt. Truxton Dougherty, Lt. Wm. E. Atwood, Ens. Alvin B. Clark, Capt. George W. Maxim, Lt. Jonathan Louder, Ens. Wm. H. Gibbs, Capt. Eliphalet Miller, Lt. Horatio Barrett, Ens. Jeremiah Lord, Capt. Nathaniel Sawyer, Capt. Nathan Ellis Jr., Lt. Isaiah Beals, Ens. John Nelson, Capt. of Cavalry Reuben S. Smart, Lt. Bidfield Plummer; Cornet Wm. B. Haws. John Sargent, Forage Master. From a handwritten roster, giving rank, regiment, corps, company letters, dates, etc., OHPMHS

body of troops.⁶¹ In an undated, secret and confidential letter to Fairfield, Hodsdon described one of his first actions, upon approaching the Disputed Territory:

> Sir, ... Considering the importance of having a suitable place to erect the necessary huts for our accommodation, in a healthy part of the country, and to have plenty of good water within the lines of our huts, and on a suitable location to protect us from surprise, capture or successful besiege by the trespassers, etc., and being unable to move in advance of the troops, I have taken the liberty to employ, for a few days, Captain Henry E Prentiss, an experienced and scientific military engineer, to fix on a place to build the huts, etc. I have sent Major Frost to attend him on this service, having first given them my own views on the subject, and I hope that this part of my arrangement may meet with your approbation.⁶²

The route Hodsdon's advanced troops travelled from Houlton to the Aroostook River area appears to have been from Houlton to the north line of the Portland Academy Grant (part of present day Bridgewater); from that point to the Bradstreet Mills, situated near the northeast corner of Bridgewater Academy Grant (present day Bridgewater); (there was a "lumberman's road," being about six miles long and stated to be quite good). From that last point there was a similar road running a

---

61 Carpenter to Hodsdon, undated, probably March 3, 1839. OHPMHS; Before General Hodsdon's troops departed from Houlton to the northward, two companies of militiamen, infantry, were organized, one at Houlton and another at Hodgdon, Linneus and New Limerick. Both companies were annexed to the Sixth Regiment, First Brigade, Third Division on March 2, 1839. *General Order Book*, Maine Militia, Maine State Archives, Augusta.

62 Prentiss served as Captain of Engineers from February 20 to April 20, 1839. AWJK; Carpenter to Hodsdon, undated, probably March 3, 1839.OHPMHS.

northeasterly direction, about ten miles, terminating at some point in Township F, Range 2, and probably some eight or ten miles distant from the new encampment, making the whole distance from Houlton to the new encampment forty miles.[63]

    Captain Prentiss wrote to Hodsdon concerning his mission:

Advanced Post, Presque Isle of St. John
March 2nd, 1839

Sir: We found a good road to Pond's Tavern, 12 miles, where we arrived at twelve o'clock. We stopped one hour only, and made all possible speed in the afternoon, but did not arrive here [Presque Isle or Prestile of the St. John] 'till dusk. We found the road bad, but little trodden and very rough, but with careful driving there is no danger by day. It would be a bad night road. There are several long and dense swamps where an enemy might, in ambush, make destructive work with our troops.

    We have been delayed some for want of a guide, among the logging roads, within two miles of this place, and as we expected that another company would come in this evening, we sent back one of the videttes to guide them. I find this place incapable of being fortified in the way expected to strengthen it. The land on the north side of the Stream, for a good distance back over the hill is cleared down to the New Brunswick line and below it, and we have no means of fortifying an open field. For the present we can only guard the Post by a judicious location of our force and by being alert. If we cannot keep an enemy out of the country, we can best give you notice when he comes in, so as to prevent you being surprised by an ambush in one of the swamps as you march in.

    The best way of fortifying this position is by not coming down into the opening, but turning off to the

---

63 Samuel Smith to Hodsdon, February 26, 1839, JFPC 145, 3/10, MHS.

left, cutting a new road to a point above here on the Mars Hill Road and then fortifying both the old roads, at points below the junctions of the old and new. By this means, our fortifications would be in the woods, but the evils would be that we would interrupt the communication of citizens and would shut ourselves out of the buildings here, which are excellent quarters for our men and which we shall want so long as we keep up communication this way.

There is a high hill on the south side of the Stream at F, on the plan on the other page. It is somewhat doubtful whether its pinnacle is in our side of the line, if so, it would make an excellent artillery post to command the River, but it is too distant for musquetry. I shall examine it. Our men are in fine spirits.

[Key to enclosed plan]:
House, e, near our line, occupied by our company.
House, b, in rear, occupied by officers and the guard.
One sentinel posted before officer's quarters
One sentinel posted on Hill D behind quarters.
One sentinel posted on road down river at c.
Line a b, possible alteration of road.
f g and j h possible lines of defense.

Sunday Morning
P S: There is a house one half mile above here that will accommodate one company, where there is hay, etc. Had I not better go on immediately to examine the country and Colonel Jarvis' Posts? I am ready for the expedition.   Yours, H. E. Prentiss[64]

---

64 Prentiss to Hodsdon, March 2, 1839, OHPMHS.

Map drawn by Captain H. E. Prentiss

Colonel Joshua Carpenter, "a good military man," appointed at Houlton as Captain of Pioneers to conduct the advance troops to the Presque Isle, went with Prentiss and Frost to the confluence of the Presque Isle and St. John Rivers. He wrote to Hodsdon:

Camp at the Presque Isle
Dear Sir, We arrived at the Post last evening at half past four, found good quarters, examined the country for a mile around. My opinion is that no fortification can be thrown better than the log houses now already built, that would be tolerable secure against small arms. If we had cannon, a fortification might be made on the south bank of the stream, that would command the stream and the surrounding country, as it is the highest ground; but with small arms we could do nothing. My opinion is, from what I can learn from those who have come into our camp, that we shall not be attacked while we keep on our side of the line, which we shall be very careful to do. The soldiers are in good spirits. Captain Maxfield is an excellent officer, knows and does his duty; also all of his officers and men. We are on hand for anything you may please to order.[65]

Orders received on March 3rd postponed Prentiss' expedition, for he wrote to Hodsdon on the 4th:

Sir: The general order of yesterday is received. We erected some breastworks with dispositions of abatis [66] at the places suggested in my letter of Sat-

---

[65] Frost to Hodsdon, March 9, 1839, OHPMHS; Carpenter to Hodsdon, undated, probably March 3, 1839, OHPMHS.
[66] abatis: fort, a defense formed by felled trees, the butts of which are secured toward the place defended and the ends of the branches, often sharpened, are directed outward, or against the enemy.

urday evening, that is, at points below the junctions of the cross road to Ketchum's with the roads to and from Bradstreet's, arranging the lines so as to concentrate three fires on the roads.

As the house here will not furnish quarters for the companies which are to come in, Colonel Carpenter, with thirty men, will proceed this morning to build camps behind the breastworks to be occupied by the companies as they arrive. The two companies now here will remain at Bradstreet's, and if driven from their quarters, will fall back on the breastworks. That on the north branch of the Presque Isle is above the Province Road on the north of the point of which I spoke yesterday. You will remember that the supplies for Captain Maxfield's Company will be expected today but they can borrow of Captain Fish for one day. I will leave here on foot this morning for the Presque Isle of the Aroostook. Pardon this ruff sheet, as I have only a half a sheet left and do not like to be destitute.[67]

While Henry Prentiss was reconnoitering in the Aroostook River area, Hodsdon was trying to cope with confusing commands and the lack of rapid communications. It took until March 3rd for enough messages to be exchanged to allow Fairfield and Thompson to be able to understand the circumstances surrounding Hodsdon's decision to use the Military Road to Houlton. They then advised Hodsdon to place his force at the mouth of the Presque Isle of the Aroostook with all possible haste. Once there he was ordered to provide a passable road to the Aroostook Road at Township No. 10, either by way of the river or by cutting a road in the most suitable direction, and to render the route from Township No. 4, on the Aroostook Road, to his position on the Aroostook, passable for troops and supplies. General Bachelder and reinforcements would soon arrive in Township No. 4.

---

[67] Prentiss to Hodsdon, March 3, 1839, OHPMHS Collection 8, 1/6.

Also, orders were issued for an express line, a line of videttes, to be established on the Aroostook Road, to meet the line between Houlton and Mattawamkeag Point, and since Hodsdon was marching to the mouth of the Presque Isle of the Aroostook, he must take immediate measures to establish posts at ten-mile intervals along that road.[68]

Adjutant General Thompson clarified misunderstandings in the chain of command by stating that Hodsdon had been instructed to aid the Land Agent, but in aiding him, it was not the intention to place him, as commanding officer of the military force, under the immediate orders of the Land Agent. The Land Agent might offer information and opinions, but Hodsdon was to make his own decisions. His duty was entirely distinct from that of the Land Agent, and they operated under different Resolves of the Legislature.[69]

British Troops Arrive in the Disputed Territory

Sir John Harvey had applied to Sir John Colborne at Quebec for a strong detachment to be sent to Madawaska, well within the Disputed Territory. By March 4, 1839, four companies of the XIth Regiment, under Colonel Goldie, were proceeding to Madawaska. Captain Hawkshaw, Royal Engineer, of the Department of the Quartermaster General in New Brunswick, was sent to Madawaska to cooperate with Mr. Milliken, the Officer of the Commis-

---

[68] Thompson to Hodsdon, second letter of March 3, 1839; Thompson to Hodsdon, March 2, 1839, OHPMHS. This second letter is incomplete and may have contained a map. General Order No. 20: Head Quarters, Augusta, March 2, 1839, Brig. Gen. John Williams, commanding officer of the Third Division, will call out such force as may be necessary to fill up the detatchment of one thousand men ordered from the Third Division. February 6, 1839, on requisition of Maj. Gen. Hodsdon stating the amount of the deficiency; and he will cause them to assemble at Bangor at such time, etc. AWJK.

[69] Thompson to Hodsdon, first letter of March 3, 1839, OHPMHS.

sariat Department, who had been sent from Quebec to prepare accommodations for the troops. Harvey, explained to Goldie that his presence in that settlement was to give confidence, encouragement and protection to Her Majesty's subjects, to maintain possession, and to protect the line of communication with Lower Canada. Therefore, his duty was strictly defensive and so long as they acted upon that principle, he had no apprehensions of any collision with the Armed Forces from the State of Maine. Harvey said that the French inhabitants of Madawaska were a timid people, whom he believed preferred a British to a Republican Constitution. They should be encouraged to remain at their homes, and not required to take up arms as Militia. ...

Harvey informed Goldie that he had stationed troops, under the command of Lieutenant Colonel Maxwell of the 36th Regiment at locations near the St. John River. A Flank Company, eighty men, were at Tobique and the Mouth of the Restook (Aroostook) with a ten-pound Howitzer and fifty Militia, with an intermediate Militia Post on the Portage and another at Buttermilk Creek. Maxwell, with the remainder of the 36th, with one hundred and fifty Militia and one Gun, was at Woodstock. This important position had been left extremely weak, but the 69th Regiment just arrived at St. John and would be pushed up as fast as possible. He asked Goldie to communicate with him regularly by means of the chain of mounted Volunteer Dragoons extending from the City of St. John to the Great Falls and would immediately be extended to Madawaska.[70]

Then Harvey explained his military strategy to Goldie :

I have managed to protract the crisis to a season of the year when the invasion of the Madawaska Settlement from the Valley of the Aroostook, by way of the Eagle Lakes may be considered as almost imprac-

---

70 Harvey to Goldie, March 4, 1839, LBGHPANB.

ticable from the risk that the invading party would incur of having its retreat cut off by the breaking up of the winter roads. From this fortunate change of circumstance I regard your force as disposable for the general defense of the Province. ... I therefore request you to hold it prepared to descend the St. John for the purpose of cooperating with the troops under Lieutenant Colonel Maxwell in repelling any attack from the State of Maine. ...[71]

    Harvey notified Colonel Maxwell, Commanding the 36th Regiment at Woodstock, on March 4th, that the 69th Regiment had arrived at St. John, and would soon join his forces and bring with them, if required, another gun. In order to give confidence to the timid French population of Madawaska, and for other reasons, Harvey wished a detachment of Her Majesty's Troops to be sent into that settlement, perhaps to Simon Hebert's, as soon as a second Company can be sent to replace the party now at the Falls. He suggested that perhaps Maxwell's Light Company should to be pushed on to the Madawaska Settlement. Harvey made plans to visit at Woodstock and Madawaska as soon as he had important communications from Washington.[72]

    On March 5, 1839, Lieutenant Colonel Allen, of the 2nd York County Militia, was directed to proceed to Woodstock and assume command of the drafted militia of the County of Carleton, acting under the orders of the Senior Officer of Her Majesty's Troops on the Upper St. John.[73]

---

[71] Ibid.
[72] Harvey to Maxwell, March 4, 1839, LBGHPANB.
[73] RG1839HIL.

CHAPTER IX

NATIONAL ATTENTION IS FOCUSED UPON MAINE

When, on March 2nd, the bill that had been the result of the "most glorious report" had just passed to the Senate from the House, United States Senator John Ruggles[1], Democrat, of Thomaston, expressed his disbelief in Presidential intent:

...*The Administration has no notion of backing Maine in the vindication of her rights.* I have just this moment offered an amendment to a bill for the protection of the Northern and Northwestern frontiers, an Amendment providing for certain military defenses of Maine. It was warmly *opposed* by Mr. Wright of New York and Calhoun and other leading members of the Administration, and the Amendment failed. Their purpose is to keep Maine crippled, naked, hamstrung and handcuffed, humbled, disgraced and dishonored, to make her the victim and the scorn of Sir John Harvey.

---

1 John Ruggles, 1789-1874, "one of the giants of Maine politics" from Westborough, MA, educated Brown University; studied law under Estes Howe and Levi Lincoln; began law practice in 1815 in Skowhegan; supporter of Governor Dunlap; Speaker of Maine House of Representatives 1825-1829 and 1831; served one term as U.S. Senator. James H. Mundy, *Speakers of the Maine House of Representatives from 1820*, Augusta, 1981.

The Amendment embraced the precise objects recommended by the War Department and reported favorably upon by the Committee of Military Affairs. We are voting millions for the southern and western states and frontier, but not a dollar for Maine. We only asked one hundred thousand dollars for a thousand miles of interior and maritime frontier more exposed than any other in the Union. Yet Maine bows down and worships the Administration from which it receives nothing but insult. ... The Resolutions passed last evening contained a degrading threat to leave Maine to the tender mercies of the British if we did not withdraw our troops and abandon the position we had assumed. They were supported with great zeal by Buchanan, Wright, Calhoun, etc, but were stricken by a small majority. Those resolutions were professedly in accordance with the views of the President, and intended to carry out his policy to compel Maine to take the back track. I am curious to see what Maine will say to the manner in which the President and his confidential friends treat the call of her Governor for aid in vindicating its rights.

The South boasts that they have a northern President with Southern feelings and principles. The explanation is that the south is opposed to all our interests and jealous of our prosperity. Mr. Van Buren looks to the South and West for re-election and must therefore act in all things in accordance with their wishes.[2]

Van Buren, a Democrat, in his bid for Presidency in 1836, had defeated three Whig candidates including Daniel Webster. With regard to Ruggles' attitudes and beliefs, history shows that from statehood well into the 1860's, Maine, as well as the nation, was whirling in the maelstrom of the coming Civil War. Statesmen Henry Clay, Daniel Webster and John C. Calhoun were the great influencers of attitudes in this period.

---

2 John Ruggles to Isaac Hodsdon, March 2, 1839, OHPMHS.

Shortly before the War of 1812, Henry Clay had become the most influential and popular man in the United States. In the summer of 1814, he had resigned his position as Speaker of the House of Representatives, to become a member of the peace commission that would finally produce the Treaty of Ghent. John Quincy Adams, James A Bayard, Jonathan Russell, and Albert Gallatin had worked with him. The British delegation had demanded that the northwest territory, which would become the states of Indiana, Michigan, Illinois, Wisconsin and part of Ohio, be set apart for the Indian tribes and be made an English protectorate; that the United States should keep no armed vessels on the Great Lakes; that no changes be made in the British "right" to impress sailors, and that a part of Maine should be ceded to Great Britain to make a road and communication route from Halifax to Quebec. Clay had been indignant and would rather have the war go on for several more years, but was restrained by Adams and Gallatin. Finally, on December 14, 1814, the British commissioners had given up their demands for Maine's territory, the northwest territory and fishery claims, and had concluded to leave things as they had been before the war. Clay labelled the Treaty of Ghent as "a damned bad treaty." During this time he had become thoroughly educated in the matter of Maine's boundary claims.

Daniel Webster, after the death of Alexander Hamilton, became the most prominent American political genius. Since 1820, his influence had been all pervasive. He was an expert on the interpretation of the United States Constitution and was its staunchest defender against disunion. Webster and John C. Calhoun, both orators, opposed each other, Calhoun representing the South and Webster the North. As Webster had opposed the War of 1812, he would also oppose an Aroostook War, if such a possibility existed.

While Daniel Webster put forth his strong defense of the Constitution, the Executive Branch had, as "their strong right arm" the "diplomat General," trouble-shooter *par excellence*, Winfield Scott. He was as devoted to preserving the American Union as his more voluble counterpart. He had evolved the technique of bringing a big stick, but then speaking softly, which had found success with Black Hawk in 1832, with the Nullifiers in South Carolina in 1832-33, with the Seminole Indians in 1835, and with disturbances on the Canadian Frontiers in 1837-38. In May, 1838, upon the insistence of President Jackson, and in the face of a Supreme Court ruling that removal of the Cherokees to western reservations was unconstitutional, Scott again carried out Executive wishes. Early in 1839, he had been sent to deal with Canadian insurgents in the eastern Great Lake area, and succeeded in persuading the populace to desist in any act that would violate United States neutrality with Britain. Now he was called to mediate in the confrontation between the State of Maine and the British Colony of New Brunswick.[3]

Major General Winfield Scott, the Great Pacificator

When Winfield Scott reported to Secretary of War Poinsett, he found all branches of the Government in a state of alarm. Under duress from the rapidity with which things were happening on Maine's frontier, for several days Scott met with the chairmen of the committees on foreign and military affairs, urging passage of the aforementioned bill to authorize President Van Buren to call out the Militia for six months instead of the usual three, to accept fifty thousand volunteers, and to place to his credit ten million dollars in extra monies. This accomplished, in taking leave of Van Buren and Poinsett, Scott respectfully said,

"Mr. President, if you want *war*, I need only to look on in silence. The Maine people will make it for you, fast and hot enough; I know them. But if peace be your wish, I

---

3 Scott, loc. cit., 332. Wright, loc. cit., 138-139.

can give no assurance of success. The difficulties in its way will be formidable." "Peace with honor," was the reply from the President.

Accompanied by Captain Robert Anderson and Lieutenant Keyes, Aides-de-Camp, with *carte blanche*, Scott stopped in Boston to arrange a contingent call for militia and volunteers from Governor Edward Everett and then hurried to Maine. When he arrived in Portland on March 5th, the Mayor introduced him to the population from the balcony of the Cumberland House. In favor of war or the peaceful possession of the Aroostook, they expected him to conquer the disputed territory at once. They were tired of the interminable delays of diplomacy. On the 6th, in company with several companies of militia, the Major General was on his way to Augusta.[4]

Governor Fairfield wrote to his wife:

General Scott is here, and is now the lion of the day. He is often at my rooms, and I find him to be very agreeable. Last night some twenty of us were at Daniel Williams'[5] and had a splendid treat. Today we dine with Major Ripley [senior officer at the United States Arsenal at Augusta.] ...Great anxiety is manifested here, to hear from me on the subject of our difficulties and the *Memorandum*. On Monday I shall send a message to the Legislature. I hope I will be able to take a course which will preserve our honor and yet not provoke hostilities. ...[6]

---

[4] Scott, loc. cit., 332-35; The *Portland Transcript*, March 9, 1839. Fairfield to his son, March 6, 1839; Fairfield to his wife, March 9, 1938, Staples, Ed., loc. cit.

[5] Daniel Williams had been a member of the Maine House of Representatives in 1831, and would be State Treasurer in 1840.

[6] Fairfield to his wife, March 9, 1839, Staples, Ed., loc. cit.

Sir John Harvey

Daniel Webster

General Winfield Scott

Francis Ormond Jonathan Smith

Governor John Fairfield

Governor Edward Kent

Rufus McIntire

Reuel Williams

Scott had taken rooms in Augusta, at the same house as Governor Fairfield and other leading Democrats, and took meals with them. He had allowed himself to be known to them as the representative of the Democratic Administration at Washington. He soon became aware that the only hope of pacification depended on his "persuading the local belligerents to stand off the territory in question," for a time, and to allow the Governments at Washington and London to settle the question. He felt that *The Memorandum* greatly aggravated the problem. It gave great offense to Maine; they were required to withdraw their forces from the territory in dispute simply on the promise that British officers would not seek to expel them by force, without any reciprocal obligation, the other party being left free to fortify themselves, continue their depredations undisturbed for an indefinite time.[7] This "bungle" had first to be adjusted between Democratic authorities, State and Federal, he himself being a Whig.

To bring those leading Whigs and Scott together, Scott induced George Evans,[8] just in from Washington, to invite the Whigs, the Governor and several State Councillors to sup with him at Gardiner. Scott took charge of his Democratic friends in a government sleigh. All the topics he intended to urge upon the Whig leaders were given and discussed in the vehicle. In Gardiner, Evans, a distinguished Whig, placed his Democratic guests at his end of the table, and Scott, with the Whigs around him, at the other. Scott's blandishments failed to open the way to the main business of the evening, but Evans came to

---

7 Scott, loc. cit., 337-343.

8 George Evans, born in Hallowell in 1797, graduated Bowdoin College, studied law with Frederick Allen, practiced law in Gardiner. Thought to be the best criminal lawyer in New England, his reputation as a speaker rivaled that of Clay, Calhoun and Webster. State Representative from 1826 to 1829 and Speaker of the House in 1829, he was elected to Congress six times and then served in the Senate. James H. Mundy, *Speakers*, loc. cit.

the rescue; he whispered to the Whigs that Scott was as good a Whig as the best of them! Cordiality ensued and business was discussed together to the content of all parties. As Scott said, "The work was done!"[9]

The Winfield Scott - John Harvey Relationship

Events of history had and would continue to entwine the lives of Winfield Scott and John Harvey. Both had been high level military combatants in the War of 1812. Scott was with American forces that were bitterly contesting possession of the Niagara frontier. At the battle of Stony Creek, June, 1813, Harvey and his men, at two o'clock in the morning, approached the American camp, quietly bayoneted the sentries, and advanced into the center of the American camp where they fell upon the artillery and bayoneted the men at the guns. This attack on the Americans at Stony Creek saved the Niagara District and Kingston for the British. American prisoners had been taken, but reports of Colonel Harvey's kindness to them brought him the respect of the American military establishment.[10]

It was in September of 1813, that Scott, with a detachment, went with Commodore Chauncy's fleet, to seize materiel and stores from the British army at York, now Toronto. They drove out the garrison and formed a

---

9 Scott, loc. cit., 343-345. Scott had received much assistance from Albert Smith, born in Hanover, Massachusetts in 1793, graduated from Brown University, studied law and was admitted to the Portland bar in 1817. A member of the Maine House of Representatives in 1820, and U.S. Marshall of Maine from 1830 to 1838, he served in Congress 1839 to 1841; and as a U.S. Commissioner to lay out the northeast boundary under the Webster-Ashburton Treaty, 1842-1847. Died in 1867. *Biographical Directory of the American Congress, 1774-1961.*

10 J Hannay, loc. cit., 175, from a report written by Lieutenant Colonel Harvey; H J Morgan, loc. cit.; Sir James Carmichael Smyth of the Royal Engineers under Duke of Wellington wrote of situation at Stony Creek and of the participation of Harvey. Scott, loc. cit., 338-343.

cordon of guards, while Chauncy loaded booty aboard his ships. After the ships were under way, Scott learned that trunks belonging to English officers had been taken. He investigated, and purchased from a sailor a miniature painting of a beautiful lady, set in gold, taken from a trunk labelled Lieutenant Colonel Harvey. Scott and Harvey, as the chiefs-of-staff of their respective armies, had corresponded about official business and had personally met with escorts under flags of truce. Concluding this to be a portrait of Harvey's young bride, Scott sent it to him.[11] Also, in the campaign of 1813, Scott saved Harvey's life, when Harvey, out reconnoitering, was cut off from his party by Scott's escort. A soldier, taking deadly aim, would have killed Harvey if Scott had not knocked up the rifle, saying, "Don't kill our prisoner!" Harvey escaped unhurt, amid a hail of rifle balls.

Recently, during the conclusion of the removal of the Cherokees to Indian Territory, Scott had received a letter from Harvey, which remained unanswered until the former arrived at Augusta:[12]

> Government House
> Fredericton, New Brunswick
> January 13, 1839:
>
> Major General Scott, U. S. Army
>
> My Dear General, In a letter which doubtless failed to reach you, I assured you of the high degree of satisfaction which I had individually derived from hearing of your selection for the very delicate and difficult command on the frontier of the northern states opposite the British Provinces. From the high opinion I had formed of your character during the late war of 1813-1814, I felt that the circumstances of your nomination to that command involved the most satisfactory assurance of the sincerity of your General Govern-

---

[11] Scott, loc. cit., 100.
[12] Scott, loc. cit., 338-343.

ment in their wish to preserve peace and friend-ship with England. ...
My mind often reverts with great satisfaction to the interview in the Niagara Frontier and its immediate consequences. If the social history of those campaigns had been given to the world, you and I would stand crowned with the most glorious wreath which can encircle the head of a soldier, viz: that of having softened the savage character of warfare and faced it with the usages of civilized nations.
I should rejoice in renewing my personal acquaintance with you. ... Let that meeting be under my roof, in this House, and believe me you have no friend who could feel a higher degree of pleasure than myself in the opportunity of evincing towards you and yours the warm recollection which I retain of your friendly feelings and action towards myself.[13]

Scott's reply:

Head Quarters, Eastern Division
Augusta, Maine, March 9, 1839

Sir John Harvey, ...

... How happy may we esteem outselves, if a personal friendship commenced in the field and in opposite ranks can be made in any degree conducive to the preservation of peace between our countries! For, if an immediate conflict of arms about the disputed territory can be avoided, to allow time to the two governments to adjust, at London or Washington, the great question in controversy, which I am persuaded may readily be done, I see no reason to apprehend another cause of serious misunderstanding between the two portions of the great Anglo-Saxon race for centuries to come. *The ties of common blood* [emphasis added],

---

[13] Harvey to Scott, January 13, 1839, PAC COP 188 B16. In Harvey to Maxwell, March 8, 1839, LBHGPANB, Harvey referred to Scott as a gallant and honorable, high-minded gentleman.

language, civil liberty, laws, customs, manners and interests must, in a reasonable period, that is, as soon as we can forget past wars, and they are almost forgotten, work out a strong compact for reciprocal feelings far more binding than written engagements, which the other nations of the world would be wholly unable to dissolve or resist. Such a compact, although the two portions of the race are, and probably ever will remain, under separate Governments and of different forms, is necessary to both, in war as in peace, for who shall say what hostile combinations, in the next one hundred, seventy or even thirty years may not take place among other nations to require the united strength of England and America for the safety of their common principles and interests?

But how to avoid a conflict of arms on the Disputed Territory between the proximate troops of Maine and Great Britain under the purpose distinctly avowed in your letter of the 18th Ultimo, addressed to the Governor of the former? With that declaration held up *en terreur,* it is felt here that Maine cannot withdraw her troops with honor.

Entertaining a lively hope that you may have been induced by *The Memorandum* signed at Washington, ... to suspend the purpose of "seeking to expel by military force the armed party which has been sent by Maine into the District bordering on the Aroostook River" and of taking military occupation of that district, may I request a declaration from you to that effect? Should your answer be favorable, I do not doubt that the troops of Maine would be immediately recalled and the detachment in march thither from the interior of the State be at once ordered to halt. ... It is due to candour to say that, by the term "troops" Maine would not understand as included, the civil *posse,* under a Sheriff and a Land Agent, which she now has in the Disputed Territory. Such *posse,* however, would be limited to a small number of persons and restricted to certain spe-

cific duties. ... To show clearly the pacific dispositions of the United States, I will add that I have not assumed, and do not expect to assume any command over the forces which Maine has in the field, and if we can avoid collision on the Northeastern Frontier it is not likely that the United States will proceed to send a single regiment under a recent Act of Congress. I remain, my Dear Sir John, With highest respect and esteem,
        Your Friend and humble Servant,
                Winfield Scott[14]

Harvey's response:

My Dear General,   Few circumstances of recent date have afforded me so much satisfaction as the receipt of your most friendly and acceptable communication of the 9th, from Augusta. ... With the confidence and the frankness due from one soldier to another, I place myself unhesitatingly in your hands as regards the following communication. ... In saying to you that by confining myself to the valley of the St. John, including the Madawaska Settlement, indispensable as is that line to our communications with Canada, and settled as it is wholly by British subjects, and abstaining from any offensive operations against the armed force on the Aroostook until reference can be made to England, I hope and believe that I shall be considered as fulfilling the spirit of the "Memorandum." ... Effect these objects, my dear General, and a Border Peace *pro tempore* will be established. ... In the meantime depend upon my avoiding collision by every means in my power. ... Remember that I have relays of Provincial Light Dragoons by which any communication from Houlton (if sent to the Commanding Officer at Woodstock) will reach me in six hours.[15]

---

14 Scott to Harvey, March 9, 1839, PACCOP 188 B16.
15 Harvey to Scott, March 12, 1839, LBGHPANB.

The *Memorandum* that Scott considered a "bungle" had also been unacceptable to Governor Fairfield. It was strongly attacked by the latter in his Message to the Legislature on March 12th, as being "inadmissable because of its inequality of terms", and Maine would not now "voluntarily forge new shackles for herself." He proposed:

> Under these circumstances I recommend that when we are fully satisfied that the Lieutenant Governor of New Brunswick has abandoned all idea of occupying the disputed territory with a military force, and of attempting an expulsion of our party, the Governor be authorized to withdraw our military force, leaving the land agent with a *posse*, armed or unarmed, as the case may require, sufficient to carry into effect your original design. ...[16]

Major General Hodsdon with the Militia at Houlton

Hodsdon's detachment from the Third Division, Maine Militia, including one company of Cavalry, which formed the line of videttes from Bangor northward, one company of Artillery, four companies of Light Infantry, four companies of Riflemen and four companies of Infantry, including all officers, numbered one thousand and sixty-nine.[17] Hodsdon addressed the units that were at Houlton, on the Northeastern Frontier, on March 5, 1839:

OFFICERS AND SOLDIERS OF THE DETACHMENT:
The Commander-in-Chief, in the due exercise of the powers vested in him by the Constitution, has called into the actual service of the State, a portion of its physical power; and he has conferred upon you the

---

16 ROSM III, 157-165.
17 Abner Thompson, *Report of the Adjutant General*, 1839, hereinafter referred to as RAGAT 1839.

distinguished honor of being the first troops ever placed under Martial Law by the State, or called out to enforce the supremacy of the civil law.

You are already apprised that a band of lawless depredators, principally the subjects of a foreign power, have, in defiance of the civil authority and with shodden feet, entered upon this holy ground, and have been, and still are, destroying and plundering the almost invaluable timber on our public domain. Your aid is now invoked to assert the majesty of the Law, and give a practical illustration of the declaration that, "the way of the transgressor is hard." To this end, fellow soldiers, it is only necessary to remind you that you are the heirs and descendants of those patriots whose blood has enriched and whose valor has purchased this goodly land for an everlasting inheritance for you and your children. ...

... Your commanding General embraces this opportunity to remind you that you have, for a limited time, merged the character of a citizen with that of a soldier, and that for the present you will be guided and governed by the requirements and the injunctions of the Martial Law. ... No military corps can long be respectable as such, were subordination, discipline and respect for the laws and the rights of individuals not objects of paramount consideration; and your Commanding General is too ambitious to deserve your confidence and esteem, to neglect carrying into effect these principles to the word and to the letter, against every incorrigible offender. The rights of a soldier under Martial Law are few, and should be studiously guarded and faithfully administered. No punishment will be inflicted, other than restraint of liberty preparatory to trial, except by fair trial and sentence of Court Martial, unless, in case of physical resistance of orders. Irreverence at Divine Service, drunkenness, profane swearing, card playing, raffling and every kind of gambling is forbidden, and will be punished indiscriminately. No political arguments or disputations will be permitted. Reproachful, contemptuous and disrespectful words spoken against the principal officers of Government are offences against Martial Law and will be punished, more especially if spoken against the Commander-in-Chief, under whose orders we are acting. ...

The fervent prayers of absent parents, wives, children and affectionate and dearly beloved friends are daily and hourly ascending to the God of Armies, for the protection of these good men and true; and these prayers, it is hoped and trusted, will be mercifully heard and graciously answered. ...[18]

Political Intrigue Reaches the Frontier

Opposing political interests worked without constraint throughout the border crisis. Captain William H. Mills, commanding officer of the Bangor Rifles, and member of Hodsdon's staff, warned Hodsdon of such intrigue in a confidential letter, from Bangor, on March 6, 1839:

I arrived here last evening, and found General Bachelder with about five hundred troops from the Kennebec. The troops appear very well, but not so well as ours, and their discipline will not begin to compare with that of ours. In coming down from Houlton, I was happy to learn that our troops, with one or two exceptions, were universally well spoken of wherever they had been quartered. I was frequently gratified, where I was not known, to hear remarks in praise of the Bangor Rifle Corps.[19]

---

18 Hodsdon's address to Militia at Houlton, March 5, 1839, OHPMHS
19 Mills to Hodsdon, March 6, 1839, OHPMHS.

... Every movement you make is watched by the Locos[20] and some of them are in hopes to get something against you in order to have you removed or superceded. It cuts them to the quick to think that you are at the head of the army, destined to reap laurels. I need not tell you that to General Bachelder, and to the Locos, wherever I have thought it proper, I have represented you to be the very man for the station, the best qualified in the State, efficient, energetic, prompt and influenced by the right feeling. ...[21]

In 1838, the Conservative Democrats had met in Bangor, with General James Irish of Gorham as President of their Convention. Two secretaries, Oliver Frost of Bangor and F. P. Ingalls of Frankfort, were chosen. Among those present were John Hodgdon, William Emerson, Benjamin Shaw, Henry Warren of Bangor, Jonathan Burr of Brewer, Thomas Hill, Allen Haines; and John Sargent and Samuel Sylvester who reported the name of F. O. J. Smith as their candidate for Governor. A County Committee nominated Paul Ruggles, Nathaniel Treat and Samuel Strickland for Senators.[22]

Labelled by his opposition as a Loco Foco, Gorham Parks had been the Democrats' standard bearer in 1837, and had almost defeated Edward Kent. Parks had defended Sheriff Joshua Carpenter, of Penobscot County, who had been tried and convicted of adultery, and removed from office by Governor Robert P. Dunlap. Partly because of

---

20 On the national level, in 1830's, "Locos" was a name applied to the faction within the Democratic Party which vociferously espoused the doctrine of equal rights. Aligned with the movement of Jacksonian democracy, it emerged about 1835. The "Loco Focos" soon disappeared, but the name was long used for the Democratic Party in general, by its opponents.
21 Mills to Hodsdon, March 6, 1839, OHPMHS. Mills added: The New York Legislature has passed a Resolution approving the doings of Maine and pledging the State to sustain us.
22 *Bangor Daily Whig and Courier*, July 20, 1838.

this, Parks' nomination had offended the pro-banking wing of the Democratic party in Penobscot County, led by Samuel Veazie and John Hodgdon[23], both of Bangor, and closely allied with F. O. J. Smith. The *Bangor Whig and Courier* denounced Parks as "a leveling, destroying, revolutionizing Fanny Wright Loco Foco!"[24] ... Parks was uncomfortable with the "Loco Foco" label but he did not deny sharing a partiality for hard money, and a dislike for chartered bank monopolies and their banknotes.[25]

Oliver Frost, Secretary for the Conservative Democrats, was Isaac Hodsdon's Aide-de-Camp. Interestingly enough, Hodsdon had employed Joshua Carpenter, the man the "Locos" had championed, to prepare the way for the arrival of his troops on the Aroostook.

On March 6, 1836, Hodsdon wrote to Governor Fairfield that rumors had circulated through the streets of Houlton that a report had been made to the Governor that a large portion of the officers and soldiers under Hodsdon's command were "either in confinement or under arrest, and that anarchy, insubordination, disaffection and discontent were raging with unabating influence." Hodsdon admitted that he felt "rather sensitive on the subject," and appealed to the Governor to protect him.

---

23 Born in Portland in 1787, General Veazie had risen from humble origins to become one of Maine's great lumber barons, a man of extraordinary wealth. Hodgdon, like Veazie, was deeply involved in banking and land speculations.

24 Frances "Fanny" Wright was an American reformer and free thinker, b Scotland, 1795. A lecturer, she criticized the prevailing system of education, the role of churches in political affairs, etc. She demanded equal rights for women, birth control, and emancipation of women and of Negro slaves. *The New Century Encyclopedia of Names*. New York: Appleton-Century-Crofts, 1954, Vol. III, 2493, 4180.

25 Gaffney, loc. cit., 197-199, cites *History of Penobscot County*, H. A. Ford, Ed.; *Maine, A History*, Louis Hatch, Ed., 227-28; *Bangor Whig and Courier*, August 18, 1837; *Lincoln Patriot* (Waldoboro) July 21, 1837.

Major Oliver Frost went to Head Quarters at Augusta on a confidential mission.[26] Frost met with the Governor and the Adjutant General on March 9th and began his interview by informing the Governor that rumor had it that at least some of the Hodsdon's officers were considering superceding him in command. Fairfield replied that no complaint of dissatisfaction among the troops, on account of discipline or insubordination, had been made since the troops had been mustered.

Frost checked out the rumor that Hodsdon was constantly in ill humor, cross and rabid, finding fault and using disrespectful and reproachful language toward the Commander-in-Chief and the Adjutant General, in a manner unbecoming an officer in the army. Frost defended Hodsdon, stating that on the contrary he had repeatedly heard him speak in high terms of the course adopted by the Governor.

Another subject of complaint was the appointment of Dr. Watson as an assistant Surgeon. Frost explained that the appointment had been made at the earnest request of a respectable portion of the Detachment, but that Hodsdon had also appointed another surgeon, and that every soldier was at liberty to employ either as a physician. The Governor was satisfied.

Still another rumor was that Hodsdon and his staff had drawn invidious comparisons between the Land Agent's *Posse* and the Militia as to disparity in amount of their pay, in a manner calculated to create a disaffection among the troops. Frost had not heard Hodsdon make such a remark, but he admitted that he and the officers at Hodsdon's Head Quarters had frequently spoken of the force now with the Land Agent as being under good pay for soldiers, and they would probably continue so to speak of them, whenever they deemed it prudent, without fear of having their right to do called into question. How-

---

26 Hodsdon to Fairfield, March 6, 1839, OHPMHS.

ever, Frost stressed that to his knowledge this subject had never been discussed in the presence of a soldier so that the inequality of their pay might lead to murmuring among the troops.

Another problem dealt with was the charge that Hodsdon's appointments had been made, generally, from the most obnoxious men in the community where they resided. Colonel Carpenter was singled out. Frost replied that whatever Carpenter's reputation might be in public estimation, he was a good military man, and that he was appointed at Houlton as Captain of Pioneers, to conduct the advance troops to the Presque Isle, with the approbation of the officers attached to Hodsdon, including himself, and for this purpose he considered him to be as good a man as could be found.

Frost discovered that not a single complaint had been made by any member of the Detachment, and that none of the complaints from other sources had been filed as charges. Fairfield and Thompson expressed their highest confidence in Hodsdon's ability as a military commander.

After completing his inquiry, Frost's advice to Hodsdon was that as he appeared to be in the midst of enemies on every hand, it might be wise for him to caution his officers to be circumspect in their conversations.[27]

Land Agent Rufus McIntire and the Civil Force at Fort Fairfield

On March 7, 1839, Land Agent Rufus McIntyre returned to the frontier. At the time of his arrival at Fort Fairfield, Charles Jarvis was a mile down the river, superintending the quarrying of a ledge for stone to be used in building a boom across the Aroostook River. He heard McIntire's arrival announced by a previously

---

[27] Frost to Hodsdon, March 7 and March 9, 1839, OHPMHS.

arranged salute of thundering cannons to demonstrate the high respect entertained for him by the *posse*.[28] There were six hundred and sixty privates in this civil force, well armed, with fifty days provisions and spirit up to the proper pitch. They had cut one road from the shore of the river to the Portage road, a mile or more from the bank of the river at the lower end of the portage road, and another from the other end of the portage, some distance from the bank, to Fairbanks' on the Presque Isle, so that there was a direct land communication to Presque Isle from Fort Fairfield. They had built barracks, a guard house, and a store house. Some were employed in throwing up breastworks on an excellent elevation, and another opening had also been made on an elevation on the opposite side of the river, where it was intended to erect a blockhouse.[29]

Captain William Parrott, praised by McIntire as "a man of rare scientific as well as other qualifications," had immediate supervision of the construction of the Aroostook Boom on Township Letter D, Range 1. It was situated about one mile from the point where the north line of that township crossed the Aroostook River, and measuring by the river, about three miles from the boundary line. Parrott and Jarvis had chosen this location, described by Colonel John T. P. Dumont as "one of the most commanding locations he had ever witnessed," because the river spreads out at this place to be nearly double its average width; therefore, the current would not be accelerated by putting in the necessary piers, as

---

28 Jarvis to Oliver Frost, March 8, 1839, OHPMHS.
29 McIntire to Fairfield, March 7, 1839, JFPC 145B MHS; Wiggin to Fairfield, March 8, 1839, JFPC 145, 4/2, MHS; William Parrot, *Report of the Assistant Land Agent*, 1839 hereinafter referred to as RLAWP. Wiggin had served as an aide to Col. Jarvis. This boom was to be constructed to carry into effect the Resolve of the Legislature of February 20, 1839, to "preserve the timber and other lumber cut by trespassers and to prevent its removal without the limits of the State.

it might have been to a greater degree where the channel was narrower. The whole length of the Boom would be four hundred and forty-seven yards. The seven piers would be placed in the form of a triangle, with the vertex up river, at which point the largest pier would be placed. The dimensions of the main pier would be sixty by thirty feet on the base, and the other six, each forty by twenty feet, all slanted on the up-river end, generally to an angle of twenty degrees. These piers would be loaded with tons of stone, brought from a ledge down river. Intended to prevent the passage of rafts of timber, the Boom would hold loose timber just as well.[30]

Under the impression that there would be no immediate collision with New Brunswick forces, a large part of the *posse* was anxious to be discharged, especially as many were afflicted with colds and coughs. McIntire discharged a few who were unwell, but planned to retain enough to build the Boom, and perhaps to aid in making the St. Croix section of the proposed Houlton Road. Dr. Mason, of Bangor, who had been employed with the militia at Houlton, "a man of good qualifications and great energy," joined the medical staff at Fort Fairfield.[31]

---

30 John Dumont to Fairfield, February 9, 1839, JFPC 145, 4/1, MHS. Dumont, special agent for Fairfield, member of the Maine House of Representatives from 1833-1836, and State Senator from the 4th Senatorial District (Augusta, Waterville, Readfield, and vicinity) in 1838 and 1839. RLAWP. Preparations had begun on the 4th of March, by a small crew engaged in looking for timber and clearing roads, and on the 11th construction commenced. It would be completed April 3rd. Local historian, W. T. Ashby, *A Complete History of Aroostook County and its early and late Settlers* MS, stated: A high ledge was found east of Fitzherbert Brook, and enough ledge rock was blown out with gun powder to finish the piers and stone up the well in the fort. The piers were built on the ice and sank with their own weight. The boom was built double, of long pine timber, fastened together with silver birch "through-shots," and attached to the piers with heavy chains.
31 McIntire to Fairfield, March 7, 1839, JFPC 145B MHS.

McIntire commended the spirit and alacrity of his *posse*, some of whom, at his first call, had started from where they happened to be without first visiting their homes. They had cheerfully made a winter campaign, performed an immense labor without a murmur and had "shown no little skill, intelligence, vigor and disposition to act together and with harmony."[32]

Colonel Dumont visited the *posse* at Fort Fairfield and then all the advance encampments of the militia on the road between Houlton and the Aroostook and instituted all proper inquiries into their health and feelings. He reported to Fairfield that the men had responded, "give us good rations and we have no complaint to make." I am satisfied that it will not do for the *posse* and Militia to meet together. The Land Agent's men suppose that they have had to "beat the bush and the Militia will catch the bird." I have corrected this impression.[33]

Hodsdon Moves His Troops from Houlton to Fort Fairfield

Three days after Hodsdon had addressed the troops on the Square at Houlton, on March 8th, he had been ordered to place his force at the Mouth of the Presque Isle as soon as possible, and to open a road from there to the Aroostook Road, for communication by that route with Brigadier General Bachelder and his detachment.[34] The Land Agent had arranged that after he had information of the Militia having been concentrated at the mouth of the Presque Isle of the Aroostook, all of the *posse* not required as actual laborers would be dismissed. The remainder of his camps would then be vacated for the occupation of the Militia.[35] Two companies of militia were

---

32 McIntire to Fairfield, March 7 and March 11, 1839, JFPC 145B MHS. Official documents do not support scurrilous attacks made upon the reputations of these men in contemporary and later publications.
33 Colonel Dumont to Fairfield, March 9, 1839, JFPC 145 4/2.
34 Thompson to Hodsdon, March 8, 1839, OHPMHS.
35 McIntire to Fairfield, March 11, 1839, FPC 145, MHS.

already stationed at the Presque Isle of the St. John, under the command of Lieutenant Colonel Cummings, to guard a defile necessary to be passed near the mouth of the river. This Post was twenty-five miles north of Houlton, on the Bridgewater Academy Grant, and a little south of Mars Hill. It was within a few rods of the east line of the State, and a hill a short distance from the camp was occupied by sentinels of both Maine and New Brunswick units. The companies stationed there had erected camps for their own accommodation.[36]

There were nine militia companies remaining at Detachment Head Quarters at Houlton on March 8th. Hodsdon ordered four companies under Colonel Walker, including Captain Daniel Dority's Company of Light Infantry, Captain T. Doughty's Company of Light Infantry under the command of Lieutenant W. E. Atwood, Captain C. R. Hamblet's Company of Infantry, and Captain N. Sawyer's Company of Riflemen to march to the Presque Isle of the Aroostook on March 9th, with twenty rounds of fixed ammunition and three days' rations to each man.[37] The Quar-

---

36 RAGABT 1839.

37 Hodsdon was notified on March 8th, that he would receive three companies of Artillery: one then on the march from Augusta, another next week, and one from Thomaston the following week. Thompson to Hodsdon, March 8, 1839, OHPMHS. Regimental Order No. 9 and Detachment Order No. 4, March 8, 1839; Regimental Order No. 11, BRCR. As to subsistence, the ration consisted of 3/4t lb. pork or bacon, or 1 1/4 lbs. of fresh or salt beef, 18 oz. of bread or flour, or 12 ozs. of hard bread or 1 1/4 lbs. of corn meal, and at the rate of 4 lbs. of soap, 1 1/2 lbs. of candles, 2 qts. of salt, 4 qts. of vinegar, 8 qts. of peas or beans, and when practicable, 2 lbs. tea and 12 lbs. of sugar or the equivalent in molasses to every hundred rations. General Order No. 25, March 11, 1839, OHPMHS. At Encampment Houlton, rations were drawn at three day intervals. There were 44 men in Rifle Company A, commanded by W. H. Mills. From March 4th through March 13th they attempted to draw rations of flour, pork, beef, salt, soap, candles, vinegar, coffee and sugar. Notations in the "Remarks" column of the record book read: salt and vinegar sugar, candles, none. BRCR.

ter Master Department, under guard, furnished transportation for camp equipage, for additional subsistence and for those on the sick list. Men who, in the opinion of the Surgeon, were unable to move with the troops, were provided good quarters, and were attended by a member of the medical staff.[38]
    The Land Agent had already established a Post near the mouth of the Presque Isle of the Aroostook, fifty miles north of Houlton, on Letter G, Range 2 (Maysville in present-day Presque Isle). Colonel Walker's companies, upon arrival, occupied the camps that were available. All men except those required for extensive picket duty, camp guard, patrol and police, proceeded, under the direction of Henry E. Prentiss, Engineer, to construct temporary quarters for the whole detachment. Two of Wood's four companies were posted there indefinitely. They were later joined by three companies from Bachelder's Second Division.[39]
    The remaining five Companies at Houlton were preparing to move north on March 11th. Lieutenant Colonel John L. Hodsdon and the Quarter Master and Sergeant Major would move with them.[40] While awaiting orders to march, non-commissioned officers and privates were permitted to use two rounds of ammunition each day in competitive target firing. They were not without their amusements. On a singular occasion, an effigy of Queen Victoria was used for target practice. Upon receiving a complaint, General Hodsdon apologized to Sir John Harvey, who assured him that he was very willing to believe

---

38 BRCR.
39 Regimental Order No. 9 and Detatchment Order No. 4, March 8, 1839, BRCR; RLAMI 1839.
40 Ibid. McCrillis also ordered that previous to this march, each commanding officer should make out and deliver to citizens who may have furnished quarters for himself and his company during their stay at this place, an official certificate of the number of men and days for which quarters had been supplied.

that such feelings and conduct were not generally characteristic of the troops under his command.[41]

By March 11th, Hodsdon had two companies on the Aroostook, at the mouth of the Presque Isle, and two more camped in the woods above, near Mr. Fairbanks. McIntire had temporarily suspended the discharge of some of his men, to their disappointment, until he could ascertain whether the militia would be permitted to come to Fort Fairfield.[42] An alarmed McIntire reported to Fairfield on March 11th:

> Sir: Since I wrote to you this morning by express, various rumors have reached us of the movement of Provincial and Regular troops that seem to indicate a concentration of forces not far from the Grand Falls of the St. John. Reports say that a large number of axes (expert axe-men, choppers) have been sent up river. The New Brunswick Militia are in this vicinity and the Regular troops above. It is suggested that a movement may be made through the woods from Madawaska, to some point on the Aroostook, above or possibly through the Fish River to the Little Machias River, while their Militia may move directly to this Post. Under these circumstances, I have given a direct order to the commanding officer at Presque Isle to send at least two of his companies here, and have addressed a letter to General Hodsdon, acquainting him with the facts and the reasons for it and inquiring if I am to have any support from the force under his command.
>
> It is impossible to conceal from the British our true position, condition and strength, as most of the inhabitants on the Aroostook are concerned in the trespassing and are strongly interested in having us driven

---

[41] Regimental Order No. 10, March 8; Detatchment Order No. 3. BRCR. Classen, loc. cit., 57; Harvey to Hodsdon, March 13, 1838, OHPMHS.
[42] McIntire to Fairfield, first letter of March 11,'39, JFPC 145, 4/3.

off. In two hours, at any time, they can come through the woods and communicate with the Tobique [Post].

Our men are by day busy on the Boom, then fatigue duty, or are scattered in the woods for timber, in the quarries for stone, at the Boom, etc., and at night, after a laborious day's work, are not in the best condition to repel an attack. ... I would suggest that it might be well to hold the Militia on this ground, where the first colors will probably be struck.[43]

McIntire's call for the militia was answered the next day, by Lieutenant Colonel Lysander Cutler. He was at the Presque Isle of the St. John, when he received orders from Hodsdon to proceed with all possible dispatch to Fort Fairfield, leaving the troops at the Presque Isle of the Aroostook to complete the building of huts.[44] On the 13th, two Companies from the Presque Isle of the St. John arrived at Fort Fairfield, one more was on the way and Cutler was waiting for four companies still to come.

McIntire, on the 13th, discharged about two hundred of the *posse*, all except those engaged in building the Aroostook Boom. The departing men were in good spirits and generally in good health; one man had died, but all the sick and injured would soon be able to leave. McIntire made up rolls for paying the *posse*, and expected to leave upon the return of Colonel Jarvis. By the 16th, all of the *posse* except those building the Boom and a few to guard the two cannon that Sheriff Strickland had brought up the preceeding month, and for which the militia as yet refused to accept responsibility, had left Fort Fairfield.[45] Colonel David Walker and the Riflemen had just arrived; Major James Smith's Artillery was expected at any time. The barracks would be full and would not accommodate the whole force. The Land Agent had plans to erect more

---
43 McIntire to Fairfield, 2nd letter of March 11, '39, JFPC I 45, 4/3.
44 Cutler to Hodsdon, March 12, 1839, OHPMHS.
45 McIntire to Fairfield, March 14, and March 16, 1839, JFPC I 45 4/3.

barracks for the Militia and a separate barracks at the Boom for his boom men, as well as a guard house near the Boom, after which another portion of the *posse* would be discharged. Meanwhile, he had men out reconnoitering the woods between the encampments and the St. John River and Madawaska Settlement.[46]

All remaining troops at Houlton were on their way to the Aroostook on March 13th, except Head Quarters Company, the Bangor Rifle Corps, retained by Hodsdon as his body guard. On the 15th, Hodsdon and the Bangor Rifles, under Lieutenant James Henry Carleton, took up the line of march from Houlton at 11 o'clock. By a fatiguing forced march of thirty miles through the dense forest they arrived late at night at the Presque Isle of the St. John and took up rough quarters under the guard of the Castine Rifles, commanded by Captain Charles H. Wing. The next day, carrying their our own baggage, they got as far as Smith's Camp, 14 miles. They resumed their march on the 17th, arrived at a clearing, and to their surprise they came in sight of a three-story house, which the boys greeted with three rousing cheers. The owner of the house and small gristmill was Mr. Fairbanks, who, upon further acquaintance at camp, they found to be "a true specimen of a Yankee, rough in appearance but a true man clear through." They stopped for refreshment (stationed one Militia company to guard a depot of provisions there) and departed at noon.[47] Through a dense forest, at 5:30 PM, they entered Fort Fairfield under the salute of Artillery and a cheering welcome from the military band stationed at the main entrance, near the river front. The excitement "made the boys feel as if they could tread up to their knees through the frozen ground."[48]

Major General Isaac Hodsdon's Head Quarters of the Maine Militia, Army of the Aroostook, was established at

---
46 Ibid.
47 ELL.
48 BRCR.

Fort Fairfield, on March 17, 1839. The fort had two six-pounder and two four-pounder field artillery.[49] Behind the breastworks, and from the fort to the river was an intervale or plane of sufficient width for quite a village. ... In the south, trees had been felled for half a mile, forming an impenetrable abatis for the rear, and on the north a dense forest. The parade ground required the constant work of large details of men daily, in fatigue duty, to grub and grade the frozen earth, stumps and roots. The officer's quarters were on the south line; the company quarters on the west and north side, the Rifle Detachment on the front and rear of the Artillery Battery. Some quarters were built of logs covered with long split shingles with center openings through the roof for smoke and no glass windows.[50]

Elijah Lowe, Jr., Provost Marshall, wrote that "the militia found Major General Hodsdon to be a very considerate commander. He told the Chaplain one day that he might take his duties as light as possible, he need not pray much, only occasionally. Sunday morning the Military Band marched through the encampment, escorting all those who chose to fall in, to the lower picket post at Fitzherbert's, one and a half miles toward Tobique, for divine worship. Attendance was not very large; it did not crowd a small, one story house. ... Fifty men in one camp will not spend their leisure hours idly. All schemes and devices to amuse and entertain for fun and frolic, consistent with strict discipline, were resorted to. The arrival of a vidette was hailed with joy, as we could hear from home and the outer world."[51]

Shepherd Cary, at Houlton, criticized Hodsdon for not leaving any guard at the Quarter Master Store at Houlton; he thought it imprudent, as it might be broken open or burnt up, if any desperadoes were so disposed.

---

49 RLAMI 1839.
50 ELL.
51 Ibid.

Apparently Cary did not feel that this was his duty under his appointment as Assistant Quarter Master. Cary was, however, interested in the creation of the new County of Aroostook, and stated that if the bill should finally pass it would be necessary to appoint County officers before the Council adjourned. It was his wish that no appointments should be made until a Democratic convention could be held in Houlton, which would be done as soon as the local Democrats heard of the final passage of the bill.[52]

The new County of Aroostook had been created on March 16, 1839, but the news had not yet reached Cary, who was anxious to get on with his lumbering business on the northern rivers. He told Governor Fairfield:

> I think our Provincial friends are disposed to yield the jurisdiction of the Aroostook if they can truly bring about a temporary arrangement with the State of Maine. If this should be done, I think there would be no difficulty in the Land Agent's obtaining good security for the stumpage of the timber cut by trespassers, at such prices as you should see fit to exact. I think that if such an arrangement was made, it would enable myself and others who are largely interested in timber cut under regular permits, to get the same to market.[53]

Brigadier General George W. Bachelder
Leads Troops to Hodsdon's Western Flank

Rufus McIntire, who had been alarmed at British troop movements on March 11th, had pointed out a cer-

---

52 Cary to Fairfield, March 17, 1839, JFPC 145 4/4 MHS.
53 Cary to Fairfield, March 17, 1839, JFPC 145 4/4 MHS. For insight into the situation existing for local lumbermen, see Richard W Judd, *Aroostook: A Century of Logging in Northern Maine*, 1989, Orono: University of Maine Press, 36.

tain military strategy involving the troops of Brigadier General Bachelder's Second Division:

> With regard to the conjectured [British] movement through the woods to some point above us, I would suggest the propriety of a strong force to be stationed at the mouth of the St. Croix on No. 10, say General Bachelder's command, who would be ready to fall on the rear of the British if they attempted to march down the river upon us.[54]

Bachelder's "Kennebec Detachment" had been on the move from Augusta to Bangor with one company of Artillery, one company of Light Infantry, one company of Riflemen, and nine companies of Infantry. About five hundred of his men had arrived in Bangor by March 3rd, where they stopped to be supplied with arms, clothing, blankets, etc. Bachelder had plans to march in two companies, by easy stages of fifteen to twenty miles per day, to support Hodsdon on his western flank.[55]

Oliver Frost, at Bangor, had reported to Hodsdon that Bachelder's advance troops were at Oldtown on the evening of the 7th, and had commented:

> This makes their first day's march. I understand that three companies refused to march today, according to his order, and he was obliged to call his other forces to arrest them. All but three individuals finally concluded to march, and I understand these three have been tried today by a Court Martial. This looks like mutiny in good earnest. This, however, had better not be made known, ... a little more distressing criticism over small things.[56]

---

54 McIntire to Fairfield, 2nd letter of March 11, 1839, JFPC 145, 4/3.
55 RAGABT 1839; Mills to Hodsdon, March 6, 1839, OHPMHS.
56 E G Rawson, ADQM, to Hodsdon, March 3, 1839; Mills to Hodsdon, March 6, 1839; Frost to Hodsdon, March 7, 1839, OHPMHS.

Bachelder left Bangor on March 11th, with the remainder of his troops, and on the 12th, he reported to Hodsdon from Township No. 4, explaining that he would put three companies upon the march to Township No. 10 Range 5 (Masardis) in the morning, the remainder to follow as soon as practicable. His object was to establish posts from Township No. 7, on the Aroostook Road, through to the Aroostook River, and down that river as far as the Presque Isle. Many of his troops were unused to marching, and suffered severely from over-exertion and exposure, but still they were all in good spirits.57

When Bachelder's detachment arrived at No. 10, at the junction of the St. Croix and Aroostook Rivers, it occupied temporary works erected by the Land Agent's force. His Artillery, which remained at that post, were furnished with two four-pounder field ordnance. This post was one hundred and thirty miles northerly from Bangor, and fifty two by way of the Aroostook River, west south west from Fort Fairfield. The troops proceeded to erect suitable camps.58

George Stanley, in the process of moving supplies to Hodsdon's and Bachelder's troops, informed Adjutant General Thompson of the necessity of throwing a bridge across the branch of the Mattawamkeag that Bachelder had crossed on the ice. He foresaw that as soon as the ice had broken up it would be impossible to cross this stream with teams. There was no other route to the Head Quarters of Bachelder's Detachment. Charles Jarvis sent

---

57 Thompson to Bachelder, March 6, 1839, OHPMHS; Bachelder to Hodsdon, March 12, 1839, OHPMHS. His messenger to Hodsdon was Colonel S S Simons of the Regiment of Cavalry in the 1st Brigade, 2nd Division, and his Aide de Camp and orderly officer was David B. Boman. Colonel Stanley would forward supplies by this route and Bachelder would prepare suitable places for their deposit. Colonel Pike would take charge of stores on the Aroostook Road and Aroostook River.
58 RAGABT 1839.

Joseph Maddocks, of the *posse*, with a detail of men, to construct a bridge at that location.⁵⁹

In support of Major General Hodsdon, the Seventh Division, four companies of Infantry and one company of Light Infantry, numbering with the officers three hundred and sixty-nine men, had assembled at Calais on the 3rd and 6th days of March, and were comfortably quartered in that town. Major General Foster, in command of this Post, had instructions to resist any attack and to protect the eastern frontier as far north as the headwaters of the St. Croix.⁶⁰

Political and Military Affairs in New Brunswick

Under the terms of the *Memorandum*, Sir John Harvey had agreed only that Maine forces would not be disturbed in the Aroostook River Valley. He had agreed with the Right Honorable H. S. Fox, British Ambassador at Washington, to defer all offensive measures related to the disputed territory until Fox could receive the decision of Her Majesty's Government. He told Fox that his measures would be confined to the protection of the communication between this Province and Lower Canada, through the Valley of the St. John, and of Her Majesty's subjects of the Madawaska Settlement.⁶¹ On March 6th, Harvey informed Lieutenant Colonel Maxwell, at Woodstock that the 69th Regiment would be pushed up in successive divisions of one hundred each day until Maxwell found himself in sufficient force to defend his position against all comers.⁶²

---

59 Stanley to Thompson, March 13, 1839, OHPMHS; Report of Charles Davis [Daveis] to R. McIntire or Hastings Strickland, *Land Agent Materials*, Maine State Archives, Augusta.
60 RAGABT 1839.
61 Harvey to Fox, March 6, 1839, in response to Fox's letter of February 27th. RGFNB 1839.
62 Harvey to Colonel Maxwell, March 6, 1839, LBGHPANB.

The *Quebec Gazette*, March 6, 1839, ridiculed the "absurdities of the bobadil rule of the pugnacious State of Maine" and reported that two more companies of the 11th Regiment had arrived in Quebec from Sorel, on their way to New Brunswick, accompanied by a detachment of the Royal Artillery, with a field piece and several sleighs loaded with ammunition, rockets, etc., and that the two remaining companies of the 11th would follow on Friday.[63]

Then, on March 11th, Harvey confidentially informed Colonel Goldie, at Madawaska, that he had just received advice from Her Majesty's Minister at Washington, as to the very great importance of avoiding collision with the Maine Militia. He told Goldie to "endeavour to confine himself to the left Bank of the St. John, in the Madawaska Settlement, and that should the hot-headed Mainists approach the settlement in overwhelming numbers, he was to retreat to the Grand Falls. That Post being within three miles of our *acknowledged* territory, there will be no pretense for saying that we continue in the military occupation of the Disputed District."[64]

A week later, Harvey was pleased to find that the whole XIth Regiment, six hundred men and a gun, under Goldie's command, was strong enough, by calling on the two flank companies of the 36th from the Falls and Tobique, with their two six-pounder field pieces, to defy all Maine. He advised Goldie "to consult the wishes of the excellent Priest at Madawaska" in regard to quarters for the troops, but with such a force, he might venture to place them on the other side of the River. He hoped to be able to send Goldie back to St. Andrews before the winter roads broke up. He told Goldie to horse his guns if necessary, by hire, per day or week.[65]

---

63 Reprinted in the *Royal Gazette*, Fredericton, New Brunswick, 1839.
64 Harvey to Goldie, March 11, 1839, PAC COP 188 B16.
65 Ibid.; Harvey to Goldie, March 18, 1839, LGJHPANB.

Harvey reported to Lord Glenelg that the troops on the St. John, on March 13th, had been posted as follows: At the Madawaska Settlement: Colonel Goldie's Detachment, XIth Regiment with a six-pounder and rocket, 350. At Grand Falls: Light Company, 36th Regiment, 80 strong, with a six-pounder and Militia, 90. At Tobique and Mouth of the Restook: the _ Company, 36th and 80th, with a six-pounder and 50 Militia, 90. Eighteen miles below, troops that could be rapidly concentrated: At Holton (Houlton) Mill Creek (Meduxnekeag Stream), intermediate between Woodstock and the Aroostook, a party of Militia to open up a road. At Woodstock: the remainder of the 36th Regiment, two companies of the 69th Regiment, with two twelve-pounders, Howitzers and a six-pounder and about 300 Militia, amounting to about 650, under Lieutenant Colonel Maxwell. A line of (two troopers every ten miles) Volunteers and Dragoons extended from the Madawaska to St. John, enabling him to receive reports and send orders in 6 hours from Woodstock, 15 hours to the Aroostook, 18 hours to Grand Falls and 26 hours to the Madawaska. One fourth of the two Battalions of Carleton County Militia had been called out. (The French at Madawaska, 3rd Battalion, had been exempted.) The sedentary militia, Carleton County, amounted to at least 1200. To these might be added the 3rd Battalion of the 6th York Militia, of at least 800, totaling a Reserve Militia Force of 2000, only requiring arms to be placed in their hands.[66]

On the 19th of March, Harvey ordered into service, from the New Brunswick Regiment of Artillery, four companies of one officer, two non-commissioned officers and nine gunners per Company, together with the Adjutant, at Fredericton, Woodstock, St. John, and St. Andrews.[67]

---

66 Harvey to Glenelg, March 13, 1839, PAC COP 188 B16.
67 RG1839HIL.

PART FOUR: ARMISTICE WITH CONFRONTATION AND NEGOTIATION

CHAPTER X

ARMISTICE

Governor Fairfield, on March 12th, recommended that, upon assurance from Lieutenant Governor Harvey that he would "abandon all idea of occupying the disputed territory," Maine Militia would be withdrawn from the Line. This plan would be approved by the Legislature on March 23, 1839. Meanwhile, Winfield Scott invited Sir John Harvey to make a general declaration to the effect that it was not his intention, without renewed instructions to that effect from his Government, to seek to take military possession of the Disputed Territory, or to seek to expel the armed civil posse or the troops of Maine from that area. Scott assured Harvey that his declaration would be met by a similar declaration from Governor Fairfield, to the effect that it was not his intention, without renewed instructions from the Legislature, to attempt to disturb by arms, the Province of New Brunswick in the possession of the Madawaska settlements, or to attempt to interrupt the usual communications between that Province and Her Majesty's Upper Provinces. With this understanding, Fairfield would withdraw the Militia, leaving a small civil posse under the Land Agent, armed or unarmed, to protect the timber recently cut and to prevent future depredations. This arrangement would

allow time for the United States and Great Britain to settle the question of limits.[1] Videttes carried Scott's message to Harvey, who signified his concurrence. In return, John Fairfield, "because the exigency for calling out the Maine Militia had by this agreement ceased, signifed his acquiescence."[2]
While there had never been, during this boundary dispute, a "shooting war" between Maine and Great Britain, there had been animosity, enmity, antagonism, and legal and verbal battles that approximated "hostilties." With the signing of the above agreements there came a supposed cessation of hostilities, an "armistice," an uneasy peace, but tension would continue well into 1842.

Governor Fairfield began the recall of the Maine Militia on March 25, 1839. Major General Hodsdon was ordered to retire with his troops from the valley of the Aroostook as soon as a civil force suitable to protect the timber and public property was furnished by the Land Agent. Then he would return the militia, by way of Houlton and the Aroostook Road, to Bangor. Stand-by troops from the Fifth and Sixth Divisions, under Colonel Orison Ripley were recalled.[3]

After completing what he termed "The Arrangement," General Scott proceeded by way of Gardiner, to Portland, and by steamer to Boston, where he attended church with General H. A. S. Dearborn. He would leave Boston the next day, for as he wrote:

he had much to do in the way of preparation for war, if negotiations should fail to settle the boundary question. If that, too, could be left to my excellent friend, Sir J. Harvey, I am persuaded that we might settle it over the first bottle, and exhaust a second in

---

[1] Chapter 111, March 23, 1839, ROSM III, 113-14; Scott, loc. cit. 347-350.
[2] ROSM III, 350-351.
[3] General Order No. 29; General Order No. 28, AWKJ.

drinking to perpetual peace between our countries. Poor devils we are! By smoothing the way for diplomatists, he has lost a peerage, and I another vote of thanks with a gold medal! Such are the sacrifices we have made to the general good of the mighty Anglo-Saxon race, divided into two great nations.[4]

Demilitarization in New Brunswick

In Fredericton, New Brunswick, the *Royal Gazette* reported that on the 23rd of March, 1839, at twelve o'clock, his Excellency the Lieutenant Governor proceeded in state from the Government House to the Chamber of the Legislative Council, and being seated on the Throne, the Gentleman Usher of the Black Rod was sent with a Message from his Excellency to the House of the Assembly, commanding their attendance. When the members had assembled, he closed the session thanking them for their liberality in funding the Militia and Volunteer Force and the improvement of the line of communication with Lower Canada by way of the Valley of the Saint John and Temisquata Lake.[5]

On the same day, at Fredericton, Mr. Wilmot, from the Joint Committee, prepared an Address to Queen Victoria, inviting her special attention to the question of the northeastern boundary of the United States of America, involving as it did the future union, welfare and prosperity of Her Majesty's North American Possessions. They called her attention to "the actual invasion of this Colony by an armed force from the adjoining State of Maine" and tendered their "lives and property, in aid of the maintenance of Your Majesty's rights, and for repelling the invader from our soil.[6]

---

4 Winfield Scott to H. A. S. Dearborn, March 27, 1839, *Collection 420*, Fogg, Vol. V, Maine Historical Society Archives, Portland.
5 RG1839HIL.
6 Ibid.

Sir John Harvey and suite journeyed from Fredericton to Woodstock on Monday, March 25th, escorted part of the way by Major Wilmot's Cavalry. His visit was reported in the *Woodstock Times*:

Never since the axe of the woodman was first heard to sound amidst the depth of our forest, has the little town of Woodstock seen so much stir and bustle as during the last week. ... His Excellency arrived at about five o'clock, P M, and was received by a salute from the Royal Artillery, and a guard of Honor of the 69th Regiment with the Band of the 36th. An immense concourse of people of all classes were assembled to welcome his arrival, as the ark-like stage, drawn by four excellent horses decorated with ribbons, dashed through the streets, escorted by the the Troop of York Hussars with their gay and extremely handsome uniforms, the scene was most animating. ... The Officers of the Garrison entertained his Excellency at dinner that evening, ... and the Band of the 36th, led by the excellent musician, Mr. Seaume, enlivened the evening, with a variety of the most pleasing airs.

On Wednesday the whole Garrison, under the command of Colonel Maxwell, received his Excellency on the ice of the Meduxnakeag Creek and were drawn up in line facing and parallel to the right bank of the River: Royal Artillery on the right, 36th Regiment, 69th Regiment, Militia Artillery, 1st Carleton Infantry, Woodstock Rifle Company and the York Hussars, making in all an imposing military spectacle. The column marched past in slow and quick time, and the manner in which the Volunteer and Militia Corps performed their part elicited the praise of His Excellency. ...

During the week, His Excellency entertained in his never failing hospitable manner, the principal inhabitants of the neighbourhood and officers of the garrison; and on Thursday [the 28th] held a Levee at which it was gratifying to see Major Kirby and two other American officers from the Garrison at Houlton. ... His Excellency left Woodstock [on the 29th] under a salute of fifteen guns from the Royal Artillery.[7]

What Harvey termed "a most desirable arrangement," allowed him to notify Goldie that he might return to Canada the detachment of Her Majesty's Troops in the Madawaska Settlement. Then he ordered the return to their homes of the Militia and Volunteer Forces of New Brunswick. The York Light Dragoons were continued on duty to the 30th day of April.

Lieutenant Colonel Robinson, in taking leave of the Embodied Militia of York County, expressed his approbation of their good conduct, of their willingness in learning to use their arms in defending their country from a foreign and grasping enemy, and of the unanimity which existed between Her Majesty's Troops and the Embodied Militia.[8]

The Civil Posse Prepares to Cope with Maine Militia Withdrawal

Friction between Maine's civil force and militia showed itself when Charles Jarvis, Provisional Land Agent, was once more present at his headquarters in Mr. Dorsey's house at Fort Fairfield, and in need of men to protect timber from trespassers. He sent a note to Major General Isaac Hodsdon, stating that his men had discovered trespassers on River des Chutes and he needed to

---

[7] *Woodstock Times*, March 30, 1839, reprinted in RG 1839 HIL.
[8] Harvey to Goldie, March 27, 1839, Harvey to Scott, March 27, 1839, LBGHPANB. District General Order, Woodstock, March 27, 1839; RGHIL 1839; Militia General Order of March 30, 1839; The Non-commissioned officers, drummers, fifers, buglers, and Privates were allowed the bounty and marching money agreeable to the provisions of the Militia Law. All Arms, accoutrements, axes, blankets, bedding, great coats, pea jackets, etc, were returned. The men were permitted to retain their shoes and forage caps. Militia General Order of April 1, 1839.

send a detachment of thirty or forty men, early the next day, to arrest them. He would supply the guide, but requested that Hodsdon send some of his men. Hodsdon detailed thirty-five men from the Bangor and Dexter Rifle Companies to accompany Thomas Bartlett, Esq., to the River de Chute to look for trespassers. Almost immediately the men grumbled about their respective services, pay, etc., and after marching about a mile, returned. They had not absolutely declined to march under Bartlett, but when he learned of their feelings, he declined going with them. Bartlett left with some of the *posse*; Hodsdon immediately made another draft of twenty men, who acted as a reinforcement, and performed to the entire satisfaction of Mr. Jarvis.[9]

Elijah Hamlin, Superintendent of Videttes, feared it would not be possible to keep up the line of videttes between that place and Houlton, beyond the middle of April, as there was only a winter road from Mr. Fairbanks' to the Presque Isle of the St. John, and it would not be passable for a horse after the ground opened. There would be, however, no difficulty in keeping open the communications to No.10 (Masardis), by water, after the ice left the river. He had placed all spare videttes on the Aroostook Road. The health of the troops at Fort Fairfield was good, only twelve reported sick on the 17th, all slight cases. The soldiers were engaged in erecting new huts because those left by the *posse* were "wet, cold, very smoky, and unfit to live in." They lacked teams and proper tools, but showed ingenuity in making their huts convenient and comfortable. General Hodsdon had gone to the Presque Isle, to inspect road building between Mr. Fairbanks' and No.10.[10]

In the midst of these activities, an order reached Fort Fairfield that the militia troops be withdrawn from

---

9 DLWP; Jarvis to Hodsdon, March 22, 1839, OHPMHS; Hamlin to Fairfield, March 27, 1839, JFPC 145 4/4 MHS.
10 Hamlin to Fairfield, March 27, 1839, JFPC 145 4/4 MHS.

the Disputed Territory. At that time, Colonel Jarvis was at No.10, directing the Fish River expedition. He had dispatched Alvin Nye, an Assistant Provisional Land Agent, to Fish River, with instructions to fortify himself upon that river and place a boom across it in order to prevent illegally cut timber from passing down that river, into the St. John River, and on to markets at St. John, New Brunswick. Jarvis informed Hodsdon that his force consisted of about sixty men whose enlistment would expire on the 10th of April, and asked that he grant leave of absence to one hundred militia men to enlist as Volunteers, under the direction of the Land Agent, to act as a guard for the Boom, or to undertake any other service that might be required. Jarvis explained that this had been the mode adopted by General Bachelder as to the men detached for the Fish River expedition, and he felt that if this method were adopted, the remainder of the militia could be immediately withdrawn, and great expense saved to the State, arising from the enlistment and bringing a new Corps of Volunteers to the territory.[11]

    Hodsdon replied that he had no discretionary power to allow his troops to enlist under the Land Agent. Also, if Bachelder had done so, he alone was responsible; such a procedure was not covered in his orders. He, Hodsdon, had issued orders at the Regimental level to Bachelder at No.10, to withdraw his troops from the Disputed Territory, but on March 29th, as he was going south to Post No. 8, at the Presque Isle of the Aroostook, Hodsdon countermanded those orders, in order to give Bachelder time to call in his patrols and scouting parties and to detail a commissioned officer to conduct those of his troops then at Fish River back to the garrison. Bachelder was then to march to Bangor. Upon departure, he was to leave a guard at No.10, on the Aroostook Road, to protect

---

11   General Order, March 25, 1839.; Jarvis to Nye, March 27, 1839, JFPC I 45B 4/4 MHS; B Wiggin, Jr., to Fairfield, February 27, 1839, JFPC 145 B 3/10 MHS; Jarvis to Hodsdon, March 30, 1839, OHPMHS.

stores left behind. In the absence of Brigadier General Bachelder, Colonel Philbrook was to carry out these orders.[12]

Since it would require about ten days to remove his units from the Aroostook River, Hodsdon agreed to leave, during this period, sufficient militia to protect the Boom. He asked Jarvis to fix a date upon which he would have a sufficient civil force. Jarvis replied that this was impossible, that there was no alternative, but that the militia at Fort Fairfield must remain until explicit orders were received from Augusta by express.[13]

By March 31st, Hodsdon had received orders from Fairfield to leave enough militia to protect the Boom, supplies, etc., and that the officer left in command at Fort Fairfield and at the Presque Isle, when notified by the Land Agent that a sufficient civil force had been procured, would retire to Bangor.[14]

Plans Are Laid for Blockhouses at Fort Fairfield

Jarvis suggested to Fairfield that the season was rapidly approaching, when, if ever, an attack might be expected on the Boom, and that no time should be lost in preparing defenses to enable a small number of men to resist a much larger force. He recommended the erection of a blockhouse on the hill then occupied by militia troops as a guard and storehouse; another blockhouse on the hillock on this side of the River near the Boom, and a third on the eminence on the other side of the river. The reduced number of Volunteers (formerly the *posse*), fully employed on the Boom, would not have the required

---

12 Hodsdon to Jarvis, March 30, 1839, JFPC 145B 4/5, MHS; General Order No. 29; Hodsdon to Bachelder, March 29, 1839, OHPMHS; Jarvis to Hodsdon, March 31, 1839, JFPC 145, 4/5, MHS.
13 Jarvis to Hodsdon, March 31, 1839; Jarvis to Hodsdon, March 30, 1839, OHPMHS; Hodsdon to Jarvis, March 30, 1839, JFPC 145B 4/5, MHS.
14 Hodsdon to Jarvis, March 31, 1839, JFPC 145B 4/5 MHS. Gen. Order, March 30, 1839 AWKJ.

strength to erect these works in due season. Jarvis wrote that he would be pleased to confer with Fairfield as to the details.[15]

Maine Militia Withdrawal Begins

Head Quarters of the State Troops
Army of the Aroostook
April 1, 1839

ORDERS:

The Troops of the Third Division, now in service in the State, will resume their march, and return to the City of Bangor in the following manner:

The Company commanded by Captain Wing will march from the Presque Isle of the St. John on Wednesday morning, [April 2,] at an early hour. The Company commanded by Ensign Burnham will march from the Presque Isle of the Aroostook on the same morning. The Companies commanded by Captain Leighton and Captain Maxim will move from Fort Fairfield at Reveille.

The Company commanded by Captain Maxfield will march from Presque Isle of the Aroostook on Thursday morning, [April 3.]

Captain Fish and Company will march on Friday [April 4,] from the Presque Isle of the St. John

Assistant Division Quarter Masters Rawson and Wood and Quarter Masters Miller and Jewett will furnish transportation for the necessary subsistence for this march and for the camp equippage and baggage; and also quarters and fuel.

It is strictly enjoined on all officers, non-commissioned officers and soldiers to preserve the most perfect good order and soldier-like deportment toward each other and all the citizens of the State, or whomsoever they meet during this march. Every departure

---

15 Jarvis to Hodsdon, March 31, 1839, JFPC 1454 /5, MHS; Gen. Order No. 30, March 30, 1839.

from this requirement will be suitably noticed and severely punished. No excuse will be received in palliation of any insulting gestures or language toward any citizen, nor any trespass against their rights. Every commanding officer of a company or detachment will use all possible means of expediting this march, and at the least possible expense to the State. They will certify in writing to the Quarter Master's Department, the number of men quartered on each day, and by whom, and will make up each day a morning report of the State of their company or detachment, and the regular provision returns for the use of their troops during their march. By the Commanding General

                      Oliver Frost, Aide de Camp[16]

    Governor Fairfield, informed that some of the men under Hodsdon's command would be willing to remain upon the ground as a part of the Land Agent's force, modified previous orders so as to authorize the discharge of such men at their encampments.[17]

    Major General Isaac Hodsdon, on April 7th, from temporary Head Quarters at Monticello, ordered Major James Smith to assume command of the troops at Fort Fairfield and at the Presque Isle of the Aroostook, stating that Captain Maxfield, commanding at the Presque Isle should report to him.[18]

    Hodsdon and his staff were encamped at Houlton on April 8th, where Adjutant General Thompson found that Hodsdon had consolidated his companies in such a way that two companies would be a sufficient force to protect the public property at Fort Fairfield and on the river, so two more companies of Infantry were ordered to return to Bangor. Three companies were then at Houlton,

---

16 JFPC 145B 4/6 MHS.
17 Fairfield to Hodsdon, April 2, 1839; Cahoon to Fairfield, April (2?), 1839; Thompson to Fairfield, April 1, 1839, JFPC 145B 4/6 MHS.
18 Hodsdon to Major James Smith, April 7, 1839, JFPC 145B 4/7, MHS.

waiting for transportation of subsistence. The rest of the Detachment were on the march between Houlton and Bangor. The Major General watched the departure of all troops from Houlton, to see that they were suitably provided and supplied for their march, but planned to leave for Bangor in season to arrive there with the advance Companies.[19]

Charles Jarvis had been furious about what he considered to be Hodsdon's ill-advised order that Brigadier General Bachelder call in his patrols and scouting parties from Fish River in preparation for returning to Bangor. He held that the militia was there in support of the Land Agent, and should, therefore, meet his needs. The military commanders were subject to strict obedience to orders, and the amount of time required for the transmission of orders from Augusta to the frontier made it difficult for orders to be amended fast enough to adapt to changing needs.

Colonel Jarvis and Captain Nye Lead the Civil Volunteers

Adjutant Tarbox had been sent by Bachelder to recall the men who had been with Nye on the Fish River expedition. Nye's party was returning to Fort Machias when Jarvis overtook them and ordered them back to Fish River. The next morning, Calvin Carver, of the Militia, who had been appointed second in command to Nye, with Captain Tucker and Captain Anthony, started secretly back for Fort Machias. Jarvis caught up with them and an animated contest ensued about who should have the services of the militiamen; "the terrors of martial law prevailed"; only two remained.

Jarvis left for Fort Fairfield, determined to appeal to the *esprit de corps* of the boom men to raise a party of twenty men for the expedition. He arrived at noon, his

---

19 Hodsdon to Fairfield, April 8, 1839, JFPC145B 4/7, MHS, DLWP, RAGABT 1839.

call was promptly answered, and a little before sunset they were on their way, with two teams to carry their arms and baggage. They traveled twenty miles, being on the road until twelve o'clock at night, and by three the next day, they joined Nye at Fort Machias. Two hours later they resumed their march up the Little Machias, to reach the nine-mile encampment on that river, fifty three miles, in a little over twenty-four hours.[20] Though the expedition had been retarded, it had not been broken up. Jarvis sent orders to Nye:

> You will now move on with your men, (those) who have not been degraded by being attached to Hodsdon's command. Your force, with the exception of the two fine fellows from the militia, who remained when all the rest abandoned you, will be composed of the Volunteers who never flinched from the encounter of any danger or the braving of any hardship.[21]

Nye and his men resumed their expedition to Fish River.

Jarvis, when traveling south found the bridge at the Mattawamkeag (probably between present-day Moro and Knowles) to be as durable as any wooden bridge in the State. The Boom at Fort Fairfield was almost completed, all but putting on a few irons that had been deficient due to some mistake at Bangor. These irons would be obtained from Houlton.[22]

Governor Fairfield clarified his orders to Colonel Jarvis concerning the extent to which he should go in defense of the Boom:

> If I were in the place of the Land Agent, and any number of British subjects should come over the Line

---

[20] Jarvis to Fairfield, April 5, 1839, JFPC 145B 4/6 MHS.
[21] Jarvis to Nye, April 3, 1839, JFPC 145B 4/6 MHS.
[22] Jarvis to Fairfield, April 5, 1839, JFPC 145B 4/6 MHS.

with a design to cut away the Boom or take possession of the timber, I should make use of such means as I deemed sufficient and necessary to prevent the accomplishment of such purpose, even at the sacrifice of human life.[23]

After the men assigned to the Fish River expedition had departed and the boom men had been discharged, the Land Agent's Volunteer force consisted of only eighteen men, but they were soon joined by the builders of the Mattawamkeag Bridge and three new recruits. Jarvis left to procure more men and to obtain definite instructions from Land Agent McIntire for newly deputized Assistant Land Agent William P. Parrott, in command of the Volunteers at Fort Fairfield, so that the discharge of his duty should "not be at the peril of his neck." On April 9th, Parrott's men began digging very hard ground, frozen two and a half feet deep, to build the blockhouse at the Boom.[24]

Two days previously, Colonel Jarvis had sent a note to Major Smith asking for twenty militiamen and an officer to go with a civil officer and two guides to obstruct the River de Chute, but Smith's orders did not authorize him to comply with that request. On the 9th, Jarvis sent Captain Thomas Bartlett with ten Volunteers, each armed with horse pistols and an axe, to River de Chute to arrest and bring off any trespassers and their teams found at work west of the east line of the State. He was to burn their camps and hovels, and obstruct the stream so that it would be impossible to run timber that season.[25] Bartlett returned and reported that at noon on the 10th, they arrived at the camps of the trespassers, one of whom was a man named House, a deserter from

---

[23] Jarvis to Fairfield, April 9, 1839, JFPC 145B 4/6 MHS.
[24] Ibid.; DLWP.
[25] Jarvis to Smith, April 7, 1839; Smith to Jarvis, April 8, 1839; Jarvis to Bartlett, April 9, 1839, JFPC 145B 4/7 MHS.

General Hodsdon's troops, who was working as a cook. Through him Bartlett learned the names of the trespassers and their location. He left House under guard and proceeded to arrest eight men and seize two double-horse teams. With prisoners to guard, he did not have force enough to block up the river. The distance to the fort was about twelve miles through an unbroken forest; the snow was about two feet deep. He sent out two of his men and a boy whom he had taken prisoner, to ascertain the practicability of swamping through to the Houlton and Aroostook Road, which he judged to be about four miles. They returned about dark, saying that it would be utterly impossible and that the boy had escaped by "showing a clean pair of heels."

From the moment Bartlett heard of the escape of the lad, he feared an attempted rescue of the prisoners. He proposed that Asa Harvey and John Karney, the owners of the teams, give a bond of $400 for their horses, payable on demand to the Land Agent at Fort Fairfield. They readily assented. Disencumbered of the horses, on the morning of the 11th, Bartlett was about to march his prisoners to Fort Fairfield when he heard the shouting of an advancing mob. He instructed his men as to their bearing in presence of the mob, and waited. Upon the arrival of twenty-eight men with muskets and two fowling pieces, Bartlett asked the leader, John Vanning, an officer of the Provincial Militia, the reason for his visit. Vanning replied that they came to demand the horses and prisoners. Upon being asked by what authority, Vanning replied, "that of ownership." Vanning was informed that the prisoners and horses were taken in execution of the laws of the State of Maine, and that if he rescued them he did it at his peril. The mob made a push toward the hovel for the horses. Bartlett decided not to risk the lives of the good fellows who were with him by attempting to drive them off with pistols. After possessing the horses, Vanning informed the prisoners that they were at liberty to return with him. Bartlett told Harvey and

Karney that if they would go with him as prisoners to Fort Fairfield, they might induce the Land Agent not to destroy their timber; but that if they joined with the mob, a sufficient force would be sent to destroy every ton of timber on the river. As it was their only chance of saving anything, they consented and urged the mob to depart without violence. Bartlett returned with his prisoners to Fort Fairfield.[26]

Jarvis attributed the failure of Bartlett's expedition to the refusal of Major Smith to answer the requisition of twenty men. As to the trespassers, he commented that the rescue of the men and teams was an "evident infraction of the agreement of Sir John Harvey, which, of course, *a la mode Angleterre*, would be disavowed and the authors rewarded." He feared that the success of that mob would encourage future attacks upon Nye at Fish River and upon the Aroostook Boom, before he could be in a state of readiness.

Since the 19th of March, the Militia unit that included the Bangor Rifle Corps had done camp duties and stood guard at the Boom.[27] By the 16th of April, Captain Parrott had seventy-four Volunteers employed in the erection of the block house on the hillock adjacent to the Boom. Jarvis planned another blockhouse on the highest part of the encampment and perhaps a third on the hill on the other side of the River. He felt that all of these should and might have been built by Hodsdon. He refused to authorize withdrawal of the militia until the arrival of precise orders for Mr. Parrott from McIntire.

---

26 Thomas Bartlett Jr., to McIntire, undated, JFPC 145B 4/7 MHS. Other prisoners: George Smith, Martin Gallagher, George Upham, John Morehouse, Michael Gallagher. The mob: John Venning, Jonas Fitzherbert, ___ Robinson, James and Anthony Merrithew; Morris Pickard, deserter, U. S. Army; Lewis Bloodworth, James McCoy, schoolmaster; Adam Beard, Justice of the Peace; Michael Sommers, George Beard, Alexander [Wilson?], James Wright, James Heart, James Sawyer.
27 April 10th, Battalion Order No. 1, BRCR; Smith to Hodsdon, April 11, 1839, OHPMHS.

Jarvis, still angered by various refusals of militia officers to come to his assistance, had forwarded charges to the Division Advocate against Major General Hodsdon concerning "conduct unbecoming a gentleman and the neglect of every duty of a soldier." Hindsight shows that in a large measure the problems between Jarvis and Hodsdon were due to delays in communication and lack of an early explanation to the Land Agent that even though the Militia had been sent in support of the Land Agent, the Land Agent's force and the Militia were two separate entities, neither authorized to command the other.[28]

The Militia Units Return to Bangor

The Militia unit guarding the Boom waited word from Colonel Jarvis that the Land Agent's force was large enough and had authority to defend the Boom at Fort Fairfield. That word was slow in coming; the approach of spring brought melting ice and muddy roads; so when it seemed that the necessity of a longer stay had passed, and the streams were breaking up, the excess baggage from Fort Fairfield was sent out to Houlton.[29]

In the meanwhile, Major General Hodsdon had arrived in Bangor on April 12th, and was making preparation for the arrival of the Army of the Aroostook. State Treasurer Jeremiah Goodwin was at Bangor complaining to Governor Fairfield that Hodsdon was unnecessarily expending money for seventy thousand feet of boards and had employed a large gang of men to erect barracks on Thomas Hill at Bangor. He had been told by Colonel Stevens that it was Hodsdon's intention to detain all troops in Bangor for a grand military display after all had returned. Goodwin was vehement in his objections, saying that the moment two or four companies arrived they should be mustered, discharged, and paid the following

---

28 Jarvis, to Fairfield, April 16, 1839, JFPC I 45B 4/8.
29 BRCR.

day. He demanded that Fairfield send orders to Adjutant General Thompson and Hodsdon to this effect. By April 9th, the barracks had progressed rapidly enough to accommodate Captain Wing's Company.[30]

Governor Fairfield wrote to Hodsdon that there must be some misunderstanding; that it was intended that the troops would return to Bangor by single companies and be mustered and paid as they arrived. However, it seemed that the Major General's plan was to have *all* of the troops at Bangor at one time, for many days. Fairfield hoped that it was not too late to regulate the movement of the troops in accordance with his understanding of General Order No 30. He wished Hodsdon a happy return to his family after his excellent service in protecting the rights and honor of the State.[31]

Isaac Hodsdon sent Fairfield a confident defense of his arrangements. He assured the Governor that if his suggestions had been received in time he would have complied, but the barracks, if it be proper to call them such, were already completed. Upon the receipt of Order No 30, after a careful estimate of the expense of quartering the troops in the city, he had concluded that a temporary barracks would be more economical and much more to the comfort of the troops than by any other means and had ordered Lieutenant Colonel J. C. Stevens to Bangor to superintend their erection. In the spring, with muddy streets, citizens were very unwilling to admit troops into their houses at any price. Besides, with troops scattered through the city there could be no camp police sufficient to prevent those with intemperate habits from visiting places where temptation would be irresistible. The moral effect upon the community would be lamented by all. Also, the principle expense attending the erection of these huts had been the cost of the

---

30 J Goodwin to Fairfield, April 8, 1839, JFPC 1458 4/7 MHS; Francis T. Wheeler to Hodsdon, April 9, 1839, OHPMHS.
31 Fairfield to Hodsdon, April 10, 1839, JFPC 1458 4/7 MHS.

boards; they have not been cut or broken much, and but few nails had been used; they would sell for two thirds or more of their original cost.[32]

Adjutant Thompson stated that the Kennebec Division would not occupy any quarters that Hodsdon had prepared; he would not, however, interfere with General Hodsdon's plans, but would not pay for his buildings without consulting the Governor.[33]

On April 12th, the *Bangor Whig and Courier* reported:

> Tuesday evening, the Hancock Guards, a rifle Company under command of Captain Wing, arrived. This is a fine company, from Castine and Blue Hill. They were furnished for the campaign with Hall's Patent Rifles. On Wednesday evening, about six o'clock, the Bangor Independent Volunteers marched into the city under the command of Lieutenant Dunning. The Company numbered about fifty, principally young men, who are known as among the most respectable and enterprising of the city. We were rejoiced to perceive so much interest and spirit manifested at their return home. They marched with a firm and elastic step to the tune of *Home Sweet Home*!
>
> The appearance and bearing of these Companies do honor to the Militia of the State, and to their commander, General Isaac Hodsdon. They have discipline and skill almost equal to the regular troops, and perform the duties of the soldier in a manner deserving great praise. Let those who have been induced to speak lightly of the Militia System view these men and ask themselves where else they would look for defence of our country against foreign aggression; and who are the men who deserve sympathy and respect if not those

---

32 Thompson to Fairfield, April 12, 1839; Hodsdon to Fairfield, April 12, 1839, JFPC 145B 4/7 MHS.
33 Thompson to Fairfield, April 12, 1839, JFPC 145B, 4/7.

who so willingly have borne the hardships and privations of a winter campaign. ... They will rendezvous at the temporary barracks on Thomas Hill. ... We think General Hodsdon deserves much praise for his forethought in this matter. We all recollect the inconvenience of quartering six hundred men under General Bachelder's command, in the midst of the city. Besides, these soldiers deserve better treatment after their long march through the mud, than to be crowded in large companies of fifty or sixty men, into a room or two, fifteen by eighteen, at this season of the year. We suppose they will be reviewed here by General Hodsdon, and our citizens gratified by a display of their military discipline.[34]

It can be deduced from the *Bangor Whig and Courier's* report, that Abner Thompson had been partially correct when he told Fairfield that handling of the troops in Bangor was being made a political question, and that "the Whigs had taken up General Hodsdon, and supported him in all his wild rehearsal."[35]

Militia Units Are Inspected, Mustered and Discharged

Adjutant General Thompson issued orders that the detachment of troops from the 2nd Division, in active service under command of Brigadier General George W. Bachelder, would, on arrival in the City of Bangor, occupy such quarters as may be furnished by Assistant Quarter Master George W. Stanley. The "A" Company of Artillery, under Lieutenant Bates, and the Company of Infantry under Captain Crane, would be mustered on Saturday, the

---
34 *Piscataquis County Historical Society*, loc. cit., Volume I.
35 Thompson to Fairfield, April 17th, Ephriam Moulton came to Hodsdon's defense in Moulton to Fairfield, Apr 17, '39, JFPC I 45B 4/7 MHS.

13th. They would be paid by companies and then marched to Augusta to be discharged.[36]

Major General Hodsdon, from Head Quarters of State Troops, Bangor, April 16, 1839, announced that men of the 3rd Division would be inspected and mustered by companies for discharge on such days as suited the Acting Paymaster. The company of Cavalry, under the command of Captain Smart, would be inspected, mustered and discharged on Tuesday, the 16th day of April.[37]

Adjutant General Thompson, unhappy with General Hodsdon, was also having angry confrontations with the State Treasurer about funds. Rufus McIntire advised Fairfield that probably an advisory letter from him would help. He also told the Governor that passengers in the *Great Western*, on their way to the Provinces, mentioned a rumor that the English ministry had resigned; that it might change affairs in the boundary dispute.[38]

J. C. Haynes, Esq., presented a Bangor Democrat's evaluation of the political maelstrom:

> There is some excitement here in relation to General Hodsdon's conduct. The Whigs have adopted the man as one of the family; he appears to be an especial favorite. There can be no question of the impropriety of his acts, but still his Whig friends sustain him in every movement, and justify him in every step he has taken.
>
> ... General Hodsdon had a display yesterday (April 19th), paraded in our muddy streets, and broke some seventy five dollars worth of glass by firing. He performed duty himself, intermediately from a corporal to a general. He has not the slightest self control, and is superannuated.[39]

---

[36] General Orders Nos 32 and 33, April 12, 1839, AWKJ.
[37] General Order No. 34, April 15, 1839, AWKJ.
[38] Goodwin to Fairfield, April 19, 1839; Goodwin to Thompson, April 18, 1839, Thompson to Fairfield, April 18, 1839, McIntire to Fairfield, April 18, 1839, JFPC 145, 4/7 and 4/8 MHS.
[39] J. C. Haynes to Fairfield, April 20, 1839, JFPC 145B 4/8, MHS.

Hayne's opinion notwithstanding, Major General Isaac Hodsdon addressed his troops, with the exception of the few still remaining at Fort Fairfield, on April 20, 1839, exactly as he had planned:

> The Governor of this State, in execution of the important trust reposed in him, ... deemed it his duty to call on you to vindicate the honor of the State, and to wipe from its escutcheon the foul stains that a protracted diplomacy of more than fifty five years has rendered almost indelible. This call was made upon you under circumstances most unpropitious. In the dead of winter, in a high northern latitude, you were called from your businesses, your homes, and all the ties of social friendship and the endearments of your domestic firesides; to relinquish the character of citizens and assume that of soldiers. ... You have endured fatiguing marches, exposed to the inclemencies of the season and the very worst travelling; you have suffered much from want of suitable quarters; ... you have obeyed the orders and instructions with great alacrity; and you are now being discharged from the public service, to return to your friends and the enjoyments of domestic society. Your Commander derives great pleasure from the reflection that all the Officers and soldiers which he has had the honor to command have discharged their important duty to his entire satisfaction. It has been his constant endeavour to obey the orders and instructions of the Commander-in-Chief, and having done this, whatever consequences may be the result from the campaign, no dishonor can be charged upon the Troops. You are not chargeable with any neglect of duty, nor with any diplomatic compromise which may have rendered your services less important to the State than at first anticipated.
>
> Your patient endurance of fatigue, your vigilance as sentinels, and your undeviating urbanity to your

Commanding General is to him a rich reward for the sleepless nights devoted to your comfort and instruction; and if anything can enhance the value of this reward, it is the knowledge he has of your gentlemanly and moral deportment towards each other, and towards all the good citizens of the country through which you have marched, and your respect for their rights and feelings. To the Officers of the detachment collectively, the Commanding General tenders his grateful acknowledgements for their aid in executing the orders of the Commander-in-Chief, and his confidence in their devotedness to duty.

To Brigadier General George W. Bachelder, commanding the Troops of the Second Division, he tenders a high respect for the knowledge he has evinced of his duty, and the manner in which he has performed it, and through him the Major General begs leave to present the officers of the Second Division his confidence in their officer-like behavior and his esteem for them as military officers and private gentlemen.

Officers and Soldiers, you are about to retire from the public service to your ordinary pursuits and the various avocations of private life. *If you return with your brows unadorned with wreaths of victory, it is not because you were unwilling to earn them* if the exigencies of the State and the orders of the Commanding General had required this at your hands. You have discharged your duty.

In bidding adieu to the Officers and Soldiers with whom he has been associated, the Commanding General tenders to them, collectively and individually, his best wishes for their temporal and eternal felicity, and that they may again meet their families and friends in the perfect enjoyment of everything that can conduce to their mutual happiness.[40]

---

40 OHPMHS.

CHAPTER XI

WAITING FOR A TREATY

Return of the Bangor Rifles

After the withdrawal of all Militia except the two units stationed at Fort Fairfield and at the Presque Isle of the Aroostook, the supervision of the Disputed Territory devolved upon Land Agent Rufus McIntire at Bangor and his Assistants, Colonel Charles Jarvis, in charge of road construction projects in Aroostook County, Captain Alvin Nye, in command of Volunteers on Fish River, and Captain William P. Parrott, in charge of the Aroostook Boom and the building of two blockhouses. Jacob Johnson was master workman on the blockhouses, assisted by Isaac Sanborn and John Nottage. Their work was so highly rated that Parrott requested of McIntire that they also build the bridges between Fort Fairfield and Houlton. When the boom men finished their work, on April 6th some left for home, but by then enough men had signed up to increase the Volunteer Corps to eighty-one.

William Parrott's headquarters was moved from Mr. Dorsey's house to the space in the Fort vacated by General Hodsdon and his staff. On the 12th of April, when the river was nearly clear of ice below the piers, the boom irons arrived and some Volunteers finished ironing the Boom. Others made charcoal for the blacksmith and finished the cellar of the blockhouse at the Boom. Six men went to the ridge to make maple sugar. Four Redcoats from the Tobique Settlement visited the Fort on the 13th. Parrott discovered that trespassers were making preparations for driving timber on River de Chute, but he could not spare the men to guard timber, so four or five hundred tons were stolen. Work continued on the guard house at the Boom and on the blockhouse. On the 18th, in the rain, ice started to move above the Boom. Four men on one of the piers of the Boom were in great danger for some time, but escaped injury. About twenty tons of timber escaped from the Boom. The next day, a small mass of ice came down river and about eighty to one hundred tons of timber ran out with it. Then the weather cleared, the crew repaired the Boom and were hanging it, when the guardhouse caught fire. The loss of the Militia stores was about $3,500.[1]

After the fire, from April 23rd to April 30th, the Bangor Rifles guarded timber cut under permits when it arrived at the Boom. New Volunteers from Bangor began to arrive on the 2nd of May, and for the next two months the Land Agent's force of one hundred and seventy-one men performed many duties including building the blockhouses.

On May 2, 1839, the long awaited announcement came from the Land Agent: Captain James Clark's company of Light Infantry and the Bangor Rifle Corps were relieved of the charge of guarding the public property on the Aroostook Territory.[2] In anticipation of that order, on the previous day, the Bangor Rifle Corps had taken up the line of march at four P M. Their first encampment was at Johnson's Portage, eight miles below Fort Fairfield. The next day, after a fourteen-mile march, they were at Smith's camp. On May 3rd, they had their dinner at the Presque Isle of the St. John, and arrived at Pond's Tavern

---

1 DLWP, RAGABT 1839; RLAWP 1839.
2 RLAWP 1839.

at three P M. On the 4th, it took them four hours to march from Pond's to Houlton. After a stopover, on May 6th, with the baggage and wagons, they marched 25 miles and arrived at Mattawamkeag Forks at 6:00 PM. They reached Mattawamkeag Point on May 7th, after eleven and a half hours of forced marching, 29 miles. To Passadumkeag it was a twelve-hour march. On the 9th they reached Upper Stillwater (Orono), having marched from four o'clock in the morning until four thirty in the afternoon.

On May 10th they left Upper Stillwater at 9:00 AM, and arrived at Bangor at 3:00 P M. They were received, after so long an absence, "in a manner truly gratifying to their feelings and worthy of the citizens of Bangor." They were welcomed home by an escort under command of Captain Charles G. Bryant, with Lieutenant Pitcher second in command. After marching into the city and saluting General Hodsdon and Captain Mills, and having partaken of the liberality of the Major General at the Bangor House, they took up quarters at a tavern on Main St. They were inspected, mustered and discharged on the 11th day of May, by Lieutenant Colonel Joseph C. Stevens, Division Inspector, 3rd Division.[3]

The militia received the same pay and allowances as the army of the United States, with an addition to the non-commissioned officers and privates of two and a half dollars to their monthly pay, agreeable to the Resolve of March 25th. Military expenses incurred by the State, for the protection of her territory would be reimbursed by the General Government. A great effort had been made to preserve the health of the troops; and although sickness in various forms prevailed to a limited extent in each of the detachments, and a few deaths occurred, yet it was believed there was less disease and suffering than is usual with the same number of persons

---

3 BRCR; General Order No. 58, May 10th, 1839.

at that time in the year, employed in the ordinary occupations of civil life.[4]

Trespassing on the Disputed Territory Continues

On May 2nd, upon the departure of the Militia, Deputy Land Agent Parrott issued the following warning:

No person, either in a boat or on the land, is to be permitted to come within ten rods on either side or end of the Boom. All persons are to be challenged and examined who come after dark, and if any suspicious circumstances are seen, they are to be detained and reported immediately to the officer of the day. Any attempts at violent assault upon the Boom or timber in the Boom, by men armed in any manner whatever, with probable intent to cut the Boom, is to be repelled by force, and any approach of a body of men within the limits above mentioned, who do not desist from further progress when hailed, will be prevented from going to the Boom by force, and fired upon if they cannot be stopped otherwise.[5]

Shortly after Parrott posted this notice, he was forced to deal with what became known as the Molasses Riot. This mutiny, the result of an alarming dissatisfaction among the Volunteers at Fort Fairfield, nearly destroyed Parrott's command. The alleged cause was that they had no molasses, and that they would have it. Ten of the ring-leaders were discharged as unfit and unfaithful men. Disciplinary problems continued to plague Parrott; references were made, in his Log, to men discharged for drunkenness, laziness and lack of discipline.[6]

---

[4] Resolves of March 21, 1839 and March 25, 1839; RAGABT.
[5] DLWP.
[6] RLAWP 1839, DLWP.

The Boom continued to be under armed guard night and day, and construction continued on the defenses. Captain Elisha Towle of the Volunteers, moved the boom guards into quarters in the new guardhouse, and potatoes were planted nearby. It became Parrott's duty to send Captain Joseph Maddock, with a force, to River De Chute, to prevent the timber stolen the past season from being driven out. Also, in July, a group under Captain Towle was sent to seize and sell nine thousand tons of timber illegally cut on public lands on the Little Madawaska.[7]

Early in the fall of 1839, Maine Land Agent Rufus McIntire complained to Governor Fairfield that George Coffin, Land Agent for Massachusetts, was granting permits to New Brunswick citizens and others to cut timber on lands lying on both sides of the Aroostook River. If this practice were continued, McIntire believed, it would be impossible to prevent trespass on public lands, as these permits could be used as a cover for depredation. Fairfield authorized that "the utmost rightful power be exerted to counteract these plans." By September, many persons were making preparations for trespass on territory on or near the St. John and the Aroostook. Parrott took action to allow no one whom he had reason to believe intended trespassing, whether with teams or provisions for lumbering, to pass Fort Fairfield. He published a notice to that effect.[8]

The Attack on Fort Fairfield

Vigorous enforcement of anti-trespassing measures brought about the long-feared attack by angry lumbermen on Fort Fairfield. It came on September 8, 1839,

---

[7] DLWP.
[8] Governor Fairfield's address to the Legislature, January 3, 1840, *Acts and Resolves of the State of Maine* Vol. IV, hereinafter referred to as AROSM IV, 228-242; McIntire to Fairfield, August 30, 1839 and August 31, 1839, JFPC145B, MHS; Parrott to McIntire, September 5, 1839, DLWP.

at 3:00 in the morning. About forty men from New Brunswick, with government arms, were discovered by the sentinel. He fired upon them immediately, without challenging, and they took to their heels, leaving behind some hats, powder, muskets and bayonets.[9]

Many of the men in the attack force had come up from Woodstock and assembled at Tibbetts' on the Tobique River, under the leadership of Captain McKenzie and Lieutenant Colonel Dwyer.[10] Some came from fifty or sixty miles away. It was said that while three hundred had been enrolled for the enterprise, one hundred had actually come and some of these were probably left in reserve at the Line. James Maclauchlan investigated what he termed a "most disgraceful affair." He had been at the Grand Falls with the Boundary Commissioners. Rumors had come to him that Fort Fairfield had been burnt by a party of men from Tobique Settlement. He considered the reports "altogether fabulous," but soon discovered something *had* been attempted. He reported to Parrott that a number of "reckless persons" had broken open a depot of arms at Tobique; in order to prevent the possibility of any further annoyance to the armed *Posse*, he had removed the arms to Grand Falls.[11]

---

[9] DLWP; Parrott to McIntire, September 9, 1839; Parrott to McIntire, September 9, 1839, JFPC 145B MHS.

[10] Ibid. Parrott sent a list of suspects to McIntire: Names of persons said to have been engaged in the invasion of this State, Sept 8, 1839. John Vanning, Woodstock; Mick Sullivan and George Wright, River de Chute; James Lloyd, Munquat; Abraham Finnemore; John Craven and John Nevers, Woodstock; Jonathan P. Taylor and Benjamin Beveridge, Tobique; ___McFee, Scotch Corner; Peter (Fee?), (Monquart?), Edward (Susey?); (J S ?) Dwyer, Woodstock; Charles and James Wright, River de Chute; Alex Bates, River de Chute; Charles Hartgrove, Andover; and PendersonBeardsley, Woodstock.

[11] McIntire to Fairfield, November 18, 1839, JFPC 145B MHS; Tibbetts to Maclauchlan, September 8, 1839, Maclauchlan to Harvey, September 9, 1839; Maclauchlan to Parrott, September 9th, 1839, LBGHPANB

Sketch of Fort Kent, December, 1842

The Original Fort Jarvis-Fort Kent Block House

Sketch of the Larger of the two Blockhouses at Fort Fairfield

The Reproduction of the Smaller of Two Blockhouses at Fort Fairfield

In Parrott's opinion, the persons most deeply engaged in the attack on the Fort were men who had largely been engaged in trespassing on the public lands. He cited as examples, Benjamin Beverage of Tobique, J. P. Taylor of Tobique, and John Venning of Woodstock. Parrot believed that as Fort Fairfield was the only obstacle in the way of trespassing upon the waters of the Aroostook and vicinity, their object had been to destroy it and to plunder the Public Lands. Tibbetts of Tobique was an abettor, he felt; and beyond doubt had supplied the arms, directly or indirectly. He was pleased that Provincial authorities had taken early and efficient measures in this matter, and he had no fear that another attempt would be made from that quarter.[12]

The Volunteer Corps had been gradually reduced; on the tenth day of July, their number was forty-seven. This remained the average number until the fifteenth of November. The blockhouse they had built, located within a musket shot of the Boom, was twenty feet square on the lower story and twenty-six on the upper story. The walls of the lower story were twenty-two inches thick and had loop holes all around. The upper part of the walls were built of timber nine inches thick. This blockhouse was large enough to quarter sixty men. Nearby was a small cook house and below on the riverbank was another building, thirty by twenty feet for storing boat rigging and tools used at the Boom. In the vicinity of this block house, the ground had been cleared of trees, and about twenty acres had been planted with oats and potatoes.

They had built the second blockhouse at a distance of one hundred and thirty rods in a southeasterly direction, upon a hill. This one was larger than the one at the Boom, being six-sided, and twenty feet on a side on the lower story and twenty-six feet on a side in the upper story. It was pierced with loopholes in each story and in the roof, and was surrounded by one hundred and eighty

---
12 DLWP.

yards of stockade that was built of timber and filled in with earth. Also, within this enclosure was a barracks building and cook house. This fort could easily accommodate three hundred and fifty men. The hill upon which this block house was situated, had been cleared, and a large part of the land was planted with a sufficient quantity of oats, potatoes and barley to supply the men to be stationed there during the next winter. Both block houses had good cellars for storage of provisions. After July, a barn, thirty by forty feet, was built and the road that ran between the two block houses to the beginning of the Houlton Road was bridged and turnpiked.[13]

The Fish River Expedition, Soldier Pond and Fort Jarvis

New Brunswick's Lieutenant Governor was strong in his praise of Winfield Scott's abilities to quell border problems. He was no less strong in his disapproval of Colonel Maclauchlan's failure to keep Americans out of the lands north of the Aroostook River. He sent a stern reprimand to the Warden of the Disputed Territory on April 13, 1839:

> Dear Maclauchlan, I am rather surprised at not hearing direct from you upon the subject of any proceedings by the armed *posse* of the State of Maine on the Fish River, if there be any truth in it. ... You would appear to have no one to watch over the territory or to convey information of anything that may be proceeding in your absence. If you do not show yourself alert and vigilant I cannot possibly retain you in that or any other office. The eyes of far more than the Province are upon you, and if proper and efficient arrangements be not made for the seizure of all timber cut upon the St. John and its tributaries, the responsibility must

---
13 RLAWP 1839.

rest with you. I have repeatedly authorized you to employ assistance to any extent.
I am of the opinion that any interference on the part of Maine, with the Valley of the Upper St. John, is contrary to the meaning of the late agreement; they should confine themselves wholly to the Valley of the Aroostook. On the other hand, it is encumbent on me, through you, to do all that may be in my power to seize the timber unlawfully cut on the Upper St. John River, and to protect the Valley from further depredations. I cannot give you more explicit instructions as the Warden. I hope you will fulfill them, but it will require all your energy. The road building business you had better commit to some Agent or deputy in whom you can confide after making your contracts.[14]

In the face of this reprimand, Maclauchlan, on the 20th of April, submitted his resignation. Then Harvey's private secretary, Samuel Tryon, conveyed Harvey's peremptory command that he continue in his post until his Excellency saw fit to relieve him. He must report what amount of assistance he had engaged, and also superintend the improvement of communication with Canada.[15]

The proceedings of the Maine Land Agent's Volunteers on the Fish River, that had so alarmed Harvey, had been brought about by the movements of Captain Alvin Nye. When the Maine Legislature passed the Resolve of February 24,1839, that the Land Agent be required to employ a sufficient force to arrest, detain and imprison all persons found trespassing on the territory of Maine as bounded and established by the Treaty of 1783, it had done so in response to reports of widespread depredations, especially in the Fish River area.

It will be recalled that one of the first acts of Provisional Land Agent Jarvis, when he had first arrived

---
14 Harvey to Maclauchlan, April 13, 1839, LBGHPANB.
15 Tryon to Maclauchlan, April 26, 1839, LBGHPANB.

on the Disputed Territory, in February, 1839, had been to send Alvin Nye with George Buckmore and a party of twenty-five men, up the Little Machias to Fish River to investigate and arrest trespassers. In March, with his *posse* reduced to about sixty men, Jarvis still could not relax his vigil; he feared that the threat of encroachment was very real. McIntire's men had been reconnoitering the woods between Fort Fairfield and the St. John and Madawaska Settlement and reporting movements of the Provincial and Regular British forces and that a large number of axes[16] had been sent up river. It had been rumored that a movement of the Regulars might be made through the woods from Madawaska, to some point on the Aroostook, above or possibly through the Fish River to the Machias River, while the New Brunswick Militia might move directly to the Aroostook River posts.[17]

A suggestion had been made from Head Quarters at Augusta to Major General Hodsdon that should he deem it proper to establish a post on the St. John, it should be effected by way of the Fish River.[18] Hodsdon had not had time to be involved in this project, but Jarvis had known of Fairfield's interest and had pursued that course by placing Nye in charge of the Fish River expedition. His orders had been:

> Confluence of the Aroostook and St. Croix, No. 10,
> March 27, 1839
>
> Mr. Alvin Nye, Assistant Provisional Land Agent:
> Sir: You will proceed, with the volunteers under your direction, to Fish River with the least possible delay. You will then send back your teams. Your first object will be to determine on the best location for a boom to effectually stop the passage of the timber

---

16 meaning axe-men, expert choppers.
17 Jarvis to Hodsdon, March 30, '39, OHPMHS; McIntire to Fairfield, March 16, '39; McIntire to Fairfield, March 11, '39, JFPC145B 4/3 MHS.
18 Jarvis to Hodsdon, March 31, 1839, JFPC145B.

down the river. Having determined on the location, you will prepare good accommodations for the men, so as to make them comfortable. You will so calculate your camp, as that it may be, by building upon it, used as a blockhouse for defense of the boom, and secure you effectually against the attack of a mob. You will then construct the boom in the best manner you can, with the means at your command.[19]

Should you be threatened by an English Government force, exercise your own discretion. Situated on the Territory under the jurisdiction of Maine, the honor of your State will be, in a manner, entrusted with your keeping. You are not rashly to sacrifice the lives of brave men in hopeless defense; neither are you to yield your ground if there is a probability of making effectual resistance. [With] a good blockhouse, with the men under your direction, you can defend against a force of one hundred and fifty of the best troops in the British service, unless furnished with Artillery. Against a force so provided, no blockhouse within your means to erect would be defensible. If threatened by such a force, you must make the best terms you can, and if no better can be obtained, surrender at discretion, as prisoners of war. Your country will then take cognizance of your situation and govern itself accordingly.

In no event, and on no pretense, will you cross the River St. John to the northward. Determined to maintain her jurisdictional limits, Maine, pending the negotiation between the United States and Great Britain, will not excuse any officers of hers, either civil or military, in violating the jurisdictional limits of New Brunswick. Your obedient servant,
Charles Jarvis, Provisional Land Agent[20]

---

19 It has been construed that this was a camp and a boom at what is now known as Soldier Pond, built by Nye and Bachelder's "soldiers."
20 Jarvis to Nye, March 27, 1839, JFPC I 45B 4/4 MHS.

A week later Jarvis instructed Nye:

> After executing the work designated, you will select the best tract of land adjacent to your post, and employ the men in making a large clearing, the larger the better. This cleared off and sowed to grass seed, the ensuing fall will furnish the State with abundance of forage, for the purposes of the road builders, without additional costs.
> Immediately on your arrival at Fish River, you will send a trusty man to John Baker, and request him to hire two of the Madawaska Frenchmen who can be depended upon and are acquainted with the making of sugar, and to send to you some iron kettles or anything else you may want for that purpose. You will also obtain from him fifty to one hundred bushels of potatoes and one pound of Lapland or English turnip seed; you will save the seed ends of the potatoes, which you will use for planting, and you will have them into the ground as soon as possible, also some of the turnip seeds. Manage the forces under your command, the same as if they were in your employ for commencing a large farm, having their arms at hand, to resist any attack. Manage, in a word, as our fathers did on the first settlement of this country, when they had to labor for their bread, with their guns by their sides, to resist their savage foe. I conclude by saying that Maine expects every son to do his duty, and that she will never forget those who discharge it manfully.[21]

As a result of these orders, Nye and his Volunteers proceeded to the Fish River and erected a fortification and a boom about four miles down Fish River from Eagle Lake, presumably at a place presently known as Soldier Pond. Information concerning this works is given by Jarvis, who reported that during the fall of 1839, while

---

21 Jarvis to Nye, April 3, 1839, JFPC 145B 4/6 MHS.

on an inspection tour of road building in that area, he travelled from the Aroostook River up the Little Machias River to the portage between that River and Portage Lake. Following the eastern Bay of Portage Lake, he entered and descended the thoroughfare that connects it to the second Fish River Lake, and passing through Long Lake (St. Froid Lake),[22] he descended a second thoroughfare into Eagle Lake. Proceeding by the western bend, ten miles, he came to Fish river, and following Fish River four miles, arrived at the *upper block house* and boom erected by Alvin Nye, in April last. Leaving the blockhouse and boom, he descended Fish River four miles, and came to the Grand Falls (of the Fish River.) By these falls he followed a portage, and again took the river. He descended the river one and a half miles, and arrived at its mouth, where it enters the St. John at a right angle.[23]

On April 23rd, Nye reported to Jarvis on his move to *a lower blockhouse and boom* at the confluence of the Fish River and the St. John River:

> Fort Jarvis, Fish River
> April 23, 1839
>
> Charles Jarvis, Esquire
> Dear Sir: I take this opportunity to inform you of my doings which is according to order. We arrived here after a hard siege. We then went to work on the blockhouse and boom. The boom is completed. It is four hundred feet long and is in a good place. The only chance there is from the lake to the mouth of the river is a small Isle with about nine acres of land in it, and

---

22 This "Long Lake" is not to be confused with the Long Lake in T17 R4 and T18 R4, W.E.L.S. This lake, located in T15, R7, Winterville, is shown on modern maps as St. Froid Lake, but it was designated on older maps as Long Lake. See the map titled *Plan of the North Eastern Part of the State of Maine*, 1858, which accompanied A Circular from the Land Office, *Description of the Public Lands of Maine, 1858*, Noah Barker, Land Agent, printed at Bangor by Bartlett & Burr.
23 RLACJ, 1839.

would be a good chance for a boom to stop the timber that comes down the St. John. The English have surveyed the ground on the opposite bank and say they shall build barracks there.

I have been down to Mr. Baker's, but did not see him as he was gone away in the woods. I have two boats there now, after potatoes, which will be there tonight. It is fourteen miles from Fort Jarvis,[24] to Baker's. I have hired two Frenchmen to build us some canoes. I have six built already, found ten in the woods, and we have been finishing them off so that we have quite a fleet. The men are all well and hearty and satisfied with their situation, which is very pleasant. We shall move into the block house tomorrow. It is very strong built; it is principally built of hewn timber twenty inches thick, and on a high point of land. We can reach both ends of the boom with a musket, from the house. The French have been here and they are glad that we Americans are going to have their land. They are all friendly. ...Your obedient servant, Alvin Nye, A. L. Agt.[25]

When Alvin Nye moved down to Fort Jarvis, he began to enforce Maine's jurisdiction of the lands west of the Madawaska Settlement and south of the St. John River. He succeeded in stopping between six and eight hundred tons of timber, and all the logs on Fish River, by means of a slight temporary boom stretched across the

---

[24] The belief that "Fort Jarvis" was located at the mouth of Fish River, is substantiated by the heading of the letter from Nye to Maclauchlan, May 10, 1839, which read: Fort Jarvis, St. Francis Settlement, South Side of the St. John River; references in Williams to Fairfield, July 30, 1841, Williams to Fairfield, August 22, 1841, JFPC 145-86 MHS. Fort Jarvis is definitely located on: *Sketch of the Disputed Territory, showing the Military Posts occupied by the British and Americans in 1840*, which see. Fort Jarvis would eventually be renamed Fort Kent. See Chapter XII.

[25] DLWP

channel between the island and the southern mainland.[26] Then an occasion arose where Nye, with armed men, forced one of Maclauchlan's log driving crews out of the Disputed Territory.

More than two weeks had passed since Maclauchlan, in response to orders from Tryon on April 28th, had resumed his duty as Warden. He received at Allagash from Alvin Nye, at Fort Jarvis, St. Francis Settlement, *South Side of the St. John River*, a letter dated May 10th. Nye had written that he had received information that Maclauchlan had ascended the St. John River with a party of men with the intention of driving timber and logs from within the jurisdiction of the State of Maine into the Province of New Brunswick. Nye explained that he had been under the disagreeable necessity of informing Maclauchlan that such an act would be in violation of the right of the State; he had requested him to desist, as his instructions were to not permit timber to be moved from the Territory.[27]

Maclauchlan sent to Fredericton for advice. Deputy Surveyor of Crown Lands William J. Burton, a seizing officer, had just left the Warden at (Little) Black River, (a tributary of the St. John entering that river from the north, some distance west of the Allagash River) and was going down the St. John to make arrangements for collecting and guarding timber below Grand Falls. About eight miles below the Black River, he had met a party of about thirty men, eighteen of whom were armed with muskets and rifles with fixed bayonets. Burton had found the party to be Americans under command of Captain Nye. John Baker was with them. Nye was on his way to see Maclauchlan, whom he had warned that "he thought the timber had better remain where it was." Maclauchlan was

---

26 RLACJ1839
27 Alvin Nye to Maclauchlan, May 10, 1839, *Papers of John Fairfield*, mss.19254, Library of Congress, (from microfilm at Dyer Library, Saco), hereinafter referred to as PJFDL.

about one and a half miles up the Allagash, marking timber. Burton hurried up river to warn the Warden of Nye's approach.[28]

That same day, Elias Yerxa, of Fredericton, who had been hired by Maclauchlan to drive out timber cut on the banks of the St. John and its tributaries, was sent with a party of twenty men, in canoes, down the river to Baker's Brow,[29] near the St. Francis, to heave some timber into the River. About half a mile below the Allagash, Yerxa met Nye's armed party coming up river, but proceeded to Baker's Brow and camped. While supper was in preparation, Captain Nye arrived, armed with a pistol and dagger and backed up by twelve men with muskets and fixed bayonets. He ordered Yerxa and his men to be off down the River in their canoes. He did not allow them to finish their supper. His men formed a line from the door to the River, and forced them, at bayonet point, into their canoes. Then Nye and party followed them down river.[30]

On May 14th, Lieutenant Governor Harvey related this latest attempt by Maine to enforce her jurisdiction of the lands west of the Line of the Treaty of 1783 to Winfield Scott:

My Dear General Scott,
You will, I think, be hurt and distressed [by Nye's actions.] ... I instantly sent away the Troops by which the Madawaska Settlement was occupied. If these proceedings are persisted in I fear I shall have to replace them, as Mr. Baker's residence, visited by an armed party from the Fish River, is actually within what is called the "Upper Settlement of Madawaska." I have, however, instructed Mr. Maclauchlan to withdraw into

---

28 Maclauchlan to Tryon, May 10, 1839; Document A, Maclauchlan to Tryon, May 11,'39; Dep. of William James Burton, May 11,'39, PJFDL.
29 A "brow" is a high bank from which collected logs are rolled into a river preparatory to a "log drive". Baker's Brow belonged to John Baker, and apparently the Warden was seizing his logs.
30 Deposition of Elias Yerxa, May 11, 1839, PJFDL.

the settlement rather than risk collision. ... My construction of the spirit of the Agreement was that the armed *posse* of the State of Maine would confine its presence to the Valley of the Restook, [Aroostook] leaving that of the St. John River undisturbed.[31]

Whether Maclauchlan received Harvey's instructions or not, before the 15th of May he had led "a gang of trespassers" in an attack on Fort Jarvis, but had been repelled by Nye's men. Then he set off down river to procure reinforcements. John Baker went to Fort Fairfield on the night of May 15th, to get reinforcements for Nye. Captain Nymphas Turner refused to go, but Captain Thomas Bartlett readily volunteered and with twenty-five men, started early on May 17th. Bartlett carried a letter from Captain Parrott to Nye, stating that with regard to Baker's suggestion that another post be built on or near the St. John, that would be left to Nye's discretion.[32]

Nye followed through with Baker's suggestion and took possession of the Island at the entrance of Fish River, at its intersection with the St. John. A camp was erected and two sentinels with fixed bayonets were constantly on guard, one at each end of the island. When Captain John Sutton, from New Brunswick, visited Fort Jarvis, Nye told him that he was empowered to protect and detain the timber and logs made on all parts of the Disputed Territory. Sutton asked him whether, in case he should send up a New Brunswick civil officer to execute a writ, Nye would interfere. Nye told him that no Provincial civil officer had any right to execute a writ there, and that any of the settlers claiming his protection as a citizen of Maine, would be protected by him.[33]

---

31 Harvey to Scott, May 14, 1839, LBGHPANB.
32 RLAWP 1839; Parrott to Nye, May 16, 1839, DLWP.
33 Maclauchlan to Tryon, May 26, 1839; John Sutton to Maclauchlan, May 27, 1839, to JFPC 145B 5/1.

The upshot of this confrontation was a conference that took place at the Bangor House at Bangor on June 6th, 1839. Thomas Baillie, Commissioner of Crown Lands for the Province of New Brunswick and Rufus McIntire discussed Nye's act of returning Yerxa and his party back down the St. John River, and their differences in opinions about jurisdiction. Baillie exhibited certain documents [34] and remarked that it appeared that a breach of the agreement between Sir John Harvey and Governor Fairfield had been committed by Mr. Nye and his party. McIntyre replied that he believed some difference of opinion existed between the two governments respecting what constituted the Madawaska Settlement, the Americans supposing that only the north Bank of the St John was properly so called. Baillie observed that Great Britain considered that all her subjects on the St. John River, both on the Right and Left Banks above the Great Falls constituted the Madawaska Settlements. McIntire then observed that Nye had received his instruction from Mr. Parrott, a Provisional Land Agent, during Mr. McIntire's absence, that Nye had exceeded his instructions, that Nye's party had been reduced in numbers, that he had been told to confine his duties to the Fish River and not to interfere with the St. John. However, the Fish River, not being a part of the Madawaska Settlement, would be held by an American Party until a settlement was reached. McIntire also told Baillie that he was then surveying and would commence bushing out a road from the Aroostook River to the Fish River. Baillie argued that this proceeding was an interference with British jurisdiction.[35]

    Charles Jarvis visited Fort Jarvis and noted that the island that Nye had taken possession of in May, might

---

[34] Document A, Tryon to Harvey and depositions, May 11th, 1839; Document B, Maclauchlan to Tryon, 26 May, 1839, and Document C, Sutton's Report, May 27, 1839. From Parrot to McIntire, June 18, 1839, it appears that Parrot was in Bangor and attended these consultations.
[35] Minutes: Conference between Baillie and McIntire, June 6, 1839, JFPC 145B 5/1 MHS.

be connected with the mainland on the south by a 300 foot boom. To sustain this boom, only one pier would be required. Another boom of about the same length, could be extended from that pier across the mouth of the Fish River. About eighty rods above the upper end of the island, the St. John River made a short turn to the north, which caused the currents to set upon the southern shore, although the main channel of the river was on the other side of the island. Jarvis conjectured that a guide boom extending from the upper point of the island towards the point made by the north bend of the river, not halfway across the main channel, and standing end-ways to the current, would direct timber into the southern channel without posing any obstructions to the navigation of the River on the north side of the island.

On the 27th of July, Thomas Bartlett, Jr. with three of Nye's men and about twenty Madawaska Frenchmen, moved on to the ground and commenced constructing booms. On August 14th, Colonel Jarvis replaced Nye with Assistant Land Agent Captain Stover Rines. When Rines assumed command at Fish River, he concluded not to begin on the piers for the boom until the river froze over; then it could be done more easily and cheaply. He rebuilt the blockhouse, making it more defensible and comfortable for quarters.[36]

On November 18, 1839, McIntire defended the construction of the boom on Fish River. He explained that it was a side boom; it embraced a portion of the St. John River, at or above the mouth of Fish River, and received not only the timber floating down the St. John, by having it conducted into the boom, but the timber from the Fish River as well, as there was no boom across the Fish River, nine miles above, at this time.[37]

---

36 RLACJ1839; Jarvis to McIntire, August 14, 1839, LBWP.
37 McIntire to Fairfield, November 18, 1839, JFPC145B MHS.

CHAPTER XII

CONTINUED FRICTION IN THE DISPUTED TERRITORY

Ever since the agreement to the *Memorandum*, in March, 1839, both British and Maine authorities had endeavored to enhance their claims to jurisdiction.

Our true policy is to proceed silently and quietly, strengthening ourselves on the Territory, and while the two countries were negotiating we should decide the question.

These confidential words, written by Charles Jarvis to John Fairfield, reveal a strategy to prevent the British from pushing back Maine's boundaries and to prepare for the eventuality that Britain and the United States might fail to arrive at a satisfactory settlement.[1]

For the general exercise of jurisdiction of Maine's territory according to the Treaty of 1783, intensive road and bridge construction in the areas south of the St. John River had taken place in 1839. These roads, necessary for year-round communications and to enable Land Agents to sustain themselves against trespassers and possible invasion, were opened by Land Agent's Volunteers and other hired laborers under the general supervision of Charles

---

1 Fairfield to Jarvis, January 7, 1840, JFPC 145 MHS.

Jarvis.[2] In 1840, Zebulon Ingersol, joint Land Agent for Maine and Massachusetts, contracted with Abner Coburn and Oliver Frost[3] to construct the Aroostook Road across No. 7 to the center of No. 8 Range 5 WELS, and finish a road in No. 6. By the end of 1840, under the supervision of Ira Fish, the Aroostook Road was finished to within twelve miles of No. 10, Masardis.

British Troops Are Stationed at Temiscouata

Governor Fairfield, at the beginning of 1840, announced to the Legislature that Maine territory had

---

[2] Charles Jarvis, *Report of the Land Agent*, 1839, hereinafter referred to as RLACJ1839. Roads opened under Jarvis' supervision in 1839: Houlton Road, from Fort Fairfield to Portland Academy Grant, 31 miles and 36 rods, passing through Letter D, Range 1, Letters G and F, Range 2, Deerfield Academy Grant, Mars Hill Township, Letter B, Range 1, and Bridgewater Academy Grant, to Houlton. Fish River Road, from the Aroostook River to the St. John River, 44 and 1/2 miles, passing through Nos 11 and 12, Range 5; Nos 12, 13, 14, and 15, in Range 6; and No. 16, Range 7, and the undivided lands north of the Norris Survey. The St. Croix Road, from the Houlton road, crossing the Presque Isle River at Fairbanks's on the south side of the Aroostook River, to the Aroostook Road, previously partially opened by Purrington, 23 miles, 96 rods, passing through Letter F and Letter G, Range 2; No. 12, Range 3; No. 12, Range 4; and No. 11, Range 5. Also, a road had been laid out from the mouth of the Presque Isle, 1 1/2 miles, to the Houlton Road at Fairbanks's, to be finished in 1840. Two and a half miles of road have also been made and a bridge built across the Meduxnekeag, on Letter A, and 12 miles of road from the Aroostook to the St. Croix Rivers, in part opened by Purrington. One hundred and fourteen miles of road had been opened in 1839, on the Territory and 17 bridges, averaging 113 feet in length, had been built.

[3] Abner Coburn would become Governor of Maine during the Civil War, in 1863. The son of Eleazer Coburn, he and his brother Philander, in 1845, formed a powerful lumbering firm. Coburn began surveying timber tracts of northern Maine in 1825. *Just Maine Folks*, Maine Writers Club, Lewiston Journal Printshop, 1924, 120-130. Oliver Frost of Standish was active in making surveys for the State of Maine.

actually been invaded; that two companies of British troops had been stationed at Temiscouata Lake. The British had built barracks on the Disputed Territory at two places: one at the outlet of the Temiscouata Lake and the other at the northwest side, where the road strikes off across the headwaters of the St. Francis and the highlands to the St. Lawrence. They had also improved the towpath on the Madawaska River, and made anew the road from Madawaska across the highlands. These facts were communicated to the President and action on the part of the General Government had been requested.[4]

Informant Mark Little wrote to the Governor on February 8, 1840:

... The movement at the mouth of the Madawaska River has been to engage a couple of houses for the reception of troops and the stationing a couple of men there, in charge. ... At the head of the Madawaska River they have built two large timber buildings capable of containing four hundred men, and a storehouse, and stationed a man there with a quantity of supplies. At the head of Temiscouata Lake they have built two timber buildings eighty feet long, thirty feet wide and two stories high, for barracks; one building for officers quarters and one for the Commissary Department, besides a number of smaller ones. Their buildings were completed last October. Stationed there last June was part of one company, a surgeon, commissary and bar-

---

4 Fairfield's address to Legislature, January 3, 1840, AROSM IV, 228-242; McIntire to Fairfield, Nov 18, 1839 JFPC 145B MHS. In the 1839 election, Fairfield, with 41,038 votes, had defeated former Governor Kent, who received 34,794 votes. In 1840 Fairfield's Governor's Council: Gowen Wilson, John Webb, Benjamin F. Eastman, Alpheus Lyon, Nathan C. Fletcher, John Burnham, and Micah J. Talbot. Philip C. Johnson was Secretary of State; Daniel Wilson was Treasurer, Abner B. Thompson was Adjutant General, Rufus McIntire, Land Agent, and Thomas Sawyer was Surveyor General. Stephen C. Foster was President of the Maine Senate and Hannibal Hamlin was Speaker of the Maine House.

racks master, with all necessary apparatus and a years supply of provisions for two hundred men. They were the first men ever stationed there, and their force has been increased to two companies. They have built four gunboats, capable of holding twenty five to thirty men each, for the navigation of the Lake. The authorities of New Brunswick have made a towpath[5] the whole length of the Madawaska. ... Their buildings are of permanent and durable character, bulletproof by actual experiment. The position at the head of the Lake is a commanding one. They have plans to surround their works by stockade and make it a strong military post.[6]

The Mudge-Featherstonhaugh Fluff

In March, 1839, a proposition had been made by the British to the Americans for establishing a joint Commission to explore and survey the Disputed Territory, but its limitations and conditions brought immediate rejection by President Van Buren. Then, in July, the Americans submitted a counter project. Pending this negotiation, Lord Palmerston, planning for a new diplomatic offensive, dispatched two surveyors, Richard Z. Mudge and G. W. Featherstonhaugh, who were to go over the Disputed Territory once again in search of suitable highlands.[7]

Sir John Harvey, well acquainted with the region, commented that the success of the survey might be "a

---

5 Wiggin, *History of Aroostook*, p 194, describes towpaths: The boats used were large flat bottomed scows with a cabin built upon the after end, upon the top of which the helmsman stood and steered the boat by means of a huge rudder. They were drawn up the river by two horses attatched by a long warp and guided by a rider on the back of the near horse.

6 PJFDL. In the opening paragraph of this letter, Little stated that he had formerly worked for the Maine Land Agent. On October 1, 1839 he had been at Fish River.

7 Fairfield's message to Maine Legislature, January 3, 1840; Classen, loc. cit., 70-71.

misfortune rather than an advantage." An irate Palmerston, commented, "the less Sir John Harvey occupies himself with the Boundary question the better, as his views and notions upon that question appear ... by no means calculated to advance British interests." Featherstonhaugh and Mudge mapped out "an uninterrupted line of Highlands and true axis of elevation" precisely along the line of the British claim.[8]

When President Van Buren received the report and maps made by Mudge and Featherstonhough, on June 27, 1840, he told the Senate:

> The British commissioners express an opinion that the true line of the Treaty of 1783 is not materially different from that so long contended for by Great Britain. The report is altogether *ex parte* in its character, and has not yet, as far as we are informed, been adopted by the British Government.[9]

The maps and survey presented by Featherstonhaugh and Mudge had been so obviously constructed to support the British claim that an irate Charles S. Daveis vehemently castigated it for "its impudence, its audacity, and its mendacity; of its sophistries and evasions, of its assumptions and its suppressions, of its profligate perversions and of its presumptuous and extravagant pretensions." The survey was such an embarassment to the British government, that it was not used in further boundary negotiations. Palmerston, was replaced by Lord Aberdeen in 1841.[10]

President Van Buren, expecting that the Mudge-Featherstonhaugh survey would be used by the British government in negotiation, determined that another Am-

---

8 Ibid.
9 MPP, 594.
10 Charles S Daveis, *Report of the Joint Select Committee of the Senate* March 30, 1841.

erican survey of the northeast boundary should be made.[11] An Act of Congress of 20th of July, 1840, authorized his appointment of James Renwick, James D. Graham and Captain A. Talcott as Commissioners. The work would continue until the middle of December, 1840 and their Report would be submitted on January 6, 1841.

British Troops Are Stationed At Madawaska

Coincidental with the American survey, in August, 1840, the federal census was being taken in the Madawaska Settlements by Gorham Parks and in areas south of Madawaska by Thomas Bartlett Jr. Harvey, considering that this was Governor General, Lord Sydenham's responsibility, merely protested.[12]

No doubt prompted by Parks, John Baker, highly respected by Maine's Land Agents as an authority on the Disputed Territory, summarized his views concerning the boundary dispute:

Bakersville, September 15, 1840
Honorable Gorham Parks, United States Marshall
Sir: I would inform you that I have resided in the northern part of the United States for twenty four years, on what is improperly called the Disputed Territory, and have travelled over the whole frontier of Maine, and from the Connecticut [River] to Cape Rosier

---

11 MPP, 594.
12 Gorham Parks had been narrowly defeated in the election at the end of 1836; Parks, 33,879 votes and Kent 34,350 votes. Parks was a member of the U. S. House of Representatives from 1833-37. Brunelle, loc. cit., n. p.; Raymond, loc. cit., 364; Official United States Census Records, 1840. Lord Sydenham, formerly Charles Edward Poulette Thomson, was a liberal British statesman who was created Baron Sydenham of Kent, in England and of Toronto in Canada, and reappointed Governor General and Governor of the Province of Canada. Norah Story, *Oxford Companion to Canadian History and Literature*, 1967, Oxford University Press, New York. SEE Appendix I, for 1840 census.

to Gaspe, and in consequence of my situation have taken great interest in the boundary question. The policy of the British Government has always been procrastination, to get possession of the country, raise difficulty where then did none exist, to involve in diplomacy what was perfectly plain and simple, and get us to acknowledge that there were real difficulties existing in the Boundary Question. And the Provincials intentions were, in the meantime, to strip the state of its valuable timber, and I am sorry to say that they have been very successful in their attempts. I find that the American Government has not been in possession of all the circumstances relative to the country. They have given too much credit to the British statements, which have been very incorrect. The British Government, for fifteen years, has kept a special agent in the Territory to overawe the inhabitants and make such reports as they would wish. This agent has not protected the timber, as was expected, but has been active in keeping back the American authorities and turning the timber to the benefit of New Brunswick. At Tamiscouata Lake, where he had full control, he suffered large quantities of timber to be taken away last winter, and on the Restigouche, there has been twenty cargoes cut annually for many years, within the State. The British have no right to keep troops at the Tamiscouata Lake in consequence of former usages. There has been no trace of any military establishment there, until last summer, for twenty years. The Highlands that the Americans claim comports with the words of the Treaty in every particular. ... The Boundary is perfectly marked by the unchanging law of nature. Any native of the forest will follow it with precision enough for any practical purpose. Were there a boundary of that description between tribes there would be no difficulty. ...

It is extremely desirable and is to be expected that Maine will redeem her pledge in protecting the inhabitants from foreign encroachment and establish

able authority and give us the rights and privileges that other citizens of Maine enjoy. ...
With much respect, I am, Sir, Yours, etc., John Baker[13]

In October, 1840, John Baker was presiding at a town meeting at the house of Joseph Nadeau, next above the blockhouse, at the mouth of Fish River. According to Maclauchlan, those who attended were "chiefly Americans and the lowest order of Canadians, who have been but a short time in the settlement, and are, generally speaking, without principle or property." Maclauchlan commended the peaceable attitude of the Acadians, whom, he said, took no part with the Americans. In this they may have been influenced by Monsieur Langevin, their priest, who about that time or a little later, wrote to Sir John Harvey:

As regards political matters, we live at one time in hope, at another in fear of what the outcome may be in regard to the boundary; but come what may, we will rather prefer war than to yield an inch of the soil of Madawaska to the Americans.[14]

Another town meeting was held by the American colony at the mouth of Fish River on November 2nd, 1840. At this meeting, in which John Baker was active, Captain Rines, threatened Warden Maclauchlan with arrest if he attempted to interfere.[15]

On November 13th, Harvey reported the town meetings to Lord Sydenham, asking if he thought military occupation desirable, and if so could it be managed from Temiscouata. Sydenham immediately ordered two companies of infantry into the Madawaska settlements, with orders to keep the Americans out of the Disputed Terri-

---

13 Baker to Gorham Parks, September 15, 1840, PJFDL.
14 Raymond, loc. cit., 364.
15 Ibid.

tory north of the St. John. Sydenham's swift movement was unexpected by Harvey, who tried to intercept the march of the troops from Temiscouata.[16]

Harvey wrote to Fairfield on December 10, 1840, to acquaint him that the troop movement made by Sydenham had no other object than to give support to the Magistrates, Francis Rice and James Maclauchhlan. His suggested solution was that he might raise an armed civil *posse* corresponding in amount and description with that maintained by Maine to prevent interference by the Americans; then, he supposed, the British troops would be withdrawn to their former stations. However, New Brunswick legal officers ruled that the civil power had no right to create an armed body of men without consent of Parliament. Harvey was mortified; Sydenham was pleased with this additional evidence that his opinion concerning Sir John's ineptness had been correct.[17]

Contributing to Harvey's embarrassment was the fact that Warden Maclauchlan, apparently having lost confidence in Harvey's determination to defend the territory, had appealed directly to Sydenham for military assistance.[18] Maclauchlan was unhappy about the indignities he suffered from Americans who refused to accept his authority, but he had also found it difficult to carry out Harvey's orders in such a poorly defined jurisdiction. By writing directly to Sydenham, whether deliberately intending to or not, he had taken revenge on Harvey for earlier reprimands.

Fairfield responded to Harvey, December 15, 1840, that he regarded the quartering of troops at Madawaska Settlement as a direct infringement of their arrangement

---

16 W. S. MacNutt, "New Brunswick's Age of Harmony, The Administration of Sir John Harvey", loc. cit., 120-22.
17 The Volunteers under George W. Towle, at Fort Fairfield, had been reduced to eight persons. At Fish River, the Volunteers under Stover Rines numbered fourteen men. RLAMI 1840; MacNutt, loc. cit., 120-22. AROSM IV, 641-641;.
18 MacNutt, loc. cit., 120-122.

and the situation was aggravated by the fact that it was a repetition of a similar movement, the stationing of two hundred troops at Temiscouata Lake.[19]

Governor Fairfield reported the quartering of British troops at Madawaska to President Van Buren on December 15, 1840, stating that Maine had again been subjected to the mortification of having foreign troops quartered upon her territory. Again, on December 23, he called upon the Federal Government for the protection from invasion guaranteed in the constitution.[20]

At the end of December, Sydenham wrote to Colonial Secretary John Russell of his surprise at Harvey's change of opinion with respect to the advance of a company into the Madawaska settlements and the regret he felt at various inconsistencies in his correspondence and his indiscreet declaration of opinion to the Governor of Maine. He blamed the unsatisfactory state of things on Harvey. For Russell this was sufficient. On January 25, 1841, he informed Harvey that his successor would shortly arrive, and on February 24th, Harvey[21] received a dispatch stating that the interests of Her Majesty's service required that Harvey should not continue in the administration of the government of the Province of New Brunswick. This news was received with regret at all levels, for his policies had made more friends than enemies. A gift of a service of plate valued at £1500 was presented to him as a farewell gift.

---

19 Fairfield to Harvey, December 15, 1840, AROSM IV, 642-644
20 Fairfield to Van Buren, December 15, 1840, AROSM IV, 644; Fairfield to Van Buren, December 23. 1840 USD 107.
21 MacNutt, loc. cit., quotes: Series G12, Vol. 27, Sydenham to Russell, December 28, 1840; 120-122; Classen, loc. cit. Harvey was appointed Lt. Gov. of Newfoundland, and later of Nova Scotia. He died, in high esteem, at 74, in NS. A few months after his dismissal, Sydenham, injured in a fall from a horse, contracted tetanus and died.

The new Lieutenant Governor of New Brunswick, Sir William MacBean George Colebrook, entered upon his office on April 27, 1841.[22]

Edward Kent Wins a Second Term as Governor

The situation in which the State of Maine found itself, at the end of 1840, was dismal indeed. An actual military and naval armament had been established upon the shores and waters of the Madawaska region. Her territory had been made a thoroughfare for the passage of British troops. But still Maine had no national fortifications, other than Houlton, nearer than at the Forks of the Kennebec, or the mouth of the Mattawamkeag.[23]

In the fall election, Governor Fairfield, had been defeated by his Whig opponent, Edward Kent, by 70 votes. On January 15, 1841, Kent began his second nonconsecutive term as Maine's Governor by reiterating Fairfield's request that the General Government take military possession of the territory in dispute.[24]

John Baker once more became the center of jurisdictional controversy on April 21st, when two magistrates near the British post, tried, sentenced, and compelled him to pay a fine of eighty dollars for the alleged offence of harboring a British deserter.[25]

John Baker had requested, in his letter to Gorham Parks that the state "establish able authority and give us

---

22 Classen, loc. cit., 76. Colebrook had been Lt. Governor of the Bahamas from 1834-1837, and of the Leeward Islands in 1837-1841.
23 State of Maine, *Maine Senate Document No. 19*,Charles S. Davels, *Report of the Joint Select Committee upon the State of the Northeastern Boundary*, March 30, 1841, 626-627.
24 Kent got 45,574 votes and Fairfield, 45,507, so Kent was chosen Governor by the Legislature. Isaac Hodsdon replaced A. B. Thompson as Adj. General and Elijah Hamlin replaced Rufus McIntire as Land Agent; Edward Kent, Address to Legislature, January, 1841.AROSM IV.
25 Elijah Hamlin, *Report of the Land Agent*, 1841, dated January 1, 1842, hereinafter referred to as RLAEH 1841.

the rights and privileges that other citizens of Maine enjoy." Now Baker's arrest provided only one of the reasons for Maine to institute legal jurisdiction on the west side of the Line, as Maine understood its location to be, according to the treaty of 1783. The laws of Maine provided that persons who, under the authority of any foreign government, served any civil or criminal process within the limits of the State, was guilty of a misdemeanor. Therefore, Samuel Morrison, of Bangor, was sent to Fort Jarvis, prepared to serve criminal process, to arrest offenders and take them to Bangor for trial.[26]

The civil force retained at Fort Jarvis consisted of Captain Rines and eight men. Captain Wing, with three men were in charge of the public property at Fort Fairfield. New settlers were fast taking up lots in the vicinity of that fort, and the Land Agent felt they could be summoned to aid the *posse* in case of emergency.

At the mouth of the Madawaska River the British were engaged in erecting a strong blockhouse upon an eminence on the north east side of the St. John, about one hundred rods from the shore. A New Brunswick agent was signing contractors to build sections of a forty-five mile long turnpike road from the Grand Falls to Madawaska; all of the inhabitants on the St. John, above Grand Falls, including those above Fort Jarvis, would be assessed and tax bills would be committed to a collector with instructions to enforce the payment. £5000 were expended between the Grand Falls and the Madawaska on the North side of the St. John, and £5000 from the Madawaska to the River Du Loup on the portage from Tamiscouata. A bridge across the Aroostook River, near its mouth, had been completed, and a new road cut out and grubbed from the bridge to the Grand Falls. It was planned, during the next year, to finish this new road and also one from the Grand Falls to and over the portage from Tamiscouata to the St. Lawrence. On this route, the British, in 1841, had

---

26 Ibid.

six military stations: one at the Grand Falls, another at the termination of the portage on the St. Lawrence, in lower Canada and near the west line of the State. The other four were within the supposed limits of Maine: one at the portage on the Tamiscouata, with a garrison of two hundred soldiers; one at the Degele or foot of Temiscouata, with one hundred soldiers; one at the new blockhouse at the mouth of the Madawaska, and another on the south side of the St. John, with one company of soldiers divided between the two.

U. S. Artillery Is Stationed on the St. John River

Because of Baker's arrest, increased British fortification, and the possibility of enforcement of tax levies, etc., the Land Agents of Maine and Massachusetts petitioned the governors of their respective States to make a renewed call upon the general government for relief from the expense of maintaining an armed civil *posse* and for the immediate installation of federal troops in Forts Jarvis and Fairfield.[27]

When this request was referred to the President, it had caused some anxiety with the Cabinet. Daniel Webster and the President conferred with Major General Scott.[28] On July 19th, Senator Reuel Williams reported:

> It seemed to have been settled to order one company of United States Troops to Fort Fairfield, and another to Fort Jarvis, but the order had not yet been given. ... [one of the reasons for this arrangement] was

---

27 Ibid. Note: "Fort Jarvis" has been here substituted for "Fort Kent," as Hamlin had written it, because the name was not changed until the fall of 1841, and this report was dated January 1, 1842, after the name change had taken place.

28 By Executive Order from the War Department, Washington, July 5, 1841, Brevet Major General Winfield Scott was appointed Major General of the Army of the United States. MPP, 1925; Williams to Fairfield, June 21, 1841, JFPC 145B6 MHS.

that by placing the borders under the charge of national troops, collisions would be less likely to occur, and trespasses would be prevented, and another was to relieve Maine from the expense of keeping up a *posse*, and further, pending the negotiations the territory south of the St. John would remain in custody of the United States and that north of it in custody of Great Britain, each denying the other's right to do so. ... [The opinion of Mr. Fox is that] Great Britain will not assent to it, because it would throw that portion of Madawaska, south of the St. John, under the jurisdiction of the United States, and that, in his belief, nothing short of giving the Valley of the St. John to the custody of Great Britain will answer.[29]

The so-called McLeod affair was assuming a more threatening aspect. (Harking back to 1837, the *Caroline*, a small American steamship had been captured by those involved in the Canadian rebellion. In the process they had killed one of the crew. Time passed, and, in a New York tavern, a man named Alexander McLeod bragged that he had killed the American. His arrest set off a serious diplomatic problem between United States and Britain, and nearly, by itself, set off war between them.) Williams thought hostilities might be near at hand.[30]

Fort Jarvis Becomes Fort Kent

As he had in his letter of the 19th, Williams was still referring to the fort at the mouth of Fish River as Fort Jarvis, when on August 22, 1841, in a letter to Fairfield, he wrote:

---

29 Williams to Fairfield, July 19, 1841, JFPC 145B6 MHS.
30 Williams to Fairfield, July 30, 1841, JFPC 145B6 MHS; Classen, loc. cit., 77-8. Macleod was not convicted, and the resolution of his case cleared the way for Lord Ashburton to come to Washington to meet with Daniel Webster.

General Scott told me a few days ago that the order had gone out for one company to be stationed at Fort Fairfield and another at Fish River, Fort Jarvis.[31]

On the 14th of August, 1841 two companies of United States Artillery were ordered to invest the forts on the St. John River. Captain David Van Ness commanding Company H, 1st Artillery, on the 7th of September, 1841, marched north from Hancock Barracks and manned the United States Military Post at Fort Fairfield on the 10th.[32]

Then the name, Fort Kent, was placed in official usage when Captain L. B. Webster, commanding Company C, 1st Artillery, wrote in his Muster Roll that the Company marched from Hancock Barracks, Houlton, September 7, 1841 and arrived at Fort Kent, Fish River, Maine, September 17, 1842.

The block houses and defences at both locations were formally delivered to the respective commanding officers by Mr. Ingersol, and all provisions, tools, etc., not needed for the *posse* and wanted by the commissary were sold to them. The Volunteers had all been discharg-

---

31 Williams to Fairfield, July 30, 1841, Williams to Fairfield, August 22, 1841, JFPC 145B6 MHS; See map: *Detail from Sketch of the Disputed Territory, showing the Military Posts occupied by the British and Americans in 1840*, compiled from Reports and Sketches of Lieutenants Bainbridge and Simmons, Royal Engineers, and other sources, under the direction of Lieutenant Colonel Oldfield, K. H., Commanding Royal Engineers in Canada, Head Quarters at Montreal, 12 August, 1840, National Archives, Washington, D.C. Map locates Fort Jarvis and Baker's Mill on the St. John River.

32 NARG 94, Muster Roll, Regular Army Companies, Records of the Adjutant General's Office, 1780-1917, Roll 357. See Appendix III, Federal Troops in Aroostook County, Maine.

ed, with the exception of Captain Rines and one man at Fort Kent and Captain Wing at Fort Fairfield.[33]

Sir Richard Downes Jackson, who had been Commander-in-Chief of the Forces in British North America, became Acting Governor General after Sydenham's death on Sept 19, 1841. He ordered a seven-man detachment of the Madawaska Garrison to cross the St. John and establish itself in the barrack on the south bank.[34]

Tyler, too! A Post Script to this Period

In the election of 1840, President Van Buren was defeated by Whig candidate, William Henry Harrison. Harrison offered Henry Clay the office of Secretary of State. When he refused, Daniel Webster was induced to accept. President Harrison died on April 4, 1841, a month after his inauguration, and was succeeded by John Tyler.

Because, among other reasons, President Tyler refused to sign a bill to re-charter of the United States Bank, in September, 1841, all members of his cabinet resigned except Daniel Webster. Webster was then deeply involved in boundary negotiations. Tyler's new cabinet were his personal friends, who had been Jackson Democrats. The Whig victory was lost; the Democratic Party began its ascendancy. President Tyler became involved in negotiations concerning Maine's boundary problems.[35]

---

[33] RLAEH1841. A part of the lot at Fish River belonging to Maine and Massachusetts was leased to the United States, and Lot No. 12, on Township Letter D, belonging to Maine, was also leased to the United States. The Fort Jarvis-Fort Kent blockhouse, as rebuilt by Rines, still stands in the town of Fort Kent. A reproduction of the smaller of the two blockhouses built at Fort Fairfield now stands near the river in Fort Fairfield. An cannon is displayed on the lawn at the Fort Fairfield Public Library.

[34] Classen, loc. cit., 76.

[35] John Lord, *Beacon Lights of History*, New York: William H. Wise and Company, 1921, Vol. VI, 127-131.

PART FIVE: RESOLUTION

CHAPTER XIII

FINAL NEGOTIATION

The Influence of Francis Ormond Jonathan Smith

John Fairfield was elected to a third non-consecutive term as Governor of Maine. On January 7, 1842, he spiritedly advocated the forcible expulsion of the British from Maine territory.[1] However, the winds of war had been adjusted to blow from a different quarter, to carry sentiments of peace. The idea of changing the attitude of the people of Maine and their elected representatives, by the careful use of propaganda, had been suggested to President Van Buren by Francis Ormond Jonathan Smith

---

[1] John Fairfield's address to the Maine Legislature, January 7, 1842, ROSM V, 96-101 A margin of ten thousand votes had brought defeat to Governor Kent. Philip C. Johnson was Secretary of State, James White was Treasurer, Alfred Redington, Adjutant General; Levi Bradley, Land Agent. The Governor's Council included Gowen Wilson, Dominicus Jordan, Atwood Levensaler, Jonas Parlin, John Burnham, Greenlief White and John Stickney. Samuel H. Blake was President of the Maine Senate and Charles Andrews was Speaker of the House. Maine sent Reuel Williams and George Evans to the U. S. Senate and Benjamin Randall, Virgil D. Parris, Nathan Clifford, Joshua A. Lowell, Elisha Allen, William P. Fessenden, Nathaniel S. Littlefield, and Alfred Marshall to the U. S. House of Representatives. ROSM V; Brunelle, loc. cit.

of Portland, as early as December, 1837, but it was not until the spring of 1841 that his idea's time had come.2

Prince Von Otto Bismark is reputed to have said that a statesman can't create anything; he must wait until he hears the footsteps of God. F. O. J. Smith, who called himself a deist, had a marked talent for listening for God's footsteps. Moving in and out among the layers of political, financial and religious establishments, he exerted tremendous influence. He was ever watchful for events that could advance his schemes for making himself more powerful and affluent. He used various Maine newspapers to manipulate as much as he could of Maine's political scene. His nickname, "Fog," suited his ability to cloud or transform issues to suit his own ends.3

F. O. J. Smith would make the Whig Secretary of State, Daniel Webster, his unseen collaborator in manipulating a boundary dispute solution. Much of the credit for having authored the "grand stroke" in which Webster later exalted, goes to Smith.4 In Washington, he found a welcome audience in President Tyler and Daniel Webster, and he most surely had the approval of General Scott.

Prompted by Webster's expression of concern over the boundary dispute, Smith proposed a plan for a solution. He was taken into Webster's confidence and into employment as a secret agent to the State Department. An advance payment of five hundred dollars was made to him from the President's secret fund. He sent his plan to Webster on June 7, 1841. Excerpts:

Mr. Webster: ... The mistake and inefficiency of all past efforts upon this subject has laid in directing

---

2 Its implementation was researched and explained by Frederick Merk, in *Fruits of Propaganda in the Tyler Administration*, Boston: Harvard University Press, 1971, 63.

3 Gaffney, loc. cit. Thomas Gaffney traced Smith's career from his birth in Brentwood, New Hampshire on November 26, 1806 to his death in Portland on October 14th, 1876.

4 Merk, loc. cit.; Gaffney, loc. cit., 379.

negotiations at the wrong end of the dispute. The dispute, in reality, has not been so much with the federal government and the British government as with the people of Maine and the people of the British provinces. ... Now my plan is to prepare public sentiment in Maine for a compromise of the matter through a conventional line, founded partly in consideration of an exchange of territory, and partly in a pecuniary indemnity to Maine and Massachusetts for the difference in the exchange of territory. ... Public sentiment on this matter can be brought into the right shape in Maine by enlisting certain leading men of both political parties (yet not politically) and through them, at a proper time, guiding aright the public press.

Having obtained the favorable opinion of the leading political men of Maine ... and drawing after this an appropriate expression of the public press, the same work could be accomplished in a much less time among the citizens of the interested provinces; and the whole may be combined into corresponding and reciprocal resolutions of the Legislative Assemblies of the two local governments at their next winter sessions, in ample season for Congress to confirm all at its next regular session.

A few thousand dollars expended upon such an agency will accomplish more than hundreds of thousands expended through formalities and delays of ordinary diplomatic negotiations and surveys, and more than millions would if the parties shall be brought into belligerent attitudes. ... My own compensation I should expect to be definitely fixed upon at the rate of $3500 per anum, and my necessary travelling expenses, postage and incidental expenses paid by the government.[5]

Smith's general plan was that propaganda would result in successful negotiation based upon the principle of an exchange of equivalents in territory, with the understanding that any losses to Maine would be compensated in cash, and Great Britain would cede to the United States free navigation to the Lower St. John River. Smith was authorized to employ assistants.[6] Compensation was to be paid from the President's secret fund upon completion of the work. Webster and Tyler approved.

"To adjust the tone and direction of the party presses, and through them, of public sentiment," Smith held conferences with editors and advanced the cause by writing a series of three articles, bearing the general title, "Northeastern Boundary – Why Not Settle It?" under the pseudonym "Agricola." He persuaded the editor of an influential religious journal, *The Christian Mirror*, of Portland, to publish them. The first appeared on Novem-

---

[5] F.O.J. Smith to Daniel Webster, June 7, 1841, Merk, loc. cit., 143-144; Gaffney, loc. cit., 334, citing "The Deposition of Francis O. J. Smith, taken before the Select Committee of the House of Representatives Appointed to Investigate Certain Charges made by C. J. Ingersoll against Daniel Webster," in U. S. Congress, House, *Official Misconduct of the Late Secretary of State*, H R 684, 29th Congress, 1st Session, 1846, p 1. F. O. J. Smith, on June 12, wrote to his long-time friend John Hodgdon of Bangor, to enlist his active participation. He told Hodgdon that those who assisted would be "amply compensated." Hodgdon thought well of the proposal, but had serious doubts about carrying it into effect. Smith's influence was reflected in the columns of the *Eastern Argus*, which, at his urging, had been purchased by Eliphalet Case, his wife's brother-in-law. Gaffney, loc. cit., 336, 338, 339, 347.

[6] Merk, loc. cit., page 10., states that among these agents were Jared Sparks, Peleg Sprague, Albert Smith and C. S. Daveis.

ber 18, 1841; the others followed at intervals. They were repeated in similar vein in other journals.[7] A sampling of Smith's rhetoric is found in his November 18th article signed "Agricola":

> Our boundary dispute ... may be adjusted by the contending parties without the concession of any disputed *principle* on either side. It is undoubtedly true that Great Britain wanted only a small part of the territory to which she advances claim. It is no less true and obvious that the actual and practical value of that portion which she really wants is to her very much greater than it is, or ever can be to either Maine, as a State or to the United States. To Maine it is valuable for timber and settling purposes. It is, except in reference to a condition of peace, and for the support of quiet industry, of comparatively no value to Maine. But for this it is of great value, and cannot, and ought not to be parted with by Maine, except for a corresponding benefit. ... To me it is obvious that while that territory is of very great convenience and value to the British government in a military point of view it is of but little value to the United States or Maine in the like point of view. And then, again, while in a civil point of view, it is of very little or no value to Great Britain, to Maine it is of very great value. ...[8]

Final Negotiations

Smith, alias "Agricola," had been at work on his plan since June 7, 1841. Early in 1842, Maine heard

---

[7] Merk, loc. cit., 63-64, F. O. J. Smith to Webster, August 12, 1842; Joseph Griffin, in *The Press of Maine*, 1872, Brunswick, 64-65, stated that Reverend Asa Cummings pastor of the church at North Yarmouth "assumed the conduct of the paper and remained its proprietor and editor from 1826 to 1855."

[8] Ibid, 158-161.

rumors of England's decision to send a special minister to Washington.

In Great Britain, in 1841, Lord Aberdeen had become Secretary of Foreign Affairs. A Conservative, he replaced Palmerston, who had foiled all attempts at a solution to the boundary question. The new Peel government had many "hot spots" to deal with on the American-Canadian border. Any one of the areas on the upper waters of the Connecticut, at Indian Stream, on the New York frontier, on the Grand Portage west of Lake Superior or in the Oregon territory, threatened to erupt into violence at any time. As soon as the British government received an indication from Webster that he was ready for a new negotiation on the Maine boundary, a special mission was named. Alexander Baring, Lord Ashburton, an investor in Maine lands and a personal friend of Daniel Webster, was appointed to head the mission.[9]

Baring, born 1774, had been groomed for his role as financier for his family banking firm, Baring Brothers and Company, at the Dutch merchant-banking firm of Hope and Company. As a partner of Hope and Company, in 1795, he represented the interests of that company, as well as Baring Brothers, in America. He associated with the highest levels of Philadelphian society, including Judge Thomas Willing, founder of the Bank of Pennsylvania and President of the Bank of North America. Willing's daughter Anne was wed to William Bingham, also of Philadelphia, wealthiest man in the United States in the post-revolutionary period. As a member of the Continental Congress, Bingham, with the cooperation of Willing, had been actively involved in financing and arming the revolutionary forces and had close friendships with George Washington, Alexander Hamilton, John Adams, Thomas Jefferson, Benjamin Franklin and other patriots. Alexander Baring's first mission to America had been to look into the purchase of part of William Bingham's

---

9 Merk, loc. cit., 56-59

District of Maine lands as an investment for the Hope and Baring firms. Early in 1793, Bingham had acquired three million acres of land in the District of Maine of Massachusetts, divided into three tracts; the Kennebec Million, the Penobscot Million and the Upper Penobscot Tract. After much deliberation and bargaining, Baring had purchased half of each tract from Bingham. Baring became a business partner of the then United States Senator Bingham, and by 1798 he had married Bingham's daughter Anne. Alexander Baring and his wife had departed Philadelphia for a new life in England in 1802, leaving his interests in Maine lands under the supervision of Bingham's land agent, General David Cobb. Cobb was, at this time, President of the Massachusetts Senate and Chief Justice of the Court of Common Pleas. Baring Brothers, Hope and Company and William Bingham had financed the American purchase of the Louisiana Territory from France in 1804. In 1806, Baring, having been appointed to the Court of the Bank of England, had begun a long term of service in the House of Commons.[10]

    Lord Ashburton arrived at Annapolis on April 1, 1842. Tyler and Webster conferred secretly with him. Not until April 11th, was Governor Fairfield notified of his presence and purpose. The Maine Legislature had adjourned. Webster told Fairfield that Ashburton had authority to "treat for a conventional line on such terms and conditions and with such mutual considerations and equivalents as may be thought just and equitable." He proposed that the governments of Maine and Massachusetts appoint commissioners to confer with federal authorities about a conventional line; no line was to be agreed upon without their unanimous consent. Governor Fairfield convened an

---

10   Robert C. Alberts, *The Golden Voyage, the Life and Times of William Bingham, 1752-1804*, Houghton Mifflin Company, Boston, 1969, 232, map, 349, 415, 423, 433; Baring soon despatched John Black, a young English accountant, as clerk to his land agent. In time Black married the daughter of General Cobb and became a prominent citizen with a mansion in Ellsworth, ME.

extra session of the Legislature on May 18th, and recommended that course.[11]

In anticipation of an upcoming special session of the Maine Legislature, Daniel Webster had sent Jared Sparks, a distinguished historian, soon to be President of Harvard, to Augusta. In 1841, in the archives of the French Foreigh Office, Sparks had found a map on which the boundaries of the United States were marked by a strong red line. Benjamin Franklin had mentioned such a map having been marked by himself in December, 1782. Upon his return to Cambridge, Sparks wrote to Webster about the map and enclosed a recently published map of Maine on which he had drawn a strong black line corresponding with the red line he had found on the French map. Endorsed by Webster, "Very Confidential," it was in the State Department files two months prior to Ashburton's arrival in Washington. It supported the claim of Great Britain in the northeast.[12] This map and a "Steuben map," were exhibited confidentially in Augusta. Neither had been proven to be an authentic map used by the negotiators of the Treaty of 1783. They produced the intended apprehension in Augusta.[13]

---

11 William Leo Lucey, S. J., in *Edward Kavanagh, Catholic Statesman, Diplomat from Maine* nd, Francestown, New Hampshire, 107-108; ROSM V, 128-130 and 16-19.

12 Merk, loc. cit., cites a letter of Sparks, February 15, 1842, and the map, to be found in the State Department file M-179, Roll 96, National Archives.

13 Merk, loc. cit., 65-67; Sprague, a federal judge in Massachusetts, was a supporter of Maine. Albert Smith, former federal marshal in ME; congressman, 1839-41. Merk, fn 52, p 66, cites *Select Committee on Charges against Mr. Webster made by Mr. C. J. Ingersoll*, labeled HR 29, No. 684, A-D, 241, National Archives, and cautions that this manuscript report is not the committee's published report in House Reports, 29 Congress, 1st session, (Ser 490) No. 684. In fn 53, page 67, Merk notes that details of expenditures from the secret fund and a lot Tyler's testimony were suppressed in the published report.

The Maine Legislature, during a special session on May 26, 1842, re-affirmed Maine's traditional position, but concluded that in an endeavor to terminate a controversy, there should be chosen, by ballot, four persons to be commissioners on the part of Maine, to give assent to any conventional line, with such terms, conditions, considerations and equivalents as they deemed consistent with the honor and interests of the state.[14] Their assent must, however, be unanimous. Elected were William P. Preble and Edward Kavanagh, Democrats and Edward Kent and John Otis, Whigs.[15]

Maine's Governor Fairfield and the Legislature as a whole, were not aware of F. O. J. Smith's collaboration with Webster in the preparation of Maine's public for what would be forthcoming. Lord Ashburton, as well as President Tyler and Secretary of State Webster, had employed funds from secret accounts for propaganda purposes, to expedite a quick settlement. Ashburton gave £2998 (approximately $14,500) to someone, secretly. He disclosed this to Lord Aberdeen in a note that was apparently destroyed on arrival, but on August 9, 1842, he referred to it again in a letter marked "private and confidential":

> The money I wrote about went to compensate Sparkes, to send him, on my first arrival, to the Governors of Maine and Massachusetts. My informant thinks

---

14 Merk, loc. cit., p. 68, footnote, quotes from a letter from Webster to Jared Sparks, of March 11, 1843, in which he jubilantly described these preliminary stages of negotiation: "As to the conduct of the negotiation, there is one point on which I wish to speak to you very freely, even at the hazard of a well founded imputation of some vanity. The grand stroke was to get the previous consent of Maine and Massachusetts. Nobody had attempted this; it had occurred to nobody else; it was a movement of great delicacy, and of very doubtful result, ... and it succeeded, and to this success the result of the whole negotiation is to be attributed." *Jared Sparks Papers*, Harvard College Library.
15 Chapter 111, ROSM V, 16-17.

that without this stimulant Maine would never have yielded.

The use of funds for disseminating propaganda was not an unusual governmental procedure.[16] Maine's peacemakers, Preble, Kavanagh, Kent and Otis, in a report to Daniel Webster, summarized the negotiations and their eventual acceptance of the agreement that became the Treaty of Washington of 1842. They explained that early in 1842, assurances were held out that Lord Ashburton was clothed with ample powers and furnished with the most liberal and conciliatory instructions for the settlement of our northeastern boundary.[17] These assurances gave rise to an expectation in Maine and in the United States, that an honorable adjustment could be made, if Maine would exhibit a proper spirit of magnanimity and conciliation. It developed that Lord Ashburton had no authority to concede a single acre of British territory adjoining Maine, not even to the smallest of her islands in Passamaquoddy Bay.

The arrangement fell short of the expectations of the Legislature and the people of Maine. It was a proposition deliberately made by President Tyler in the role of mediator. The whole country seemed to be insisting that the controversy be adjusted. They left it to the people of the State to decide whether the honor of the State had been protected. The negotiators found it ex-

---

16 Merk, loc. cit., 71-72.
17 Merk points out that Ashburton's successive instructions are summarized in E. D. Adams, "Lord Ashburton and the Treaty of Washington," *American Historical Review*, XVII, July 1912, 764-782. Ashburton's instructions on the negotiations changed from time to time. Those of February 8, 1842, had been flexible. He was directed merely to avoid a settlement less favorable than the Dutch award had been. Much hardened instructions were sent at the end of March. At the wish of the military experts and the Colonial Office, he was directed to obtain the whole area. Ashburton protested. A month later, Aberdeen returned to the original instructions. Merk, loc. cit. 72-73.

ceedingly difficult to bring their minds to consider it, but they were satisfied that the terms ultimately engrafted into the treaty were the most favorable terms to Maine to which Great Britain would accede.[18]

The Treaty of Washington, 1842

The articles of the Treaty of Washington of 1842, between the United States of America and Her Majesty, the Queen of the United Kingdom of Great Britain and Ireland, known in the United States as the Webster-Ashburton Treaty and in Canada as the Ashburton Treaty was concluded and ratified, August 9, 1842. The parts that pertain to Maine read as follows:

Article I
It is hereby agreed and declared that the line of boundary shall be as follows: beginning at the monument at the source of the river St. Croix, as designated and agreed to by the commissioners under the fifth article of the treaty of 1794, between the governments of the United States and Great Britain; thence north, following the exploring line run and marked by the surveyors of the two governments in the years 1817 and 1818, under the fifth article of the Treaty of Ghent, to its intersection with the river St. John, and to the middle of the channel thereof; thence up the middle of the main channel of the said river St. John, to the mouth of the river St. Francis, thence up the middle of the channel of the said river St. Francis and of the lakes through which it flows, to the outlet of the lake Pohenagamook; thence southwesterly, in a straight line to a point on the northwest branch of the river St.

---

[18] William P. Preble, Edward Kent, Edward Kavanagh, John Otis, *The Report of the Commissioners Chosen to Confer with Authorities in Washington D.C. Concerning the Settlement of the Northeast Boundary on January 4, 1843, etc,* ROSMV

John, which point shall be ten miles distance from the main branch of the St. John, in a straight line, and in the nearest direction; but if the said point shall be found to be less than seven miles from the nearest point of the summit or crest of the highlands, that divide those rivers which empty theselves into the river Saint Lawrence from those which fall into the river St. John, then the said point shall be made to recede down the said northwest branch of the river St. John to a point seven miles in a straight line, from the said summit or crest; thence, in a straight line, in a course about south eight degrees west, to a point where the parallel of latitude of 46° 25' north intersects the southwest branch of the St. John; thence, southerly, by the said branch, to the source thereof in the highlands at the Metjarmette portage; thence, down the said highlands which divide the waters which empty themselves into the river St. Lawrence from those which fall into the Atlantic ocean, to the head of Hall's stream; thence, down the middle of said stream, till the line thus run intersects the old line of boundary surveyed and marked by Valentine and Collins previously to the year 1774, as the 45th degree of north latitude, and which has been known and understood to be the line of actual division between the States of New York and Vermont on one side, and the British Province of Canada on the other; and, from said point of intersection, west, along the said dividing line as heretofore known and understood, to the Iroquois, or St. Lawrence river.

Articles III, V and VII provided for the free navigation of the St. John River, for the disposition of money in the Disputed Territory fund and for the running and marking of the boundary, respectively.[19]

---

[19] Articles VII, VIII, IX, X, XI and XII have been omitted, as not pertaining expressly to the Maine's northeastern boundary dispute.

The respective plenipotentiaries signed the treaty, on August 9th and it was signed by President Tyler on November 10, 1842.[20]

After a twenty-year struggle, the Treaty of Washington conveyed to Great Britain from Maine 3,207,680 acres. Maine received half of the $3,000,000 awarded jointly to Maine and Massachusetts.[21]

Repercussions

Governor John Fairfield, at the beginning of his fourth term, stated:

The result and final adjustment of this question, even if it should be regarded by the people of this state as preferable to further procrastination and another foreign arbitration, is far different from what they had anticipated. *For myself, I can truly say that I am deeply disappointed.* By this, however, I would not be understood as intending to cast censure upon the commissioners of this State. They were selected by the legislature as gentlemen of elevated standing, commanding, in high degree, the confidence of the public, and eminently qualified for such a service. The correspondence on their part was conducted with signal ability, and the embarrassments of their position, and the circumstances by which they were ultimately induced to submit the question to the determination of the Senate of the United States are fully appreciated.

But, however their course may be regarded, the result is a subject of deep disappointment. The course of the British Government ... was marked by an unyielding and grasping spirit. Its liberality, if any was evinced,

---

20 The Treaty of Washington, 1842, MD 1843
21 Shepherd Cary, John W. Dana, Cullen Sawtelle, Amasa Stetson, Leonard Pierce and William Frye, *Report of the Joint Select Committee of the Maine Senate, March 21, 1843,* MD 1843.

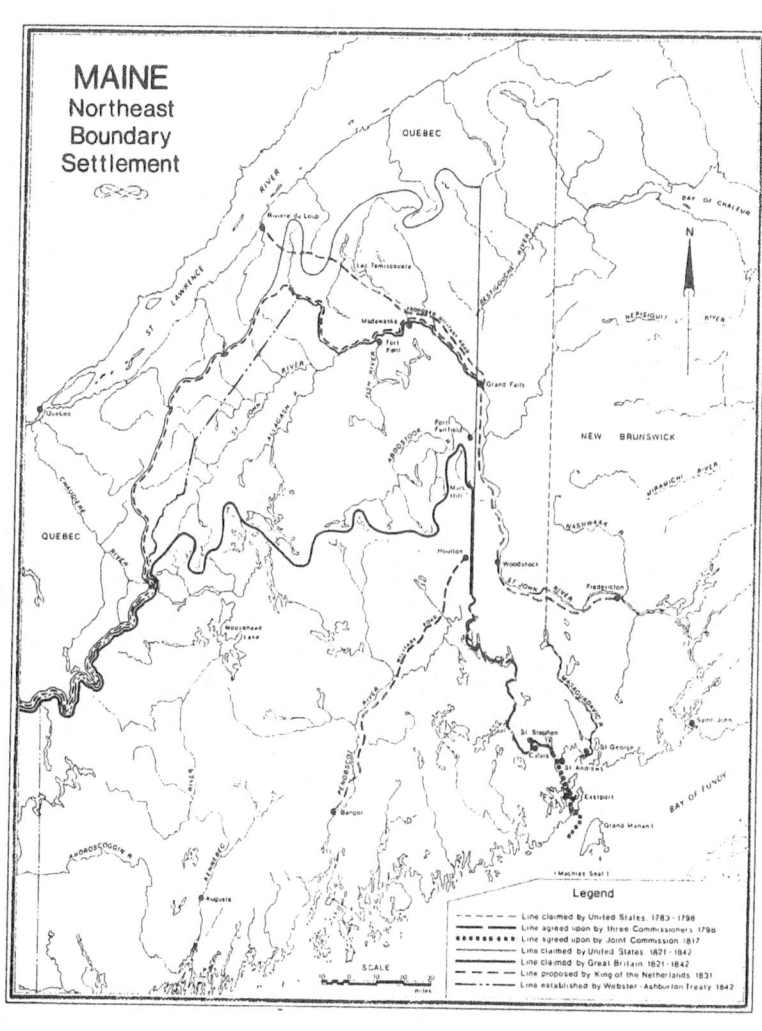

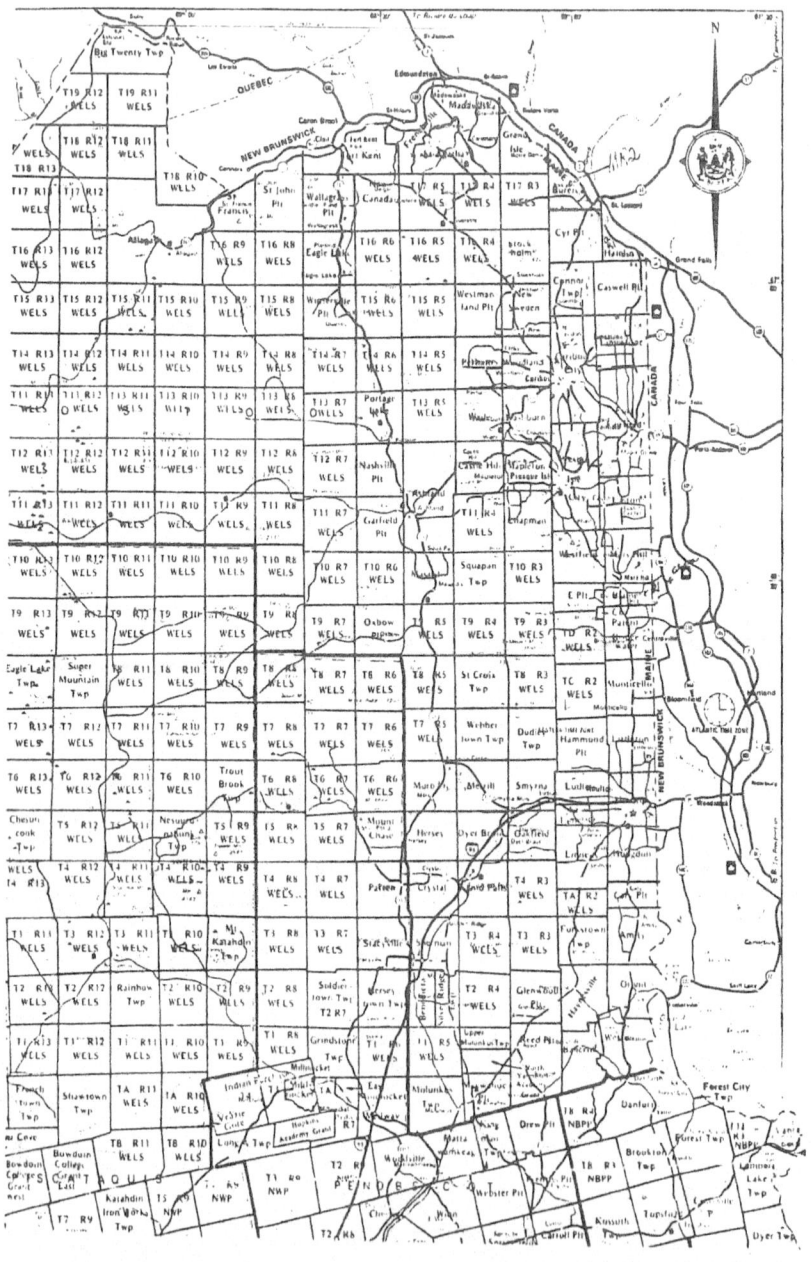

Northeastern Maine, Showing Township Designations,
Maine Department of Transportation

was in unmeaning diplomatic compliments, while its exactions were in acres and substantial privileges. For this State can never admit that the case presented was of doubtful title, in which the adversary parties might reasonably be expected to compromise by "splitting the difference."... If in this, Maine "has not been treated as she has endeavoured to deserve," it is far from being the first instance. All her injuries, however, cannot shake her sense of duty. As a member of the Union she will continue to be, as she has ever been, faithful and true. And if she could be satisfied that the sacrifice was necessary, for the good of the country, she could in that find ample consolation. To insolent and unfounded pretension she can yield nothing; to the cause of patriotism and union, everything![22]

Almost as if in rebuttal, Daniel Webster, in his speech before the New York Historical Society April 15, 1843, explained his motivations, defended his diplomatic course:

... I am willing to maintain everywhere, that in regard to the States of Massachusetts and Maine, they are better off this day, than if Lord Ashburton had not signed the treaty, but had signed a relinquishment of the claim of England to every square foot of the territory, and gone home. The States get more, by the opening of the navigation of the rivers, and by all the other benefits obtained, than all the territory is worth north of the St. John. ... It does not follow ... that the treaty must be disadvantageous or dishonorable to the other party to the treaty. By no means. ... England has no reason to complain. She has obtained all she wanted - a reasonable boundary and ... "a convenient communication," the line of intercourse between her own Provinces. Who is therefore to complain? Massachusetts

---

22 ROSM V, 237-245.

and Maine ... have adopted the treaty. It has been ratified by the English Government, and though in party times and in contests of men, some little dust may be thrown in the air, some little excitement of the political elements may be produced occasionally, yet as far as we know, no considerable fermentation in the subject exists.[23]

Maine and the United States had made a large concession in order to keep the peace. In 1933, a copy of Franklin's red boundary line, traced on a 1775 Mitchell map, for the Spanish Government, by its ambassador in France in 1782, was discovered in Madrid. It conformed perfectly to Maine's claim, as did Jay's copy of Mitchell's 1755 map, which was found after negotiations were concluded. It is believed that had these maps been available in 1842, no surrender of land would have been required.[24]

Shortly after the treaty was signed, Charles J. Ingersoll of Pennsylvania, chairman of the House Committee of Foreign Affairs, found, in the State Department's secret archives, correspondence and vouchers relating to the boundary dispute. In 1846, the Committee brought charges against Daniel Webster and F. O. J. Smith. Webster was charged with having personally taken money from the president's secret service fund, possibly misappropriating it, and, through Smith, using public money to corrupt the party press of Maine.[25]

Both Smith and President Tyler testified before the Committee. Webster was exonerated.

---

23 Albert Gallatin,"A Memoir on the Northeastern Boundary," New York Historical Society, 95.
24 Bemis, loc. cit., 164.
25 Gaffney, loc. cit., 370. Gaffney cites *U.S., House Report* No. 684, 1-8; and Merk, loc. cit., 69-70. See Gaffney, loc. cit., 371-379 for the analysis of Smith's influence upon the settlement of the boundary dispute.

CONCLUSION

Reflections

One hundred and fifty years have passed since the crisis on the Maine-New Brunswick border took place. The foregoing chronology is the first detailed study of what actually happened at the local, and state and provincial levels, from 1820-1842.

Highlighted against a background of former wars and real or imagined injuries, dynamic people, the moving forces in this conflict, were involved in an economic, ethical and patriotic struggle. For the first time, the use of archival information brings the actions and reactions of the participants in the boundary dispute to public view. Like candles in darkness, their letters and conversations illuminate this dimly lit era. We become acquainted with unique personalities. We begin to understand their motivations.

This scenario brings insights into the uses of power and the value of having loyal adherents to a cause. Men from Maine and men from New Brunswick marched to their frontiers as bravely as in any previous war, with every expectation of doing battle. The fact that they did not engage in a shooting war does not dim their devotion to their respective causes. In the face of almost certain bloodshed and despair, they held fast until a settlement was reached.

The final solution brought not blood but sacrifice, by Maine, of land her people truly believed was their rightful property. Ties of common blood seem, on the surface, to have availed little, so far as the boundary dispute was concerned. The unknown quantity is the extent to which those ties contributed to the restraint shown through all those years of dispute. However, at present, at the local level, on the Maine-New Brunswick border, ties of common blood avail much. The people living there have been and continue to be a community of bloodlines and of spirit. Bonds of marriage between Maine and New Brunswick residents were and are so prevalent that it would be difficult to find families native to that area that do not share common ancestry with those involved in both sides of the old dispute.

A century and a half later, ties of common blood have prevailed, both along the boundary line and on the international scene. We have, as Winfield Scott had hoped, "worked out a strong compact for reciprocal feelings far more binding than written engagements, which the other nations of the world would be wholly unable to dissolve or resist."

BIBLIOGRAPHY

MANUSCRIPTS:

Maine Historical Society:
Mss *John Fairfield Papers*, Collection 145.
Mss *Collection of Official Papers, Northeast Boundary Dispute*.
Mss *Official Hodsdon Papers*.
Mss *Collection 420*, Fogg, Vol. V.
Mss *Documents Relating to the Public Lands in Maine*.

Maine State Library:
Mss *Bangor Rifle Corps, Records from its Organization in 1835 to June 20, 1840, Including the Aroostook War*, Maine State Library, Augusta, Maine.
MS *Correspondence and Documents Relating to the North East Boundary Dispute*

Maine State Archives:
Mss *Aroostook War Vouchers*, Land Agent Materials.
Adj. Gen. Rufus C. Vose, *General Order Book, Maine Militia*
Mss *Report of Charles Davis [Daveis] to R McIntire or Hastings Strickland*, Land Agent Materials.
Mss *The Journal of George W. Coffin, Massachusetts Land Agent, September and October, 1825*
Mss *Diary and Letter Book of William P. Parrott*.

Cary Library, Houlton, Maine:
Mss *Letters*, Joseph Treat to Samuel Cook, April 28,
   1828; Parris to Joseph Houlton, March 31, 1828;
   Elijah M. Lowe Jr., to Francis Barnes, February 14,
   1890, by permission of Joseph Inman, Librarian.

American Antiquarian Society, Worcester, MA:
Mss *Lincoln Family Papers*, Octavo Vol. 35, American
Antiquarian Society. Used by written permission.

Library of Congress:
Mss *The Papers of John Fairfield*, Mss 19264.

National Archives, Washington, D C:
Register of Enlisted Men in U. S. Army, Vol. 76, #5937.
NARG 94: *Monthly Returns of the Commanding Officers of the Second Infantry at Hancock Barracks, Houlton, Maine, from 1828 to 1839* Muster Roll, Regular Army Companies, Records of the Adjutant General's Office, 1780-1917; National Archives Microfilm Publications, Microcopy 617:
   Roll 448, Monthly Returns of the commanding officers of the 2nd Infantry, Hancock Barracks, Houlton, ME;
   Roll 448, Monthly Returns of the commanding officers of the 1st Artillery, Hancock Barracks, Houlton, ME;
   Roll 357, Monthly Returns of the Commanding Officers of the 1st Artillery, Fort Fairfield, Maine;
   Roll 571, Monthly returns of the commanding officers of the 1st Artillery, Fort Kent, ME.

Public Archives of Canada:
Microfilms: COP188, B12, B13, B16
The Queen versus McIntire, Cushman, Bartlett and Webster, February 18, 1839, PAC COP188 B16.
Lumber Mills, New Brunswick, 1831, Film B 1265.

Public Archives of New Brunswick:
Mss *Letterbook of Governor Harvey.*
An Alphabetical Listing of Militia Appointments, etc., arranged by County, compiled by David Facey-Crowther, MC279.
Mss *New Brunswick Militia: General Correspondence and Papers,* No. 599.

Public Archives of Nova Scotia:
Memorial of the Halifax Committee of Trade to Bathurst, October 8, 1813, Vol. 304, Document 6, No. 66.

DOCUMENTS:

Commonwealth of Massachusetts:
Report of the Joint Committee on Public Lands for the Commonwealth of Massachusetts, Document no. 67, February 7, 1838.
George W. Coffin, *The Journal of George W. Coffin, Massachusetts Land Agent, September and October, 1825,* Maine State Archives, Augusta.
_____, *The Journal of George W. Coffin, Massachusetts Land Agent, September and October, 1825,* Maine State Archives, Augusta.
_____, *Report of the Land Agent of Massachusetts,* Boston, December 8, 1828.
_____, *The Report of the Joint Committee on Public Lands for the Commonwealth of Massachusetts,* February 7, 1838.

State of Maine:
George W. Buckmore, *Report of the Land Agent,* submitted January 22, 1839, for an inspection done in December, 1838.
Shepherd Cary, John W. Dana, Cullen Sawtelle, Amasa Stetson, Leonard Pierce and William Frye, *Report*

of the Joint Select Committee of the Maine Senate, March 21, 1843.

Charles Stewart Daveis, Esq., *Report*, Executive Department Records, 1828, no. 16.

———, *Report of Charles S. Daveis, Esq. Agent appointed by Gov Enoch Lincoln of Maine to enquire into certain facts relating to aggressions upon the rights of the State of Maine and of individuals citizens thereof, by inhabitants of the Province of New Brunswick*; January Session, 1828, Legislature, document no. 18.

———, *Report of the Joint Select Committee of the Senate*, March 30, 1841.

———, *Report of the Joint Select Committee upon the State of the Northeastern Boundary*, March 30, 1841, Maine Senate Document No. 19.

———, *North East Boundary Collection*, Maine Historical Society, Portland.

John G. Deane, *Report to the Maine Legislature*, 1825

———Document no. 13, January Session, 1828, *The Report of the Joint Select Committee of the Senate and House of Representatives of the State of Maine, in Relation to the Northeastern Boundary of the State*, January 26, 1828.

——— *Report of the Joint Select Committee of the House of Representatives*, March 30, 1831.

Oliver Frost to Elijah Hamelin, Esq., *Land Agent's Report*, December 30, 1838.

Elijah Hamlin, *Report of the Land Agent*, for 1841, dated January 1, 1842.

Mr. Holmes of Alfred, ME, *Report in the House of Representatives, February 2, 1837, on the North Eastern Boundary*, Smith and Robinson, Printers.

James Irish, *Report of the Land Agent*, 1825-1826.

Charles Jarvis, *Report of the Land Agent*, 1839.

Rufus McIntire, *Report of the Land Agent*, 1839.

M Norton, *Report of the Land Agent*, 1830.

William Parrot, *Report of the Assistant Land Agent, 1839.*

Joseph Parlin Jr., Chairman, *Report of the Committee on Public Lands*, January 18, 1825.

William P. Preble, Edward Kent, Edward Kavanagh, John Otis, *The Report of the Commissioners Chosen to Confer with Authorities in Washington D.C. Concerning the Settlement of the Northeast Boundary*, January 4, 1843.

Daniel Rose, *Report of the Land Agent*, for 1829, dated January 1, 1830.

Abner B. Thompson, *Report of the Adjutant General of the Militia of Maine*, December 31, 1839, in *Documents of the Legislature*, 1840.

Report of the Land Agent, January 5, 1827 in *Maine Documents*, Vol. II, 1825-1828

The Report of the Joint Standing Committee on State Lands, in *Resolves of State of Maine*, in *Resolves of Maine*, Vol. I, Wm. R. Smith & Co., Augusta.

Report of the Joint Select Committee of the Senate and House of Representatives of the State of Maine, 1828.

Report of the Joint Select Committee of the Maine Legislature on the Northeast Boundary, February 2, 1837.

The Commissioners Report of the Survey of the Northeast Boundary, 1838.

Maine Documents, 1831-32.

Resolves of the State of Maine, Vols. I-IV, Augusta, Maine, W. R. Smith, Printers to the State.

Acts and Resolves of the State of Maine, Vol. IV.

Private and Special Laws of the State of Maine, Vol. II, 1829-1835.

Historical Collections of the Piscataquis County, Maine, 1910.

United States Congress, Documents:

House of Representatives, [Executive] document no. 222, 25th Congress, 3rd Session, *Message from the President of the United States upon the Subject of* the present state of affairs between the State of Maine and the British Province of New Brunswick, February 26, 1839.

House of Representatives Report no. 314, 25th Congress, 3rd Session *Disturbance in Maine*

House of Representatives document no. 684, 29th Congress *Select Committee on Charges against Mr. Webster made by Mr. C. J. Ingersoll*,.

House of Representatives, document no. 684, *Official Misconduct of the Late Secretary of State*, 29th Congress, 1st Session, 1846, including "The Deposition of Francis O. J. Smith, Taken before the Select Committee of the House of Representatives Appointed to Investigate Certain Charges made by C. J. Ingersoll against Daniel Webster."

House of Representatives, [Executive] Document no.3, 25th Congress, 2nd Session, *Message from the President of the United States to the Two Houses of Congress at the Commencement of the Second Session*, December 5, 1837.

House of Representatives, [Executive] Document no. 31, *Message from the President of the United States transmitting the information required by the resolution of the House, of the 13th instant, on the subject of the Northeastern Boundary of the United States*, September 26, 1837.

House of Representatives, Document no. 90, 1827.

House of Representatives, [Executive] no.126, 25th Congress, 2nd Session, 1838.

House of Representatives, document no. 119, 38th Congress, 1st Session, *Defenses of the Northeastern Frontier*, June 28, 1864.

Senate document no. 35, John E. Wool, Brigadier General, "The Wool Report," 1838 and "The Graham Report," November 16, 1838.

Senate document no. 71, [Executive] 30th Congress, 1st Session, *Report of the Joint Commission of Bound*

ery, appointed under the *Treaty of Washington, August 9, 1842.*
Senate document no. 130, 20th Congress, 1st Session, in the United States Congressional Serials Set, Vol. 166, March 3, 1828; *Statements relating to alleged aggressions on the rights of citizens of the United States by the authorities of New Brunswick on the territory in dispute between the United States and Great Britain.*
Senate document no. 319, 25th Congress, 2nd Session, *Message of the President of the United States, transmitting all the Correspondence between the United States and Great Britain on the subject of the Northeast Boundary, March 21, 1838.*
Senate documents no. 414, 451, and 502. *Statement on the part of the United States, of the case referred, in pursuance of the Convention of 29th September, 1827, Between the said States and Great Britain, to his Majesty, the King of Netherlands, for his Decision thereon,* printed but not published, Washington, 1829.

PUBLISHED SOURCES, BOOKS:

A Compilation of the Messages and Papers of the Presidents, Fifty Second Congress, 1897, Bureau of National Literature, Inc., NY.
Thomas Albert, *The History of Madawaska*, Madawaska: Northern Graphics, English translation by Sister Therese Doucette and Dr. Francis Doucette.
Robert C. Alberts, *The Golden Voyage, the Life and Times of William Bingham, 1752-1804,* Houghton Mifflin Company, Boston, 1969.
Robert G. Albion, *Forests and Sea Power, 1652-1862,* Cambridge: Harvard University Press, 1926.
F. S. Allis, Jr., Ed., *William Bingham's Maine Lands, 1790-1820,* The Colonial Society of Massachusetts, 1954, Vol. XXXVI.

American State Papers, Foreign Relations, Washington, 1831-1859. [Six volumes.]

Aroostook War, Historical Sketch and Roster of Commissioned Officers and Enlisted Men Called into Service for the Protection of the Northeastern Frontier of Maine From February to May, 1839, Augusta, Kennebec Journal Print, 1904.

Stanley B. Atwood, *The Length and Breadth of Maine*, Orono: U. of Maine Press, 1971; H. W. Richardson.

Ronald F. Banks, *Maine Becomes a State*, Portland: Maine Historical Society.

Francis Barnes, *The Story of Houlton*, Houlton, Maine, Will H. Smith, publisher and printer, 1889.

Francis Barnes, Editor, *Spauldingania, Autobiogaphical Sketch of Reverend Royal Crafts Spaulding, and Extracts from Letters of Himself and His Wife, Jerusha Bryant Spaulding*, Houlton, ME, William H. Smith, 1891.

F. F. Bierne, *The War of 1812*, New York: E. P. Dutton and Company, Inc., 1949.

Alden Bradford, *History of Massachusetts for 200 Years*, Boston: Hilliard, Gray and Co., 1835.

Samuel F Bemis, *A Diplomatic History of the United States*, 1955, New York, Henry Holt and Co.

Henry Sweetser Burrage, *Maine in the Northeastern Boundary Dispute*, Portland: printed for the State of Maine, 1919.

Jim Brunelle, *Maine Almanac*, Portland: Guy Gannett, 1978.

H. George Classen, *Thrust and Counterthrust, the Genesis of the Canada-United States Boundary*, 1965, Longmans, Canada, Ltd.

Albert B. Corey, *The Crisis of 1830-1842 in Canadian-American Relations*, New Haven, Yale University Press; Toronto.

Alfred DeCelles, *Papineau*, Morang and Company, 1906.

Dictionary of Canadian Biography, Vol. IX, 1976, University of Toronto Press.

Harold A. Davis, *An International Community on the St. Croix, 1604-1930*, Orono: University of Maine, 1974.

Diplomatic Correspondence of the United States: Canadian Relations, 1784-1860, Vol. II, Washington: Carnegie Endowment International Peace, 1942.

Edgar, Lady, *General Brock*, Toronto: Morang and Co. Ltd.

Thomas Gaffney, *Maine's Mr. Smith, A Study of the Career of Francis O. J. Smith, Politician and Entrepreneur*, Doctoral thesis, University of Maine, Orono, 1979.

John E. Godfrey, *Annals of Bangor*, in *History of Penobscot County, Maine*, Cleveland: William Chase and Company, 1882.

George Hiram Greeley, *The Genealogy of the Greely-Greeley Family*, Boston, 1905.

Joseph Griffin, *The Press of Maine*, 1872, Brunswick, ME.

James Hannay, *The War of 1812*, in *Nova Scotia Historical Society*, Vol. XI, 1901.

Howard Jones, *To the Webster-Ashburton Treaty, A Study in Anglo-American Relations*, 1783-1843, Chapel Hill: University of North Carolina Press, 1977.

Richard W. Judd, *Aroostook, A Century of Logging in Northern Maine*, 1989, Orono: U. of Maine Press.

Lower, Arthur M., *Great Britain's Woodyard, British America and the Timber Trade, 1763-1867*, Montreal: McGill-Queens University Press.

C. Prestwood Lucas, *The Canadian War of 1812*, Oxford: Clarendon Press, 1906.

William Leo Lucey, S. J., *Edward Kavanagh, Catholic Statesman, Diplomat from Maine*, Francestown, NH.

W. S. MacNutt, *New Brunswick, A History: 1784-1867*, Toronto: Macmillan of Canada, 1963, 157-160.

_____, *The Atlantic Provinces*, Mc Clelland and Stewart, Ltd., 1965.

Frederick Merk, *Fruits of Propaganda in the Tyler Administration*, Boston: Harvard University Press, 1971.

Samuel Eliot Morrison, *The Maritime History of Massachusetts*, Boston: Houghton Mifflin Co, 1941.

Henry J. Morgan, *Sketches of Celebrated Canadians*.
Moscow History Committee, Moscow, ME, Editors, *Makers of Moscow*, 1966.
James H. Mundy and Earle G. Shettleworth, *The Flight of the Grand Eagle: Charles G. Bryant, Maine Architect and Adventurer*, Maine Historic Preservation Commission, Augusta, ME, 1977.
James H. Mundy, *Speakers of the Maine House of Representatives from 1820*. Clerk of the House, printed by J. S. McCarthy, Augusta, 1981.
———*Presidents of the Senate of Maine from 1820*, Secretary of the Senate of Maine, J. S. McCarthy, Augusta, ME, Printer.
Stanley Plummer, *History of Dexter*: Dexter Historical Society, Dexter, ME, 1976.
Joseph Porter, Ed., *Bangor Historical Magazine*, 6 vols.
W. O. Raymond, Editor, *State of the Madawaska and Aroostook Settlements in 1831, Report of John G. Deane and Edward Kavanagh to Samuel E Smith, Governor of the State of Maine*, (the Deane-Kavanagh Report) in *Collections of the New Brunswick Historical Society*, Vol. III, No. 9, 1914,
———,Ed., *Winslow Papers*, St John, New Brunswick, 1901.
H. W. Richardson; *York Deeds*, 1887, Portland, ME.
James D. Richardson, *A Compilation of Messages and Papers of the Presidents*, Washington, D. C.: Government Printing Office, 1896, Vol. III.
Winfield Scott, *Memoirs of Lieutenant General Winfield Scott*, New York: Sheldon and Company, 1864.
Marion Jacques Smith, *General William King*, Camden: Down East Books, 1980.
Arthur G. Staples, Ed., *The Letters of John Fairfield*, Lewiston Maine: Lewiston Journal, 1922.
Norah Story, *Oxford Companion to Canadian History and Literature*, 1967, Oxford University Press, N Y.
H. C. Williams, *Biographical Encyclopedia of Maine of the 19th Century*, Boston: Metropolitan Publishing and Engraving Co., 1885.

William Willis, *Law Courts and Lawyers of Maine*,
Portland, Bailey and Noyes, 1863.
William D. Williamson, *History of the State of Maine*,
Hallowell: Glazer, Masters & Co, 1839.
Richard G. Wood, *A History of Lumbering in Maine, 1820-1861*, Orono: University of Maine Press, 1961.

PUBLISHED SOURCES, ARTICLES:

E. D. Adams, "Lord Ashburton and the Treaty of Washington," *American Historical Review*, XVII, July 1912
J. Chris Arndt, "Maine in the Northeast Boundary Controversy: States' Rights in Antebellum New England," *The New England Quarterly*, June, 1989, 205-223, The Colonial Society of Massachusetts and Northeastern University.
Llewellyn Deane, "John G. Deane, A Sketch of his Life," *Collections of the Maine Historical Society*, Series II, Vol. I.
Edward H. Elwell, "Enoch Lincoln," in *Collections of the Maine Historical Society*, Ser. II, Vol. I.
Albert Gallatin,"A Memoir on the Northeastern Boundary," New York Historical Society.
William Frances Ganong, "A Monograph of the Evolution of the The Boundaries of the Province of New Brunswick," *Transactions of the Royal Society of Canada*, [Series II, Vol. 7.]
D. C. Harvey, "The Halifax-Castine Expedition" *Dalhousie Review*, July, 1938.
Edward Kavanagh, "Wilderness Journal", *Maine History News*, Maine League of Historical Societies and Museums, Vol. XVI No. 2 and No. 4.
Barry J. Lohnes, "A New Look at the Invasion of Eastern Maine, 1814," Portland, 1975, Maine Historical Society *Quarterly*, Vol. XV, No. 1, Summer.
W. S. MacNutt, "New Brunswick's Age of Harmony", *Canadian Historical Review*, Vol. XXXII, No. 2, 1951.

Harriett W. Marr, "Grants of Land to Academies in Massachusetts and Maine," *Historical Collections of the Essex Institute*, Vol. 88, 1952.

Dale R. Steinhaurer " 'A Class of Men': United States Army Recruits in Maine, 1822-1860", Maine Historical Society *Quarterly*, Vol. 30, No. 2, pp. 92-119.

Harvey Strum, "Smuggling in Maine During the Embargo and the War of 1812," *Colby Library Quarterly*, Vol. XIX, No. 2, 90-97.

Donald B. Webster, Jr., "Penobscot Expedition of 1814," *Tradition*, Vol. IV, No. 1, [January 1961], 58.

Donald A. Wise, "Surveying and Mapping the International Border of Northeast Maine, 1817-1818," from *Surveying and Mapping*, Vol. XL, No. 4, 1980

"The One Hundred and Fourth," Vol. I, *New Brunswick Magazine*, July, 1898.

"Memorial of the Halifax Committee of Trade to Bathurst," October 8, 1813, *Public Archives of Nova Scotia*, Vol. 304, Document 6, No. 66.

BROCHURES

"The Habitation, Port Royal National Historic Park," Minister of Environment, Ministry of Supply and Services, Canada, 1981.

MAPS

Gerald E. Morris, Ed. *Maine Bicentennial Atlas, An Historical Survey*, Maine Historical Society, 1976.

Sketch of the Disputed Territory, showing the Military Posts occupied by the British and Americans in 1840, Lieutenant Colonel Oldfield, K. H., Royal Engineers Montreal, 12 August, 1840. National Archives, Washington, D. C.

Bouchette-Johnson Survey Maps, Collection of the Maine Historical Society Archives, Portland.

APPENDIX I

SETTLERS IN THE DISPUTED TERRITORY AND IN NEIGHBORING AROOSTOOK COUNTY TOWNS, IN 1820, 1830 AND 1840

1820

Source: Census of the United States for the District of Maine, in 1820 in *Statement on the Part of the United States, of the case referred, in pursuance of the Convention of 29th September, 1827, Between the said States and Great Britain, to his Majesty, the King of Netherlands, for his Decision thereon* Printed but not published, Washington, 1829, Appendix L.

[Editor's note: To decipher many names in the 1820 lists, it must be remembered that a New England census taker, with no knowledge of the French language, and possibly with a "Boston accent," with its soft "r's" and a tendency to pronounce a final "a" as an "er" syllable, wrote these names down phonetically. He would probably have pronounced "farmer" as "famah" and "Madawaska" as "Madawasker."]

Holton [Houlton] Plantation: Wm. Averel, Edmund Core [Cone], Samuel Kook [Cook], Jacob Harrow, George Hart, James Holton, Joseph Holton, Samuel Holton, Joshua G. Kendall, Samuel Kendall, Ephriam McCondar, Micajah Morrell,Thomas Osbon [Osborn], Eleazer Pickard, Amos Put-

nam, Abraham Peirce, Amos Peirce, Eleazer Packard, Aaron Putnam, Josiah Putnam, James Taylor, Ebenezer Warner, Wm. Williams, Lewis Wright.
New Limerick Plantation, 1820: Samuel Drew, Joseph Goodenouf, Isaiah Morrison, Samuel Morrison, Samuel Morrison Jr., Stephen Morrison, Edmund Webber, Moses K. Wells.
French Settlement and Matawascah [Madawaska] Parish, 1820: Charles Adet, Joseph Albare, Vincent Albert, Albert Albert, Jr., Joseph Albert, Michael Babert, Nathan Baker, Vasion Bare, Lewis Belflour, Leon Belflour, Lewis Belflour Jr., Lario Bellgley, John Betisiere, Charles Bolio, Bartholomew Burgoin, John Betuke, Barnum Bushiere, Alexander Camio, Peter Camio, Francis Carney, Colemarkee Chrint, Gruino Chasse, Levy Clare, Alare Ann L. Clare, Alexander Crock, David Crock, Jeremiah Crock, Peter Crock, David Cyer, Elecis Cyr, Joseph Cyr, Christopher Cyer, Christost Cyer, Joseph Cyer, Xasrie Cyr, Loron Sear, Jean Sier [Cyr], Demeque Dagle, John Betis Dagle, Joseph Dagle, Mermeit Dagle, Gumain Debe, Jeremiah Dubey, Peter Duperre, Pherman Dusett, Francis Dousett, Anthony Gagne, Augustus Gavah, John B. Gavah, John Harford, John Hitchambow, Joseph Jenian, Lorent Jenian, Jeremy Jermer, Betis Joshia, Jeremere Joshia, Harris Laushiere, Honerd Larassaus, Lewis Leebore, Benjamin Lerassaus, Betis Lewsure, Peter Lezert, Michael Man, Paul Markee, Joseph Markure, Paul Marquis, Andrew Martin, Bazell Martin, Belon Martin, Charles Martin, Francis Martin, Jr., John B. Martin, Joseph Martin, Michael Martin 3rd, Simon Martin, Chrystatine Marton, Joseph Mashaw, Joseph Mashaw, Peter McCure [Mercure?], Michael Mercure, Lewis Mercure, Joseph Michaud, Joseph Michaud, John Miresheir, Jereman Morio, Jarom Morio, Batis Morris, Firmen Nadard, Benjamin Nedar, Joseph Nedow, Ely Neecchoson [Nickerson], John B. Parser, Nicholas Pelchey, Joseph Pelkey, Ran Pelkey, Nicholas Peltiere, Nicholas Peltiere Jr., Peter Peltihey, Michael Serene, Clemo Shimon, Phinney Stepheddo, Frederic Tareo, Siomon Tareo,

Joseph Tarrio, Lawrance Tarrio, Alevey Tibedore [Thibodeau], Betis Tibedore, David Tibedore, David Tibedore, Francis Tibbedo, John B. Tibedore, John B. Tibedore, Jr., John B. Tibedore 3rd, John Tibedore, John B. Tibedore, John Betis Tibedore, John B. O. Thibedore, George Tibedore, George Thibedore, Greguire Thibedore, Joseph Tibedore, Joseph Tibadore, Lewis Tibedore, Michael Tibedore, Michael Thibedore, Oliver Thibedore, Paulet Tibedore, Susan Tibedore, Henry Turdey, Chement Sausiere, Joseph Somphisaw, Lewis Sumpheysaw, Lewis Stephed, Germanis Sawuire, Benjamin Versier, Henry Versier, Alexander Violet, Augustus Violet, Francis Violet, Francis Violet, Isaac Violet, Isaac Violet 3rd, John Violet, Larison Violet, Lewis Willet.

True Bradbury, Assistant to the Marshal, found 1,256 people to be living in his Division in October, 1820.

1830

Source: United States Census of 1830, for Washington County, Maine, part of which would become Aroostook County, in 1839:

"**Aroostook**" [Aroostook River Valley area], 1830: Ferdinand Armstrong, Peter Bull, Thomas Beckwith, Wm. Brown, Elias Brown, Henry Bradley, John Bradley, Charles Boobar, Nathaniel Churchill, Joshua Christa, David Cook, Alexander Cochran, Patrick Conley, Anthony Cain[e?], James Campbell, Alexander Downey, Gabriel Davenport, John Dorsey, Joseph Davenport, Dennis Fairbanks, Peter Fowler, James Fitzherbert, Thomas Goss, Francis Guilier, Bela Gardner, Nehemiah Hooper, Charles Johnson, Lewis Johnson, James [Viah? Kiah? Vial?], John Knowles, Laura Kelley, Wm. Lovely, Alex McDoodle [Mc Dougald], Peter Mc Doodle [McDougald] Barnard McLaughlin, Daniel McLaughlin, Nehemiah Mumford, George Manser, James McNelly, John Owens, Wm. Pyle, Jonathan Parks, James Powers, Mrs. Parker, Jno. Rafford, Jno. [Rieul? Rieux?], Thomas Rogers, Michael Russell, Thomas [Tilly? Libby?],

Isaac Thomas, Wm. Thompson, Charles [Walters?], Nathaniel Bradstreet.

Houlton, 1830:
James Belyea, Abraham Bigelow, Wm. Bloodgood, B. A. Boynton, John Bradford, C. Brannin, Alex Caldwell, Elijah Carr, Wm. Cary, Isaac Chase, Peter Chase, Levi Clark, Martin Collier, Samuel Cook, John Cox, Ebenezer Crosby, Wm. Daley, Greenleaf Dearborn, James A. Drew, Jonah Dunn, Frederick Emmons, Hiram Estey, John Farley, Wm. [Fohniby?] Nathan Gibson, [Jere?] Goodwin, Jonathan Greenleaf, Ralph Holden, James Houlton, Joseph Houlton, Samuel Houlton, Joshua Kendall, Robert Kerr, Samuel Kidder, James Lander, Peleg Lander, Lewis [Lessman?], John McIntosh, Wm. Moore, Louis Morrill, Michael O'Brien, Thomas Osborne, Eleazar Parker, Abraham Pierce, Stephen [Powels?], Benjamin Prosser, Stephen Pullen, Aaron Putnam, Amos Putnam, Joshua Putnam, Joshua Putnam 2nd, Sterritt Putnam, Philip Roach, J. B. F. Russell, Daniel Ryan, Thomas Saniford, Putnam Shaw, Francis Shining, Edmund Shorey, Isaac Smith, Jeremiah Sprague, Gould Stanley, Francis Taggert, Richard Tidswell, James Thomas, John Tourney, James Van Pelt, Eben Warner, Wm. Williams, John Wilson.

Westford Grant [south half of **Hodgdon**], 1830:
John Tidd, Hugh Cosgrove, John Darrell, James Daggett, Isaac Gerow, Charles Lyons, John Outhouse, Daniel [David?] Smith.

Hodgdon, [north half] 1830:
Catherine Benn, Daniel Brackett, Thomas Brown, Noah Clough, James Dilling, James B. Doyle, Chesley Drew, Joseph Furze, Abraham Gerow, Jacob Goodnight, Samuel Grant, Wm. Green, E. C. Hall, James Hammond, Patrick Harding, Nathaniel Harrington, Wentworth Herrick, Sylvanus Howes, John Jones, Joseph Kendall, Thomas Landers, Stephen Lathrop, Jeremiah Lyon, Jul Lyons, Andrew MacCaslin, Wm. McDonald, Isaac Putnam, Jacob Russell, Charles Smart, Lewis Stone, James U. Taylor, Alfred Todd, Ebenezer Towne, Thomas Tripp, Isaac White, Jacob

White, Jesse White, John White, Wm. White, Wm. White, Charles Wilson, Aloniso Welch, Thomas Whorley, Isaac [Yonea?] [Yerenton?].
Linneus, 1830:
Hugh Alexander, Moses Burly [Burleigh], James Hamilton, Jacob Martin, Daniel Neal, John Rich, John Shields, Samuel Shields, Daniel Spaulding, John Stevens, Silas Varney.
Cary Plantation, [No 1, Range 1], 1830:
Wm. Clark, Israel Davis, W. L. Dow, Edward Doherty, John Mathison, David Moore, James McGlinch [McGlinchy?] John Reed, George Robinson, Hugh Smith, Jonathan Tracy.
Amity, [No 10, Range 1], 1830:
Wm. Clark, Jonathan Clifford, Edmund Cone, James H. Curtis, Columbus Dunn, Seth Farrar, Jonathan Greenleaf, Samuel Newman, Jacob Russell, Asa Tracy, Almond Wilkins, Benjamin Winship, Thomas Winship.
Dolls Township, 1830:
George A. Bennett, Wm. Gilkey, Wm. Hinds, Edward Henderson, Stephen Jones, Joseph Jones, Joseph Jones, Jr., [Austin?] Knight, John Logan, Wm. Lee, Frances Milton, Israel Oaks, John Pritchard, Frederick Perley, David Poor, Heywood Reed, James Russell, John Staples, Stephen Spencer, John Watson.
Weston, [Hampden Academy Grant], 1830:
Wm. Butterfield, Calvin Clark, Samuel Cleaves, John Davenport, Joseph Foss, Thos. Gillson. Thos. Gilpatrick, John Haskell, Wm. Pollard, Simon Scribner, Samuel Skinner.
Schoodic Lakes, 1830:
Wm. Deering, Wm. Moore.
Haynesville, 1830: At Mattawamkeag Forks:
Thomas Hall, John Knowles [Knowlen?], Jonathan Wilson. At Mattawamkeag River: Charles Gilson.
Ludlow and New Limerick, [Belfast Academy Grant] 1830: Edgar Anderson, Robert Blaisdell, Ebenezer Bradbury, Jabez Bradbury, True Bradbury, Reuben Chase, David Clark, Isaac Clark, Seth Cleaves, Bradford Comings, John Commings, Royal Coolbroth, David Corless, Wm. Dalton, Isaac Dickinson, Moses Drew, Samuel Drew, George Gill-

eland. Jesse Gilman. Joseph Goodenow, Oliver Gould, Samuel Gould, Jonathan Hayes, George Howe, Rufus Jamieson, Alfred Marshall, Edmund Morison, Isaiah Morrison, Samuel Morrison, Samuel Morrison Jr., Stephen Morrison, M_ Philpot, Stephen Randall, Andrew Rogers, Paul Smith, John Stewart, John Sylvester, James [Thomas?], Edmund Webber, Washington W[ebber?].
Wellington Grant, 1830:
Hugh Grimes, George Pond.

1840

Source: United States Census for Aroostook County, 1840, [Enumerated by Gorham Parks, assistant Marshall, appointed to take the census of the town of Madawaska North, in the State of Maine, certified by Stover Rines and John Baker.]
Madawaska, 1840:
Freeman Albert, Joseph Albert, John Baker, John Barribee, Nathaniel Bartlett, Vacon Bell, Jr., Vaison Bell, Louis Bellfleur, Antoine Belfleur, Louis Bijot, Alexander Bonnefas, Ephriam Bootot, Eneas Bornay, Oliver Boucher, Ashur Boulier, Etienne Boulier, Charles Boulier, Jacob Boulier, Martial Boulier, Bartholomew Burgoyne, __ Burke, Bullier [B?]uttry, Paul Carcaus, Joseph Careaux, Samuel Carney, Joseph Chary, Henry Chasse, Joseph Chasse, Francis Cher, John Cloquet, John Connet, Leonard Coombs, Freeman Cormier, Alexander Cornea, Alexis Cyr, Alvan Cyr, Billaud Cyr, Christopher Cyr, Eli Cyr, Elias Cyr, Fabian Cyr, Frederick Cyr, Henry Cyr, James Cyr, Joseph Cyr, Laurent Cyr, Laurier Cyr, Pascal Cyr, Pascal Cyr, Peter Cyr, Theodore Cyr, Auguste Daigle, Larion Daigle, Frederick Davenport, George Demot, Francis De-mot, __ Demo, Marca Demot, Abraham Diblee, Joseph Dominick, Joseph Doosto, George Dowell, Firman Ducet, Freeman Ducheme, Abraham Dufour, Freeman Duplessis, Jere Dumond, Andre Elbert, John Emerson, Miles Emery, James Foley, Joseph Fornier, John Gardiner, Ave Garnier, Bat-

tiste Gavais, _?_ Germat, James Glorin, Daniel Godain, Joseph Godain, Newell Godrow, Francis [Goestia?], Jerome Gornier, Antoine Gonyou, Bosal Gonyou, Christopher Gouvain, James Grew, John Hayford, [Hafford] Jr., Phineas Hayford [Hafford], Andrew Hammond, Francis Harvey, Leazel Hebert, John Henderson, Barnabi Hunnewell, John Johnson, George Johnson, Pascal Johnson, Wm. Johnston, Marble Kerba, Thomas Kennedy, Michael Lablanche, John Labree, Francis Lable, Auguste Landry, Laurence Landry, Paul Landry, Gregorie Langevane, Louis Lapointe, Edward LeBlanc, Peter Lecompte, Edward LeClerk, Ballazer Legarnier, Oliver Legasse, Daniel Leveque, Peter Livy, Louis Lizert, Olwan Lizert, George Long, Memen Long, Michel Longboy, Joseph Louce, John R. Loveway, Edward Loveway, Laurence Loveway, __ McCrea, Henry McDaniel, Widow McDonald, Charles McFarson, James Maly, Jere Marceaux, Nicholas Marceaux, Francis Martin, Patrick Martin, Simon Martin, Andre Micheaux, Joseph Micheaux, Andre Mijeaux, Edwin Mizeaux, Seriam Mizeaux, Andrew Martin, Basil Martin, Billand Martin, Cyril Martin, Frederick Martin, John Martin, John B. Martin, Joseph Martin, Joseph Martin, Lawrence Martin, Michele Martin, Pillaud Martin, Raze Martin, Thomas Martin, Henry Marture, Louis Marture, Vatel Marture, A. Mereau, Cephas Micheaux, Charles Micheaux, Freeman Micheaux, James Micheau, Laurient Micheaux, Marcel Micheaux, Rean Micheaux, Joseph Moreau, Joseph Moreau, Louis Moreau, Wm. Mullen, Frederic Musarod, David Nadeau, Freeman Nadeau, John Nadeau, Joseph Nadeau, Louis Nadeau, Louis Nadeau, Oliver Nadeau, Electus Oakes, Joseph Olude, Frances Pacet, John M. Paron, Peter Paradis, Vanson Paradis, Paulet Parquee, Alexander Pelkay, Augustes Pelkay, Eluy Pelket, Lavier Perot, Francis Piquet, Marin Pleide, Peter Pliede, Peter Plue, John Pilkay, Cyril Potter, Patrick Powers, Walter Powers, John Rabetai, John Ramoux, Peter Rasin, Louis Reinhart, Herod Rey, Francois Rice, Pattazer Rousseau, John Sanioy, Gallon Santon, Daniel Savage, Wesley Savage, Francis Searway [Sirois?], John Searway, John P.

Searway, Wm. Shorette. Dennis Smith, James Smith, Joseph Souci, Samuel Searway, Horace Souci, Clement Soucier, Jere Soucier, Cylestine Soucy, __ Strichman, Henry [Tadu?], Billaud Tallieux, Joseph Tallieux, Joseph Tallieux, Laurent Tallieux, Rame Tallieux, Raymond Tallieux, Joseph Thaddee, Adolph Thibodeaux, Battiste O. Thibedeaux, David Thibedeaux, Firman Thibedeau, Francois Thibedeaux, Francis Thibodeau, John Thibodeau, John B. Thibedeaux, Joseph Thibodeaux, Louis Thibedeaux, Micheal Thibedeau, Simon Thibedeaux, John Thomas, __ Tighe, John Vassal, Nore Vassicur, Phinehas Viancourt, Augustus Vilet [Violet], Larrier Vilet, Razamon Vilet, Thadee Vilet, Augustus Webster, Wm. Welsh, Jesse Wheelock, Alexander Willet, Andre Willet, Anthony Willet, Auguste Willet, Battiste Willet, Battiste Willet, Charles Willet, Charles Willet, George Willet, John Willet, Joseph Willet, Battiste Yaret, Isaac Yerenton, Conti You, Willelm __, Jack__.

LETTER A 5TH RANGE, 1840:
Elias Jourdon, Nathaniel Lord?, Levi Wheeler.

NO 1, 5TH RANGE, 1840:
Andrew Bonny, Stephen Cobb.

NO 2, 5TH RANGE, "Irish Township," [Benedicta?], 1840:
Nicholas [Bivdinch?], Patrick Brady, Thomas Bran, David Bracken, Wm. Brown, John Byrone, John Burke, Martin Carey, Thomas Casey, Wm. Crogan, Timothy Darcey [Daicey?], James Dee, Edwin Doyle, Henry Farrell, Cornell Gallagher, Henry Grover, David Harding, James Hawks, John Hayes, John Holland, John Bagley, Jeremiah Kane, John Karnes, Christopher Kegan, Nicholas Larkin, Martin Lawler, John McMan, John McNamara, Michael Mahau, John [Millmoc?], John Perry, Peter Plunket, Martin Qualy, John D. Rush, John Ryan, Francis Smith, Barney Stairs, Edward Sweeney, [Rev'd?] W. Tyler, John Woodlocke.

NO [1?] 5TH RANGE, 1840:
Samuel B. Chandler, John Cram, Alfred Cushman, Alfred Foss, Wm. Hunt, Edward Kimball, Henry Kimball, Joseph D.

Kimball, James Lock, Samuel [Mauthis?], Edwin Parker, Spaulding [Robinson?], John T. Spofford, James S. Stacey.
NO [4?], 5TH RANGE or "FISH'S TOWNSHIP," 1840:
Henry Barker, John Bell, Ebenezer Blackburn?, Oliver Blackwell, Henry Blake, Henry Boswell, John Carpenter, Bela Chesley, Silas Coburn, Wm. Cunningham, Ephriam Fairfield, Horatio Garland, Samuel Garland, Andrew Grant, Josiah Hall, Levi Holman, Samuel Huston, Eli Kellogg, Nathaniel Leslie, Almond Lewis, Wm. Lovejoy, Jared McKea, Ichabod Morrell, Jonathan Palmer, Jacob Pearley, Benjamin L. Pierce, Perrin S. Reed, Solomon E. Reed, George Rigby, Oliver Robinson, America Robbins, Lucinda Robins, Joseph Scarlett, Joseph Sprague, Isaac Webber, Hanson Weeks, John Weeks, Daniel Whitehouse, Samuel Wiggin, Hiram Willie, Willard G. [N or ?] emew.
NO 6, 5TH RANGE, 1840:
Nicholas Cooper, Jonathan Fairbrother, Charles Farewell, George H. Inman, Esia [Esra?] Myrick.
NOS 7 and 9, 5TH RANGE, 1840:
Calvin Bradford, Isaac Lewis, John Shepard, John Matherson, David [Daniel?] D. Smith.
NO 10, 5TH RANGE, [Masardis], 1840:
Eb_ Boltnoh, Wm. Coperthwaite, Charles Ellis, Ebenezer Estey, Samuel Fogg, Thomas Goss, Jr., George Grantham, John Hickey, Leonard Jones, Ephriam Knight, John Knowland, Abiel McCollister, Thomas McDaniel, Cyrus McKenney, Isaac McKenney, Thomas Neil, Sanford Noble, Wm. Parsons?, John Phinney, Isaiah Pishim [Pishon?], Joseph Pollard, George Sawyer, Solomon Soule.
NO 11, RANGE 5, [Ashland], 1840:
David G. Cooke, Wm. Cumming, Wm. Dalton, Jabez [Devincia?], Thomas Goss, Rufus Kelley, Elbridge G. Wakefield.
NO 13, 3RD RANGE, [Washburn], 1840:
Thomas Beckwith, Peter Bull, Joshua Christie, Nathaniel Churchill, Wm. Stover?, Wm. Westford.
LETTER [G] 2ND RANGE, [South side of Aroostook River, Maysville, now Presque Isle], 1840:

Henry Bradley, Louis Bradley James F. Cumins, Luther Dwelley, Nathan Gardiner, Amos Heald, John Rafford, James [ellols?].

LETTER [G?] 2ND RANGE, [North side of the Artoostook River in Maysville, now part of Presque Isle?], 1840: Wm. Elliot, Dennis Fairbanks, David [Daniel?] Fenderson, George Field, Wm. Field, Thomas Hobart, Nehemiah S. Hooper, Louis Johnson, John Oaks, James Pomroy, Wm. Pyle, Peleg Spenser, Isaac Thomas.

PLYMOUTH AND EATON GRANTS, 1ST RANGE, [Plymouth Grant became part of Fort Fairfield] [Eaton Grant was part of Township H, Range 2, which became Lyndon and then part of Caribou], 1840: John Benjamin, Thomas Fales, Wm. Hamilton, Benjamin Hicks, Isaac McDonald, Alexander McDougal, James Nichols, Andrew Scott, Solomon Pyle.

LETTERS [? AND ?] 1ST AND 2ND RANGES, [Maysville? now part of Presque Isle], 1840: Thomas Armsdell, Ferdinand Armstrong, Wm. Bishop, Wm. Boobar, Anthony Cane, Alexander Cochran, Patrick Conley, Samuel Davenport, David [Duty?] [Doody], Samuel Farley, Patrick Finley, Peter Fowler, Thomas [Giney?], Justus Gray, Boynard Guiggey, James Guiggey, Dennis Heald, Lawrence Kelley, Patrick Kelley, Wm. Lovely, Isaac Morris, Collingwood Murphy, John Noland, Jonathan Parks, James Rogers, Paul Turner, John Twaddle, Andrew Walsh, Samuel Works, Wm. Works.

PLYMOUTH GRANT, [Fort Fairfield], 1840: Francis Boles, Thomas Boles Charles Boobar, David Burchell, Charles Butler, David Cambell, [Veranes?] Chandler, Solomon Deane, Nicholas Dee, John Dorsey, John Dorsey, Jr., Job Everett, James Fitzherbert, Henry Heard, Wm. Holman, Wm. Johnson, Jonathan Johnston, John Lovely, Mitchell McCarty, Michael McKenney, Martin Murray, Barney McLaughlin, John Radiker, Michael Russell, Jesse Tarbell, Joel Tucker, Thomas Whitaker, Gowen [Wilson?].

LETTER [E? F?], [Township F, Range 2 is Presque Isle], 1840: John Amons, Philo Bean, Joseph Bickford, Ephriam

Clark, Ephriam Hall, John McCurdick, John Wade, Emmons Whitcomb, Orris Whitney.

FORT FAIRFIELD, 1840:
Samuel Bailey, Moses C. Burley, Samuel K. Burley, Wm. Carter, Calvin W. Cottin, Mahalia Crocker, Ebenezer Daggett, Gideon [Decoring?], John B. Dolley, Richard Foss, Joseph Fox, David Jameson, Oliver H. Jewell, Robert Kirbey, Isaac Leach, Dudley Leavitt, George W. Leavitt, David Mc Neil, Joseph Nelson, Chaplin Nelson, David Pratt, Henry Reed, John B. Wing, Thomas Woodlock.

NO 3, 6TH AND 7TH RANGES, 1840:
Charles C. Boynton, Augustus Howard, James Howard, Lydia Howard, Benjamin [Kirk?], [Wynn?] Rice, John Saunders, Albert Hale.

Amity, 1840:
James Austin, Peter Bedec, Wm. Clark, Edmund Cone, Benjamin Corliss, James H. Curtiss, James Daggett Jr., Waterman Daggett, John Dakin, Isaac Davis, Isreal Davis, Edward Dorethy [Dority], Edward Dorethy Jr., Columbus Dunn, Seth Farrar, Jonathan Greenleaf, David Harmon, Seth Kempton, James Merrill, David Moore, Israel Nason, Daniel Neal, John V. Putnam, John Read, Jacob M. Russell, Aaron Scott, Wm. Sheighen, Samuel Shephard, Hugh Smith, Sylvanus Steward, Asa Tracy, James Tracy, Edmund Watson.

Cary Plantation, 1840:
Edward Dorety Sr, Edward Dorety Jr., David Moore, James Merrill, Daniel Neal, John V. Putnam, John Reed, Sylvanus Steward, Hugh Smith, Wm. Sheighen, Aaron Scott, Jonathan Tracy.

Bancroft, 1840: Daniel Bean, Wm. Collins, Nathaniel Downs, Merritt C. Foster, Atwell Jellison, Josiah Jellison, Joseph Greene, Simeon Irish, Shubael Kelly, Wentworth Lombard, Jacob Lord, Joseph Rollins, Joseph Shorey, Jeremiah Skillinger, Alpheus Spaulding, Jeremiah B. Thompson, Nathaniel Thompson, John Travers.

Bridgewater, 1840:

Joseph Bradstreet, Nathaniel Bradstreet, John H. Bridges, George Flewellen, Joshua Fulton, Joseph Ketchum, Dennis Nelson, Orrin Nelson, David Packard, John Young.
Forkstown, [Township 3, Range 2,] 1840;
Samuel Ellis, Sweet Ellis, Jeremiah Kelley
Glenwood [Township 2, Range 3] 1840:
Jonathan Plummer, Seth Spaulding, Asa Straw.
Hodgdon, 1840:
[Note: This Hodgdon list only includes residents of Hodgdon in both 1830 and 1840.]
Isaac Adams, Wm. Addington, Sarah Anderson, John Bell, Catherine Benn, Edward Benn, Ephriam Benn, Solomon Benn, Abraham Benn, Francis Bird, Wm. Blisard, Daniel Brackett, Christopher C. Bradbury, Edwin Bradbury, Jabez Bradbury, Alexander Brown, Asa Brown, Thomas Brown, Thomas J. Brown, Jane Brown, Michael Cassidy, Noah Clough, Hugh Cosgrove, Major James Daggett, James Daggett Jr., Waterman Daggett, Robert Daggett, John Darrell, Hartley Deering, James Dilling, Patrick Dinen, James B. Doyle, Chesley Drew, Wm. Fisher, Noah Furbush, Joseph Furze, Abraham Gerow, Joseph Gerow, Jacob Goodnight (Goodenough?), Samuel Grant, James Grant, Wm. Green, Abraham Green, E. C. Hall, Abner Ham, James Ham, James Hammond, Patrick Harding, Nathaniel Harrington, Joseph B. Haven, Wentworth Herrick, Daniel Hilton, Willard Howard, Sylvanus Howes, Francis P. Hunter, John Hutchinson, John Hutchinson, Isaac L. Hutchinson, Christopher C. Hutchinson, John C. Ingraham, Samuel E. Jackins, John W. Jackins, John Jones, Daniel Jones, Thomas Kimball, Thomas Lander, Thomas Lane, John Lincoln, John P. Lincoln, James Lindsay, Hezekiah Lindsey, Thomas Lloyd, Stephen Lothrop, Charles Lyons, Jeremiah Lyons, Jul Lyons, Andrew McCaslin, Malcolm McCollum, Wm. McDonald, Samuel McIntire, Stephen Martin, Louis Morrill, James Nolen, John Outhouse, Nicholas Outhouse, Thomas P. Packard, Jonathan Paine, Aaron Perley, Wm. Peters, Luke Petit, Gilman Philbrick, Aaron Plummer, Stillman Pollard, Luther Porter, David H. Porter, Capt. Luther

Quint, Gardiner Read, Samuel Rhoda, Alphonzo Rogers, Frances Scott, Putnam Shaw, Charles Smart, David Smith, Daniel Smith, Jeremiah Sprague, Wm. Sterritt, Peltiah M. Stevens, Lewis Stone, Wm. Stone, James U. Taylor, David Tidd, John Tidd, Alfred Todd, Ebenezer Towne, Thomas Tripp, Cushman Walker, Alonzo Welch, Isaac White, John White, Wm. White, Jacob or James White, Jonathan White, Thomas White, Thomas White 2nd, Jesse White, Isaac White, John White, Thomas White, Jonathan Whitney, Moses Whitney Jr., Samuel Whitney, Thomas Whorley, Rufus Wiggins, Charles Wilson, Matthew Wilson.

Houlton, 1840:

[Brigadier General Eustis, United States Army, Commanding, at Hancock Barracks, took the census.]

Heads of households: Deborah Adams, Edmon Banks, John Basford, George A. Bennett, Dennis Boil, James C. Burrows, Cyrus Bray, Horace Broad, Maryann Baker, John Brown, Benjamin Burley, Shepherd Cary, [?erbon] Creasy, Joseph Creasy, Samuel Cook, David W. Clifford, Reuben Chase, Ephriam M. Condra, Isaac Chase, Patrick Collins, Wm. [P.?] Collins, James A. Drew, [Malisa Doll?], Mikiel Donovan, [Homer?] S. Daggett, Jeremiah Donivan, Job Edminster, Hyrum Esty, Green Evins, Jonas Eaton, Ezekeil French, Timothy Frisby, Christopher Foss, Jacob Frisby, Samuel Frisby, David Foster, John A. Fernald, Samuel Gooch, John Garvey, John H. Green, Isaiah Gould, James [Ginden?],Wm. H. Gibson, Alvin Gould, Wm. B. Gilkey, Rice Gosland, Christopher Gross [Cross?], Freeman Gilkey, Patrick Hardin, George Haslett, Luke Hastings, Albion P. Haywood, Wentworth Hall, Elias Hiscock, Charles Herrington, John Hogan, Harrison Houlton, James Houlton, Joseph Houlton, Edward Henderson, Zelotes Haskell, Alonzo Haskell, Batchelder Hussey, Bartholomew [Howles?], Wm. Hasey, Wm. Hews, Garrett Hews, John F. H. Hall, Philip B. Holden, Zebulon Ingersoll, Richard Jolley, John H. Jones, Joseph Jones, Hendrik Judson, Phillip Keen, Green Kendall, Arstron Knight, Thomas Knox, Peleg Lander,

David Libby, John Libby, John Louring, Wade Litchfield, John Logan, Samuel Lambert, Wm. McGrouty, John Mann, Allen Morrison, Alexander Moor, Rufus Mansur, George Morrell, Thomas McKelpin, James McBrine, Elexander Mac-Caslin, Philip Morey, Catherine Machin [Maclin?], Wm. McDonald, Reuben M. Mancer, Charles McClusky, Mary Mallory, Wm. Martin, Jonas McKinney, John Martin, Margaret Mahoney, John McVicar, John Niles, Wm. Nye, Nelson Oliver, Israel Oaks, John Owen, Rufus Orn, Mitchel O'-Brine, Stephen Pettee, Eleazer Packerd, George Parks, Wm. Parson, Joseph Parks, Aaron Putnam, Joshua Putnam, Lysander Putnam, Andrew Porter, James Perrington, Amos Putnam, Abrahan Pierce, Romain L. Putnam, Stephen Pullen, Leonard Pierce, Moses Person [Parson?], Stern Putnam, Thomas Parks, Jesse Quinton, Francis Rice, James Russell, Charles H. Shepherd, Henry Skidgels, Prescott Spaulding, Ezor Smith, Wm. Skidgels, Andres Stitham, Stilman Stone, John Staples, David Sypher, Isaac Smith, Robert Sanborn, Bartlett Smith, Joseph Spencer, ___ Stackpole, Isaac Tabor, Benjamin Treadwell, [Dennis T.?arney], Jeremiah Trueworthy, Stephen Thomas, Francis Targett, Nathaniel G. Treat, James Tull, Wm. Vandine, Ezekiel Vandine, Augustus Varnum, Robert Vernon, Sally Whittier, James Williams, John Wilson, Isaac White, Daniel Wyman, Ebenezer Warner, Moses White, James Webb, Jonathan Watson, Mathias Whalin, Wm. Williams.

Linneus, 1840:
Hugh Alexander, Jesse B___, Edmund Bickford, Benjamin Bither. Wm. D. Bither, David W. Boobar, Samuel Brown, Harrison Buck, Thomas Burton, Moses Burleigh, Winfield G. Carpenter, John H. Clough, Isaac Cochran, Ebenezer Collins, David Corless, Jackson Corson, Dennis Coye, Joseph Downes, Hiram Eaton, James Elliot, Alexander Gamble, Alexander Gamble 2nd, Nathaniel Goodhue, John C. Hamilton, Richard Hamilton, Jonathan Hayes, Elijah Hersey, John Homan, Jesse Joward, John Jones, Isaiah Keith, Nathan Lamb, James McGary, Daniel McMullen, Jacob Martin,

Joshua Merrill, Edmund Morrison, Isaiah Morrison, Samuel Morrison, Wm. Morrison, James Niles, Charles Norcross, Freeman Pike, Lawson Pratt, Benjamin Rackliff, John Russell, James Ruth, Isaac Sawyer, James Sawyer, William Scott, Ezra Shields, John Shields, Thomas Shields, Luther Simmons, John Stevens, David Veal [Vail], George W. Webber, Mary Whitney, Christopher Williamson.

Littleton 1840:
[Framingham Academy Grant:] James Thorncroft.
[Williams College Grant:] Thomas Asbin, Lewis DeLate, Charles Durning, Oliver Fletcher, Samuel B. Gilkey, Rufus Hambleton, Andrew P. Jones, Samuel P. Kelley, Jerome Moor, Edmond Shorey, Mark Staples, James Sutter, Thomas Trip, [Adrian?] H. Turner.

Ludlow, 1840:
Henry G. Allen, Zebidiah Barker, Robert Blaisdell, John Chase, Isaac Clark, John Commings, Wm. Farwell, Thomas Fields, Andrew Graham, [Joseph or Jesse?] Gilman, Peter Haggita, Silas Hilton, George How, Cyrus Hutchings, Robert Ingram, Alfred Marshall, Frances Milton [Mitton?], Samuel Morrison, Jacob Pickerd, James H. Stephens, John Stewart, David Weston.

New Limerick, 1840:
Cyrus Bradbury, Ebenezer Bradbury, Hall Bradbury, Moses Bradbury, True Bradbury, Daniel Cookson, Royal B. Colbroth, John Dowe, Moses Drew, John Fitch, Oliver Gould, Simeon Lougee, Samuel Morrison Jr., Stephen Randall, Charles Spooner, Abner Stimson, Joseph Stimson.

North Yarmouth Academy Grant, [T1, R4,wild land township, bounds Macwahoc, Molunkus and Reed], 1840:
Daniel C. Berry, Franklin Butterfield, Humphrey Chadbourn, Noah Jordan, Charles Kimball, Stephen Leavitt, James Libbey, Richard Libbey, John Rollins, John Weston, Jacob Wheeler, Simon Wheeler.

Oakfield, 1840:
Daniel Spaulding.

Orient, 1840:

Bela Betts, Wm. Butterfield, John Collier, Robert Collier, Thomas Collier, Sarah Deering, Wm.. Deering, James Hanesy, James Lambert, Thomas J. Maxwell, Samuel Newman, Marcus Peters, Francis F. Towle, Wm. Trask.

Reed Plantation: [Wytopitlock, T1, R3], 1840: John Clifford, Joel P. Corson, Otis Froshey, Lavinia Prouty, John Rollins.

Smyrna, 1840: Thomas Adams, Andrew Drew, Joseph Goodenow, Mikiel Lyons, Jarvis Perkins, Ivory Webber.

Township A, Fifth Range, 1840: Daniel Howard

Weston, 1840: Henry Brackett, Hiram Brackett, James Brackett, Luther Brackett, Samuel Cleaves, Seth Cleaves, Coridon Butterfield, Joseph Butterfield, Samuel Butterfield, Wm. Butterfield, Charles Clapham, Charles Clark, Thomas Gilpatrick, Elijah Gove, Samuel Guthrie, John Davenport, Timothy Desmond, Patrick Faulkner, Elijah Ford, Joseph Foss, Frances Frost, Hezekiah Harris, Robert Hinch, Thomas Jellison, Wm. Jellison, Isaac Loveland, Samuel Marle[y?], Charles Megguier, Alexander Miller, Thomas L. Pratt, Wm. Russell, Hugh Sheridan, Lewis Smart, Barney Smith, Gilford Smith, Joseph Smith, Joseph O. Smith, Leonard Smith, Nathaniel Smith, Stephen Smith, Alpheus Spaulding, John Springer, George Springer, Samuel Springer, Studley Springer, Alexander Taylor, Ira Watson, Ambrose Webber, Joseph W. Webber.

***

Danforth, Washington County, ME, 1840: Frances Butterfield, Hugh Carroll, John P. Decker, Alexander Jacobs, Amaziah Harden, Edward Haskell, Wm. Hinds, George Hows, Daniel Moor, Jr., James Pumroy, Angus Robinson, James Russell, Moses Scott, Reuben Snow, Seth Stinchfield, Parker Tewksbury.

APPENDIX II

CANADIAN TIMBER HARVESTERS ON THE ST JOHN AND AROOSTOOK RIVERS IN 1825

Samuel Cook, Esq., of Houlton, who was employed by the Maine Land Agent in the spring of 1825 to ascertain how much depredation was being done, reported that the following amounts of timber had been cut* under British permits at the Aroostook River:

James Sloat, a merchant of Fredericton, and a manager named Greenlaw, an American now living in New Brunswick, had cut eighteen hundred tons on the Machias Stream and twelve hundred tons on the Madawaska Stream.

Isaac Smith of Woodstock, N B and manager James Stinson of New Hampshire had cut one thousand tons, five miles up the Machias Stream.

Wilmot and Peters, merchants of Fredericton, with manager William Pyle, a settler on the Aroostook River, had cut seventeen hundred tons at Brewer Brook and seven hundred tons at Beaver Brook which is a little below Presque Isle Stream. Also they have, with manager Lewis Johnson, a settler on the Aroostook River, cut one thousand tons a little below Salmon Brook; and with a manager named Smart, one thousand tons on the Madawaska Stream and four hundred tons a little below the Aroostook River.

William Black, a merchant of St John City, with a manager by the name of Hinkley, has cut at Beaver Brook eight hundred tons of timber and one hundred logs.

John and Walter Beedle, merchants of Woodstock, with manager Warren Snow, a British subject now residing in Hodgdon Plantation, have cut two thousand tons on Salmon Brook. They have also cut two thousand five hundred tons at two locations on the Carriboo [Caribou] Stream.

William Hallett of Tobique Settlement with manager George Fields, a settler on the Aroostook, cut five hundred tons near the mouth of the Madawaska Stream.

Timber cut above the Grand Falls:

Wilmot and Peters, with a manager named Golden, have cut sixteen hundred tons, and logs equal to one hundred and eighty-four tons. Also, with a "gang of Irishmen" they have cut eight hundred tons, and they have bought of the French settlers eleven hundred tons, six hundred of which were cut without a permit.

Long and Gordon have cut five hundred tons

Baker and Goldthwaite have cut four hundred tons and logs equal to one thousand tons and these logs were cut without permit but settlement has been made with the New Brunswick government.

Belfleur, a Frenchman, cut without permit five hundred tons but since settled with New Brunswick government.

Burgoin and Company, Frenchmen, have cut five hundred tons.

*First named individuals obtained permits and furnished supplies. Source: Refer back to footnote 8, page 40.

APPENDIX III

FEDERAL TROOPS IN AROOSTOOK COUNTY

The impact of the extended presence of military units in small frontier towns can hardly be overestimated. Economic conditions, social life and personal relationships were profoundly affected.

Mr Wiggins, in *History of Aroostook*, pointed out that "it was a sad day for Houlton when its citizens bade adieu to the soldiers and saw them march off down the Military Road. Among those officers who afterward obtained military fame were Lieutenants Hooker, McDowell, and Ricketts of the Union Army. Lt. Magruder, afterwards of Rebel fame, was remembered by the older citizens as a dashing and popular young officer."

[Source: *Monthly Returns of the Commanding Officers of the 2nd Infantry at Hancock Barracks, Houlton, Maine, from 1828 to 1839,* National Archives, Record Group 94, Muster Roll, Regular Army Companies, Records of the Adjutant General's office, 1780-1917. National Archives Microfilm Publications, Microcopy 617, Roll 448, Hancock Barracks, Houlton. Microfilm has been placed on file at the Maine Historical Society, Portland, ME.

[Excerpts from U. S. Army Returns for the 2nd Infantry at Hancock Barracks have been selected at intervals to best represent staff changes and recruits. Records of this unit begin in Chapter IV, p 69.]

PART A:

FEDERAL TROOPS, UNITED STATES 2ND INFANTRY, HANCOCK BARRACKS, HOULTON, MAINE:

February, 1829: Bvt. Maj. N. S. Clark, commanding. Post; Capt. Greenleaf Dearborn[1] c'm'd'g. Co. K; Capt. Thomas Staniford, c'm'd'g. Co. F and ANCS and AAQM; 2nd Lt. J. R. Smith on duty, Co. C; 2nd Lt. Wm. Bloodgood c'm'd'g. Co. E; 2nd Lt. A. B. Eaton, Co. K, Adj. of Post; Ass't Surgeon Robert K. Kerr on duty; 1st Lt. C. F. Morton, Co. K., on recruiting service in New York; S. L. Russell at St Albans, Vermont; and Lt. Abner Hetzell, Co. F, absent, cause unknown; 2nd Lt. L. E. Morrison, Co. F, AWOL.

May, 1829: Bvt. Maj. N. S. Clark, reported the same staff listed for February, 1829, with the following additions: Abner R. Hetzell, Co. F on duty; 2nd Lt. J. S. Gallagher, Co. C, ACS at Bangor, Aug, 1829; Bvt. Lt. Antes Snyder, Co. F; Bvt. Lt. Richard B. Scriven, on duty.

August, 1829: Clark reported the following additions to his staff: 1st Lt. Thompson Morris, Co. C; 2nd Lt. I. H. K. Burgwin, Co. K; S. P. Simonton, Co. C.

January, 1831: Clark reported the presence of Dearborn; Staniford; Boynton, c'm'd'g. Co. E; Morris, Bloodgood, Hetzel, Simonton, Burgwin, 1st Lt. S. L. Russell on recruiting duty in New York; 2nd Lt. Richard B. Scrivener of Co. F in pursuit of deserters; Kerr, Joshua Brante, station unknown; 2nd Lt. A. B. Eaton of Co. K, transferred to Co. G, 15 January, 1831, and 2nd Lt. Abraham Van Buren, attached to Co. D, on duty at Washington. Aggregate, 183 men.

---

[1] See: Dale R Steinhauer, " *A Class of Men:* United States Army Recruits in Maine, 1820-1860," Maine Historical Society Quarterly, Vol. 30, No. 2, Fall, 1990, for Dearborn's recruiting activities, etc.

August, 1832: Roster same as January, 1831, except that Joshua B. Brante was promoted to 1st Lt., Co. E, and Lawrence Sprague was Ass't. Surgeon. Van Buren was on duty at the Post and Thompson Morris was on duty in Washington. Elbridge G. Eastman was 2nd Lt. in Co. C and John G. Harvey, 2nd Lt. in Co. E.

1833: The staff had a few additions: I. P. Gilmanton, Co. C; 1st Lt. Hannibal Day, Co. F; 2nd Lt. G. W. Patten, Co. K; Bvt. 2nd Lt. James W. Anderson, Co. E.

December, 1833: Post Commander N. S. Clark, Bvt. Maj., reported the presence of Capt. Greenleaf Dearborn, Capt. Thomas Staniford, Capt. Benjamin Boynton; 1st Lt. S. L. Russell, 1st Lt. Thompson Morris, 1st Lt. Hannibal Day, 2nd Lt. James Hill, 2nd Lt. George M. Patten, Bvt. 2nd Lt. Henry M. Wessels, Bvt. 2nd Lt. James N. Anderson; C. A. Waite and J. P. Simonton, absent on duty; A. R. Hetzel, on recruiting service. Aggregate: 204.

June, 1834: C. S. Trippler assigned Ass't. Surgeon.

May, 1835: Captain N. S. Clark was promoted to a Majority in the 6th Infantry, per Gen. Order No 24. He relinquished command of Hancock Post, May 12th, 1835.

[Note: In 1835 there was a contract between the U. S. Army and Elias Hiscock, Zebulon Ingersoll and William Wiliams for 400 cords of wood for fuel for troops at Hancock Barracks. This is reported by Elizabeth Ring in her *Bibliography of Maine*. Williams family tradition has it that William Williams was paid in gold coins for his firewood.]

June, 1835: Capt. Greenleaf Dearborn, Co. K, commanding the Post; 1st Lt. S. L. Russell ACS; 1st Lt. Thompson Morris c'm'd'g. Co. C; 1st Lt. Hannibal Day c'm'd'g. Co. F; 2nd Lt. James M. Hill c'm'd'g. Co. E and AQM; 2nd Lt. G. W. Patten, c'm'd'g. Co. K; I. Brown, Co. C; Bvt. Lt. 2nd Lt. H. W. Wessels, Co. F, acting Adj.; J. W. Anderson, Co. E; C. S. Tripler, Ass't. Surgeon on duty; J. Bradley, promoted to Captain, absent; B. Boynton on leave; Bvt. Maj. Thomas Staniford, Co. F; 1st Lt. C. A. Wait, Co. E, on recruiting duty in Chester, Pa.; 2nd Lt. A. R. Hetzel, Co. F, on duty with the Engineering Department, Washington.

December, 1835: Bvt. Maj. Greenleaf Dearborn, Co. K, assumed command of Post 16 December, 1835; 1st Lt. S. L. Russell, c'm'd'g. Co. K; 1st Lt. T. Morris, c'm'd'g. Co. C; 1st Lt. H. Day, c'm'd'g. Co. F; 2nd Lt. J. M. Hill, c'm'd'g. Co. E; 2nd Lt. G. W. Patten, Co. K; 2nd Lt. J. Brown, Co. C; 2nd Lt. J. V. Bamford, Co. F; Bvt. 2nd Lt. H. W. Wessels, Co. F, acting Adj.; Bvt. 2nd Lt. J. W. Anderson, Co. E; Bvt. 2nd Lt. J. W. Scott, Co. C; L. Sprague, Ass't. Surgeon. Absent on Staff duty, C. A. Waite, on topographical duty, R. L. Smith. Absent: B. A. Boynton and J. Bradley.

February, 1836: Command of the Post returned to Maj. N. S. Clark. Officers present: 1st Lt. Thompson Morris, c'm'd'g. Co. C; 2nd Lt. J. M. Hill, Co. E, and ACS and AAQM; Bvt. 2nd Lt. J. W. Anderson c'm'd'g. Co. E; L. Sprague, Ass't. surgeon. Absent on staff duty: C. A. Waite. Absent: B. A. Boynton, J. Bradley, J. Brown, and J. W. Scott.

January, 1837: Maj. N. S. Clark c'm'd'g. Post; Capt. J. J. B. Kingsbury c'm'd'g. Co. E; 2nd Lt. T. Johns, c'm'd'g. Co. C and Post Adj.; L. Sprague, Ass't. Surgeon. Absent, Capt. John Bradley, on leave, surgeon's certificate; 1st Lt. James W. Penrose, Co. E, four months leave; 1st Lt. E. R. Long, Co. C, on recruiting service in Louisville, Ky; 2nd Lt. J. M. Harvie, Co. E, joined company 26 January, 1838, absent serving in Florida.

On the 3rd of August, 1838, Maj. Clarke forwarded the last return of his detachment of the 2nd Infantry at this Post, "for the purpose had been formed to remove the Infantry and replace them with the 1st Artillery Regiment." Clark was promoted and transferred to the 8th Regiment of Infantry. On August 12,1838, J. J. B. Kingsbury took command. He made his last return on October 4th, 1838.

On October 14th the arrival of the new force was reported to Brig. Gen. R. Jones, Adj Gen., at Washington, by Maj.Kirby.

PART B:

FEDERAL TROOPS: UNITED STATES 1ST ARTILLERY HANCOCK BARRACKS, HOULTON, MAINE AND AT FORT KENT AND FORT FAIRFIELD, MAINE

On October 14th, 1838, Maj. R. M. Kirby reported the arrival of the 1st Artillery at Hancock Barracks to Brig. Gen. R. Jones, Adj Gen., Washington. The 1st Artillery replaced the 2nd Infantry, which had occupied the post for ten years.
[Source: The National Archives, Record Group 94, *Muster Roll, Regular Army Companies, Records of the Adjutant Generals Office, 1780-1917,* National Archives Microfilm Publications, Microcopy 617, Roll 448, Hancock Barracks, Houlton, Maine. Microfilm has been placed on file at the Maine Historical Society, Portland, ME.]

HANCOCK BARRACKS, HOULTON, MAINE

Excerpts from United States Army Returns for the 1st Artillery at Hancock Barracks have been selected to best represent staff changes and recruits.

Muster Roll, Company C, 1st Artillery, Hancock Barracks, Brig. Gen. Eustis c'm'd'g., 31 December, 1838 to 28 February 1839:
Capt. L. B. Webster, 1st Lt. T. Green, 1st Lt. J. L. Donaldson, 2nd Lt. J. **McDowell**, 1st Sgt. James Davidson, 1st Sgt. Charles Atkins, 1st Sgt. William Clement, 1st Sgt. James Madden, Cpl. Oliver Lewis, Cpl. Jerome More, Cpl. James McMillin, Cpl. Augustus Ambreicht. Musician Edward Dyer, Musician Edward Griffith, Artificer William McGregor, Artificer George W. Creed. Privates: John Anderson, Michael Brynan, Abraham Blakesley, William Campbell, John Crofts, William Carr, David C. Carr, Peter Dempsey, Peter Duffy, Thomas Fisher, George M. Griffin, John Gragg, Charles Harper, David Holman, John Holman,

Richard Jones, Thomas Key, James Lanagan, James McGoulick, Michail McDermott, John McNeal, James Martin, James O'Brien, William Striebe, James Todd, Robert Wedding, Robert Wilson. Died: John Lyle and William Hewitt. Deserted: Thomas Henly and John Muny.

Muster Roll, Company E, 1st Artillery, Hancock Barracks, Brig. Gen. Eustis c'm'd'g., 31 December, 1838 to 28 February, 1839:

Capt. [Bvt. Maj.] Henry Saunders, 1st Lt. James R. Irvine, 1st Lt. Bennett H. Hill, 1st Sgt. George Weightmans, Sgt. Charles Mayberry, Sgt. William Wendall, Sgt. Robard Burrows, Cpl. Joseph Woodhead, Cpl. John Ward, Artificer Benjamin Adsite. Privates: Horatio Anderson, John Blum, Wm. Brandolla, John Bradyman, Orrin V. Comstock, William Connor, Florence Crowley, Richardson Cole, John Caffrey, Michale Fox, Daniel Geary, William Gentry, George Hunter, [Trew?] Hayes, John Hurd, William McGee, Patrick McAllean, Michael McMahone, John Maul, Matthew Leachead, Hugh O'Donnell, Patrick Purdy, James Sanford, James Whitaker, Hugh O'Donnell, Patrick Purdy, John Partridge, John Reynolds, John Wilson, Daniel Douglas, Eben Knight, George Paine.

Muster Roll, Company E, 1st Artillery, Hancock Barracks, Brig. Gen. Eustis c'm'd'g., 31 December, 1838 to 28 February, 1839:

Capt. George Nauman, 1st Lt. E. S. Sibley, 1st Lt. Isreal Vogdes, Ord. Sgt. Robert Gray, 1st Sgt. John Lovejoy, Sgt. Joseph Bond, Cpl. George W. Cooke, Cpl. Nathaniel Billings. Privates: Robert Allison, John Barry, John Bilby, Lyman Brown, Robert Cunningham, Thomas Dalton, William Davids, James Dobbins, John Duffie, Robert Duffy, Daniel Eastwood, John Ferris, James Fitzgerald, John Lamptford, William Leycroft, Henry E. Martin, David McMahon, Edward Mullen, Felix McElthone, Henry O'Brien, John H. O'Connor, John Roache, William Ready, Robert Seaborn, Michael Tolan. Discharged: Martin Huyler and James Irvine.

In January and February, 1839, Capt. [Bvt. Maj.] R. M. Kirby of the 1st Artillery reported that he was in command of Company G, cm'd'g the Post, under G. O. of October 20, 1837. L. Sprague, Ass't. Surgeon; Capt. L. B. Webster c'm'd'g. Co. C; Capt. G. Nauman c'm'd'g. Company F; 1st Lt. B. H. Hill, c'm'd'g. Co. E and ACS and AQM; 2nd Lt. J. McDowell, Co. C.; absent from Post, H Saunders, I. R. Irwin, E. S. Sibley, J. Vodgdes, T. Green and J. L. Donaldson. Aggregate:120 men.

December 1839: Bvt. Maj. George Saunders, Co. E, c'm'd'g. the Post; L. Sprague, Ass't. Surgeon; Capt. L. B. Webster c'm'd'g. Co. C; Capt. G. Nauman c'm'd'g. Co. F, 1st Lt. B. H. Hill, Co. E; 2nd Lt. J. McDowell Co. C, Post Adj.; Absent: T. Green, I. R. Irving, E. S. Sibley, J. L. Donaldson, I. Vogdes and J. A. Haskins.

April, 1840: Lt. Col. B. K. Pierce c'm'd'g. regiment and detachment; Adj. W. W. Mackall, on duty; Capt. R. M. Kirby, c'm'd'g. Co. G; 1st Lt. John B. **Magruder**, c'm'd'g. Co. B, and AQM and ACS; 1st Lt. E. A. Capron, c'm'd'g. Company I; 1st Lt. W. E. Asquith, Co. B, on duty; Joseph Hooker, 1st Lt., Co. A, temporarily attached to Co. G; 2nd Lt. A. R. Lawton, Co. G, on duty; 2nd Lt. J. B. **Ricketts**, c'm'd'g. Co. H; 2nd Lt. S. K. Dawson, Co. I, on duty. Absent: D. D. Tompkins, James H. Prentiss, George Waggaman, W. H. French, J. K. Ruvis, F. Whiting, D. Van Ness, and H. C. Wayne.

May, 1840: [Bvt. Brig. Gen.] Col. Abraham Eustis, c'm'd'g. M. Department on North East Frontier and c'm'd'g. Post; 1st Lt. James H. Prentiss, Co. G; Bvt. Capt., Co. G, AAG.; Capt. E. B. Babbitt [of the 3rd Infantry], AQM; Maj. B. K. Pierce, Bvt. Lt. Col., c'm'd'g. the Regiment; 1st Lt. W. W. Mackall, Co. H, Adj.; Capt. Giles Porter, c'm'd'g. Co. A; 1st Lt. John H. Winder, Co. A, ACS; 1st Lt. Joseph Hooker, Co. G; 2nd Lt. M. S. Culbertson, Co. A; 1st Lt. W. E. Aisquith, c'm'd'g. Co. B, relieved Lt. Magruder May 12, 1840; 2nd Lt. H. C. Wayne, Co. B; Capt. L. B. Webster, c'm'd'g. Co. C; 2nd Lt. J. H. McDowell, Co. C; Capt. Henry Saunders, Bvt. Maj., Co. E, Acting Maj. of the Regiment; 1st Lt. B. H. Hill, c'm'd'g. Co. E; Capt. George Nauman, c'm'd'g. Co. F; 2nd Lt.

J. A. Haskin, Co. F; Capt. R. M. Kirby, Co. G, Bvt. Maj. c'm'd'g. Co. G; 2nd Lt. A. R. Lawton, Co. G; Capt. D. Van Ness, c'm'd'g. Co. H, relieved Lt. Ricketts, May 4, 1840; 1st Lt. W. H. French, Co. H, on duty, joined Co. H on May 4, 1840; 2nd Lt. James B. Ricketts, Co. H, relieved of command of Co. H on May 4, 1840; 1st Lt. E. A. Capron, Co. I; 2nd Lt. S. K. Dawson, Co. I. Absent: D. D. Tompkins, J. B. Magruder, Tim Green, J. L. Donaldson, J. R. Irwin, E. S. Sibley, Israel Vogdes, G. G. Waggaman, F. Whiting, and S. K. Reeves.

September, 1840: Brig. Gen. Eustis reporting: New recruit, Michael McCarthy, 1st Artillery, temporarily attached to Company G. Under detention, Timothy Lyons, Second Infantry, Co. C, sentenced to served remainder of his term of enlistment with ball and chain. He was enlisted 27 June, 1832 and deserted 16 August, 1833, and apprehended 19 July, 1840. Company G, aggregate, 37, marched to Fort Sullivan, September 14, 1840.

November, 1840: Maj. B. K. Pierce, Bvt. Lt. Col., c'm'd'g Regiment and Post, relieved Gen. Eustis in his command on November 1, 1840. Adj. W. W. Mackall, Co. H; 1st Lt. C. O. Collins, [of the 4th Artillery] AQM; A. N. McLaren, Surgeon; 1st Lt. W. E. Aisquith, c'm'd'g. Co. B; Capt. L. B. Webster c'm'd'g. Co. C; 1st Lt. J. F. Donaldson, Co. C; 2nd Lt. Irwin McDowell, Co. C; Capt. H. Saunders, Bvt. and acting Maj. of Regiment; 2nd Lt. James G. Martin, c'm'd'g. Co. E., relieved Lt. Hill 20th November, 1840; Capt. George Nauman, c'm'd'g. Co. F; J. A. Haskins, 2nd Lt., Co. F; 1st Lt. W. H. French, Co. H, Ass't. Commissary, Post Order of July 12, 1840; 2nd Lt. James B. Ricketts, 2nd Lt., c'm'd'g. Co. H, relieved Capt. Van Ness November 2, 1840; 1st Lt. E. A. Capron, c'm'd'g. Co. I; 2nd Lt. S. K. Dawson, Co. I; Transferred: S. K. Dawson, 2nd Lt., Co. I, to Co. G, R. O. No 8, 22 August, 1841, left this post 26 January, 1841. On Staff duty: D. D. Tompkins, J. R. Irwin, E. S. Sibley, Tim Green, W. H. French. On recruiting duty: D. Van Ness, J. B. Magruder. On special duty: Israel Vogdes and S. K. Reeves. On furlough: F. Whiting, L. B. Webster and B. H. Hill. Aggregate no of men, 249, in companies B, C, E, F, H and I.

Hancock Barracks at Houlton, in January of 1841, had an aggregate of 364 personnel. In July, 1841, post returns noted an aggregate of 344 men in Companies B, C, E, F, H and I. New enlistee: Benjamin L. Center. Joseph Burton on July 3rd was listed as a recruit joined from desertion [from the British Army?]. Patrick Durken was temporarily attached to Company C.

On September 20, 1841, Lt. Col. Pierce relinquished command of Hancock Barracks to Lt. E. A. Cassrow. Adj Mackall left his post for Fort Fairfield. New Enlistees included I. M. McIntosh: M. M. McCarthy, Pvt., Co. G; P. Durkin, Pvt., Co. A; Wm. Tyrrell, Pvt., Co. C; B. L. Center, Pvt., Co. D; [J.?] Remington, Pvt., Co. H; J. Langan, Pvt., Co. C. G. Dittmar, Pvt., Company C. J. Burton was discharged. Temporarily attatched to Co. I: S. Connor; to Co. C: P. O. Donovan and A. Blakely. Deserted: Timothy Lyons, while in confinement, December 5, 1841.

February, 1842: Aggregate: 258.

May, 1842: Col. Abram Eustis, 1st Artillery, Bvt. Brig. Gen., c'm'd'g. post, assumed command May 9, 1842. Maj. B. K. Pierce, Bvt. Lt. Col., relieved of command of Post and Regiment May 9, 1842. Capt. C. O. Collins, QMD; Capt. H. Saunders, 1st Artillery, Co. E, Bvt. Maj., c'm'd'g. company as of May 1st, 1842, on extra duty as Maj. of the Regiment. Capt. George Nauman c'm'd'g. Co. F; 1st Lt. E. A. Cassrow c'm'd'g. Co. I; 1st Lt. M. J. Burke c'm'd'g. Co. B; [1st Lt. J. S. Hatheway relieved of command of Co. E on May 1, 1842.] 1st Lt. Wm. H. French, Co. I, ACS, Acting Adj.; 2nd Lt. J. S. Haskins, Co. F; 2nd Lt. J. G. Martin, Co. E; 2nd Lt. Samuel Jones, Co. I; John D. Blake, Chaplain. Dr D. E. French, Acting Ass't. Surgeon for this post during the absence of Surgeon A. N. McLaren,. U. S. A. Absent: D. D. Thompson, J. R. Irwin and J. H. Prentiss. On recruiting service, J. B. Magruder. On special duty, H. C. Wayne. On furlough, A. N. McLaren, J. Hooker and F. Whiting.

June 16, 1842: W. Jacobs was taken as a deserter.

July, 1842: Maj. B. K. Pierce, 1st Artillery, commanding. C. O. Collins, QMD; 1st Lt. J. Hooker, Co. F, Adj.; Capt. H. Saunders, c'm'd'g. Co. E, on extra duty as Maj. of the Regiment; Capt. George Nauman, c'm'd'g. Co. F; 1st Lt. E. A. Cassron, c'm'd'g. Co. I; 1st Lt. M. J. Burke, c'm'd'g. Co. B; 1st Lt. J. S. Hatheway, Co. E; 1at Lt. W. H. French, Co. I, ACS; 2nd Lt. J. S. Haskins, Co. F; 2nd Lt. Co. E; 2nd Lt. Samuel Jones, Co. I; John Blake Chaplain and Dr French, citizen of Houlton, Acting Ass't. Surgeon during the absence of Surgeon A. N. McLaren U. S. A. Staff Officers: Capt. D. D. Thompkins, Co. B, AQM; 1st Lt. J. R. Irwin, Co. B, AQM. 1st Lt. J. H. Prentiss, Co. E, Bvt. Captain, Ass't. Adj. Gen: 1st Lt. J. B. Magruder, Co. F, on recruiting service in Boston; 2nd Lt. H. C. Wayne, Co. B, on duty at Military Academy. A. N. McLaren, Surgeon, M. D., on leave of absence for two months. Bvt. Maj. S. Whiting, Co. F, arrived at this post July 1, 1842, left July 27, 1842, on leave of absence.

November, 1842: The Garrison was reinforced on the 19th by a detachment of 45 recruits from the G. R. Department, New York. The detachment for Fort Fairfield and Fort Kent arrived on the same date. Those for Fort Fairfield left on the 21st; the state of the roads at present understood impracticable for those destined for Fort Kent to leave this post for some time.

December 1842: Saunders c'm'd'g. The detachment of recruits, [16], destined for Fort Kent, left this post on the 21st of December, 1842, in charge of Lt. Martin. Recruit Casidy was assigned to this company. Recruits: to Co. C: Pvts: John Newell; Ed I. Edwards; Sol Morrison.

January, 1843: Maj. L. Whiting, 1st Artillery commanding, having assumed command on the Post January 4, 1843. General and Regimental Staff present at the post at this time: A. N. McLaren, Surgeon, MD; Capt. E. B. Babbett, QMD; Capt. H. Saunders, 1st Artillery, Bvt. Maj., c'm'd'g. Co. E, having relinquished command of the Post on Jan 4, 1843; Capt. G. Nauman, c'm'd'g. Co. F; 1st Lt. J. B. Magruder, Co. F; 1st Lt. E. A. Cassron, c'm'd'g. Co. I; 1st Lt.

M. I. Burke c'm'd'g. Co. B; 1st Lt. I. S. Hatheway, Company E, ACS, and Post Adj.; 1st Lt. W. H. French, Co. I; 2nd Lt. J. S. Haskins, Co. F; 2nd Lt. Samuel Jones, Co. I; 2nd Lt. J. M. Brannan, Co. B; John Blake, Chaplain. Staff Duty: Capt. D. D. Thompkins, 1st Artillery, Co. B, AQM; Capt. J. H. Irwin, Co. I, Ass't. QM; 1st Lt. J. H. Prentiss, Co. E, Bvt. Capt. and Ass't. Adj Gen.; 1st Lt. J. Hooker, Co. F, Adj., Head Quarters, 1st Artillery, Portland, Maine. Special duty: Lt. Col. B K. Prince, c'm'd'g. 6th Military Department; 1st Lt. H. C. Wayne, Co. B, on duty at Military Academy, West Point. On Furlough: I. G. Martin. Aggregate: 284. Mustered on rolls, I. G. Martin.

April, 1843: Recruits: Pvt. Thomas Mills, Co. C; Sgt. James O'Brien, Co. G; Pvt. Eugene Brady; William Simmons, Co. F.

May, 1843: Recruits: Cpl. C. O. Donnell, Co. D; Pvt. J. G. Fly, Co. H; Pvt. T. W. Pauley, Co. H; Pvt. Christopher Parker, Co. H; Pvt. James Green, Co. D; Pvt. Wm. Wendell, Co. C.; Pvt. Orrin Butterfield, Co. C; Pvt. G. Sunderland, Co. A; Pvt. M. Franklin, Co. C. Sgt. James O'Brien, Sgt. of a detachment ordered to the Boundary Line.

28th of June, 1843: A detachment of Co. I ordered to the Boundary Line in charge of 1st Lt. French.

August, 1843: Enlistees, Pvt. William Smith, Co. H, in confinement for desertion; J. A. Fernald, Co. H. Aggregate, 269.

September, 1843: Present at Hancock Barracks, Capt. D. Van Ness, Co. H, c'm'd'g. Co. and Post, joined post ohn the 5th of September and assumed command of the Post September 23, 1843. A. P. McLaren, Surgeon, MD; Capt. E. B. Babbett; Ass't. Surgeon C. E. Isaacs; Capt. L. B. Webster, command Co. C, joined Sept 23, 1843; 1st Lt. J. B. Magruder, Co. B; 1st Lt. J. S. Hathaway, Co. C, ACS; 2nd Lt. J. A. Haskin, Co. B, transferred from Co. F, Sept 3, 1843; 2nd Lt. J. B. Ricketts, Co. H, joined this Post Sept 5, 1843, Post Adj.; 2nd Lt. J. G. Martin, 2nd Lt., Co. E. J Bowen, Co. C, joined 23rd Sept, 1843; Bvt. 2nd Lt. D. H. Hill, joined September 23, 1843; Bvt. 2nd Lt. J. H. Greland, joined from leave of Absence on Sept 30, 1843; Bvt. 2nd Lt. J. A. Hardis, Co. B, joined from leave of absence on Sept 30, 1843; John Blake, Chaplin. Staff Duty, Capt. D. D. Thompkins, Co. B, AQM; 1st Lt. E. L. Sibley, AQM; 1st Lt. J. H. Prentiss, Ass't. Adj Gen., appointed May 24, 1839, Co. E; 1st Lt. G. G. Waggaman, Co. H, Captain in the Staff. Special Duty: 1st Lt. H. C. Wayne, on duty at Military Academy; 1st Lt. J. McDowell, Co. H; On Furlough: Maj. L. Whiting, on leave 20 days; Capt. H. Saunders, on leave for three months; 1st Lt. J. L. Donaldson, leave of absence 3 months. Transferred, Bvt. 2nd Lt. C. L. Kilburn, Co. E, transferred to the 3rd Artillery, Co. H, left this post Aug 10, 1843. Sgt. Maj. Cantwell transferred to 3rd Artillery. The Garrison was reinforced on the 5th of September by Company H and on the 23rd by Co. I of the 1st Artillery.

October, 1843: Maj. L. Whiting, 1st Artillery, c'm'-d'g. Enlistees: [Garrett?] Sunderland; Norman Thorner, Co. F; Christopher Parker, Co. D. Co. E left this post on the 17th of October for Fort Sullivan, Maine and the Garrison was reinforced on the 31st of October by Co. G, 1st Artillery.

December, 1843: Enlistee, George Dennison.

April 1844: Company I, aggregate 62, left for Fort Kent, Fish River, April 1, 1844 with the exception of 2nd Lt. Dawson, who remained at this post until the 12th instant. Pvt. Jeremiah Sullivan, Co. F, is in confinement, undergoing sentence. George McFarland, Co. F, Edward Mulligan and John W. Steinhall, Co. G, are sick in hospital.

August, 1844: Maj. Levi Whiting reported that a detachment of the 1st and 2nd Artillery, under the command of Lt. S. J. Donaldson, arrived on the 2nd of August and left on the 22 of August, 1844.

September, 1844: Pvt. Alexander Galusha of Co. I, was apprehended as a deserter on September 10, 1844. Thirty dollars was paid as a reward. Pvt. John Rutledge, Co. K., surrendered as a deserter 20 September, 1844. Aggregate: 181.

October, 1844: Co. H, Aggregate 58, left this Post on 5 October, 1844, for Fort Sullivan, Maine. Co. E, 1st Artillery, arrived at this Post October 16, 1844.

November, 1844: Pvt. Alexander Galusha of Co. I and Pvt. John Rutledge of Co. K., in confinement, undergoing sentence.

February, 1845: Maj. Levi Whiting, joined from special duty, February 2, 1845, and resumed command of Post 2 February, 1845. Adam N. McClaren, Surgeon, Medical Department; Capt. Lucien B. Webster, Co. C, joined from special duty, 2 Feb, 1845, resumed command of Co. C, 3 Feb, 1845; Capt. Ebenezer S. Sibley, joined from leave of Absence on 20 Feb, 1845, and resumed command of Co. E on 26 February, 1845. 1st Lt. John S. Hathaway joined from Special duty, resumed command of Co. C, 3 February, 1845 and relinquished command of Co. E to Capt. Sibley 26 February, 1845; 1st Lt. Joseph a Haskin, Co. C, relinquished command of Post to Maj. Whiting 2 Feb, 1845, and command of Co. C to Capt. Webster on 3 February, 1845; 2nd Lt. James G. Martin, Co. E, relinquished command of company to 1st Lt. J. S. Hathaway, 3 February, 1845; 2nd Lt. Isaac Bowen Co. C; 2nd Lt. Seth Williams, c'm'd'g. Co. B.; Bvt. 2nd Lt. Thomas J. Curd, Co. B.; John Blake, Chaplain. On Staff Duty, Daniel Thompkins and James H. Prentiss. Other special duty: John B. Magruder, James S. Donaldson, Henry C. Wayne and James A. Hardie.

May, 1845: Capt. Ebenezer S. Sibley, Co. E, relieved Capt. Webster in command of Post May 25th, 1845, AQM; Adam McLaren, Surgeon, Medical Department; 1st Lt. John H. Hatheway, Co. E, ACS; 1st Lt. Joseph A. Haskin, Co. C. relieved Capt. Webster in command of Co. C May 25th, 1845; 2nd Lt. Seth Williams, c'm'd'g. Co. B; Bvt. Lt. Thomas S. Curd, Co. B.; John Blake, Chaplain. On staff duty: Daniel D. Tompkins, James H. Prentiss; Recruiting Service: Isaac Bowen. Other special duty: Maj. Levi Whiting, Member, Board of Inspectors, West Point; 1st Lt. J. B. Magruder, Co. B, ordered, 19th February, 1845, to report in person to the recruiting service, New York; 1st Lt. James L. Donaldson, 1st Lt. Henry C Wayne, Bvt. 2nd Lt. James A. Hardie. On leave of absence, Capt. Lucien B. Webster and 2nd Lt. Samuel K. Dawson.

June, 1845: Captain Lucien B. Webster, Co. C, joined from leave of absence June 21st, and relieved Capt. Sibley in command of Post and Lt. Haskin in command of Co. C the same day. Adam N. McLaren, Surgeon, Medical Department; 1st Lt. John H. Hatheway, ADS; 1st Lt. Joseph A. Haskins, relinquished command of Co. C to Capt. L. B. Webster, June 21st; 2nd Lt. Seth Williams, Command Co. B., relinquished command of Co. B to Lt. Magruder, 23 June and relieved Lt. Magruder in command June 27th; Bvt. 2nd Lt. Thomas S. Curd, Co. B; John Blake, Chaplain. On staff duty, Daniel D. Tompkins, James H. Prentiss. On recruiting service, 2nd Lt. Isaac Bowen on Regimental Recruiting Service at Bangor, Maine. Other special duty, Levi Whiting, member of the Board of Inspectors at West Point; John B. Magruder, summoned to appear as a witness before the General Court Martial convened at Fort Adams, Rhode Island. Resumed command of Company June 23, 1845. Relinquished command to Lt. Williams and left Company June 27, 1845; 1st Lt. James L. Donaldson, Co. C assigned to duty with Maj. Graham, topographical Engineers, Feb 12, 1844 and left Company July 2, 1843; 1st Lt. Henry C. Wayne, Co. B, at Military Academy, left Company 20 August, 1845; Bvt. 2nd Lt. James A. Hardie, Co. B, At Military Academy, left Company 26 August, 1841.Leave of Absence: 2nd Lt. Samuel K. Dawson, Co. C.

July, 1845: Capt., [Bvt. Maj.] Lucien B. Webster reporting Companies B and E, 1st Artillery, Field and Staff had an aggregate number of 113. These companies left "without delay," for Boston Harbor on July 30, 1845, under the command of Maj. L. Whiting.

August, 1845: The Post had an aggregate total of 54 men including new recruits, Patrick Price and Richard F. Wallace, Pvts.

THE UNITED STATES MILITARY POST AT FORT FAIRFIELD

Source: *National Archives Microfilm Publications* Microcopy 617 Roll 357, Fort Fairfield, Maine. [This microfilm has been placed on deposit at the Maine Historical Society, Portland, ME.]

Company H, 1st Artillery, Capt. Van Ness commanding, marched from Hancock Barracks to Fort Fairfield to man the Garrison on the 7th of September, 1841. Returns of Company H at the Post at Fort Fairfield, Maine, September, 1841 reported: One Company, Co. H, of the 1st Artillery, with 29 privates, 1 Ass't. surgeon, 1 Captain, 1 First Lieutenant, 1 Second Lieutenant, 4 Sergeants, 2 Corporals one drummer and one Fifer, with a total of 49 non-commissioned officers, musicians, farriers, blacksmiths, artificers, and privates. Pursuant to Regimental Order of August 29, 1841, this Company left Hancock Barracks at Houlton, Maine on the 7th and arrived at Fort Fairfield on the 10th of September, 1841. With David Van Ness, Capt. c'm'd'g. Richard Coolidge, Ass't. Surgeon; Wm. W. Mackall, 1st Lt. and AACS and AQM. [Isaac L. Reeves, 1st Lt., detatched to duty at West Point, New York.] Officers at Fort Fairfield: Capt. David Van Ness, c'm'd'g.; Ass't Surgeon Richard H. Coolidge; 2nd Lt. James B. Ricketts, Ass't. Commissary of subsistence and Acting AQM. 1st Lt. I. M. Dowell, detatched to duty at Military Academy; total of 57 personnel.

May, 1843, 1st Lt. G. G. Waggeman transferred to H Company from K Company, 1st Artillery. Lt. Mackall transferred to Company K. 1st Lt. Irvine McDowell was on duty at the Military Academy.

On 22 August, 1843, Capt. Van Ness received Department Order No 11 to withdraw the Garrison from Fort Fairfield to Hancock Barracks at Houlton.

THE UNITED STATES MILITARY POST AT FORT KENT

Source: NationalArchives Microfilm Publications Microcopy 617, Roll 571, *Fort Kent, Maine.* [This microfilm has been placed on deposit at the Maine Historical Society, Portland, ME.]

First investment of Fort Kent: Company C, 1st Artillery, Capt. L. B. Webster c'm'd'g., marched to Fort Kent to man the garrison on the 7th of September, 1841.

Returns of Company C at the Post at Fort Kent, in September, 1841: This company consisted of 1 Captain, 1 Ass't. Surgeon, 1 First Lieutenant, 1 Sergeant, 3 Corporals, 1 Drummer, 1 Fifer, and 16 Privates, a total of 48 non-commissioned officers, musicians, farriers, blacksmiths, artificers and privates. Company C marched from Hancock Barracks, arrived at the post at Fish River on the 17th of September, 1841.

Officers present at Fort Kent in September, 1841, were: C. E. Isaacs, Ass't. Surgeon, J. L. Donaldson, 1st Lt., c'm'd'g. Capt. L. B. Webster, absent on duty visiting English posts in the neighborhood; T. Green, 1st Lieutenant, detached to Fort Monroe, Virginia; I. McDowell, 2nd Lieutenant, detached to duty at the Military Academy.] In October, 1st Lt. E. L. Sibley was AQM.

In January, 1842, Federal troops, Company C, 1st Artillery at the United States Military Post at Fort Kent included Capt. L. B. Webber, c'm'd'g.; C. E. Isaacs, Ass't. Surgeon; I. L. Donaldson, 1st Lt.; Isaac Bowen, 2nd Lt.; D. H. Hill, Bvt. 2nd Lt.; E. L. Sibley, 1st Lt. [Bvt. Lt.] D. H. Hill was attached to Company C in August, 1842. In November, 1842, 2nd Lt. Bowen joined Co. C at Fort Kent.

Fort Kent was evacuated in September, 1843.

Second investment of Fort Kent:

On April 5 1844, Company G of the First Artillery arrived at Fort Kent. Officers were: Capt. John H. Winder, c'm'd'g., with Alex W. Witherspoon, Ass't. Surgeon; W. E. Asquith, 1st Lt.; Israel Vodges, 1st Lt.; John F. Irons, 2nd Lt.; 3 Sergeants, 3 corporals, 1 Drummer, 1 fifer, 1 artificer, and 34 privates, a total of 52 non-commissioned officers, musicians, farriers, blacksmiths artificers and privates. They arrived at Fort Kent and occupied the Post, according to Order 21, dated Hancock Barracks, on 25 March, 1844. On September 24, 1844, a new recruit, Benjamin Webster, was "learning music" [fifer?] and he was assigned to Company G on December 1, 1844. 1st Lt. Henry D. Grafton, was promoted to Capt. on 24 February, 1845, and attatched to Co. G at Fort Kent in April, 1845.

May 18, 1845, Lt. Grafton was put in charge of the detachment of recruits, to march to Hancock Barracks.

APPENDIX IV

SETTLERS ON THE DISPUTED TERRITORY IN 1831
Exclusive of the Acadian Community at Madawaska

Information in this section comes from various sources, including the Deane-Kavanagh Report of 1831.

American settlers on the **St John River**, 1831:

Bacon, James, son of Timothy Bacon of Gorham, ME, his land on north side of river conveyed to him by deeds of Maine and Massachusetts, many improvements, had died in 1830. **Baker**, John, claims a lot on north side of St John, and another one hundred acre lot and an island in the St John, claimed since 1826. His residence, bounded on the east by the Madawaska River, and on the south by the St John River, originally claimed by Harford, and in 1831 was entangled with claims of Simon Hebert; his property located at the mouth of the Meriumpticook stream. **Bartlett**, Nathaniel, residence on north side of river, owns land on Fish river and owns part of the Savage Mill. He is married and works at Baker's sawmill. He cultivated a lot half a mile below the Peters and Wilmot sawmill, on the south side of the river, (in 1831?) and he claimed an unoccupied lot on south side, next to Hunnewell and Landry. **Cannon**, Cyrus, absentee owner of lot near John Baker; lot in Baker's care. **Clements**, Ezekiel,(Yankee?) abandoned claim on north bank, has blacksmith shop and house and a few acres cleared; lives near

Powers. **Harford**, John, located six miles below the mouth of the St Francis River; had begun improvements on this lot in 1816; had been at Madawaska Point in 1815; cleared land at the west point of the Madawaska River in 1817, and sold it to John Baker. **Harford**, Phineas Randall, son of John Harford. **Hunnewell**, Barnabas, of Madison, Somerset Co, Maine, bought (in 1827) his house and land on north side of St John from Charles **Stetson**, who had begun improvements on lot in 1825. New Brunswick Historical Society records state that he had resided in Oromocto, New Brunswick in 1823. In 1830 he began to cut four acres on the south side of the river, below Landry. **Kenny**, Thomas, a Canadian, who bought a place on north bank from Jonathan Cyr, who had claimed it in 1823. In 1831, Kenny lives in John Bacon's house and is a miller for John Baker's grist mill. **Maddocks**, Amos, nationality unknown, resides at Savage's mills in 1831, on the Fish River, and owns land on north side of St John River which was previously owned by Stephen Grover and Owen Fitzgerald. **Powers**, Walter, works on land John Baker bought from John Harford, at Madawaska Point. **Smith**, Dennis, settled on north bank about 1828. **Stetson**, Charles, began improvements on lot in 1825 and sold to Hunnewell. **Webster**, Augustine, lives on land originally cleared by John Harford, Jr.

Settlers on the south bank of the **St John River**, 1831: **Emery**, Miles, cleared lot and sold to Joseph Michaud; **Essena**, David, cut three acres of trees in 1826. **Essena**, Reuben, cut three acres of trees in 1826. **Cannon**, Cyrus, cleared and took first crop on Essena lot in 1828. **Fitzgerald**, Owen, in 1829, cut trees but did not clear land. Owns two more lots just below Fitzgerald. **Fitzgerald**, Owen (Junior or same as above) claimed two lots below Fitzgerald, and left the country. **Hale**, Franklin, was on lot in 1828. **Harford**, John Jr., came Aug 3, 1827, claims 100 rods frontage south of Fitzgerald. **Ketch**, Thomas, felled two acres of trees in 1828. **McKay**,

Edward, in back settlement, of Canada, age 20, came about 1826, lives with his brother in law, Phirmain **Dumont** and supports his mother. **McPherson**, James, took crops on Essena lot in 1829 and 1830 and claims it. **McPherson**, Charles, owned lot just below Wheelock and Powers. **Oaks**, Electus, born Canaan, Me.; began settling July 1827; sold his lot which is opposite the east end of Churchill Island. **Pollard**, David, planted potatoes on Ketch lot in 1830. **Savage**, Daniel, lived two miles inland from the mouth of the Fish River. He had been employed in 1826-27 to build a double sawmill for Peters and Wilmot of New Brunswick. He sold his right to the mill to Nathaniel **Bartlett**, but occupied the mill lot in 1832. **Powers**, Walter: living on the Fitzgerald lot in 1831, built cabin about 1830. **Wheelock**, Jesse, occupant.

Irish settlers on north bank of the **St John**, 1831:
____ **Ellwood**, an improved lot. ____ **Murphy**, house, barn, 50 acres cleared, 60 rods frontage in 1831. **O'Neal**, Edward, house, barn, 50 acres cleared, 60 rods frontage in 1831. **O'Neal**, John, house, barn, 50 acres cleared, 60 rods frontage in 1831. **Pearl**, John, resides here with his son John Jr., 50 acres cleared and some intervale. **Powers**, James, 4-5 acres of cleared land. **Rice**, Francis, Irish, is a British magistrate, has been an adjutant of the British militia. **Stearns**, William, lot and an acre of corn. **Tighe**, Michael, had 15 cleared acres and a house and barn. **Whelan**, Maurice, had a house and barn and 50 acres cleared, with 60 rods frontage in 1831.

Irish settlers on south bank of **St John**, 1831:
Douglass, Dennis, left his lot in possession of M Farrell in 1827. **Farrell**, Michael, bought land from Joseph Saussfacon. **Grace**, Cyprian, began improving a lot about 1826, and has lived on the north bank. **Hagan**, James, settled here about 1827. **McRae**, William and **Keaton**, John, both Irish, of Nova Scotia, swapped land on Aroostook River for this land, with George **Manser**, who bought

it from Abraham Dubez, who had begun improvements in 1828. **O'Neal**, Edward, lives on south bank, but claims a lot across the river on south bank from his home lot.

New Brunswick settlers on north side of the St John, 1831:

Coombs, Leonard, of New Brunswick, his homestead on north side of river, previously owned by Joseph Souci, Jr., located 12 miles above Grand Falls; possessory clearing near homestead. He owns land on the south side of the river which he purchased from Michel Thibodeau and Louis Ouellette. He is in the employ of the British Government. **Long**, Phillip, (Loyalist?) came in 1828, carries mail for the English from Fredericton, to Quebec. **Long**, Marmoise, son of Phillip Long, settled in 1828. **Long**, George, settled in 1828. **Pollock**, Thomas, Scotsman, claimed land in 1829, moved to Rivier du Loup. **Theaney**, Samuel, of NB, house, barn, 20 acres, formerly an employee of British Government.

English or New Brunswick settlers, south bank of St John, 1831:

Christopher, Samuel and **Christopher**, Raphael, both of Bay of Chaleur, began improving a lot in 1824, and claimed another lot set off by their brother, who was drowned, and may have been married, but left no children. **Emerson**, John, English; he and his brothers have begun to clear lot in 1830. **Squires**, Zebedee, is building a house and has cleared four acres in 1831. **Nugent**, Thomas, Irish; began settling about 1827, has purchased land adjoining properties of James **Malone** and William **Cartwell**. **Pendergrass**, John, made a cutting but the lot appears to be abandoned in 1831. **Weeks**, Benjamin, purchased lot of John **McGuire**; this lot McGuire had begun clearing about 1826. Weeks has been there since 1829, but says he and his wife and two children are planning to move to the Tobique River. **Wilds**, Joseph, came 1828, born Fredericton, New Brunswick. **Yearnton**, Isaac, Englishman, came in August, 1828.

On the **Aroostook River**, 1831:

Settlers in No 13, 4th Range, **Wade Plantation**: **Arnold**, Joseph, was there in 1824, sold his lot to John Black of New Brunswick, about 1825. **Black**, John, of NB, bought his land from J. Arnold. This lot had been improved in 1824 by Henry Bradley. **Bull**, Peter, of New Brunswick, lives on the South Bank, since 1822. New Brunswick Historical Society records say he was the son of Captain George Bull, Loyalist, who settled at Woodstock, NB. This is the last lot in No 12, Range 3 (Mapleton,) and he also owns Bull's Island. **Christie**, Joshua, of New Brunswick, bought land from William **Dalton**, and is farming. **Churchill**, Nathaniel, lives below **David Freeman**, on an island in the Aroostook River. He had worked on the Freeman lot about 1824, and had sold it to Samuel Nevers. **Currier**, James, lives on lot cleared by Joseph **Arnold**, at the request of John Black, in 1831. **Freeman**, David, of NB, building a house in 1831, on his lot adjoining Salmon Brook. He also owns a house and barn in Maysville, on south bank of river. **Dalton**, William, and family, live in 1831 below Nathaniel Churchill, on the south bank of the Aroostook, but plans to move farther up river, near the Great Machias River, to No 11, R 5, (Ashland). **Hickey**, John, below John **Kendall**, on the south bank of the river, Irish unmarried, came here about 1826, farmer. **Kendall**, John, began work on the lot occupied by William **Dalton** about 1825, and sold it to Abraham **Hammond**, who sold it to Story **Hooper**. **Mumford**, William, of Nova Scotia, lives on an island in the river which he bought from Joshua **Christie** about 1829, who had come to the island about 1827. Plans to move to south bank of the river because of the spring flooding. **Rand**, James, and his family live in the home of John **Hickey**, above, but he is clearing his own land down river.

Settlers in **Letter G Maysville**, on the **Aroostook River**, in 1831:

Armstrong, Ferdinand, of Nova Scotia, bought this land on the south bank from Elias **Brown** about 1829. Armstrong first began a habitation on Nathaniel Churchill's island, and it has had several occupants. **Beckwith**, Thomas, of New Brunswick, lives, in 1831, in Letter G, Maysville, came about 1822. His married son lives with him, on the south bank of the river. **Bradley**, Henry, of New Brunswick, bought of John **Hickey**, who had the land from Andrew **McRae**. **Brown**, Elias, of NB came to north bank of Aroostook about 1829. **Brown**, William, of NB, claims a lot begun by James **Dennison** about 1824? and "went off." Brown came about 1828, is not married, and his mother is living with him, north bank. **Churchill**, Nathaniel of NB, owns the last island, forty acres, in letter G, Maysville, since about 1829. **Cook**, David, of NB, occupies a farm developed by Oliver **Bradley**, who drowned in 1830. The lot has had several owners. **Fairbanks**, Dennis, about 1828 he left Aroostook River area to go to Letter F, Presque Isle. **Hooper**, (Nehemiah, Nathaniel?) an American, bought land from Joseph Arnold, "some years ago," south bank; also had a small clearing on lot on north bank in 1831. **Goss**, Thomas, an American, bought his lot from original claimant, Wm. Piles (Pyles). It is on the north bank. **Johnson**, Charles, of New Brunswick, settled about 1821, south bank of Aroostook River. **Johnson**, Lewis, of New Brunswick, settled about 1821 on north bank. **Mansur**, George, an American, owns two lots; the first was bought from Dennis **Fairbanks**, who had it from James **Armstrong**, who had it from Joseph **Arnold**. The second lot he traded his lot in the Madawaska Settlement for, with Wm **McRae**. **Piles** (Pyles) William, an American (Loyalist?) came here about 1822, south bank. **Rafford**, John, on land opposite lower end of Bull's island, north bank, settled about 1828, on land abandoned by John **Wade**.

Teiling, Thomas, English, occupied lot on north bank of Letter G, Maysville, about 1827 to 1830, and left. New Brunswick Historical Society notes say he had been in the British navy, lived on the Mirimichi River and engaged in lumbering on the Eel River in NB. **Thomas**, Isaac, of NB, bought land from Joseph **Arnold** about 1828, has sold it to Dennis Fairbanks, south bank. **Thomas** also, in 1831 had a possession on the north bank of the Aroostook.
Wade, John, settled on land now owned by John **Rafford**, about 1825.

Settlers in **Letter F, Presque Isle,** in 1831:
Fairbanks, Dennis, about 1828, came to Letter F, Presque Isle from the Aroostook River and built a grist mill. **Hasey,** John, an American, began improving a lot in 1831. **McCan**, Robert, began improving a lot in 1831. **Work**, Levi, American, began improving a lot in Letter F in 1831.

Settlers in **Letter I, Caribou and Eaton Grant**, part of **Caribou**.
Cochrane, Alexander, Irish, settled about 1828 on a lot where Wm. **Piles** and John **Vaughn** had begun a grist mill on the Caribou Stream, Letter I Caribou. **Connelly**, Patrick, Irish, Eaton Grant. **Davenport**, Gabriel, NB, north bank. **Davenport**, Samuel, NB, north bank. **Gallagher**, Francis, Irish, is settling near the upper part of the Oxbow, Letter I, Caribou. Eaton Grant. **Gardiner**, Widow, American, Eaton Grant. **Kelley**, Lawrence, Irish, Eaton Grant. **Parks**, David, American, Eaton Grant. **Parks**, Joseph, American, Eaton Grant. **Stoner**, William, American, Eaton Grant.

Settlers in **Plymouth Grant, [Fort Fairfield]**, 1831:
Bobear (Bubar) David from NB, north bank. **Bobear, (Bubar)** Charles, same. **Campbell**, James, Irish, south bank. **Dorsey**, John. Irish, south bank. **Fitzherbert**, James of NB, bought of Michael **Weyland**, who had purchased from Benjamin **Weeks**, who had begun improve-

ment about 1824, on south bank. **Fowler**, Peter, Irish, north bank. **Heywood**, Charles, American, south bank, came in June, 1831. **Kean**, Anthony, Irish south bank. **Loveless**, William, from NB, south bank. **McDougal**, Peter, Scotsman, south bank, came in 1829. **McDougal**, Alexander, Scotsman, north bank. **McLauchlin**, Bernard, Irish, south bank. **McLauchlin**, Daniel, Irish, north bank. "**McRae Place**," claimed by Wilmot and Company, in Plymouth "Township" (Grant), south Bank. **Mowry**, Martin, Irish, north bank, came in 1829. **Parker**, John, American, south bank, came in 1829. **Powers**, James, Irish, north bank, came in 1829. **Rogers**, Thomas, from NB, south bank. **Russell**, Michel, Irish, south bank. **Wright**, George, from NB, south bank, came in 1831.

Settlers in **Bridgewater**, including Bridgewater Academy Grant and Portland Academy Grant, in 1831:
Bradstreet, Nathaniel, came to the Presque Isle of the St John to Bridgewater Academy grant in 1830 to build a sawmill.

Settlers in **Township A** in 1831:
General Joel Wellington was planning to build a sawmill and a grist mill in 1831. He and Samuel Whitney, in 1827, had bought from the State of Maine a township of land, of six miles square, for $3500, under the condition that they erect a saw mill and grist mill and cause at least ten families to be settled in three years and fifty settlers in ten years. As a result Township A, R1 WELS, or Wellington Township, (now Monticello) was settled in 1830 and incorporated July 28, 1846. (Chapter XXXVI, February 23, 1827, ROSM. Sale was completed on February 14, 1829.)

Settlers at confluence of the **St John** and **Aroostook Rivers**, 1831:

Tibbetts, ___, three miles below confluence, on west side of the river St John, had been lumbering under license from the British.

Settlers at the confluence of the **St John** and **Presque Isle** of the **St John Rivers**, 1831:

Tompkins, ___, had a public house two miles above the confluence, on the east bank of the St John River.

APPENDIX V

THE LAND AGENT'S CIVIL POSSE

The names of the men who volunteered to be part of the Land Agent's posse at various intervals are difficult to determine; at least part of them are found in scattered documents from various sources.

I.

One probable source is a listing found on a manuscript scroll entitled, "List of Men Furnished with Guns At Aroostook." This is a listing of names, accompanied by the numbers engraved on their rifles. The rifles were issued to each man by Captain Towle of Lincoln, Maine. The list included:

Hiram Adams, Robert Allen, Jr., Wm. Allen, Mark T. Ames, Sewel Ames, Elkins Andrews, Blanchard Austin, Cyrus Austins, Moses Austins, Henry Badger, Algenon Barrett, Stephen D. Barrett, Larange B. Battes, Reuben O. Bean, Samuel Bean, Richard Bedle, Jr., Ellexander Bell, Henry Bell, Henry Bell Jr., Addison Benjamin, Leander Benson, Phillip Blake, James Blanchard, Sylvester Bragg, George Breslin?, John Brockry, George Brown, Francis B. Bunker, John Burnham, Samuel A. Burr, David L. Busell, Hiram Busell, Horacio Butters, Harrass Butriss, John B. Butts, Asa S. Carpenter, Jonathan Carter, Andrew Cates, Joshua Chamberlain Jr., Thomas H. Chase, Alpheus A. Coburn, Ebenezer Cunningham, Wm. Cunningham, Levi D. (Cleverly?) Joseph Clough, Jr., Charles Coffin, Wm. Coffin, Robert Colberth, Gustavus Colberth, Ebenezer Collins, J. Collins, Jacob C. Comber, Edmond T. Conney (Coney?), Isaac Copland, Benjamin B. Crandlemire, Joshua Crooker, Redmond S. Cummins, James Curr, Melzer Curtis, Benjamin W. Davis, Gideon Deering, Henry F. Dicker, Albert Dilnow, Henry Dolley, Joshua Done, Noah Dow Jr., Thomas Dresser, Benjamin Drew, Jesse Dior Jr., Andrew Eaton, Levi Eaton, John Elkins, Charles Ellis, Elisha Evans, Stephen C. Elwell, Levi Engerson, John Fariher, John Farrar, Sewell Farrar, Alvin Felps, Cyrus A. Felps, Henry C. Field, Wm. C. Fillebrown, Ansel Fish, Zeddock Fish, Daniel Floyd, Aaron French, Joseph D. French, Solomon Furnal, Solon Gales [Gates?], Otis Glidden, Stephen Grander, Thomas Graves, Hiram Gray, Moses S. Greenell, John P. Guptall, Silvanus Hall, Daniel Ham, Augustus Hammond, Solomon Ham, J. Hanson, Joseph Hardy, Appleton Herrin, Wesley Harrington, Nathaniel Haskell, Benjamin Hathorne, Russel Hathorn, Isreald Heald, John Herik? [Herk?], David Hervey, David Higgins Jr., Dyer Higgins, Timothy Hodgdon, John Hohen?, Amasa Holdin, Nathaniel S. Hooper, Stephen Hoopking, L. Hudson, Charles C. Hurd, John Hurd, Miles Huzzy, Wm. Huzzy, Jedediah H. Judkins, Ezra Kneeland, Isaac Laberee, Samuel M. Laribee, Oliver Lane, Moses M. Land, Amos C. Leighton, W. H. (Y? L?esan?), George W. Levett, Wm. C. Libby, Henry W. Little of Bangor, Jacob Litton, Robert McCannery, Luther McClain, Solomon McGuire, Isaac McKinney, James Tosh, James Macumber, Isaac Millett, John Millett, Wm. Millett, Wm. Maxwell, Leander A. Merrill, Wm. B. Merrill, Wm. P. Merrill, Asa Miller, John Miller, Levi Moore, John S. Morgan, Nathaniel Muzzy, Rufus Muzzy, Orrin Nelson, George W. Oaks, Robert A. [Osnaliave?], Charles Parsons, Elijah Pease, Warren Pease, James Pennington, Martin Perce, Alphred Phillips, George Piper, Stephen Piper, George Plummer, Marstie Potter, Oliver Potter, Alexander Pratt, Sylvester Pray, Lucius Prince, Gilman Quimba, Wm. Randall, Henry Read, M. Read, Benjamin Ridlon, Silas Ridland, Jesse Robberts,

Moses Roberts, James Robbinson, Wm. Robbins, Charles Robinson, James Rogers, Charles G. Row, W. A. Row, David Ruges, Wm. Sangler, Wm. Sargeant, Asa Sawatelle, John Serrett, Isaac Shaw, J. R. Sinclair, John Smith, John Somes, Joseph Sonas? [Somes?], Asa Spencer, David Spencer, J. Spencer, Samuel Spiller, E. G. Stackpole, Winslow Staples Jr., Francis Sturtvant, James C. Thurlow, Noah Trafton, Charles M. Tuck, Andrew Tuck, John Tucker, James F. Turner, Azriah Wadleigh, James Wagg, Alfred Walker, Samuel Wentworth, Jacob Werks, N. Weston, H. White, Henry Wilson, Jesse Withman, Ansel Wood, Daniel Wright, Alfred Young.

II

Another possible source is a list of officers in the *Bangor Historical Magazine* (The editor states: "After the death of Colonel Porter, I found this roster of officers of the volunteer troops ... It may or may not be correct. It is just as I found it.")

Colonel Charles Jarvis	Acting Land Agent
*Wm. P. Parrot	Aide de Camp to Colonel Jarvis
Joseph Porter	Col. Commanding
Joshua Chamberlain Jr.	Lt.ColonelCom'ding
John Dunning of Charleston	Major Commanding
Henry W. Cunningham	Adjutant,from Swanville
++Daniel Chase of Atkinson	Quartermaster
Luther Turner Jr., of Lincoln	Artillery Captain
Benjamin Drew, of Dexter	Artillery Lt.
D. L. Bussell	" "
++Wm. Cross of Milo	" "
*Ward Witham of Bangor,	Infantry Captain
____Rollins	Infantry Lt.
George W. Towle, of Lincoln	Rifles Captain
Thomas H. Chase of Lincoln	Rifles Lieutenant
Alpheus Coburn of Lincoln	" "
Jedediah Judkins of Lincoln	" "
*Stover Rines of Orono	Infantry Captain

Thomas Hunt of Orono,	Inf. Lieutenant
Samuel Burr of Brewer	" "
Lorenzo D. Butters of Exeter	Infantry Captain
Horace Butters of Exeter	" Lieutenant
Ansel J. Wood of Stetson	" "
Calvin S. Doughty of Sangerville	" Captain
Charles Robinson of Dover	" Lieutenant
Luther Chamberlain of Foxcroft,	" "
Thomas Bartlett Jr., of Bangor,	" Captain
Simon Burnet, of Hermon	" Lieutenant
Harrison M. Crowell of Corinna	" "
Henry Williamson of Parkman	" Captain
Jacob Works of Parkman	" Lieutenant
Adams Macomb of Parkman	" "
John Ford of Hallowell	Artillery Captain
Abner True of Hallowell	" Lieutenant
Wallis McKennie of Augusta	" "
Charles T. Dunning of Charleston	Infantry Captain
Jere[miah?] Page of Charleston	" Lieutenant
Daniel Brown of Atkinson	" "
**Thomas Emery of Hampden,	" Captain
S. B. McAllister of Hampden	" Lieutenant
W. S. Booker of Hampden	" "
Daniel Billings of Monroe	Inf. Acting Captain
Caleb F. Billings of Northport	" Lieutenant
***Alvin Nye	
+Daniel Chase of Atkinson	Infantry Captain
Job Parsons of Dover	" Lieutenant
++Wm. Brown of Atkinson	" "
Nymphas Turner of Milo	" Captain
Asa Dow of Dover	" Lieutenant
Thomas Furber of Milo	" "
Franklin Hussey of China	" Captain

* Rines, Parrot and Witham were reported by the *Bangor Daily Whig and Courier* to have been the the leaders of

the three original sections of the first posse to go to the Aroostook Area.
** See Part III of this Appendix.
*** Alvin Nye was promoted and placed in command at Fort Jarvis, later renamed Fort Kent.
+Daniel Chase appears twice on this list; could have served in both capacities
++ Men with these names also appear on the Maine Militia rolls, and may or may not be the same men.
Note: This list does not include Rufus McIntire, Land Agent, so it may have been made up when McIntire was held captive in New Brunswick.

III

From the Voucher Files, *Aroostook War Vouchers*, Maine State Archives, Augusta, Maine, the following undated list:
Memorandum of Captain Emery's men:
Thomas Emery, John Cary, Samuel Cary, Cyrus Adams, Henry Snow, Benjamin Adams, Nathan Hatton, Sylvanus B. McCorison, Eben Edgerly, J. C. Wing, Joseph W. Wade, Levi Baker, Wm. S. Booker, Lewis Young, Benjamin Young, Ephriam Stuggs and team; Wm. G. Lowe, Robert Moore, Edward Doane, Ezekiel Morse, Gilbert Young, Isaac Knowles, Lendall Myrick, Amos Morrill, John T. Bragdon, Daniel Low, Philip Randall, John Clark, Benjamin Murch, Ephriam Quin, Almon E. Osgood, Simon Mudget, Albion P. Wilson, Jonathan Powers, ___Hartford and team.

IV

The following is a listing of the men on the payroll of the State in order to carry out the duties of the Civil Posse, February 26, 1841:

Erastus Adams, Wm. Arnold, Silas Barnard, Thomas Bartlett, Thomas Bartlett, Jr., Daniel Billings, Daniel W. Bradley, Charles G. Bryant, George W. Buckmore, Lorenzo Butters, Humphrey Chadbourne, Sumner Chalmers, Joshua Chamberlain, Daniel Chase, Isaac B. Cilley, C. S. Clark, C. M. Cobb, H. W. Cunningham, C. C. Cushman, G. G. Cushman,

John Devoin, Calvin S. Doughty, C. T. Dunning, John Dunning, Thomas Emery, W. End, Jesse Fairbanks, Wm. C. Fillebrown, Ira Fish, John Ford, Wm. A. Gilman, Elijah L. Hamlin, Lewis Hancock, John Hanscomb, Aaron Haynes, Alvin Haynes, Isaac Heath, Franklin Hersey, John G. Jameson, Charles Jarvis, Jacob Johnson, D. F. Leavitt, Charles Lowell, Wm. Lowell, J. T. McIntosh, Joseph Maddox, I. Mason, Wm. P. Parrott, Joseph Pollard, Joseph Porter, Francis Porus, R. S. Prescott, F. S. Remick, Amos Rines, Stover Rines, A. M. Robinson, James Rogers, Franklin Rollins, Joseph Shaw for transportation, James Simmons, Gideon R. Sinclair, George W. Stanley, Hastings Strickland, C. H. Thaxter, Prince Thomas, James W. Thompson, Elisha Towle, George W. Towle, Nymphas Turner, Nathan Weston, Benjamin Wiggin, Henry Williamson, H. Winslow and Ward Witham. AROSM V

APPENDIX VI

MUSTER ROLLS OF SOME OF THE MORE ACTIVE MAINE MILITIA UNITS ON DUTY ON THE NORTHEAST FRONTIER IN 1839

Captain Charles H. Wing's Company of Riflemen, in service from rendezvous at Bangor, on 20 February, 1839 to 22 April, 1839: Lieutenant Abram Morris, Ensign Simon P. Atkins; Sergeants: Thomas C. Crehore, Wm. B. Walker, Daniel B. Hall, Wm. H. Ginn, J. Selden Burbank, Micah P. Erskine; Corporals: Samuel Spencer, Joseph L. Buck, John G. Orcutt, Henry Balch; Musicians: John A. Heath, Zeneth W. Burrill; Privates: Harvey M. Burrill, Spencer G. Bowles, John H. Connoly, Ambros Emery, Rufus Emery, Isaac D. Emerson, John Farnham, Charles T. Fitz, Ephriam Gray, Josiah Hall, Jr., Stephen D. Holt, Samuel M. Hopkins, Benjamin F. Hutchinson, Charles Libbey, Wm. Little, Jr., Ethan A. Mason, Benjamin Moore, Isaac W. Moore, George Noyes, Gordon Perkins, John Prim, John Rea, Jr., Benjamin R. Smith, Joseph B. Smith, John Snowman, Joshua Staples, Robert C. Straw, Cyrus Stubbs, Elijah Taylor, Tobias Thompson.[1]

---

[1] *Aroostook War, Historical Sketch and Roster of Commissioned Oficers and Enlisted Men*, official State of Maine publication, printed by the Kennebec Journal, 1904, hereinafter referred to as AWOSP, p 70.

Ensign Jeremiah Burnham's Company of Light Infantry, in service from rendezvous at Bangor, on 20 February, 1839 to 22 April, 1839: Ensign James Dunning; Sergeants: John Pray, James Littlefield, Phineas Batchelder, James H. Stewart. Corporals: Horace I. Gould, Frederick K. Bartlett, Hiram G. Caridge, George W. McFarland; Musicians: Frederic Stewart, Rufus Smith; Privates: James Bragg, John Brown, Josiah Brown, Perkins Brown, Royal R. Burnham, Orrin Butterfield, Jonathan Buzzell, Benjamin Chadbourne, John Champion, Samuel Clark, John Cookson, Erastus Corson, Samuel F. Cottle, Robert M. Cumston, Ebenezer Daggett, James M. Daniels, Barsillai Dorr, Israel Douglass, Andrew G. Fitts, Oliver Ferguson, Peleg Fogg, George W. Fullerton, Daniel Geral, John Glidden, Ebenezer H. Gordon, Peter R. Gribbin, Jairus Harris, Samuel H. Holt, James Horn, Derry P. Jellison, Stephen Jones, Charles Kelley, Asa Longley, Henry B. Martin, Wm. Moores, Solomon Morey, Nathaniel Myrick, Christopher Overlock, Martin Overlock, George Paine, Wm. H. Palmer, Hiram Peavey, Jonathan Peavey, Jason R. Philbrook, Peter Pilsbury, John Puffer, Samuel Roberts, Alfred Seaman, Joseph P. Sinclair, Charles S. Sprague, Charles Stavers, Wm. Turner, Eli Wadleigh, Paul P. Wakefield, Calvin Ward, Nathaniel S. Wentworth, Nathaniel White.[2]

Captain Stephen Leighton's Company of Riflemen, also known as The Dexter Rifles,[3] in service from rendezvous at Bangor, on 20 February, 1839 to 22 April, 1839: Lieutenant Isaiah Beals; Ensign Alvin B. Clark; Sergeants: Reuben Flanders, Hiram Safford, Asa Spooner, Seth Drew; Corporals: Stephen D. Jenning, Charles Jumper, Cyrus Jumper, Calvin Safford; Musicians: John M. Shaw.

---

2 AWOSP, 40

3...AWOSP, p 57; See *History of Dexter* by the Hon. Stanley Plummer, reprinted by the Dexter Historical Society in 1976, for further details.

A manuscript in the possession of the Maine Historical Society Archives (accession number 67-633-2, catalogued as "Roster of Enlisted Men, March, 1839"), appears to be, after a comparison with names of men belonging to the Dexter Rifles (as listed in *The History of Dexter*) a list of men from Dexter who took part in the Aroostook Expedition. The list: Wm. Jumper, Simeon Safford Jr., Seba F. Leighton, Reuben Flanders, Charles Jennings, James Lane, Hiram Safford, John Ricker, John Safford, Asa Spooner, Seth Drew, Stephen D. Jennings, Charles Jumper, Cyrus Jumper, Calvin Safford, John M. Shaw, David Berry, James Crowell, Andrew C. Winslow, Eli Winslow, Levi Bridge Jr., Isaac Tucker, Curtis Sturtivant, Stephen Fish, Daniel H. Howard, Darius Sampson, Henry A. Sprague, Silas Leavitt, Joseph Gould, Benjamin Ireland, Andrew N. Day, Luther H. Shaw, Edward P. Longly, George Severance, Henry K. Sawyer, James (F.?) Burleigh, and Isaiah Beals.

Benjamin Drew and David L. Buswell had been members of the Dexter Rifles but were appointed Lieutenants of Artillery in the Land Agent's *posse* by Colonel Joseph Porter. Captain Lysander Cutler had been been elected Lt. Colonel of the 8th Regiment, Maine Militia.

Ensign Emerson and thirty-three privates were transferred to this company from other regiments. By process of elmimination (using the listing in AWOSP) it seems possible that those privates were Willard Abbott, Lemuel Arnold, Othniel Barden, Isaac Bedee, Wm. Bosworth Jr., Benjamin Brown Jr., David G. Brown, Reuben Brown, Wm. McE Brown, John Cole, David Densmore, Thompson Dyer, Levi Emerson, David R. W. Grindell, Samuel Hillman, Charles M. Hodsdon, Albert G. Hunt, Robert Johnson, Wm. L. Johnson, John Kimball, John Leavitt, Charles R. Logan, George P. Logan, George Oakes, Daniel Palmer, Daniel Pickering, Jonathan Pitcher Jr., Horatio Pratt, Harrison G. O. Thoms, John Towle, Benjamin F. Tozier, Charles D. Treworgy, Milton Twitchell, Wm. B. Walker, Burnham Wardwell, Ira Wardwell, Peleg Washburn, George Whittemore, Rufus Willard and Charles Wyman.

    Captain George Maxim's Company, Infantry, in service from rendezvous at Bangor, on 20 February, 1839 to 22 April, 1839: Lieutenant Jonathan Lowder, Ensign Wm. Gibbs; Sergeants: Wm. Averill, David Getchell, Daniel Moulton, Joel Vickery; Corporals: Dudley D. Bean, Jeremy Baker, Jacob Holyoke, Wm. W. Smith; Musicians: Greenleaf M. Fogg, George G. Patterson, George S. Herrick, Francis C. Keisor; Privates: John Ames, Levi Bagley, Enoch M. Blunt, Charles Buffam, Charles E. Chaplin, James B. Cleveland, Seth F. Cook, Reuben Cookson, John Cowan Jr., Rufus G. Curtis, Joseph B. Damon, Asa Davis, 2nd, Benjamin Dillingham, John M. Fogg, Joseph Francis, Ephriam Glidden, Thomas Gould, Thomas Gullifer, Sumner Hamilton, Wm. P. Hatch, Bradford Higgins, James S. Homans, Samuel Houston, Manassah S. Hovey, Manoah Hurd, David G. Ireland, Thomas Jenkins, Ephriam Johnson, Robert Littlefield, Moses Maynor, Ephriam B. McCondray, Isaiah McKenney, Shuber Nickerson, Jr., Simon Orff, James O'Rooke, Norman Page, John Parsons, Samuel Patterson, Enoch Peasley, Benjamin Pratt, George Pratt, Wm. Ransdell, Wilmot Riggs, Allen Rines, Jesse Russ, Asa Sawyer, Wm. Sherburn, Jr., David Shorey, Abram Sibley, Christopher Smith, Asa L. Stiles, Levi S. Torrance, Samuel S. Torrance, John Weymouth, Stephen White, Daniel Willey, Shuber N. Williams, John Witham, Francis Young.[4]

    Captain Eliphalet L. Maxfield's Company of Infantry, in service from rendezvous at Bangor, on 20 February, 1839 to 25 April, 1839: Lieutenant Horatio Barrett, Ensign Goodridge Cummings; Sergeants: Horace Banks, Carlisle Dennis, Joseph Nelson, John Abbot; Corporals: Alvin Merryfield, Thomas I. Towle, Charles Davis, Walker Darling; Musician: Nathaniel Fellows; Privates: Bradley B.

---

4 AWOSP, p. 60.

Ayers, Daniel Bailey, Philip Bailey, Wm. F. Bazzell, Enoch W. Bickford, Wm. Brown, John W. Buck, Sherburn W. Clark, Solomon Comstock, Albert Coombs, James Cooper, Joel F. Dam, Leader N. Dam, Chandler Damren, Asahel Davis, David B. Davis, James Deling, Wm. Devo, Nahalie Doe, Benjamin Eastman, Daniel W. Edgerly, John Elkins, Jr., John B. Emery, Charles Emerson, Joseph Emerson, Wm. Emerson, Stephen P. Haynes, Willmoth Haywood, Joseph Hodgdon, Moses Hodgdon, Moses Ingalls, Jr., Joseph Jordan, Wm. Johnson, Benjamin Judkins, David Kneeland, John W. Lane, Mathias Lane, Solomon P. Lankester, John Lawton, Eliphalet Leavitt, Horace Lord, Alfred S. Lovett, George W. Merrill, Samuel McPheters, James G. McTosh, Wm. McTosh, Josiah Miles, Carleton P. Moody, Rufus Moody, John Morgan, Frederic Morrill,Samuel Norton, Jr., Calvin L. Noyes, Stover Perkins, John Pratt, Josiah Richards, William G. Rogers, James Sanborn, John Scott, Charles L. Smart, Thomas Smith, Wm. A. Tosh, Israel Tracy, Joshua Warton, Mark G. Weymouth, David Young.[5]

Captain Samuel Fish's Company of Infantry, in service from rendezvous at Bangor, on 20 February, 1839 to 23 April, 1839: Lieutenant Francis I. Cumming, Ensign Gilbert Emerson; Sergeants: David C. Jellison, John P. Davis, Moses S. Page, Joseph Budson, James S. Eldridge, Jesse Hutchins; Corporals: Josiah McPheters, Charles H. Forbes, Joseph Bray, George Lincoln, John B. Bond, Kenny Snow; Musicians: Robert P. Chase, Solomon Row; Privates: Thomas Abbot, Willard Abbot, Almarin Ames, Wm. Bachelder, Wm. Ballard, Jr., David L. Billings, John Boyd, George Burns, Timothy Burton, Isaac Buzzell, Justus S. Carr, Garey Chapman,Wm. I. Chapman, Thomas Cunningham, Samuel Deering, James Dickinson, Ephriam Dorr, John Dunham, Jr., Joseph Duran, Wm. Dwelly, Jr., Elisha M. Eveleth, Amasa S. Emerton, Chester Farren, Daniel Fowles, James H. Gilmore, Shadrach Gray, John Grindel,

---

5 AWOSP, p.59.

Wm. P. Guppy, Abial Harmon, Seth Holt, Joseph James, Abel S. Jordan, Levi R. Kilburn, Gilbert Knowlton, David Lancaster, Wm. Lassell, John N. Lawrence, Ronald Lawrence, Thomas Mann, John E. Miller, Wm. B. Moody, Henry Montgomery, Charles Newcomb, Alva Osgood, Roderick R. Park, Charles Patten, Samuel Pierce, Joseph Priest, Thomas Raymond, Samuel Sheet, Jacob Simpson, Wm. C. Snow, John Southard, Jr., Samuel Spencer, Horatio N. Stinson, Joseph C. Stinson, James Stubbs, Jacob P. Swett, Timothy C. Tapley, Levi Tower, Samuel S. Trevett, Benson D. Wood.[6]

On March 2, 1841, Governor Kent sent a message to the Senate and House of Representatives:

The Governor, by advice of the Council, has caused the Third Division of the Militia of Maine to be divided, and a new Division, denominated the Ninth Division of the Militia of Maine has been created, embracing the militia in the following towns, viz: Argyle, Bangor, Brewer, Bradford, Bradley Burlington, Corinth, Charleston, Chester, Dexter, Exeter, Eddington, Enfield, Edinburgh, Glenburn, Garland, Greenbush, Howland, Lee, Levant, Lincoln, Maxfield, Milford, Orono, Oldtown, Orrington, Passadumkeag, Springfield, and Stetson in the County of Penobscot; and Atkinson, Brownville, Dover, Foxcroft, Guilford, Milo, Sangerville and Sebec, in the County of Piscataquis; and Houlton, Hodgdon, Linneus, and Weston, in the County of Aroostook. It therefore becomes your duty to elect a Major General for said division.

Edward Kent
Council Chamber, March 2, 1841[7]

---

6 AWOSP, p. 41.
7 Acts and Resolves of the State of Maine, Vol. IV, p. 678.

CAPTAIN REUBEN SMART'S COMPANY[8]
MAINE MILITIA, 1839

Captain Reuben Smart, 5' 7", age 24, r Swanville, b Swanville, hazel eyes, brown hair, ruddy c, mason.
Lt. Bidfield Plummer, 5' 10 1/2", age 22, r Frankfort, b Bristol, blue eyes, brown hair, light c, joiner.
Cornet Wm. B. Hawes, 5' 9", age 23, r Prospect, b Prospect, hazel eyes, brown hair, light c, farmer.
Orderly Sergeant Stephen O. Colson, r and b Frankfort.
Sgt. John G. Chase, 5' 4", age 20, r Monroe, b Monroe, black eyes, dark hair, dark c, blacksmith.
Sgt. Henry S. Lackey, 5' 2", age 22, r Prospect, b Prospect, blue eyes, brown hair, light c, farmer.
Sgt. Giles C. Grant, 5' 5", age 21, r Prospect, b Penobscot, blue eyes, brown hair, light c, laborer.
Cpl. Jacob Curtis, 5' 7", age 24, r Monroe, b Prospect, blue eyes, dark hair, dark c, farmer.
Cpl. Elisha Persons, 2nd, 5' 8", age 22, r Belfast, b Swanville, blue eyes, dark hair light c, farmer.
Cpl. Jonathan A. Carlton, 5' 11", age 25, r Frankfort, b Frankfort, blue eyes, dark hair, light c, farmer.
Cpl. Samuel F. Stinson, 5' 7 1/2 ", age 26, r Prospect, b Georgetown, blue eyes, light hair, light c, farmer.
Trumpeter James N. Clements, 5' 6 1/2", age 24, r Monroe, b Monson, black eyes, brown hair, light c, farmer.
Pvt. Washington Carleton [not on original listing.]
Pvt. Nathan C. Cole, 5' 8", age 23, r Frankfort, b Frankfort, gray eyes, brown hair, light c, farmer.
Pvt. Alfred Curtis, 5' 6", age 22, r Swanville, b Monroe, blue eyes, light hair, light c, farmer.
Pvt. George B. Curtis, 6', age 21, r Prospect, b Belmont, blue eyes, dark hair light c, farmer.

---

8 From an original manuscript in the possession of the Maine Historical Society Archives, compared with listing in AWOSP.

Pvt. Gideon Curtis, 5' 5", age 28, r Monroe, b Prospect, gray eyes, black hair, dark c, farmer.
Pvt. John W. Curtis, 5' 7", age 22, r Monroe, b Monroe, blue eyes, light hair, light c, farmer.
Pvt. Daniel Downs, 5' 10 1/2", age 23, r Frankfort, b Monroe, blue eyes, brown hair, light c, farmer.
Pvt. James Durham, 5' 6 1/2", age 21, r Waldo, b Monroe, black eyes, brown hair, light c, farmer.
Pvt. John Ellingwood, 6', age 26, r Frankfort, b Frankfort, blue eyes, brown hair, light c.
Pvt. Dodge N. Ewell, 5' 4 1/2", age 21, r Prospect, b Frankfort, gray eyes, brown hair, light c, farmer.
Pvt. Andrew Folsom
Pvt. Obadiah George, 5' 6 1/2", age 24, r Prospect, b Prospect, black eyes, brown hair, light c, farmer.
Pvt. Stephen [Stevens?] D. George, 5' 8", age 21, r and b Prospect, blue eyes, brown hair, light c, farmer.
Pvt. George H. Hall, 5'7", age 21, r Frankfort, b Frankfort, blue eyes, brown hair, light c, farmer.
Pvt. Nathan H. [G.?] Hichborn, 5'4", age 21, r Prospect, b Prospect, blue eyes, brown hair, light c, farmer.
Pvt. John F. Kelley, 5'11", age 21, r Prospect, b Chester, N. H.; black eyes, brown hair, dark c, farmer.
Pvt. Jesse Lambert, 5' 7 1/2", age 24, r Monroe, b Mt Vernon, Mr;, black eyes, brown hair, dark c, blacksmith.
Pvt. John C. Libby
Pvt. Elijah S. Mitchell, 5' 7 1/2", age 20, r Monroe, b Monroe, blue eyes, light hair, light c, farmer.
Pvt. Randal Morton [Moulton in AWOSP list] 5' 9 3/4". age 22, r Frankfort, b Thorndike, blue eyes, sandy hair, light c, farmer
Pvt. Elijah S. Mitchell, 5' 7 1/2", age 20, r Monroe, b Monroe, blue eyes, light hair, light c, farmer.
Pvt. Samuel Murray, 5' 10", age 23, r Frankfort, b Waterville, blue eyes, light hair, light c, farmer.
Pvt. Daniel D. Nealey, 5' 4 1/2", age 21, r Swanville, b Newfield, black eyes, brown hair, dark c, farmer.

Pvt. Freeman Nickerson, 5'9", age 17, r Swanville, b Swanville, blue eyes, brown hair, light c, farmer.
Nathaniel Nickerson, 5' 8 1/2", age 20, r Belfast, b Swanville, blue eyes, brown hair, light c, farmer.
Pvt. Isaac Patterson, 5' 8 1/4 ", age 23, r Monroe, b Belfast, blue eyes, sandy hair, light c, farmer.
Pvt. James H. Pendleton, 5'11 1/2", age 20, r Prospect, b Prospect, blue eyes, black hair, dark c, farmer.
Pvt. Thomas Perkins, 6', age 31, r Frankfort, b Frankfort, black eyes, black hair, dark c, farmer.
Pvt. Francis N. Pumroy, 5' 6 5/8", age 23, r Hampden, b Hermon, blue eyes, brown hair, light c, farmer.
Pvt. Charles N. B. Robinson, 5' 7", age 39, r Frankfort, b Deerfield, NH; blue eyes, brown hair, light c, ___.
Pvt. Richard Robertson, Jr., r Monroe
Pvt. George W. Segee, 5' 7 1/2", age 17, r Waldo, b Knox, black hair, brown eyes, light c, sailor.
Pvt. Edward B. Stafford, 5' 10", age 47, r Frankfort, b Gilford, NJ; dark eyes, dark hair, light c, farmer.
Pvt. David Sterns, Jr., 5' 5 1/2 ", age 23, r Monroe, b Monroe blue eyes, brown hair, light c, farmer.
Pvt. Wm. B. Stinson, 6' 2 1/2", age 23, r Prospect, b Georgetown, black eyes, brown hair, dark c, farmer.
Pvt. Truworthy [Timothy?] Stubbs, r Prospect , farmer.
Pvt. James Treadwell, 5'9", age 32, r Frankfort, b Frankfort, blue eues, brown hair light c, farmer.
Pvt. Levi Trundy, 5' 9 1/2", age 23, r Frankfort, b Knox, blue eyes, brown hair, light c, joiner.
Pvt. James Tyler, 5' 10", age 23, r Prospect, b Edgecomb, blue eyes, brown hair, light c, farmer.
Pvt. Wm. Verrill [not on original list]
Pvt. Samuel West [not on original list]

APPENDIX VII

COMMERCIAL AND POLITICAL ESTABLISHMENTS IN NEW BRUNSWICK

COMMERCIAL ESTABLISHMENT:

W. S. MacNutt, Canadian Historian, wrote that the politics of the timber trade had a strong determining influence upon events from about 1825 to 1845. The merchant-politicians held the seats in a legislature so powerful that it controlled New Brunswick politics. All governmental issues were dependent upon the struggle to control the Crown Lands and because the economy of the Province depended upon timber, these matters dominated the work of the Legislature.[1]

Land disposal, in the 1830's, was done through a two-tier system; 200-acre settlement lots at a price set by the Commissioner of Crown lands could be had by petitioners, upon payment of four equal installments. Land

---

[1] W. S. MacNutt, "*The Politics of the Timber Trade in Colonial New Brunswick,*" 1825-1840, 1949; *The Canadian Historical Review*, Vol. XXX, 47-65, quoting from the *St. John Courier*, April 30, 1831.

often sold at £1 per acre, but in reality was worth ten times as much.[2]

Land fever was evident, as it was in the States, and American capital was invested in large tracts of New Brunswick lands through Provincial intermediaries. One investigation revealed that an association had been formed in Boston to control all of the timberlands and mill sites on the St. Croix, St. John and Penobscot Rivers. The Lieutenant Governor suspended land sales in the southwest part of the Province in 1833 to combat this organization. Mr. Baillie, New Brunswick's Commissioner of Crown Lands, encouraged the alienation of large tracts of the Crown domain in the 1830's and much of this land was bought by American interests, and in cooperation with New Brunswick citizens, mill companies were organized to make large profits.[3]

British shipping interests, finding that their vessels were returning home with empty holds due to the failure of the cotton crop in the United States, disregarded the agreement to the contrary and petitioned for the privilege of exporting timber cut on the Disputed Territory.[4] Under these conditions, Baillie caused prices to rise at the land auctions, selected sites for mills, dams and booms, priced them exorbitantly and used his power to show favoritism to certain privileged individuals.[5] Baillie was the largest purchaser of all. He formed the New Brunswick and Nova Scotian Land Company which

---

[2] Graeme Wynn, *Timber Colony. A Historical Geography of Early Nineteenth Century New Brunswick*, 1981, U. of Toronto Press, 144.

[3] Wynn, loc. cit,.144-145.

[4] MacNutt, loc. cit. 56; citing P A C, Council Minutes, May 3, 1836.

[5] Ibid, 56; citing evidence of favouritism in land sales to Capt. Eccles and to Beckwith, a chief clerk in his office in 1837, citing PAC CO 188, Harvey to Glenelg with enclosure, Aug 18, 1837.

purchased, in 1834, 500,000 acres of land in York County, along the northern boundary of the parish of Queensbury.[6] There came to be a feeling that New Brunswick needed American capital to aid in development.[7] Limited corporations, with lawyers and merchants who were members of the New Brunswick Legislature as shareholders, multiplied. Ernest H. Lombard, "a professed American, who had been driven from lumbering operations on the Aroostook, but one who said that British institutions were best," formed the Red Rapids Company, on the Tobique River, with one hundred thousand acres of timberland.[8] Moses H. Perley,[9] of St. John, was a leader in introducing American capital, and he had several enterprises including the Lancaster Milling Corporation on the Bay of Fundy. In the United States, the Panic of 1837, caused by the failure of American banks, brought an end to buying on credit and many lumber businesses failed.[10]

---

6 Ibi., 57. After the arrival of Lt. Gov. Harvey, in 1837, Baillie was systematically degraded, lost his post as a commissioner, Crown lands became subject to liberalized legislative control. See 58-63.
7 Ibid., 56, MacNutt cites Harvey to Glenelg, June 29, 1837.
8 Wynne, loc. cit., 104-105, who wrote: "In March, 1836, the investment was placed on firmer legal grounds by the incorporation of Lombard, Berton and others into the Tobique Mill Company. ... Lombard began to organize the construction of a dam and the erection of fifteen sawmills at the Red Rapids ... At least one of these mills was in operation before 1840 and some spruce and pine lumber was sent to market. ... By midsummer, 1842, the Red Rapids dam had fallen into decay, and the Tobique Mill Company had ceased operations after five years of precarious, unprofitable existence, [due to] ... speculation expanded beyond all precedent."
9 Ibid., 106, Wynn wrote: "Moses Perley, was a prominent, if often unsuccessful speculator in this field. An ill-fated venture involving 80,000 acres to the east of the Chiputnecticook Lakes, and a similar enterprise with one million acres near the Musquash Lakes, did not lessen his enthusiasm to assist American investors, and he purchased the 32,000 acre area of Inglewood Manor, in western St. John and King's counties while acting as agent of a lumber company in 1832."
10 MacNutt, loc. cit., 56-57.

Changes made by Lieutenant Governor Harvey inaugurated the rule of victorious timber barons who held the seats of an all-powerful legislature. By 1840 it was said that the only good timber left in New Brunswick was to be found in the Disputed Territory. In New Brunswick, the issue in contention with the United States was seen as the trade of Fredericton versus that of Bangor.[11]

Lumbering Activities in New Brunswick, 1831-1832:

The following data[12] specifies the names of New Brunswick sawmill owners and the locations of their mills, in 1831:

SAINT JOHN COUNTY: Otty & Crookshank, William Black, Ward Chipman, Charles Simonds, ___ Clark, at **South Bay**; John Robertson at **Lepreau**; Ralph M. Jarvis at **Musquash**; Bell & Wilmot at **Mispeck**; George Matthews at **Black River** and **Emerson's Creek**; ___Brown at **Gardner's Creek**, ___Ratcliffe at **Loch Lommond**; Allan Otty at **Goose River**; Robert Ellis at **Teigmouth**; John Ward & Sons at **Wolfe's Cove**; T. Melville, Howard & Brown, J. Founds, William Bradshaw, David Vaughan, S. & P. Mosher, Joseph Brown, John Brown, J. Tabor, all at **Quaco**; C. M. Wheatton at **Golden Grove**; Calvin Hathaway, Archibald Menzies at **Musquash**; David Hatfield, John Conley, James & Isaac Cole, all at **Lancaster**. Estimated amount of lumber sawed in St. John County, 11,805,000. Estimated number of men employed in lumbering, sawing and delivery to ports, 320.

KINGS COUNTY: A. H. Rose, Samuel Vaughan, Joseph Sherwood, David Faulkner, Jonathan Titus, James Crawford,

---

11 Ibid, 64, 49.
12 *Official Statement of the Saw Mills and Mill Property in the Province of New Brunswick*, December 7, 1831, Public Archives of Canada, CO193/3.

Abram Baxter, John Smith, John McVay, John Darling, Samuel Fowler, John Faulkner, John Hennigar, Caleb Wetmore, Jr., James Smith, all at **Hampton**; James Wardle, Hanford Bostwick, James Peters, Gould Pickett, Walter Bates, Isaac Perry, Samuel Fairweather, Justus S. Wetmore, Samuel Kirstead, all at **Kingston**; James Brittain, Sr., Zebulon (Jones or James?), James Brittain, Jr., John Coffin, John Haggerty, all at **Greenwich**. Estimated amount of lumber sawed in King's County, 3,805, 000. Estimated number of men employed in lumbering, sawing and delivery to ports, 287.

GLOUCESTER COUNTY: John Young, Puckashaw; Romaine Doucette, Hugh Monroe at **Nipisiguit**; William Fleming, at **Addington**; Robert Ferguson, Jacob Church, William Dunbar, all at **Restigouche**. Estimated amount of lumber sawed in Gloucester County, 2,920,000. Estimated number of men employed in lumbering, sawing and delivery to ports, 114.

WESTMORELAND COUNTY: William Atkinson, Philip Palmer, Aaron Brownell, William Dickson, James Cruikshank, George Kinear, James Boyd, John Gotero, Gideon Smith, William Letes, John Humphrey, Joseph Gould, all at **Dorchester**; John McRae, John Cochran, Robert Ray, Harper Wilson, T. McFadden & Marten, all at **Hopewell**; J. &J. Woodworth, John & James Steves, William & George Taylor, John & George Steeves, Henry & M. Steeves, Jones & Colpitts, Smith & Rogers, T. Smith & John Lates, William Durphy, Andrew Steeves, all at **Hillsboro**; George Rogers and J. Hoar & John Rogers at **Sawmill Creek**; Joseph Peck, Elias Peck, Oliver Stiles, all at **Chapman Creek**; John Pearson, Stephen Stiles at **Crooked Creek**; Daniel Tingley, Jr. at **Main River**; Edward Stevens, John & Rufus Reed at **Village Creek**; Levi Elliot, Gilbert & Forsythe at **New Horton**; William Fillemore at **North River**; John Smith, David Oliver at **New Horton**; C.&T. Richardson, Isaac Turner at **Cape Earage**; Hiram Edgett at **West**

River; Thomas Taylor, Joseph Hanning, Jacob R. Grey, Thomas Gallang, Joseph Arseno, Gabriel Leshere at **Shediac**. Estimated amount of lumber sawed in Westmoreland County: 8,805,000. Estimated number of men lumbering sawing and delivery to ports, 324.

KENT COUNTY: Barnard Turner, James Long, Edwin Atkinson at **Bucktouche**; George Thomson, William Hannington, Jr., Alexander Nevers at **Cocagne**; Washington Raymond and Oliver Barrio at **Carleton**; John P. Ford, Thomas Atkinson, at **Liverpool**. Estimated mount of lumber sawed in Kent County: 2,650,000. Estimated number of men employed in lumbering and sawing and delivery to ports, 84.

NORTHUMBERLAND COUNTY: Joseph Cunard,[13] Thomas Boice, Joseph Wing, at **Southwest**; Stephen Peabody at **Sabey's River**; Betts & Miller at **Forks**; Dock & McLaggen at **Bart's River**; John Foy at **Indian Town**; Estate of the late J. Fraser & James D. Fraser at **Barnaby's River**, Northwest; Joseph Cunard at **Toser's Brook**; Patrick Henderson at **Mill Cove**; Gilmour, Rankin & Co at **Moorfields**; Alexander P. Henderson at **Bay de Vin**; Benjamin Styment, McLeod & Campbell at **Taborintuck**. Estimated amount of timber sawed in Northumberland County, 15,606,000. Estimated number of men employed in lumbering, sawing and delivery to ports, 800.

SUNBURY COUNTY: George Nevers, Thomas Harit at **Oromocto**; Andrew Smith, Stephen Peabody at **Rusagonis**; Stephen Glasier at **Lincoln**; David Tapley, Isaac Burpee,

---

13 The Cunard family fortune grew from small opportunities to immense calculated investments, along with the fortunes of Nova Scotia and New Brunswick, through trade in timber, spirits, sugar and investments in shipbuilding. Joseph Cunard, son of Samuel Cunard and grandson of Abraham Cunard, was one of three sons to inherit a vast trading empire.*Dictionary of Canadian Biography*, Vol. IX, 173-185.

at **Sheffield**. Estimated amount of lumber sawed in Sunbury County: 4,900,000. Estimated number of men employed in lumbering, sawing and delivery to ports, 103.

YORK COUNTY: Samuel Nevers, Simon Hebert, Firman Thibodeau at **Madawaska**; _Fairbanks at **Restook**; Peters & Wilmot, John Giberson at **Kent**; R. Ketchum at **Little Presque Isle**; Samuel Nevers at **Pockagomick**; Smith & Bull, _Connell at **Medersmikik** [Meduxnekeag]; Robert Phillips, R. & T. Gibson at **Northampton**; _Ingrahams at **Shugomock**; J. & A. Allan, Solomon Parent, _ Palmer at **Poqiock** [Pokiok]; _Morehouse at **Coack**, _Long at **Long's Creek**; T. C. Joslin at **Prince William**; Daniel Jewett at **Mactaquack**; _Jones at **Keswick**; _ Pickard, _ Miles at **Douglas**; A. Estey at **Nashwaaksis**; C. Murray at **Kings Clear**; James Buber, McLaggen & McLean, _ Manzer, _ Porter, _ McPherson at **Nashwaak**; Estimated amount of lumber sawed in York County: 9,000,000. Estimated number of men employed in lumbering, sawing, and delivery to ports, 300.

CHARLOTTE COUNTY: Samuel Fry, John Wilson at **Chamcook**; Richard Turner at **Buckabeck**; Allanshaw & Co, Samuel McFarlan at **Digadiguash**; Moses Vernon, J. Munroe, L. Cameron, Patrick Clinch, D. Milliken, J. Linton, Ker & Campbell, P. Baker, D. Gilmore, J. Pratt, G. McKenzie, R. Whidden, D. Brockway, at **Magaguadavic**; George Thomson at **Letang**; G. Knight, T. B. Cripps, S. Buckman at **Beaver Harbour**; John Robertson at **New River**; _ Memet at **Pope Logan**; Abraham & S. Hill, George A. Hill, Hill & Emerton, J. N. Clark at **Union Mills**; A. & L. Hill, David Wright, Todd & Hill, B. F. Waite, Austin & Jinker, R. M. Todd, John McAllister, Jr., John Mc Allister, Sr, J. Christie & T. Berry, Wm C. Scott, Pine & Porter, James Frink at **Mill Town Mills**; Gilman D. King, H. F. Richards, **Upper Mills**. Estimated amount of lumber sawed in Charlotte County: 33, 950,000. Estimated number of men employed in lumbering, sawing and delivery to ports, 1357. Laborers earned three to four shillings per day. The Official Statement concluded with: "However extensive our Mill property in this Province may be, it sinks before the still more extensive outlay of capital employed in our timber trade. In the year ending January 5, 1832, the Port of St. John and its Out-Bays exported 232,515 tons of square timber, besides a quantity of masts, staves, lathwood and other articles. ... The bulk of it finds its way to Britain, West Indies and the United States and our Sister Colonies."[14]

New Brunswick historian Ketchum furnished more information: "It is interesting to note that as far back as 1836, there were two lumbering companies organized and incorporated, consisting of New Brunswickers, one known as the Restook Lower Mill Company, with a capital of £48,000 and the other as the Restook Upper Mill Company, largely made up of residents of St. Andrews, which was capitalized at £50,000. Clearly these companies expected to do business in the disputed territory."[15]

POLITICAL ESTABLISHMENT:

The Members of the Provincial Assembly of New Brunswick in 1838 were: L. A. Wilmot, James Taylor, John Allen, Charles Fisher, Charles Simonds, John R. Partelou, John M. Wilmot, John Jordan, Thomas Wyer, George Hill, James Brown, Jr., William Fitz William Owen, William Wilson, Daniel Hannington, William Crane, Philip Palmer, Alex Rankin, J. A. Street, George Hayward, Henry A. Partelou, Samuel Freeze, William McLeod, Hugh Johnston, Thomas Gilbert, John Weldon, D. McAlmon, William End,

---

14 *Official Statement of the Saw Mills and Mill Property in the Province of New Brunswick*, December 7, 1831, PAC CO193/3
15 Ketchum, *A Short History of Carleton County*, 38.

Peter Stewart, J. M. Connell, R. Beardsley, _?_, Thomas Barlow and A. Barberie.[16]

The Executive Council in 1838 consisted of William Black, George Shore, Frederick Robinson, William F. Odell, John S. Saunders, Charles Simonds, Hugh Johnston, William Crane, A. E. Botsford, and Joseph Cunard.[17]

Members of the Legislative Council, 1838, were: Ward Chipman, The Bishop of Nova Scotia, William Black, George Shore, Thomas Baillie, Harry Peters, Joseph Cunard, James Allanshaw, William H. Robinson, John S. Saunders, Amos Botsford, Charles Peters, Thomas Lee and E. R. Chandler.[18]

The List of Civil Officers of New Brunswick, 1838, included: Thomas Baillie, Esq., Surveyor General and Commissioner of Crown Lands and Forests; Amos Botsford, Esq., Assistant Auditor; William Botsford, Esq., Assistant Judge of the Supreme Court; James Carter, Esq, Assistant Judge of the Supreme Court; Rev. George Coster, Archdeacon; Ward Chipman, Esq., Chief Justice; Sir John Harvey, KCB, KCH, Lieutenant Governor of New Brunswick; William Kinnear, Esq., Judge of the Court of the Vice Admiralty; Thomas C. Lee, Esq., Receiver General; William F. Odell, Esq., Provincial Secretary, Register of the Record and Clerk of H. M. Executive Council; Neville Parker, Esq., Master of the Rolls; Robert Parker, Esq., Assistant Judge of the Supreme Court, Charles Peters, Esq., Attorney General; William Tyng Peters, Esq., Clerk of the Circuits and Clerk of the Crown on the Circuits; Beverly Robinson, Esq., Province Treasurer; Daniel Robinson, Esq., Register of the Court of Chancery; P. Robinson, Esq., Auditor General; John M. Robinson, Esq., Register and Scribe of the Court of the Vice Admiralty; John M. Saunders, Esq., Judge Advocate;.George F. Street, Esq., Clerk of the Pleas in the Supreme Court; Samuel Tryon,

---

16 *Blue Book of Statistics*, 1838, CO 193/21,60-61.
17 Ibid, 58.
18 Ibid, 59.

Esq, Private Secretary to the Lieutenant Governor, (Juno?) Anthony, Esq., Marshall in the Vice Admiralty Court; Alexandre Wedderburn, Esq., Emigrant Agent.[19]

---

[19] Ibid., 62-63.

APPENDIX VIII

COMMERCIAL ESTABLISHMENTS IN NORTHERN MAINE

AROOSTOOK, WASHINGTON AND PENOBSCOT COUNTIES

AROOSTOOK COUNTY

1833: **Mills**: Joseph Pollard of Oldtown, ME, with seven men, had commenced building mills in Township No. 9, Range 4, WELS, at the falls, a very good site for water power, on the St. Croix of the Aroostook. This river enters the south side of the Aroostook in No. 10 Range 5, WELS, directly opposite what was at that time the Goss farm, and is crossed near its mouth by the Aroostook Road. This location was known as Goss Settlement on June 12, 1838. [E. Holmes to the *Bangor Daily Whig and Courier*, June 12, 1838; *Bangor Whig and Courier*, July 6, 1838.]

    Davis-Russell Mills: Israel Davis and Jacob M. Russel received a grant of two hundred acres of land in Township No. 10, Range 1, (Amity), on condition that they build a sawmill in 1833, and a grist mill by January 1, 1835, and keep them in good repair for eight years. Chapter 17, February 7, 1833.

1838: **Ashland Mill and Dam Co.**: to build a dam across the Great Machias River, in Township No. 11, Range 5, [Ashland]. Partners: George W. Buckmore of Ellsworth,

Wm. D. Parsons of Eastbrook, and James McCaron of New Brunswick.

1844: **Ira Fish's Mills**: The Maine Legislature granted Ira Fish sections of land in Township 8, Range 5 WELS and in Township 9, Range 6 WELS, [present day Oxbow Plantation] and the mill lot in Township No. 9, R6, on the condition that within three years he build a good saw and grist mill on the Umqualcus Stream. Chapter 255, ROSM V, 186. Note: In 1825, Fish, from Wakefield, NH, built at Lincoln ME, what was then the uppermost saw mill on the Penobscot River. [*Bangor Historical Magazine*, Vol. V].

1847: **Allegash and East Branch Log Driving Co.**: to drive logs and timber in East Branch of the Penobscot River between Telos Lake and the Grand Falls on the East Branch of the Penobscot River, to any place above the Penobscot Boom. Partners: John H. Pilsbury, Dudley F. Leavitt, Wm. H. Smith, Daniel M. Howard, Warren Brown, Henry R. Soper, Wm. F. Leavitt, Cyrus S. Clark, and Cyrus Moore. Chapter 91, August 2, 1847.

1851: **Allegash Dam Co.**: Partners: Daniel W. Bradley, G. K. Jewett, Hastings Strickland, Isaac Farrar, John Winn, E. G. Rawson, Samuel F. Hersey, C. S. Clark, Shepard Cary. Chapter 448, June 3, 1851.

1852: **Fish River Dam Co.**: Partners: Daniel W. Bradley, Joseph L. Smith, Leonard March, George K. Jewett, Gorham L. Boynton, Cyrus S. Clark, Wm. H. McCrillis. Chapter 26, April 22, 1852.

1852: **Aroostook Dam and Railway Co.**: to build booms and piers on the Aroostook River near the mouth of Lapomkeag Stream, to stop logs and take them out and transport them to Sebois Lake or Beaver Pond, and to build a dam at Godfrey's Falls on Sebois Stream in 1852. Partners: John Winn, E. S. Coe, Daniel W. Bradley, Gorham L. Boynton, Cyrus S. Clark, Thomas Howe, Wm. H. McCrillis. Chapter 628, April 22, 1852.

WASHINGTON COUNTY:

1820: **Passamaquoddy Bank**: Jabez Mowry, President; Directors: Samuel Wheeler, Horatio G. Wheeler, Jonathan Bartlett, Benjamin Bucknam, Ichabod R. Chadbourne, Jacob Penniman, Leonard Pierce, Oaks Ruggles, Life Smith, Solomon Thayer, Samuel Wheeler, Cashier: John Woodman.

1822: **Proprietors of the Great Marsh** on Pleasant River in Columbia and Addison: their plan was to make a dike around the Marsh. Partners: Ichabod Bucknam, Wm. Bucknam, Joseph Wilson, Gowen Wilson, Nathaniel Wilson, Wm. Wass, Wm. H. Ruggles, John Wass, and John McKinsey. Chapter 143, February 9, 1822.

Calais Boom Corporation: Partners: Jones Dyer, Jr., Ebenezer Reding, Salmon Gates, Robert Pike, Jonas Rice. Chapter 120, February 5, 1822.

1823: **East River Sluice Co.**: sluice to lead from mills called "Unity" and "Industry" to tide waters in East Machias River. Partners: Wm. Pope, Aaron L. Raymond, Moses Hovey, Jabez W. Foster, and Benjamin Gooch, Jr. Chapter 189, January 31, 1823.

1826: **Dennysville Tide Mill Co.**: on Damon Wilson's Stream, Dennysville. Partners: Ebenezer Wilder, Ebenezer C. Wilder, Jr., Daniel Kilby, Wm. Kilby Jr., John Kilby, Bela R. Reynolds, Wm. Mayhew. Chapter 383, February 6, 1826.

1827: **Schoodiac River Log Co.**: Partners: John Barnard, George Downes, Joseph Whitney, Wm. Vance, Rufus Lane and Neal D. Shaw. Chapter 493, Feb. 24, 1827.

Cherryfield Log Driving Co.: for more convenient navigating and transporting logs on the Naraguagas River passing through Cherryfield. Partners, Lewis Thompson, Tobias Hall, James Small and Robert Foster Jr. Chapter 438, 1827.

St. Croix Steam Navigation Co.: operate steam boats on St Croix River. Partners: Samuel Wheeler, Wm. Vance and George Downes. Chapter 463, February, 1827.

Calais Steam Boat Co.: to operate steam boats on the St Croix River. Partners: George M. Chase, John M. Clement and Joseph Whitney.

Narraguagus Co.: Partners: Charles H. Coffin, David E. Wheeler, Harmon Westervet, Newton Hayes, Ferdinand S. Wilsey, Edward Soley, James M. Quin, Daniel P. Bacon and Charles F. Green. Chapter 274, March 14, 1827.

1831: **Calais Bank**: Partners: George Downs, Wm. Delesdernier, Joseph Whitney, Abel Barnard and Wm. Pike. Chapter 202, April 1831.

1832: **Calais Railway Co.**: the line to be constructed in the town of Calais from the still-water at Milltown to the place of shipping lumber on the St Croix. Partners: Wm. Delesdernier, Jones Dyer, George Downes, Joseph Whitney and Otis L. Bridges. Chapter 238, Feb. 17, 1832.

Lubec Manufacturing Co.: to manufacture wood, cotton, wool, iron and steel products. Partners: Jeremiah Fowler, Wm. Fowler and Sanford M. Hunt. Chapter 253, March 3, 1832.

1834: **Cherryfield Boom Co.**: Partners: Amzi Curtis, Wm. Nickols, James W. Moore, Tobias A. Hall, Sabin P. Jordan, Western Merritt, and Jeremiah Burnham. Chapter 450, February 21, 1834.

1836: **Frontier Bank** (Eastport): Partners: John A. Balkam, Samuel Wheeler, Charles Peavey, Aaron Hayden, Samuel B. Wadsworth, Leonard Shaw, Samuel Stevens, George A. Peabody, John Hinkley, Joshua Hinkley, Eliphalet Y Sabine, Lorenzo Sabine, George Hobbs, Isaac Hobbs, Henry B. Williams, Jesse Gleason, Wm. Shackford, Jacob Shackford, Wm. M. Brooks, Archibald Heney, John Beckford, Henry Bates, Partmon Houghton, Charles S. Carpenter, Gilman Lamphrey, Edward Gilligan, Seward C. Bucknam, Wm. A. Sabine, Stephen Bartlett, Daniel Kilby, Isaac Ray, Zebulon Paine, Jonathan Buck, Wm. Billings, Mary Thacher, James W. Lyman, James Nason, Solomon Thayer, John Kilby, Bela Wilder, Ebenezer Wilder, Peter G. Farnsworth, Simeon Howe, James M. Balkam and John N. M. Brewer. Chapter 210, April 1, 1836.

Eastport Manufacturing Co.: to manufacture wood, cotton, wool, iron and steel and other metals, and grind grain and gypsum; to dig canals and sluice-ways, build dams to include tide waters, erect wharves, piers, mills and works, machinery and buildings. Partners: Edward Baker, Samuel Wheeler, Charles Peavey, Benjamin B. Leavitt, John Mason, Robert Mowe, and John J. Peavey. Chapter 103, March 15, 1836.

East Machias Canal Co.: to construct canals from the tide waters of East Machias River, along or near river, streams and lakes to the source, and also from the mouth of Gardiner's stream to, the sources of said streams, with proper dams, locks, piers, to be used for boats, rafts and lumber, etc. Partners: John Dickenson, Wm. Pope, John C. Talbot, M. Jones Talbot, J. A. Lowell, Peter Talbot Jr., Jeremiah Foster Jr., Wm. H. Pope, Walter Robbins, Peter T. Harris and George Harris. Chapter 173, March 29, 1836.

St Croix Bank (Calais): Partners: Jones Dyer, Cyrus Hamlen, Rendol Whidden, Luther C. White, Thomas Sawyer, Joseph Whitney, and Neal D. Shaw. Chapter 201, April 1, 1836.

Pembroke Milling Co.: to process gypsum, lumber, etc. Partners: Ezekiel Foster, Nathaniel Deering and Samuel Wheeler. Chapter 185, March 31, 1836.

Machias Bank: Partners: John Holway, Samuel A. Morse, Stephen J. Bowles, George S. Smith, Aaron L. Raymond, Jacob Longfellow, Stephen Sprague, Wm. A. Crocker, John Dickinson, Joshua A. Lowell, Walter Robbins, Benjamin Mathes Jr., George Burnham, Frances Libby, Nathan Longfellow, Wm. F. Penniman, Peter Talbot, Micah J. Talbot, Isaac Ames, Foster and Norton, George W. Simpson, John Kellar, and Jeremiah Foster. Chapter 109, April 1, 1836.

Machias Water Power and Mill Co.: Partners: Salem Towne, John Holway. Chapter 80, March 7, 1836.

Perry Manufacturing Co.: to build a dam over the tide waters in Perry from Dodge's Point to Charles

Frost's land near the State's land at Stand's Point, and cut a canal from Frost's Cove across Mark Leighton's land into Perry Harbor; to build mills to manufacture plaster of paris, flour, meal or other articles. Partners: Mark Leighton, Aaron Frost and Charles Frost. Chapter 93, March 9, 1836.

Jonesborough and Whitneyville Railroad Co.: a rail line from the mills at Middle Falls to Jonesborough. Partners: Edmund Monroe, Samuel J. Lewis, Joseph Whitney, Benjamin Mathes, Charles Ellis, Charles E. Brown, Amos Binney, James C. Dunn, Mortimer Jackson, Andrew Hinkley. Chapter 122, March 16, 1836.

Cutler Mill Dam Corporation: to build a dam across the head of Little River Harbour in Cutler. Partners; Nathaniel Stevens, Solomon Wildes, Isaac Stevens, Amos Carlton, Putnam J. Farnham, and Wm. Stevens. Chapter 123, March 16, 1836.

East Machias Sluice Co.: to repair or rebuild and operate a sluiceway for the passage of lumber from the Mills, called "Unity" and "Industry" to the tidewaters in East Machias River. Partners: John C. Talbot, Cyrus W. Foster, Wm. Pope, Jeremiah Foster Jr., John E. Sevey, Luther Hall, Walter Robbins, John Bryant, Jeremiah Foster, Jabez Norton, H. S. Chase, Silas Chase, A. M. Foster, Micah Talbot, and John S. Seavey. Chapter 86, March 9, 1836.

Narraguagus Log Driving Co.: Partners: Robert Tucker, Jr., Tobias Hall, Daniel S. Tucker, Weston Merritt, Amizi Curtis, Sabin P. Jordan, James S. Tucker, Jere O. Nichols, Ambrose Lovis, George H. Devereaux, H. G. Carter, Isaac Smith, Daniel F. Emery, Edward E. Upham, John O. Bartels, Henry Goddard, Alford Richardson, Wm. W. Woodbury, Nehemiah Cram, James B. Cahoon, Luther Dana, Charles H. Coffin, Jefferson Sinclair. Chapter 159, 1836.

Pembroke Milling Co.: to process gypsum, lumber, etc., Partners: Samuel Wheeler, Ezekiel Foster, and Nathaniel Deering. Chapter 185, March 31, 1836.

1837: **West Musquash Canal and Sluice Co.**: a canal to pass through Township No. 3 Range 2, Washington County. Partners: George Jewett, Martin Gore, Charles Mussey, Joshua Richardson, and Luther Jewett. Chapter 275, March 14, 1837.

Calais and Baring Rail Road Co.: a line from Milltown in Calais to Baring to Baileyville, through to Meddybemps Lake by Stephenson's Mills to Round Pond. Partners: Neal D. Shaw, Anson G. Chandler, Shilometh S Whipple, Joshua Veasey, Bion Bradbury Jeremiah Curtis, Otis L. Bridges and John M. Clement. Chapter 315, March 20, 1837.

Baring and Bog Brook Railway Co.: a line between the still-water in the Mill Pond at Baring and the Schoodic River at or near the entrance of Bog Brook, into the same, and to run in its course south of the Magurawock Mountain. Partners: Joseph Granger, Theodore Jellison, Anson G. Chandler, Jonathan Williams, Shilometh S. Whipple, Manley B. Townsend, Dwight B. Barnard, Gilbert Foster, James S. Pike, Otis Patterson, Bion Bradbury, Seth Emerson, Asa A. Pond, Z. E. McKusick, Eben Pratt, Charles Perkins, Matthew Fowler, Josiah Flagg, James S. Cooper, George Downes, Amaziah Nash, George F. Wardsworth, Benjamin Shattuck, Joshua Veazie, Lewis Wilson, Joel Knight, Alexander H. Weymouth, Levi L. Lowell, Royal McKusick, Wm. Goodwin, George S. Smith, Joseph Whitney and Wm. Pike. Chapter 376, March 29, 1837.

St Croix Mill and Land Co.: to lumber and improve their lands in Calais, and in two half-townships, Lenox and Amherst. Partners: Joseph Whitney, Charles E. Bowers, James T. Hobart, and Samuel J. Gardner. Chapter 389, March 29, 1837.

New York and Machias Lumber Co.: for lumbering upon, manage and improve their land, in Township No. 25, of Bingham's Purchase, to market, deal in and transport lumber to market. Partners: George N. Titus, Jesse W. Goodrich, E. H. Blotchford, Alvin Waite, S. L. Bush,

Alexander H. Dana, C. P. Gould, D. Wilder, Jr., and J. Harrington. Chapter 284, March 17, 1837.

St Croix Manufacturing Co.: to build dams, piers, railways, canals, and sluices necessary for grinding grain, manufacturing lumber, iron, steel, cotton, wool or hemp. Partners: Benjamin F. Copeland, Neal D. Shaw, Timothy Williams, Isaac Clapp, George Gray, James L. P. Orrach, Thomas Simmonds, David Dudley, and D. A. Simmonds. Chapter 320, March 21, 1837.

Baskahegan Land and Mill Co.: Partners: Horace Baker, Gardiner Ball, Benjamin L. Whitney, Joseph Haywood, Joshua Haywood, Wm. Phipps, Samuel Phipps, Henry J. Holbrook, Franklin Green, Barnabas T. Lowell, Lemuel Stetson and Wm. Brown. Chapter 386, March 29, 1837.

1841: **Ingalls Brook Co.**: (perhaps the Ingalls Brook branch of Machias River, in 36 MD BPP, 3 townships west of Crawford?) Partners: John S. Webster, Samuel Webster, Benaiah Goodwin, Samuel Swan, and Caleb Swan. Chapter 187, 1841.

Dam: at Princeton, Rolf Putnam, of Princeton, to erect a dam across the St Croix River at or near the foot of Lewis' Island. Chapter 97, 1841.

1847: **Narraguagus Steam Manufacturing Co.**: to operate steam boats from lower bridge at Cherryfield to Salt-Water Falls Dam. Partners: David Campbell, James W. Moore, and Alexander Campbell. Chapter 48, 1847.

Baskahegan Falls Dam Co.: Partners: Samuel Moore, A. G. Brown and A. W. Babcock. Chapter 142, August 3, 1847.

Cherryfield Sluiceway Co.: Partners: Wm. Nickels, Jere O. Nickels, Freeman Kingsley, Charles H. Howe, Wm. Freeman, Wm. Burnham, David W. Campbell Alexander Campbell and Francis C. Campbell. Chapter 49, July 19, 1847.

St Croix Log Driving Co.: to drive logs in the St Croix River below Louis and Chiputneticook Lakes to the booms at Baring. Partners: Lendal Tyler, Thomas G. Copeland, James S. Hall, Wm. McAllester, E. C. Gates, Samuel

Furlong, Wm. Brooks, W. E. Duren, Ephriam Whitney, Jonathan P. Dutch, John P. McAllester, S. Murphy. Chapter 85, July 1, 1847.

1848: **Baring Boom Co.**: to operate on the St Croix River in Maine. Partners: John Stickney, R. C. Stickney, Thomas Skofield, Albert Stinson, George Wills, E. McDougal, George Pierce, Reuben Smith, Robert Halsey, Ansel Daily, Horatio N. Hill, John Porter, Daniel K. Chase, Samuel T. King and Charles Hamilton. Chapter 129, July 26, 1848.

1853: **Dam**: on Lambert Lake Stream, a tributary of Schoodiac Lakes, to drive logs in that area. Partners: Robert Todd and George M. Porter. Chapter 175, 30 March, 1853.

PENOBSCOT COUNTY

1820: **Bangor Bank**: Samuel Dutton, President; Directors: Thomas H. Hill, Joseph Leavitt, Eleazer Adams, Eleashel Adams, John Barker.

Castine Bank: Otis Little, President; Directors: Leonard Jarvis, Samuel Upton, Wm. Abbot, Josiah Hook, Jr.; Cashier: John Brooks, Jonathan L. Stevens.

1822: **Orono Boom Corporation**: Partners: John Bennock, Luther H. Hills, John Peters, Sabin Pond, Daniel Pilsbury, Samuel White, Ebenezer Webster and George Read. February 4, 1822.

1823: **Augusta and Bangor Stage Co.**: Partners: Moses Burleigh and Chase Robinson, Jr. Chapter 206, February 8, 1823.

1825: **Penobscot Boom Co.**: the boom to cross the Penobscot River at Costagan's Island or such other safe place between Sunkhaze and Hemlock Island. Partners: Samuel Silsbee, Samuel Dudley, Andrew Godfrey, Daniel White, Amos Roberts, S. C. Burrill, Joseph Treat, John Benoch, George Read, John P. Davis, Amos Bailey. Budd Parsons, George Ring, David Ring, Retire Freeze, John Benoch, Jr., Ira Wadleigh, and Ebenezer Webster. February 26, 1825.

1827: **Penobscot Steam Boat Navigation Co.**: Partners: Otis Little, Thomas Adams, Hezekiah Rowell, Joseph Bryant, and Mellen Chamberlain. Chapter 451, February 6, 1827.

Old Town Bridge: Partners: Samuel Veazie, Benjamin Fiske, Wm. S. Bridge, Richard H. Bartlett, Nathaniel Haynes, Daniel Davis, Joshua Carpenter, Ira Fish, Ira Wadleigh, and Samuel Bailey. February 10, 1827.

1828: **Penobscot Mill Dam Co.**: a dam, Penobscot River from Bangor to Brewer or Eddington. Partners: Wm. Lowder, John Blake, Wm. Forbes, Joseph Burr, George Leonard and Joseph Treat. Chapter DXX, February 12, 1828.

Penobscot Manufacturing Co.: to erect and keep a dam or dams across the Penobscot River, from Bangor to Brewer or Eddington, with such canals, locks, sluices, wharves, piers and side booms between the foot or Rose's or Treat's Falls in Bangor and McMahon's Falls in Eddington, for the purpose of flowing the water a sufficient height for safe and convenient passage of rafts and boats from the foot of Eayer's Falls in Orono, to Bangor ... Partners: Wm. Lowder, John Blake, Wm. Forbes, Joseph Burr, Joseph Treat, George Leonard, and their associates. February 2, 1828, *Maine Documents*, Vol II, Document 15.

Old Town Canal Co.: to build a canal and locks on the east side of the Penobscot River at Old Town Falls. Partners: Benjamin Fiske and Wm. S. Bridge. Chapter DXII, February 5, 1828.

Stillwater Canal Corporation: Partners: John Bennoch, Asa W. Babcock, John Bennock, Jr., Moses Averell, Daniel White, Wm. Emerson, James B. Fisk, Zebadiah Rogers, Thomas A. Hill, Samuel White, and George Read. February 7, 1828.

1830: **Bangor Pier Corporation**: Partners: Wm. Emerson, Amos Patten, Moses Patten, James B. Fisk, Wiggins Hill, James McLaughlin, Samuel Lowder and Samuel Lowder, Jr. Chapter 102, March 15, 1830.

1831: **Bangor Commercial Bank**: Partners: Wm. D. Williamson, Thomas A. Hill, James B. Fiske, Jacob McGaw,

Nathaniel Hatch and Thornton McGaw. Chapter 203, April 1, 1831.

1832: **Sugar Island Side Boom Co.**: Partners: Nathan Winslow, Henry Campbell, Francis Blackman, Wm. E. Blackman, John Butterfield, Amos M. Roberts, Samuel Dudley and Amos Bailey. Chapter 283, March 9, 1832.

Bangor and Oldtown Railway Co.: Partners: Ira Wadleigh, Charles Ramsdell, Isaac Damons, Ebenezer French, Ford Whitman, and Amos M. Roberts. Chapter 276, 1832.

1833: **Bangor and Pushaw Pond Canal Co.**: Partners: Mark Trafton, Amos M. Roberts, Hermon Fisher, J. M. Woodman, Elias T. Aldrich, Joseph Treat, John Bright, Daniel W. Bradley, Peter H. Hesseltine, John Hodgdon, E. G. Rawson, Seth Emery, Isaac Hodsdon, John Berry John E. Hesseltine, John Trafton and David Nye. Chapter 321, February 10, 1833.

Penobscot Log Driving Co.: for more convenient navigating and transporting of logs on Penobscot River. Partners: Charles Johnson, Asa W. Babcock, Wm. Butterfield, Waldo T. Pierce, Samuel Moore, Heywood Pierce, Amasia Jones and Thomas Crosby. February 20, 1833.

1834: **Orrington Pier and Warehouse Co.**: Partners: Archelaus Atwood, John Wilkins, Timothy Nye, Jr., John Wentworth, Jesse Atwood, Benjamin Atwood, Warren Nickerson 2nd, Ephriam Goodale Jr., and Wm. H. Nickerson. February 26, 1834.

Kenduskeag Canal Corporation: Partners: Wm. Bradbury, Benjamin Garland, Mark Trafton, Isaac Hodsdon, Rufus Parks, Samuel Ramsdell, Romulus Haskins, Thomas A. Hill. John Bradbury, and John C. Dexter. Chapter 503, March 11, 1834.

Bangor and Dexter Stage Co.: Partners: Lysander Cutler, Stevens Davis, Isaac Hodsdon, Advardes Shaw, John Walker, George W. Sawyer, Asa Tibbets, John B. Hill, Elijah Skinner, Calvin Copeland. February 1, 1834.

Orrington Canal and Railway Co.: Partners: Timothy George, Joseph Doane, Nicholas G. Norcross, Samuel Thatcher, Jr., March 8, 1834.

1836: **Mattanawcook Rail Road** Corporation: to build a railway from Lincoln to Milford and across the river to Oldtown. Partners: Josiah Towle, Solomon Parsons, Elisha Ayer, George W. Towle, Theodore Taylor, and Joseph Porter. Chapter 170, March 28, 1836.

Newport Mill Dam and Manufacturing Co.: for the manufacture of cotton, wool, steel and iron. Partners: Martin Wilson, Benjamin Shaw, Edmund Pilsbury, John Wilson Jr., Otis Briggs Jr., John Stuart, Samuel Pratt, John Benson, Jared Harden, Luther H. Greenlief, Albert Martin, Enoch C. Shaw, James Benjamin, Albert Brooks, John H. Folsom, Wm. F. Fitch, Jeremiah Prescott, Moses Dole, Justus Kirby, Jesse Miles, Joseph Lord, Wm. L. Walker, Edward Rowe, Nathaniel Burrill Jr., L. P. Burrill, Charles P. Mason. Chapter 177, March 30, 1836.

Penobscot Bank (Bangor): Partners: Isaac Farrar, Jonathan Farrar, Wm. Emerson, E. G. Rawson, Samuel Farrar, John Hodgdon, and Eleazer Coburn. Chapter 197, April 1, 183[6?].

Bangor and Lower Stillwater Manufacturing Co. (Orono): to manufacture lumber, wool, iron. Partners: Robert McNeel Smyth, John M. Mayo, Henry Hubbard, Moses Guild, Gershom B. Weston, Thomas Hobart, Matthew Bolles Jr., Jacob Chamberlain, Wm. Durgin, Wm. E. Butter, Wm. Smyth, Charles Howland. Chapter 67, March 1, 1836.

Madaceunk Mill Co.: Partners: Jacob Fish and Asa Freeman. Chapter 107, March 15, 1836.

Penobscot Mill and Manufacturing Co.: to manufacture lumber, cotton wool, iron and steel, etc. Partners: Simon P. Green, Joseph Floyd, Walter Smith, George Kittridge, Lyman Morse, Ebenezer Chapman, Albert Foster, George W. Tole and Samuel Haley. Chapter 101, March 15, 1836.

Bangor and Moosehead Lake Stage Co.: Partners: Elias Hale, E. G. Thompson, Joseph S. Hammond, G. M.

Moore, Aaron Morse, John Monroe, Wm. K. Lucas, and Joseph Kelsey. Chapter 147, March 22, 1836.

Lafayette Bank (Bangor): Partners: Thomas A. Hill, Wm. L. Walker, Moses L. Appleton, S. H. Blake, Levi Bradley, George Starrett, Charles H. Hammond, Reuben S. Prescott, Stevens Davis, D. W. Bradley, Wiggins Hill, John A. Poor, George Waugh, Alexander Savage, Wm. B. Reed, Samuel Hudson, Daniel Emery, Joseph C. Stevens, Robert Long and Wm. Hammat. Chapter 211, April 1, 1836.

Agricultural Bank (Brewer): Partners: Edward Holyoke, Deodat Brastow, James Collins, George Blake, Lewis Howard, Watson Holbrook, Caleb H. C. Burr, Jonathan Burr, Stilman Wilson, Samuel Sterns, Samuel Thurston, Samuel K. Hart, Horatio N. Page, Joshua Chamberlain Jr., John D. Wilson, Abraham Hill, Edward Burr, David B. Doane, Zenas Lawry, Brazer Barstow, John Holyoke, Joseph W. Jordan, John Hilferty, and James Hastings. Chapter 200, April 1, 1836.

Central Market House Co.: to erect a Market House on the flats of Kenduskeag River in Bangor, between the bridges lately built by Hudson and Greenough, Samuel Smith etc., two hundred feet long and fifty feet wide, built of stone and bricks, covered with slates, ... with a passage-way for rafts and boats passing up and down the river. Partners: Samuel Hudson, Andrew W. Hasey, John R. Greenough, John Ham, Henry Little, John Hodgdon, Wm. Emerson, Jonathan Farrar, Isaac Farrar, and Ebenezer Gilman Rawson. Chapter 175, March 29, 1836.

Castine Steam Mill Co.: for grinding grains, sawing lumber and manufacturing steel and wool. Partners: John H. Jarvis, Wm. Witherle, Samuel Adams, Otis Little, Thomas Adams, Benjamin Gay, C. J. Abbott, R. H. Brigham, Noah Mead, Robert Perkins, Charles K. Tilden, Joshua Fuller, James Crawford, James B. Crawford, J. L. Stevens, George Vose, Benjamin Hook, Jr., Joshua Hooper Jr., Hezekiah Williams, Joseph A. Deane, H. Rowell and Benjamin Robinson. Chapter 24, February 18, 1836.

Union Wharf Co. (Frankfort): Partners: Albert L. Kelly, Oliver Parker, Amos Sproul, Josiah Fernald, and Jeremiah Holmes of Frankfort and Amos Patten, Willis Patten, Moses Patten Jr., Waldo T. Pierce and Hayward Pierce of Bangor. Chapter 60, March 1, 1836.

Great Works Milling and Manufacturing Co. (Bradley): Partners: Enoch Paine, Nathaniel F. Deering, E. M. Wildredge, John L. Maserve, Joseph H. Hale, Joseph B. Hervey, Josiah S. Little and Francis B. Todd. Chapter 28, 1836.

Globe Bank (Bangor): Partners: Solomon Parsons, John Appleton, J. B. Hill, N. O. Pilsbury, Dwight Allen, Josiah Towle, Elijah L. Hamlin, A. G. Brown, Henry Warren. Chapter 196, 1836.

Penobscot Steam Navigation Co.: Partners: Willis Patten, Waldo T. Pierce, Cyrus Goss, Henry Warren, Samuel Farrar, Amos Davis, Nathaniel Lord, Mark Trafton, Charles Ramsdell, Wm. Bradbury, Leonard March, Ephriam Lincoln, Charles Hayes, John A. French, Charles H. Hammond, B. C. Atwood, George Perry, Josiah Towle and Haywood Pierce. Chapter 48, 1836.

Bangor Mill and Manufacturing Co.: to manufacture lumber, cotton, wool, iron and steel. Partners: Wm. Phipps, Franklin Greene Jr., Elias Keyes, Luther Faulkner, Parker H. Pierce, Joshua Crane, Edward Smith, Wm. Hales, George Morey, Homer & Palmer, L. H. Osgood, Isaac Jackson, Samuel R. Allen, Thomas R. Sewall, Wm. P. Parrot and Z. B. Adams. Chapter 95, March 9, 1836.

Hampden and Carmel Canal Rail Road Co.: to make a canal and or railroad from the Sowadabscook River to the Penobscot River, to make the Sowadabscook River navigable for boats, to erect dams, towing paths, reservoirs, aqueducts, feeders, culverts, waste weirs, basins for boats, enbankments, piers, locks, wharves, bridges, channels etc., necessary for the transportation of lumber and merchandise to and from the Penobscot River. Partners: Moses Sanborn, Joseph L. Cilley, Jacob H. Sanborn, John Lowe Jr., George Gardiner, James Bell,

Wells Healy, S. D. Bell, George W. Chamberlain, Simeon Stetson, Reuben K. Stetson, John Crosby Jr., Elias Dudley, and Josiah Kidder. Chapter 145, March 22, 1836.

Frankfort, Bangor and Belfast Rail Road Co.: Partners: Benjamin Shaw, Albert L. Kelley, Webster Kelly, Eben S. Coffin, Nehemiah Rich, Waldo Pierce, Waldo T. Pierce, Tisdale Dean, Wm. Andrews, Lewis C. Kelly, Archibald Jones, Benjamin Johnson, Elisha Chick Jr., Jeremiah Holmes, Francis W. Rhoades, James Arey, Ephriam Lincoln, Wiggins Hill, Joseph Carr, Wm. B. Reed, Theodore B. Mc Intire, Willis Patten, James B. Fisk, Abner Taylor, Thomas A. Hill, Lot V. Bartlett and Joseph Bartlett. Chapter 148, March 22, 1836.

Bank of Old Town: Partners: Joseph Smith, Jesse Wadleigh, James Stinson, Stover Rines, John T. Davis, George W. Ingersoll, Solomon Moulton, Ira Wadleigh, Eli Hoskins, J. B. Morgan, Wm. Jameson, Jefferson Sinclair, Alvin B. Gilman, Thomas Bartlett, James Purington, Asa Smith, Henry Richardson, S. L. Hunt, Abiel W. Kennedy, George P. Sewall, Samuel Coney, Frederick A. Fuller, and Nathan Winslow. Chapter 204, April 1, 1836.

Kirkland Canal and Rail Road Co.: to construct a canal and or railroad from Little Pushaw Pond in Kirkland (the name Kirkland has been changed to Hudson) or from any point on Pushaw Stream above the falls at the centre of town, to Great Pushaw Pond. Partners: Charles W. Wilder, Winborn A. Swett, Edward Mitchell, Luke Wilder Jr., Elijah Clark, Neal Warren, Rendall Smith, Nathan L. Merrill, Heman S. Jackson, Hall Bagley, John Thissel, Samuel Blake, Matthew H. French, Harvey Hatch, Wm. Tozier, Wm. McLaughlin, Martin Ulmer, Moses Shepard, Ijay Gay and Chapman Goodwin. Chapter 172, March 29, 1836

1837: **Hampden and New York Steam Co.:** to manufacture, vend and deal in all kinds of lumber, wood, cotton, wool, paper, iron and steel. Partners: Barnabas Bartol, Thomas Hassard, Samuel McGaffey, Thomas Emery. Chapter 277, March 15, 1837.

Western Great Works Manufacturing Co.: to manufacture wood, cotton, wool, iron and steel on the Penobscot River. Partners: Charles Q. Clapp, M. P. Sawyer and Rufus Dwinal Chapter 361, March 28, 1837.

Cooper Orono Mill Co.: to construct booms, dams and mills at Pushaw Falls on Marsh Island. Partners: James N. Cooper, Alexander Cooper and Charles Cooper. Chapter 302, March 18, 1837.

Kenduskeag Manufacturing Co.: to manufacture lumber, cotton, wool, and paper, and to erect dams, mills, etc in their own land in the city of Bangor. Partners: Andrew Scott, Nathaniel Hatch, James S. Hobart, Lendel G. S. Boyd, Robert Boyd, and John Appleton. Chapter 394, March 29, 1837.

North American Lumber Co.: to erect mills and manufacture lumber, etc., in Orono. Partners, Thomas J. Oakley, Stephen A. Halsey, Samuel Stocking, John George McKeen, Samuel D. Dakin, Charles Clinton, Pliny Freeman, David Evans, Freeman Roberts, and Seth Greer of the State of New York; John Williams of Dover, New Hampshire; Wm. Smith of Virginia; and Robert McNeel Smyth, Wm. Smyth and Nathaniel Treat of Bangor. Chapter 474, March 22, 1838.

1841: **The Dexter Co.**: Partners: Samuel Farrar, Isaac Farrar, Lysander Cutler. Chapter 138, 1841.

1846: **Penobscot Log Driving Co.**: Partners: Ira Wadleigh, Samuel P. Strickland, Hastings Strickland, Wm. Emerson, Isaac Farrar, Amos M. Roberts, Leonard Jones, Franklin Adams, James Jenkins, Aaron Babb and Cyrus S. Clark. Chapter 407, August 10, 1846.

[Telos Canal Company ?]: to construct, maintain and keep open and repaired as already constructed, a proper sluiceway or canal with suitable dam or dams, gates, and other erections for passage of logs, water, lumber between Webster Pond and Telos Lake T6 R11, Piscataquis County ... and free passage from Chamberlain Lake to said Canal. Partners: Rufus Dwinel, Calvin Dwinel and their associates. Chapter 386, (1846?).

[Note: Ten years earlier, in December, 1835, John Hodgdon, Maine Land Agent, had reported a proposal for the making of the **Telos Cut**. He had accompanied the Commissioners appointed by the Legislature of Massachusetts, to investigate the subject of the public lands. He and George W. Coffin, their Land Agent, went by way of the Moose Head, Chesuncook and Allegash Lakes to the St John, and down that River through the Madawaska Settlement. They studied the comparative elevations of the Allegash Lakes and the head waters of the East Branch of the Penobscot, and found that the distance from Lake Telos, the end of the Allegash chain, to Webster's Pond, on the East Branch of the Penobscot, was a little more than half a mile. The greatest elevation of the tract intervening above the high water mark of Lake Telos, was about two feet and six inches, but in less than one hundred rods the land again fell below the level of the Lake. The surface of the lake, in October, was three feet and a half below the high water mark, as indicated by the trees upon the margin. Therefore, the greatest depth of a cut to connect this lake with the waters of the Penobscot, would have been six feet, and the length one hundred rods. Lake Telos, Telasinis and Chamberlain Lake, an ex-tent of more than twenty miles, were nearly upon the level, and could, at a slight expense, be made entirely so by erecting a low dam at the outlet of Chamberlain Lake. Thus, at a moderate cost, the timber from fifteen to twenty towns in the State could be brought down the Penobscot. The distance to market would be shortened more than two hundred miles. ... (from John Hodgdon, *Report of the Land Agent*, December 31, 1835.)

Grand Lake Dam Co.: to build a dam in T6 R8, Penobscot County, to flow the Grand Lake, in order to facilitate the transportation of logs and lumber across the lake and down the Penobscot River. Partners: John Goddard, James Jenkins, Rufus Dwinel, Ebenezer S. Coe and Associates. Chapter 388, August 7, 1846.

Katahdin Iron Works: Partners: David Pin-gree, with Samuel E. Cowes, Charles H. Ladd, John L. Hayes and Alexander H. Ladd. Pingree purchased the works and about one million dollars was expended in the ori-ginal purchase, improvements and for operating, June 26, 1846. [Trustees of the will of David Pingree of Salem, MA, were George K. Jewett of Bangor; Edward D. Jewett of St John, NB; Elbridge G. Dunn and Peter Dunn of Ashland; Thomas Egery of Bangor; Daniel Hinckley of Boston; Samuel B. Hinckley of Bangor: Mary Ann Hinckley of Boston; Edward D. Kimball of Danvers; Asa Pingree of Topsfield; Thomas P. Pingree of Salem; Ebenezer S. Coe and James H. Chandler of Bangor.]

1847: **Kenduskeag Bank** of Bangor: Partners: Waldo Brown, Waldo T. Pierce, Jabez True, Samuel H. Dole, Abner Tapley, Isaiah Stetson, James Dunning, Dorilis Morison, Albert Emerson, Thomas A. Taylor, Cyrus Goss, J. B. Foster, George W. Ladd, and John McDonald. Chapter 41, July 13, 1847.

Orono Manufacturing Co.: at Ayer's Falls on the Penobscot River in Orono, to process lumber, cotton and woolens. Partners: Courtland Palmer, Samuel Dakin and John B. Fall. Chapter 40, 1847.

Bangor Manufacturing Co.: to build mills, dams, etc, for cotton, wool, iron and steel and wood. Partners: John Fiske, Samuel Veazie, James B. Fiske, and Edward D. Peters. Chapter 39, July 13, 1847.

Bangor and Orono Rail Road: Partners: Daniel White, Israel Washburn Jr., John Benock, Asa W. Babcock, Samuel P. Strickland, Nathaniel Treat, Ebenezer Webster, John Goddard, John A. Poor, Levi Dennett, John B. Hill, Rufus Dwinell, Waldo T. Pierce, Elvator P. Butler, Wm. H. McCrillis, Wyman B. S. Moor. Chapter 89, August 2, 1847.

1848: **Veazie Bank** (Bangor): Partners: Samuel Veazie, John Fiske, James Crosby, John McDonald, Jabez True, Nathaniel Lord, Jones P. Veazie. Chapter 111, July 14, 1848.

Stage Company: between Bangor, Garland and Moosehead Lake. Partners: Leonard Howard, John Hill, Abraham True, Aaron Hill, Benjamin Lane, and Daniel Spooner. Chapter 153, August 7, 1848.

1849: **Mattawamkeag Dam Co.**: Partners: Daniel White, Ebenezer Webster Jr., Israel Washburn Jr., John Hutchins, Wm. B. Harlow, Abner R. Hallowell, George F. Marston, Jonathan A. Cushing, Jonathan Eddy, Henry E. Prentiss, Samuel F. Hersey, and Theophilis Cushing. Chapter 269, August 9, 1849.

Souednmehunk Dam and Sluice Co.: Partners: Ira Wadleigh, Samuel P. Strickland, Hastings Strickland, Oliver Frost, John Winn, Cyrus S. Clark, Daniel W. Bradley, and Dudley F. Leavitt. Chapter 230, July 12, 1849.

Kenduskeag Log Driving Co.: Partners: Jacob Drummond, Lysander Strickland, Benjamin Dudley, George Stetson, Daniel P. McInester, John Dinsmore, Elhanan Garland, John McDonald, Aaron A. Wing and Nathan Pendleton. Chapter 290, August 14, 1849.

1852: **East Branch Dam Co.**: the dam to be located at the outlet of Webster Lake with side dams in Webster Stream. Partners: John Winn, Samuel R. Bearce, Warren Brown and Wm. Cutter. Chapter 658, April 26, 1852.

Sources: *Resolves of the Maine Legislature; Acts and Resolves of the Maine Legislature; Deed Cards*, 1852-1868, Maine State Archives; *Massachusetts Deeds*, 1853, 1859, 1865, 1869, Maine State Archives, Augusta, ME.

APPENDIX IX

VERIFIED LAND CLAIMS OF AROOSTOOK LAND HOLDERS
1854 and 1857

Part I: 1854

Report of the Commissioners Appointed Under the Resolve of April 12, 1854, to locate grants and determine the extent of possessory claims under the late Treaty with Great Britain. Commissioners Ebenezer Hutchinson, Charles Whidden and Stephen Pattee reported to Governor Anson P. Morrill of the State of Maine, on March 6, 1855, on settlers' claims in Aroostook County. Schedules in this report include names of landowners, number of acres held, and comments. Following are townships with lists of land holders in each, excerpted from this report:

Township D Range 1 (Fort Fairfield): Almon S. Richards.

Township G, Range 2 (Maysville): John Allen, Jonathan E. Armstrong, Ferdinand Armstrong, Reuben Bean, Thomas W. Beckwith, Joshua Bishop, Ebenezer Blake, Joseph Blake, Peter Bull, Alexander Campbell, Adeline Chandler, Elizabeth N. Chandler, Ann Currier, heirs of James F. Currier, David B. Delano, Thomas Fields, John Finney, Joseph Hasey, Sewell Henderson, Daniel Johnson, Thomas W. Nary, John Nichols, Ebenezer Oaks, Cyrus Pomeroy, Wm. Pyle, John Raford, John E. Raymond, Hector Sutherland, Isaac Thomas, James Thompson, Andrew

Scott, Robert Scott, James Nichols, Richard Sutter, Stephen Sutter, Benjamin Weeks, Jacob Weeks.
Township No. 13, Range 3 (Washburn): Peter Bull, Wm. and Charles Bull, Job Churchill, Joshua Christie, Jeremiah Crouse, J. and A. and G. Crouse, Ebenezer Esty, Stephen Harris, heirs of John Hickey, Wilder Stratton, James Easler.
Township No. 13, Range 4 (Wade): Wm. Black.
Township D, Range 1 (Fort Fairfield): Purchasers from the State of lots improved before August 9, 1836: Alonzo Fisher, John B. Trafton, Sarah Johnson. Lots granted to encourage the erection of mills, improved before August 9, 1836: A. and J. and A. and F. Bishop, Job Everett, Mary Ann Everett, Daniel Hopkins, Henry W. Hyde, Samuel Fitzherbert, Martin Murray.
Township F, Range 2 (Presque Isle): Purchasers from the state of lots improved before August 9, 1836: Ephriam Clark, Freeman Hayden, Alanson Rackliff, Gowen Wilson. Lots granted to encourage the erection of mills, improved before August 9, 1836: David Hudley, Thomas Kennedy, Sumner Whitney.
Township 11, Range 5 (Ashland): Purchasers from the State of lots improved before August 9, 1836: Josiah Blake, Elbridge G. Dunn, John S. Gilman, Benjamin Howe, George W. Smith.
Masardis (No. 10 R5): Purchasers from the State of lots improved before August 9, 1836: Sarah E. Clayton, Amasa Goding, Charles W. Clayton, Wm. Cowperthwait, Isaac Hacker, Samuel Leavitt, Sanford Noble, Eliza Sawyer, Lydia Sutherland.
Township D, Range 1 (Fort Fairfield): Lots purchased or contracted for and improved before August 9, 1842: Amos Bishop, Frederick Bolstridge, Bradford Cummings, Henry C. Currier, Benjamin D. Eastman, Otis Eastman, Joseph Fisher, Reuben Harvey, Enoch Hoyt, Enoch W. Hoyt, Levi Hoyt, Melville C. Hoyt, Edward Johnson, James Johnson, Wm. Johnston, Patrick McShea, Stephen B. Pattee, Addison Powers, John Rediker, Axel E. Rollins, Jonathan

True. Lots granted to encourage the erection of mills, improved before August 9, 1836: Caroline Campbell, Oliver Frost or Charles R. Pratt, Stillman Gorden, Henry W. Hyde, Stephen E. Phipps, Hiram Stevens.

Township F, Range 2 (Presque Isle): Lots purchased or contracted for and improved before August 9, 1842: Solomon Adams, Moses Allen, Ephriam Clark, John E. Clark, Thomas Clark, Amzi Doe, Lavinia Fenderson, Marcellus L. Foster, Harrison G. O. Greenwood, John T. Goss, Silas Ireland, Hiram Hardison, Samuel Lamson, Peter McKenzie; heirs of Joel Munson, Benaniah Pratt, Alanson Rackliff, Francis M. Rackliff, Jesse Tarbell, Wm. Tarbell, Calvin Taylor, Benjamin Whidden, Sumner Whitney.

Township No. 8, Range 5 (located four townships west of Monticello): Wm. Burns, Richard Cliff, Benjamin Hewes, Stephen Morison, Heirs of Samuel Smith.

Masardis: Jesse C. Bradstreet, Jesse Broadstreet, Homan Bragg, Jonathan Chase, Wm. Cowperthwait, John Dean, Wm. Fitzgerald, Amasa Goding, Wm. Goding, Caroline P. Hewes, Stephen Hewes, John Knowles, Samuel Leavitt, Hugh McGilvery, Sanford Noble, Sanfield Reed, Eliza Sawyer, John Wessenger.

Number 11, Range 5 (Ashland): Calvin P. Bartlett, Guilford S. Bartlett, Septimus B. Bearse, Wm. Bigger, Josiah H. Blake, Ebenezer Bolstridge, James and Joel Boynton, Hiram Brackett, Horace Bragdon, Wm. Brown, Luther Butler, Artemas Coffin, Rufus Coffin, David G. Cook, Jabez Dorman, Joshua Dunn, Josiah Ellis, Leonard H. Ellis, Wm. Ellis, Daniel Fenderson, Nancy and Francis Foster, Edward F. Garland, John S. Gilman, Frances Guay, Dexter A. Hale, Benjamin Hawes, Benjamin Howe, George Hows, George K. Jewett, Marcus Keep, Rufus G. Kellock, Leonard March, John B. Ouilette, Thomas W. Rafford, Daniel Robinson, Jefferson Sinclair, George W Smith, Charles Stewart, Harrison Walker, Joseph Walker, Joseph Walker, Matthew White, Wm. Whitney, Alden B. Wright, Daniel B. York.

Lots granted to encourage the erection of mills, improved before August 9, 1842: Calvin P. and Joshua Bartlett, James A. Flint, Ira D. Fish, Andrew Weaver.

Township No. 9, Range 6 (located one township west of Ashland): Lots purchased or contracted for before August 9, 1842: Wm. Botting, Elias Hayden, Samuel Hayden, Isaac B. Smith, and John Winn who was had a mill lot.

Township 11, Range 6 (west of Ashland): Lots purchased or contracted for before August 9, 1842: John Eastman, Ira D. Fish, Andrew I. Flint, Robert McCann. Lots granted to encourage erection of mills improved before August 9, 1842: Ira Fish and James Flint.

Township D, Range 1 (Fort Fairfield): John Argraves, Edward Dorsey, Miles and Wm. Dorsey, James Gross, Jonathan Hopkinson, Simeon Hoyt, George Martin, Wm. Y. Merchant, Thomas Riley Wm. Riley, Alphonzo Rogers, Hiram Stevens, John B. Trafton, Wm. B. Trafton, John L. Turner, Elbridge W. Waite.

Township granted to Town of Plymouth, MA (Fort Fairfield): Samuel Dean, Patrick Finland, Richard Jordan, Wm. Haley, John Murphy, Samuel Sands, Wm. Upton.

Tract granted to Deerfield Academy (Westfield): James Thorncraft.

Township F, Range 2, (Pleasant Ridge): George P. Allen, Mark Bridges, John Clark, James Cloutman, David Foster, Silas Ireland Jr., Thomas McLain, Joseph Rackliff, Benjamin Rackliff.

Township G, Range 2, (Maysville): John Allen, George Armstrong, Charles P. Bean, Nathaniel Blake, James F. Barton, Joel Bean, Philo Bean, Joseph Beaulieu, Sewall Hill, Alexander Kennedy, George W. Martin, Calvin Morris, Isaac Morris, George Mosier, Wm. Pratt, Solomon F. Pyle, Henry Rolf, James A. Sutter, Edward Rideout, Andrew Scott, Lewis Scott, Wm. Skidgell, Leonard Thomas, Israel Todd, Jacob B. Weeks, Daniel Whitmore.

Tract granted to General Eaton (Caribou): Cornelius Gambeen, Dennis Hale, Elisha Hale, Abel Humphrey, James Keegan, James Walton.

Township H, Range 2 (Caribou): Jesse Drew, Ivory Hardison, Oliver A. Hardison, Heirs of Charles Walton, Lydia Ann Walton.

Township I, Range 2 (Caribou): Alexander Cochran Jr., John Cochran, David Collins.

Township 12, Range 3 (Mapleton): James Beckwith, John Beckwith, Wm. Bull, Samuel Casey, Wm. Clark, Jeremiah Crouse, John C. Harris, Stephen Harris, Andrew K. Packard, Ansel Packard, George Packard, George W. Packard, Shepard Packard.

Township 13, Range 3 (Washburn): Nathaniel Blake, Thomas Brennan, Samuel Bugbee, Nathaniel Churchill, Wm. Clark, Jeremiah and Abraham and Gould Crouse, Thomas Linton, Thomas McDonald, Isaac Pelkey, John Porter, Robert Porter, Charles Simpson, Charles Wilder, Isaac Wilder.

Township 12, Range 4 (Castle Hill Plantation): John Brown, Robert Milliken, Patrick Powers, John Ramsdell.

Township No. 8, Range 5 (located four townships west of Monticello): Heirs of Daniel Smith; Isaac Tabor.

Township No. 9, Range 5 (south of Masardis): Charles Campbell, Thomas McGlaughlin, John Matherson, Levi Powers.

Masardis (No. 10, Range 5): Solomon Brown, Wm. Fitzgerald, Wm. P. Gording, Ambrose Palmer, Eben Trafton.

Township No. 11, Range 5 (Ashland): Wm. Gardner, Hazen Walker.

Township No. 9, Range 6 (Oxbow): Thomas Goss, Jr., Isaac B. Smith, John N. Winslow.

Township No. 12, Range 6 (Nashville): Thomas Knowland, Charles McCormick, Ebenezer McKenzie, Lewellyn Pratt.

Township No. 13, Range 6 (Portage Lake): Nathaniel Blake, Nathaniel Blake, Samuel Brown, David Dow, Melser

Drake, Isaac Stephenson, David Sylvester, James Thompson.

Township No. 14, Range 6 (north of Portage Lake): Wm. Winchell.

Township No. 17, Range 7 (Eagle Lake Plantation): Nathaniel Blake, Cefrot Neddo, Richard Wood.

Township No. 17, Range 7 (wild land township): Ellebert Michaud, Eugene Michaud.

West of the 7th Range of townships, River lots north of the St John River: John Harford, John Henderson, John Hughes, Wm. Mullen, Martin Savage.

River lots south of the St John River: Louis Albert, Magloise Albert, Zebulon Berabe, John and Joseph Diamond, Samuel Bolton, Louis Charette, Henry D.'Aigle, Vital D.'Aigle, Paschal Gandreau, John Gardiner, Edward Gelbert, John Henderson, John Hughes, Joseph Labee, Daniel McPeace, Joseph Nadeau II, Thomas Neddo, Wm. Ouillette, Charles Pelletier, Cirville Pelletier, Martin Savage, Jesse Wheelock.

Islands: Richard Egan, John Gardner, James Grew, William Mullen, Martin Savage, Martin Savage.

Township 18, Range 7 (Fort Kent): Charles Pelletier, Joseph Nadeau II, Zebulon Berabe, Aime Neddo, Charles Bouchard, Henry D.'Aigle, Joseph Robichaud, Wm. F. Gordon, Solomon Cyr, Thomas McGlaughlin, Joseph Nedeau, Hilauin Charette.

Township No. 18, Range 6: George Laferriere, Joseph Laferriere, Augustine Madore, Ettienne Michaud, Antoine Ouilette, John Baptiste Ouilette, Thomas Pinnet.

Rear Lots: Prudent Castonye, Henry Dionne, Peter Dube, Arnable Dubois, Joseph Govin, Louis Le Blanc, John Masse, John Baptiste Roi; Bellanne Saucier, Antoine Saucier.

Township 18, Range 5 (Frenchville): *River Lots:* Benjamin Blanchette, Leander Blanchet, Charles Bouchard, Nicholas Bouchard, Richard Bouchard, Louis Cormier, Phirmain Deschene, Cynac Dube, Joseph Dube, Alexander Gagnon, Antoine Gagnon, Thomas Gagnon, Francis M. Gagnon, Prudent Gagnon, Marie A. Guerette, Louis Le

Blanc, Paul Marquis, Paschal Michaud, Marie E. Pelletier, Joseph Pelletier, Louis Pleurd, Benoni Roi, John Baptiste Roi. *Rear lots*: Basil Albert, Damien Bourgoyne, Raphael Bourgoyne, Louis Lamord, Christopher and Peter Marquis, Alexander Ouilette, Bruno Ouilette, Joseph Ouilette, Julien Ouilette, Andrew and John Raymond, Thomas Rediker.

Township 18, Range 4 (Madawaska): *Rear Lots, second range from the St John River:* Eloie Beaulieu, John Baptiste Beaulieu, Nazare, Beaulieu, William Beaulieu, Eugene Cote, Augustine Cyr, Honore Cyr, Michael Cyr, heirs of Hiliare Martin, Urbain Martin, Luke Paradise, Octave Paradise, Remi Paradis, Louis St Armand, Remi Theriault. *Rear Lots, 3rd range from the St John River*: Registe D.'Aigle, Dennis Cyr, Remi Cyr, Abraham and Simon Dufour, Benjamin Michaud, Antoine Michaud, Gilbert Picard.

Township M Range 2 (Van Buren?): Remi Boucher, Urbain Cyr, Lucian Dube, Remi Dumond, John Baptiste St Germain dit Ecureill, Anthony Gosselin, Jules Levasseur.

Township L, Range 2 (Cyr Plantation?): *Rear lots*: Urbain Cyr, Remi Dumond, John Baptiste St Germain dit Eucriell, Anthony Gosselin, Benjamin Madore, Francis Madore, George Madore.

Township G, Range 1 (Hamlin Plantation): *River lots*: Anthony Bellefleur, Octabe Cormier, Francis Cyr, Abraham Dube, Augustine Dube, Joseph Dube, Abraham and Simon Dufour, Daniel Johnston, Oliver Lepointe, Julien Levasseur, Heirs of Louis Nadeau, Maurice Sirois, Michael Sucie, Registe Thibodeau, Francis Thibodeau, Registe Thibodeau, Francis Muzeroll.

Township F., Range 1 (Pleasant Ridge): *River Lots*: Francis Cyr, Francis Muzeroll.

Part II: **1854**

PERSONS IN THE **PLYMOUTH AND ETON GRANTS**: (title to said lands to be procured, from the present owners of the fee, for two dollars per acre.) Listed here are the

owners of the lots, with the present occupants in parentheses, as of August 9, 1842:
Township granted to the town of Plymouth: Thomas Amsden; Samuel and Joseph Barnes (Edward Guigey); Joseph Barnes (J. Davenport); Thomas Beaulieu; A. and J. and A. and F. Bishop (John Lovely); Amos Bishop (Wm. Bishop); Amos and Frederick Bishop (Libby and Fox); Atherton Clark (A. and T. Rogers); Wm. and James Bishop (Amos Bishop); Samuel Davenport; Wm. Day; George Dean (Frances Carron); James and Edward Doyle (Patrick Conley); Margaret Doyle; Job Everett; Samuel Farley; Joseph Fisher; John Flannery (Daniel Bishop); Patrick Flannery (Daniel Bishop); Patrick Flannery (Edward Guigey); Thomas Flannery (Brinard Guigey); Julia Ann Giberson and the heirs of Alfred Giberson (Alfred Giverson); Thomas Givney and James Drew (Thomas Givney); Alexander Guigey (Samuel Farley); Edward Guigey (Chaplin Nelson); James Guigey; Charles Hammond (John Twaddle); John L. Higgins; Henry Hurd; John Lovely; William Lundy (Martin Murry); John McDonald (Robert Whitaker); Sarah McGlaughlin and the heirs of Daniel Mc Glaughlin (Daniel McGlaughlin); Michael McKinny (Martin Murray); Martin Murray; George Rogers, (J. and R. Rogers); John Russell (B. McGlaughlin); Thomas Russell (Michael Russell); John Sands and Thomas Walton (Michael Keane); Isaac Smith; John Sterling (Thomas Whitaker); Daniel Turner; James Upton (Anthony Keane); Wm. Ward; Samuel Wark; Eliphalet Watson (Justus Gray); George White (T. Flannery and J. White); Wm. White (John Twaddle).
Tract granted to General Eaton: Elias Brown; Solomon Brown; John Buber (Wm. Bubar); Nathaniel Buber; Charles Butler (Wm. Buber); Patrick Conley; Elizabeth Dondy (Dudy?) and heirs of David Dondy (Doody?); James and Edward Doyle (Patrick Conley); John Gallagher (Collingwood Murphy); Moses Grass; Lawrence Kelley, Patrick Kelly; Thomas Kelly (Patrick Kelly); David O. Parks; George Parks, Hannah Parks (Jonathan Parks); Jesse Partridge; Robert Richards (Dennis Shugrue); John Sands and

Thomas Walton (Michael Keane); John Sands and Thomas Walton (John Thompson); James Shea (John Thompson); Dennis Shugrue and James Corkins Patrick Somers (Collingwood Murphy); Samuel Wark; James Walton (Robert Richards) Jonah Whiteknact.

Part III: **1857**
Source: *Report of the 34th Congress, Session 3, Rep. Com. No. 323, January 23, 1857*: A. statement of claims represented by George M. Weston, Esq, Commissioner of Maine, growing out of the settlement of the northeastern boundary question, by the Treaty of August 9, 1842, submitted to the Senate Committee of Claims by N. C. Towle, under the resolve of the Senate of July 18, 1856, included an explanation of three types of claims: possessory claims, timber depredations, and variation of the boundary line (where it appears that about ten thousand acres of land, previously granted by the State of Massachusetts, and based upon the old treaty line, was cut off by the conventional line adopted by the treaty of 1842 and thereby lost to the proprietors). A. summary of the history of the dispute includes these conclusions: It appears from the records and papers exhibited that the following named persons hold the proprietary title to these lands, and are the **claimants to indemnity for loss by the operation of the treaty**, to the extent stated, viz:
Laura A. Stebbins, Catherine C. Ward, Rufus Munsen and James A. Drew, jointly, to 3,353 acres, on which the improvements are $10,711.
Edward Monroe, three quarters, and Benjamin Sewall, one quarter of 3,385; improvements, $15,229.
James A. Drew and Rufus Mansur in equal parts, 1,692 acres; improvements, $6,337.
List of settlers on the Eaton Grant (original shows number of acres and value of improvements thereon): Solomon Brown, John Buber, Nathaniel Buber, Wm. Buber, Charles Butler, Patrick Conly, J. Corkins, J. and E. Doyle, Elizabeth Dudy, John Gallaughn, C. Gambeen, Moses Glass,

Dennis Hale, Elisha Hale, Abel Humphrey, James Keegan, L. Kelly, Patrick Kelly, Thomas Kelly, D. O. Parks, George F. Parks, Hannah Parks, Jesse Partridge, Robert Richards, John Sands, James Shea, R. Shugren, Patrick Somers, James Walton, Thomas Walton, Jonah Whitenackt, Samuel Work.

Settlers on the western section of Plymouth township (Edmund Munroe and Benjamin Sewall, Proprietors): Thomas Amaden, Joseph Barnes, Thomas Beaulieu, A. and F. Bishop, Amos Bishop, W. and J. Bishop, A. Clark, Samuel Davenport, Wm. Day, J. and E. Doyle, Margaret Doyle, J. A. Drew, Samuel Farley, Patrick Finland, John Flannery, A. Giberson's heirs, T. Giveney, Alex Guigey, Edward Guigey, James Guigey, Wm. Haley, Charles Hammond, John L. Higging, Richard Jordan, John Lovely, Sarah McGlaughlin, John Murphey, George Rogers, Samuel Sands, Isaac Smith, Daniel Turner, James Upton, Wm. Upton, Sands and Walton, Wm. Ward, E. Watson, Wm. White, S. Work.

Settlers on the eastern section of Plymouth Township (Drew and Manson, Proprietors): Joseph Barnes, S. and J. Barnes, George Dean, Samuel Dean, Job Everett, Joseph Fisher, Patrick Flannery, Thomas Flannery, John L. Higgins, Henry Hurd, Wm. Lundy, John McDonald, Michael McKinney, Martin Murray, John Russell, Thomas Russell, John Sterling, George White and ___ Ward.

INDEX

ABBOT, C J 388 John 360 Thomas 361 Willard 359 361 Wm 384
ABERDEEN, Lord 64 266 283 286
ADAMS, Benjamin 355 Cyrus 355 Deborah 319 Eleashel 384 Eleazer 384 Erastus 355 Franklin 391 Hiram 351 Isaac 318 John 283 John Q 22 34 190 43-4 57 60 71 Samuel 388 Solomon 397 Thomas 322 385 388 Wm Pitt 75 Z B 389
ADDINGTON, Henry U 75 Wm 318
ADET, Charles 308
ADSITE, Benjamin 330
AGRICOLA, 281
AISQUITH, W E 331-22 341
ALBERT ALBARE, Basil 401 Freeman 312 Joseph 308 312 Louis 400 Magloise 400 Vincent Jr 308
ALDRICH, Elias T 386
ALEXANDER, Hugh311 320
ALLAN, J&A 372
ALLANSHAW, Allanshaw & Co 372 James 374
ALLEN, Dwight 389 Elisha 278 George P 398 Henry G 321 John 373 395 398 Lt Col 187 Moses 397 Robert Jr 351 Samuel R 389 Wm 351
ALLISON, Robert 330
AMADEN, Thomas 401 404
AMBREICHT, Augustus 329
AMES, Almarin 361 Benjamin

44 Isaac 380 John 360 Mark T 351 Sewel 351
AMONS, John 316
ANDERSON, H J 110 162 166-67 John 78 Robert 192
ANDREWS, Charles 278 Edgar 311 Elkins 351 Horatio 330 (J ?) Anthony 375 James W 327-28 John 329 Sarah 318 Wm 390
ANTHONY, Capt 231
APPLETON, John 389 391 Moses L 388
ARBUTHNOT, Colonel 28
ARGALL, Colonel 28 Samuel 26
ARGRAVES, John 398
ARMSDELL, Thomas 316
AREY, James 390
ARMSTRONG, Ferdinand 54 309 316 347 395 General 9 George 398 400 James 54 347 Jonathan E 395
ARNOLD, Joseph 346-48 Lemuel 359 Wm 355
ARSENO, Joseph 371
ATWOOD, Archelaus 386 Benjamin 386 B C 389 Jesse 386
ASBIN, Thomas 321
ASHBURTON, Lord 283-87 291
ATKINS, Charles 329 Simeon P 178 Simon P 357
ATKINSON, Edwin 371 Thomas 371 Wm 370
ATWOOD, Wm E 178 209
AUSTIN, Austin & Jinker 372 Blanchard 351 James 317
AUSTINS, Cyrus 351 Moses 351
AVEREL AVERELLL, Moses 385 Wm 307 360
AYER AYERS, Bradley B 361 Elisha 387
AYOTTE, Zachary 27

BABCOCK, Asa W 385-86 393 A
W 383
BABB, Aaron 391
BABBITT, E B 331 334-35
BABERT, B— 320 Michael 308
BACHELDER, George W 153 168
178 184 201-2 208 215-18
227-28 231 239 242 Wm 361
BACON, Daniel P 379 James 34
45 48-9 52 342 John 343
Timothy 342
BADGER, Henry 351
BAGLEY, Hall 390 John 314 Levi
360
BAGOT, Charles 34-5
BAILEY, Amos 384 386 Daniel
361 Philip 361 Samuel 317 385
BAILLIE, — 368 Mr 367 Thomas
72 260 374
BAKER, — 324 Abner 33
Amanda 34 Asa 33 Asahel 51-2
Barnabas 33 Dorcas 34 Edward
380 Enoch 34 Elizabeth 34
Horace 383 Jeremy 360 John 34
40-42 44-57 60-66 68 86-8 91
254-59 267-69 272-74 342-43
Joseph 33-4 66 John B 312 Levi
355 Lovinda 34 Maryann 319
Nathan 33-4 40 66 86 308 P
372 Sophia (Rice) Mrs 34 40 44
51 60 86 Sophronia 34 86
Reuben 33
BALCH, Henry 357
BALKAM, James M 379 John A
379
BALL, Gardiner 383
BALLARD, Wm Jr 361
BAMFORD, J V 328
BANGOR INDEPENDENT VOLUN-
TEERS 238
BANGOR RIFLE CORPS, 157-58
160 213 226 235 243-44
BANKHEAD, Charles 90

BANKS, Edmon 319 Horace 360
BARBERIE, A 374
BARBOUR, James 61
BARDEN, Othniel 359
BARE, Vasion 308
BARING, Alexander 30 283-84
BARING BROS, 284
BARKER, Henry 315 John 384
Zebidiah 321
BARLOW, Thomas 374
BARNARD, Abel 379 Dwight B
382 John 378 Silas 355
BARNES, J 404 Joseph 402 404
S 404 Samuel 402
BARRELL, Samuel B 57 64
BARRETT, Algenon 351 Horatio
178 360 Stephen D 351
BARRIBEE, John 312
BARRIO, Oliver 371
BARSTOW, Brazer 388
BARTLETT, — 72 Calvin P 397-
98 Guilford S 397 Frederick K
358 Jonathan 378 Joseph 390
Joshua 398 Lot V 390 Mrs 89
Nathaniel 48 89 91 312 342
344 Richard H 385 Stephen 379
Thomas 355 390 Thomas Jr 132
134-37 142-43 226 233-35
259 261 267 354-355
BARTELS, John O 381
BARTON, James F 398
BASFORD, John 319
BATCHELDER, Phineas 358
BATES, Henry 379 James 78 Lt
239 Walter 370
BATTES, Larange B 351
BAXTER, Abram 370
BAYARD, James A 190
BAZZELL, Wm F 361
BEAL, Andrew D 178
BEALS, Isaiah, 178 358-59
BEAN, Charles P 398 Daniel 88-
9 317 Dudley D 360 Joel 398

Philo 316 398 Reuben 351 395
Samuel 351
BEANES, Dr 9
BEARCE BEARSE, Samuel P 394
Septimus B 397
BEARD, Adam 235 George 235
BEARDSLEY, Paul 135 Penderson 134-35 137 248 R 374
BEAULIEU, Eloie 401 John Baptiste 401 Joseph 398 Nazare 401 Thomas 402 404 Wm 401
BECKFORD, John 379
BECKWITH, __ 367 James 399 John 399 Thomas 309 315 347 Thomas W 395
BEDEC, Peter 317
BEDEE, Isaac 359
BEDLE BEEDLE, John 324 Richard Jr 351 Walter 324
BELL, Bell & Wilmot 369 Ellexander 351 Henry 351 Henry Jr 351 James 389 John 312 315 D 390 Vacon Jr 312 Vaison 312
BELLEFLEUR BELLFLEUR BELFLOUR, __ 324 Anthony 401 Antoine 312 Leon 308 Lewis 308 Lewis Jr 308 Louis 312
BELLGLEY, Lario 308
BELYEA, James 310
BENJAMIN, Addison 351 James 387 John 316
BENN, Abraham 318 Catherine 310 318 Edward 318 Ephriam 318 Solomon 318
BENNETT, George A 311 319
BENNOCK (Benoch), John 384-85 393 John Jr 384-85
BENSON, John 387 Leander 351
BERABE, Zebulon 400
BERRY, Daniel C 321 David 359 John 386 T 372
BERTON (see Burton), __ 367

BETISHERE, John 308
BETTS, Bela 322 Betts & Miller 371
BETUKE, John 308
BEVERIDGE (Beverage), Benjamin, 248-49
BICKFORD, Edmund 320 Enoch W 361 Joseph 316
BIGELOW, Abraham 310
BIGGER, Wm 397
BIJOT, Louis 312
BILBY, John 330
BILLINGS, Caleb F 354 Daniel 354-55 David L 361 Nathaniel 330 Wm 379
BINGHAM, Anne 284 Wm 30 33 283-84
BINNEY, Amos 381
BIRD, Francis 318
BISHOP, A 396 402 404 Amos 396 402 404 Daniel 402 F 396 402 404 Frederick 402 J 396 402 404 James 402 Joshua 395 W 404 Wm 316 402
BISMARK, Prince 179
BITHER, Benjamin 320 Wm D 320
BLACK, John 284 346 Mr 85 Wm 324 374 396
BLACKBURN?, Ebenezer 315
BLACK HOOF, 8
BLACKMAN, Francis 386 Wm E 386
BLACK SNAKE, 8
BLACKWELL, Oliver 315
BLAISDELL, Robert 311 321
BLAKE, Ebenezer 395 Henry 315 General 14 George 388 John 385 John D 333-338 Josiah 396 Josiah H 397 Joseph 395 Nathaniel 98 399-400 Phillip 351 Samuel 390 Samuel H 278 S H 388

BLAKELY, A 333
BLAKESLY, Abraham 329
BLANCHARD, Charles, 170
James 351
BLANCHET BLANCHETTE,
Leander 400 Benjamin 400
BLISARD, Wm 318
BLISS, Chief Justice 62 91
BLOODGOOD, Wm 69 310 326
BLOODWORTH, Lewis 235
BLOTCHFORD, E H 382
BLUM, John 330
BLUNT, Enoch M 360
BOICE BOYCE BOIS, Thomas 371
BOIL BOYLE, Dennis 319
BOLES BOLLES, Francis 316
Matthew Jr 387 Thomas 316
BOLIO, Charles 308
BOLSTRIDGE, Ebenezer 397
Frederick 396
BOLTON, Samuel 400
BOND, John B 361 Joseph 330
BONNEFAS, Alexander 312
BONNY, Andrew 314
BOOKER, W S 354 Wm S 355
BOOTOT, Ephriam 312
BORNAY, Eneas 312
BOSTWICK, Hanford 370
BOSWELL, Henry 315
BOSWORTH, Wm Jr 359
BOTTING, Wm 398
BOTSFORD, A E 374 Amos 374
Justice 91 Wm 374
BOUCHARD, Charles 400
Nicholas 400 Richard 400
BOUCHER, Oliver 312 Remi 401
BOUCHETTE, Col Joseph 31-2
BOULIER, Ashur 312 Etienne
312 Charles 312 Jacob 312
Martial 312 Simon 67
BOURGOYNE, Damien 400
Raphael 400
BOWEN, Isaac 337-38 340

J 335 Lt 340
BOWERS, Charles E 382
BOWLES, Spencer G 357 Stephen
J 380
BOWMAN, David B 217
BOYD, James 370 John 361
Lendel G S 391 Robert 391
BOYNTON, B A 310 Benjamin A
327-28 Charles C 317 Gorham L
377 James 397 Joel 397
BRACKEN, David 314
BRACKETT, Daniel 310 318
Henry 322 Hiram 322 397
James 322 Luther 322
BRADBURY, Bion 125 380 382
Christopher C 318 Cyrus 321
Ebenezer 311 321 Edwin 318
Hall 321 Jabez 178 311 318
John 386 Moses 321 True 311
321 Wm 386 389
BRADFORD, Calvin 315 John 310
BRADLEY, Daniel W 355 377 386
388 394 Henry 309 316 346-47
J 327-28 John 309 Levi 278
388 Louis 316 Oliver 347
BRADSHAW, Wm 369
BRADSTREET BROADSTREET,
"Bradstreet's"184 Jesse C 397
Joseph 318 Nathaniel 310 318
BRADY, Eugene 335 Partrick
314
BRADYMAN, John 330
BRAGDON, Horace 397 John T
355
BRAGG, Homan 397 James 358
Sylvester 351
BRAN, Thomas 314
BRANNAN BRANNIN, C 310 J M
335
BRANDOLLA, Wm 330
BRANSON, Alice 86 Nora (Baker)
86 Sidney 86
BRANTE, Joshua B 326

BRASTOW, Deodat 388
BRAY, Cyrus 319 Joseph 361
BRENNAN, Thomas 399
BRESLIN, George 351
BREWER, John N M 379
BRIDGE, Levi Jr 359 Wm S 385
BRIDGES, John H 318 Mark 398 Otis L 379 382
BRIEN, Jean Baptiste-Henri 121
BRIGHT, John 386
BRIGGS, Otis Jr 387
BRIGHAM, Caleb R H 88
BRITTAIN, James Jr 370 James Sr 370
BROAD, Horace 319
BROCKWAY, D 372
BROCKRY, John 351
BROOKS, Albert 387 John 384 Wm M 379 383
BROWN, ___ 369 A G 383 389 Alexander 318 Asa 318 Benjamin Jr 359 Charles E 381 Daniel 354 David G 359 Elias 309 347 402 George 351 (Howard &)Brown 369 J 327-28 James Jr 373 Jane 318 John 319 358 369 399 Joseph 369 Josiah 358 Lyman 330 Perkins 358 Reuben 359 Samuel 399 402 320 Solomon 399 402 403 Thomas 310 318 Thomas J 318 Waldo 393 Warren 377 395 Wm 309 314 347 354 361 383 397 Wm McE 359
BROWNELL, Aaron 370
BRUNSIEU, Mr 126
BRYANT, Charles G 120-22 245 355 John 381 Joseph 385 Wm 111
BRYNAN, Michael 329
BUBAR BUBER BOBEAR BOOBAR BOOBER BUBIER, Charles 309 316 348 David 348 David W 320

409

James 372 John 402 403 Nathaniel 402 403 Wm 316 402 403
BUCHANAN, ___ 189
BUCK, Harrison 320 John W 361 Jonathan 379 Joseph L 357
BUCKMAN, S 372
BUCKMORE, George W 126 127 128 155 252 355 376
BUCKNAM, Benjamin 378 Ichabod 378 Seward C 379 Wm 378
BUDSON, Joseph 361
BUFFAM, Charles 360
BUGBEE, Samuel 399
BULL, Charles 396 George 346 Peter 309 315 346 395 396 (Smith&) Bull 372 Wm 396 399 Peter 127 131-32
BUNKER, Francis B 351
BURBANK, J Selden 357
BURCHELL, David 316
BURGOIN, Bartholomew 308 312 Burgoin&Co 324
BURGWIN, I H K 326
BURKE, ___ 312 John 314 M J (I?) 333-35
BURLEIGH, Benjamin 319 James 359 Moses 311 320 384
BURLEY, Moses C 317 Samuel K 317
BURNET, Simon 354
BURNHAM, Ensign 229 George 380 Jeremiah 178 358 379 John 264 278 351 Royal R 358 Wardwell 360 Wm 383
BURNS, George 361 Wm 397
BURPEE, Isaac 371
BURR, Edward 388 H C 388 Jonathan 202 388 Joseph 385 Samuel 354 Samuel A 351

BURRILL, Harvey M 357 L P 387
Nathaniel Jr 387 S C 384
Zenath W 357
BURROWS, James C 319 Robard 330
BURTON (see Berton), Joseph 333 Thomas 320 Timothy 361 Wm J 257-58
BUSH, S L 382
BUSHIERE, Barnum 308
BUSELL (see Buzzell), David L 351 D L 353 Hiram 351
BUSWELL, David L 359
BUTLER, Elvator P 393 Charles 316 402-03 Luther 397
BUTRISS, Harrass 351
BUTTER, Wm E 387
BUTTERS, Horace 354 Horacio 351 Lorenzo 355 Lorenzo D 354
BUTTERFIELD, __116 Frances 322 Franklin 321 Henry Coridon 322 John 386 Joseph 322 Orrin 335 358 Samuel 322 Wm 311 322 386
BUTTS, John B 351
BUZZELL (see Busell), Isaac 1361 Jonathan 358
BYRONE, John 314
CAHOON, James B 381
CAINE, Anthony 309
CAFFREY, John 330
CALDWELL, Alex 310 John 126
CALHOUN, Mr 163 188-90
CAMERON, James 92 L 372
CAMIO, Alexander 308 Peter 308
CAMPBELL, Alexander 383 395 Archibald 81 87 90-2 97-8 Colin 98 118 Caroline 397 Charles 399 David 316 383 David W 383 Francis C 383 Henry 386 James 309 348 James Jr 111 (Ker &) Campbell 372 (McLeod &) Campbell 371 Wm 329
CANADA, Mr 127
CANE, Anthony 316
CANNING, Cyrus 342-43 Mr 64
CANNON, Cyrus 51
CANTWELL, Sgt Maj 336
CAPRON, A 331-32
CARCAUS, Paul 312
CAREAUX, Joseph 312
CAREY, Martin 314
CARIDGE, Hiram G 358
CARLE, Mr 126
CARLETON, Governor 28 76 81 Washington 363
CARLTON, Amos 381 James 178 Jonathan A 363
CARMAN, A 133
CARNEY, Francis 308 Samuel 312
CARPENTER, Asa S 351 Charles S 379 John 315 Joshua 98 183-84 203-04 385 Winfield G 320
CARR, David C 329 Elijah 310 Joseph 390 Justus S 361 Wm 329
CARROLL, Hugh 322
CARRON, Frances 402
CARTER, H G 381 James 374 Jonathan 351 Timothy J 162 William 317
CARTWELL, Wm 345
CARVER, Calvin 231
CARY, John 355 Samuel 355 Shepard 159 178 214-15 319 377 Wm 310
CASE, Eliphalet 281
CASEY, Samuel 399 Thomas 314
CASIDY CASSIDY, __ 334 Michael 318
CASSRON, E A 333-344
CASTINE RIFLE CORPS, 213
CASTONYE, Prudent 400

CATES, Andrew 351
CATON, Mr 127
CENTER, B L 333 Benjamin L 333
CHADBOURNE, Benjamin 358-59 Humphrey 321 355 Ichabod R 378
CHALMERS, Sumner 355
CHAMBERLAIN, George W 390 Jacob 387 Joshua 355 Joshua Jr 171 351 353 388 Luther 171 354 Mellen 385
CHAMBERLAND, Abraham 47 62
CHAMPION, John 358
CHAMPLAIN, 26
CHANDLER, Adeline 395 Anson G 382 Elizabeth N 395 E R 374 James H 393 John 36 61 Samuel B 314 [Veranes?] 316
CHAPLIN, Charles E 360
CHAPMAN, Ebenezer 387 Garey 361 Wm I 361
CHARETTE, Hilauin 400 Louis 400
CHARY, Joseph 312
CHASE, Daniel 353-355 Daniel K 384 George M 379 H S 381 Isaac 310 319 John 321 John G 363 Jonathan 397 Peter 310 Reuben 311 319 Robert P 361 Silas 381 Thomas H 351 353
CHASSE, Gruino 308 Henry 312 Joseph 312
CHAUNCY, Commodore 194
CHER, Francis 312
CHESLEY, Bela 315
CHICK, Elisha Jr 390
CHIPMAN, Ward 20 62 369 374 Ward Jr 75 91
CHRINT, Colemarkee 308
CHRISTA CHRISTIE, J 372 Joshua 309 315 346 396

411

CHRISTOPHER, Raphael 345 Samuel 345
CHURCH, Jacob 370
CHURCHILL, Job 396 Nathaniel 309 315 346-47 399
CILLEY, Isaac B 355 Jonathan 123-24 Joseph L 389
CIRE, Michael 67-8 Joseph 67-8
CLAPHAM, Charles 322
CLAPP, Charles Q 391 Isaac 383
CLARE, Alare Ann L 308 Levy 308
CLARK, __ 369 A 404 Alvin B 178 358 Atherton 402 Calvin 311 Charles 322 C S 355 Cyrus S 377 391 394 David 311 Elijah 390 Ephriam 317 396-97 Isaac 311 321 James 244 John 355 398 John E 397 J N 372 Levi 310 N S 61 68-70 326-28 Samuel 358 Sherburn W 361 Thomas 397 Wm 311 317 399
CLAY, Henry 22 42 44 49 50 56 59 65 80 163 189-90 277
CLAYTON, Charles W 396 Sarah E 396
CLEAVES, Samuel 311 322 Seth 311 322
CLEMENT John M 379 382 Wm 329
CLEMENTS, Ezekiel 342 James N 363
CLEVELAND, James B 360
CLIFF, Richard 397
CLIFFORD, __153 David W 319 John 322 Jonathan 311 Nathan 162 278
CLINCH, Patrick 372
CLINTON, Charles 391
CLOPPER, Henry G 62 91
CLOQUET, John 312
CLOUGH, John H 320 Joseph Jr 352 Noah 310 318

CLOUTMAN, James 398
COBB, C M 355 David 284
Stephen 314
COBURN, Abner, 263 Alpheus A
351 Alpheus 353 Eleazer 387
Silas 315
COCHRAN, Admiral 13 Alexander 309 316 348 Alexander Jr 399 Isaac 320 John 370 399
COE, Ebenezer S 377 392-93
COFFEE, John 127
COFFIN, Artemas 397 Charles 352 Charles H 379 381 Eben S 390 George W 41-2 247 392 John 370 Rufus 397 Wm 352
COGSWELL, Frederick 125
COLBERTH, Gustavus 352 Robert 352
COLBORNE, Sir John 118
COLBROTH COOLBROTH, Royal 311 Royal B 321
COLE, Isaac 369 James 369 John 359 Nathan C 363 Richardson 330
COLEBROOK, Sir Wm 272
COLLIER, John 322 Martin 310 Robert 322 Thomas 322
COLLINS, C O 332-34 David 399 Ebenezer 320 352 J 352 James 388 Patrick 319 Wm 317 319
COLPITTS, (Jones &)Colpitts 370
COLSON, Stephen O 363
COMBER, Jacob C 352
COMINGS, Bradford 311 John 321
COMMINGS, John 311
COMSTOCK, Orrin V 330 Solomon 361
CONDRA, Ephriam M 319
CONE, Edmund 307 311 317
CONEY, Samuel 390

412

CONLEY, John 369 Patrick 309 316 402-03
CONNELL, __ 372 Charles 133 M 374
CONNELLY CONNOLY, John H 57 Patrick 348
CONNET, John 312
CONNEY, Edmond T 352
CONNOR, George W 330 S 333 Wm 330
CONY, Samuel 125 Dr 170
COOK COOKE, David 309 347 David G 315 397 Samuel 307 310 319 323 Samuel 39 61 70 Seth F 360
COOKSON, Daniel 321 John 358 Reuben 360
COOLIDGE, Richard 339 Richard H 339
COOMBS, Albert 361 Leonard 312 345 Leonard R 83 86 89 91-2 99 127
COOPER, Alexander 391 Charles 391 James 361 James N 391 James S 382 Nicholas 315
COPELAND COPLAND, Benjamin F 383 Calvin 387 Isaac 352 Thomas G 383
COPERTHWAITE, Wm 315
CORKINS, J 403 James 402
CORLESS, David 311 320
CORLISS, Benjamin 317
CORMIER, Freeman 312 Jean Baptiste 27 Louis 400 Octabe 401
CORNEA, Alexander 312
CORNWALLIS, 25
CORSON, Erastus 358 Jackson 320 Joel P 322
COSGROVE, Hugh 310 318
COSTER, Rev George 374
COTE, Eugene 401
COTTLE, Samuel F 358

COTTIN, Calvin W 317
COWAN, John Jr 360
COWES, Samuel E 393
COWPERTHWAITE, Wm 396-97
COX, John 310
COYE COY, Asa 92 Dennis 320
CRAM, John 314 Nehemiah 381
CRANDLEMIRE, Benjamin B 52
CRANE, Capt 239 Joshua 389
Wm 373 374
CRAVEN, John 248
CRAWFORD, James 369 388
James B 388
CREASY, _?_ 319 Joseph 319
CREED, George W 329
CREHORE, Thomas C 357
CRIPPS, T B 372
CROCK, Alexander 308 David
308 Jeremiah 308 Peter 308
CROCKER, Mahalia 317
Wm A 380
CROFTS, John 329
CROGAN, Wm 314
CROOKER, Joshua 352
CROSBY, Ebenezer 310 James
393 John Jr 390 Thomas 386
CROSS, Wm 353
CROUSE, A 396 Abraham 399 G
396 Gould 399 J 396 Jeremiah
396 399
CROWELL, Harrison M 354
James 359
CROWLEY, Florence 330
CRUIKSHANK, Cruickshank &
Johnson 40 James 370
CULBERTSON, M S 331
CUMMING CUMMINGS CUMINS,
Bradford 396 F I 178 G W 178
209 Ensign Goodrich 178
Goodridge 360 Francis I 361
James F 316 Redmond S 352
Wm 315
CUMSTON, Robert M 358

CUNARD, Joseph 371 374
CUNLIFFE, Capt 137
CUNNINGHAM, Ebenezer 351
Henry W 353 H W 355 Robert
330 Thomas 361 Wm 315 351
CURD, Thomas J 337-38
CURR, James 352
CURRIER, Ann 395 Henry C 396 I
F 85 James 346 James F 395
CURTIS
Alfred 363 Amzi 379 381
George B 363 Gideon 364 Jacob
363 James H 311 317 Jeremiah
382 John W 364 Melzer 352
Rufus G 60
CUSHING, Jonathan A 394
Theophilis 394
CUSHMAN, Alfred 314 C C 355 G
G 355 Gustavus G 132 134-37
142-43
CUTLER, Lysander 178 212 359
386 391
CUTTER, Wm Cutter 394
CUTTS, Dolley 123 Madison 123
Mary 123 Richard 123
CYR CYER SEAR SIER, Alexis
312 Alvan 312 Augustine
401Billaud 312 Christopher
308 312 Christost 308 David
308 Dennis 401 Elecis 308 Eli
312Elias 312 Fabian 312
Francis 401 Frederick 312
Henry 312 Honore 401 James
312 Jean 27 308 Jean Baptiste
25 Jonathan 343 Joseph 308
312 Laurent 312 Laurier 312
Loron 308 Michael 401 Pascal
312 Pascal 312 Peter 312 Remi
401 Solomon 400 Theodore 312
Urbain 401 Xasrie 308
DAGGETT, Ebenezer 317 358
[Homer?] S 319 James 310 318

James Jr 317 318 Robert 318
Waterman 317-18
DAIGLE DAGEL DAGLE D'AIGLE,
Auguste 312 Larion 312D 127
Demeque 308 John Battis 51
John Betis 308 Joseph 27 29
308 Mermeit 308 Henry 400
Vital 400 Henry 400 Registe
401
DAILY, Ansel 384
DAKIN, John 317 Samuel D 391
393
DALEY, Wm 310
DALTON, Thomas 330 Wm 54
311 315 346
DAM, Joel F 361 Leader N 361
DAMONS, Isaac 386 Joseph B
360
DAMREN, Chandler 361
DANA, Alexander H 383 Luther
381
DANIELS, James M 358
DARCEY [Daicey?], Timothy 314
DARLING, John 370 Walker 360
DARRELL, John 310 John 318
DAVEE, Thomas 110 162
DAVEIS, Charles S 55 57 64-5
75 110-11 266 281 Ebenezer
55 Mehitable 55 Elizabeth
(Gilman) 55
DAVENPORT, Frederick 312
Gabriel 309 348 J 402 John 311
322 Samuel 316 348 402 404
DAVIDS, Wm 330
DAVIDSON, James 329 John 54
DAVIS, Amos 389 Asa 2nd 360
Asahel 361 Benjamin W 352
Charles 360 Daniel 385 David B
361 Isaac 317 Israel 311 317
376 John P 361 384 John T 390
Mr 163 Stevens 387 388
DAWSON, Lt 336 Samuel K 338
S K 331-32

DAY, Andrew N 359 Hannibal
327-28 Wm 402 404
DEAN, George 402 402 404 John
397 Samuel 398 404 Tisdale
390
DEANE, John G 60 64-7 82-4 92
111 Joseph A 388 Solomon 316
M G 111
DEARBORN, Greenleaf 310 326-
28 Capt Greenlief 70 Gen H A S
222
DEBA, Gumain 308 Joseph 51
DECATUR, Stephen 5
DECENADO, Mr 127
DECKER, John P 322
DEE, James 314 Nicholas 316
DEERING, Gideon 352 Hartley
318 Samuel 361 Sarah 322
Nathaniel 380 381 Nathaniel F
389 Wm 322
DELANO, David B 395
DE LATE, Lewis 321
DELESDERNIER, W 379
DELING, James 361
DEMPSY, Peter 329
DEMO, ___ 312
DE MONTS, Sieur 25 Wm 379
DEMOT, Francis 312 George 312
Marca 312
DENNETT, Levi 393
DENNIS, Carlisle 360
DENNISON, George 336 James
347
DENSMORE, David 359
DESCHENE, Phirmain 400
DESMOND, Desmond 322
DEVEREAUX, George H 81
DEVO, Wm 361
DEVOIN, John 356
DEXTER, John C 386
DEXTER RIFLE CORPS, 159 226
DIAMOND, John 400 Joseph 400

DIBLEE, Abraham 312 Wm 51 137 140
DICKENSON DICKINSON, Isaac 312 James 361 John 380 Wm 370
DICKER, Henry F 352
DILLING, James 310 James 318
DILLINGHAM, Benjamin 360
DILNOW, Albert 352
DINEN, Patrick 318
DINSMORE, John 394
DIONNE, Henry 400
DIOR, Jesse Jr 352
DITTMAR, C G 333
DOANE DONE, David B 388 Edward 355 Joseph 387 Joshua 352
DOBBINS, James 330
DOCK, Dock (&McLaggen)371
DOE, Amzi 397 Nahalie 361
DOHERTY, Edward 311
DOIL, [Malisa Doil?]319
DOLE, Moses 387 Samuel H 393
DOLLEY, Henry 352 John B 317
DOMINICK, Joseph 312
DONALDSON, I (J ?) L 340 J 336 James L 338 James S 337 J L 329 331-32 336 340
DONDY, Elizabeth 402 David 316 402
DONNELL, C O 335
DONOVAN DONIVAN, Jeremiah 319 Mikiel 319 P O 333
DOOSTO, Joseph 312
DORETHY, Edward 317 Edward Jr 317 Edward Sr 317
DORITY, Daniel 178 209
DORMAN, Jabez 397
DORR, Barsillai 358 Ephriam 361
DORSEY, Edward 398 John 309 316 348 John Jr 316 Joseph 309 Miles 398 Mr 143 Wm 398

DOUCETTE, Romaine 370
DOUGHERTY, Truxton 178
DOUGHTY, Calvin S 171 354 356 Capt T 209
DOUGLAS, Daniel 330 Sir Howard 40-1 55 70 72 75
DOUGLASS, Dennis 344 Israel 358
DOW, Asa 130 134 136-37 142 354 David 178 399 Noah Jr 352 W L 311
DOWE, John 321
DOWELL, George 312 I M 339
DOWNES DOWNS, George 378-79 382 Daniel 364 Joseph 320 Nathaniel 317
DOWNEY, Alexander 309
DOYLE, E 404 Edward 402 Edwin 314 J 404 James B 310 402 James B 318 Margaret 402 404
DRAKE, Melser 399
DRESSER, Thomas 352
DREW, Andrew 119 322 Benjamin 352-53 359 Chesley 310 James 159 402 James A 310 319 403 Jesse 399 Moses 312 321 Samuel 308 312 Seth 358-9
DRUMMOND, Jacob 394
DUBE, Abraham 401 Augustine 401 Cynac 400 Joseph 400-01 Lucian 401 Peter 400
DUBEY, Jeremiah 308
DUBEZ, Abraham 345
DUBIE, Jeremiah 67
DUBOIS, Arnable 400
DUCET, Firman 312
DUCHEME, Freeman 312
DUDLEY, Benjamin 394 Daniel D 111 David 383 Elias 390 Samuel 384 386
DUDY (see Dondy), Elizabeth 403
DUER, Wm 30

DUFFIE, John 330 Peter 329
Robert 330
DUFOUR, Abraham 312 401
Joseph 24 Simon 401
DUMOND, Jere 312 Remi 401
DUMONT, John T P 206 208 P
333 Phirmain 344
DUNBAR, Wm 370
DUNHAM, John Jr 361
DUNLAP, Governor Robert P 96-
7 100-02 106-07 188 202
DUNN, ___ 116 Columbus 311
317 Elbridge G 393 396 James
C 381 Jonah 310 Peter 393
DUNNING, Charles T 354 C T 356
James 178 238 358 393 John
353 356
DUPERRE, Francis 34 Pierre 24
29 33-4 Peter 308
DUPLESSIS, Freeman 312
DU PONT-GRAVE, 25-6
DURAN, Joseph 361
DUREN, W E 383
DURFREE, Amos 119
DURGIN, Wm 387
DURHAM, James 364 Lord 117
DURKEN, Patrick 33
DURNING, Charles 321
DURPHY, Wm 370
DUSETT, Pherman 308 Francis
308
DUTCH, Jonathan P 384
DUTTON, Samuel 384
DWELLEY, Luther 316 Wm Jr361
DWINAL, Calvin 391 Rufus 391-
93
DWYER, Lt Col 248
DYER, Edward 329 Jones 79-80
Jones Jr 378 Thompson 359
EASLER, James 396
EASTMAN, Benjamin 361 Benja-
min D 396 Benjamin F 264 El-
bridge G 327 John 398 Otis 396

EASTWOOD, Daniel 330
EATON, A B 326 Andrew 352
Hiram 320 Jonas 319 Levi 352
Joseph178 Gen Wm 31
ECCLES, Capt 367
EDDY, Jonathan 394
EDWARDS, John 138
EDGERLY, Daniel W 361 Eben
355
EDGETT, Hiram 370
EDMINSTER, Job 319
EDWARDS, Ed I 334
EGAN, Richard 400
EGERY, Thomas 393
ELBERT, Andre 312
ELDRIDGE, James S 361
ELLINGWOOD, John 364
ELLIOT, James 320 Levi 370
Wm 316
ELLIS, Charles 315 352 Josiah
397 Leonard H 397 Nathan Jr
178 Robert 369 Samuel 318
Sweet 318 Wm 397
ELKINS, John 352 John Jr 361
ELLWOOD, ___ 344
ELWELL, Stephen C 352
EMERSON, Albert 393 Charles
361 381 Ensign 359 Gilbert 361
Isaac D 357 John 312 345
Joseph 361 Levi 359 Seth 382
Wm 202 361 385 387-88 391
EMERTON, Amasa S 361
(Hill &) Emerton372
EMERY, Ambros 357 Daniel 388
Daniel F 381 Emery 343 John B
361 Miles 312 Nicholas 55 80
152 Rufus 357 Seth 386
Thomas 354-356 390
EMMONS, Frederick 310 Micah
P 357
END, W 356 373
ENEAS, Francis 111
ENGERSON, Levi 352

ESSENA, David 343 Reuben 343
ESTEY, A 372 Ebenezer 315 396
Hiram 310 Holland 92 Hyrum
319 Wm J 92
EUSTIS, Brig Gen 319 329-33
EVANS, David 391 Elisha 352
George 78 110 193 278
EVELETH, Elisha M 361
EVERETT, Edward 192 Job 316
396 402 404 Mary Ann 396
EVINS, Green 319
EWELL, Dodge N 364
FAIRBANKS, ___372 Dennis 72
85 132 309 316 347-48
Captain 155 156 Jesse 356 Mr
211 226
FAIRBROTHER, Jonathan 315
FAIRFIELD, Anna 123-24
Ephriam 315 John 110 124-25
128 136 138 140-41 144 148
150-52 154 160-61 166 168
183 192 199 203-05 214 221-
22 228 230 232 237 240 247
252 260 262-63 271-72 278
284 286 290
FAIRWEATHER, Samuel 370
FALES, Thomas 316
FALL, John B 393
FAREWELL, Charles 315 Wm 321
FARIHER, John 352
FARLEY, John 310 Samuel
Farley 402 404 Samuel Farley
402 Samuel Farley 316
FARNAM FARNHAM, John 357
Putnam J 381
FARNSWORTH, Peter G 379
FARRAR, Isaac 377-88 391
John Farrar 352 Jonathan 387-
88 391 Samuel 387 389 Sewell
352 Seth 311 317
FARRELL, Michael 344 Henry 314
FARREN, Chester Farren 361

FAULKNER, David 369 John 370
Luther 389 Patrick 322
FEATHERSTONHAUGH, G W
265-6
FEIRIO, Wm 47
FELLOWS, Nathaniel 360
FELPS, Alvin 352 Cyrus A 352
FENDERSON, David [Daniel?] 316
Daniel 397 Lavinia 397
FERGUSON, Robert 370 Oliver
358
FERNALD, J A 335 John A
Fernald 319 Josiah 389
FERNANDEE, C 126
FERRIS, John 330
FESSENDEN, Wm P 278
FIELD FIELDS, George 53-4 316
324 Henry C 352 Thomas 321
395 Wm 316
FILLEBROWN, Wm C 352 356
FILLEMORE, Wm 370
FINLAND, Patrick 398 404
FINLEY, Patrick Finley 316
FINNEMORE, Abraham 248
FINNEY, John 395
FISH, Ansel 352 Ira 146 356
377 385 398 Ira D 398 Jacob
387 Samuel 178 229 361
Stephen 359 Zeddock 352
FISHER, Alonzu 396 Charles 373
Hermon 386 Joseph 396 402
404 Thomas 329 Wm 318
FISK FISKE, Benjamin 385
James B 385 390 393 John 393
FITCH, John 321 Wm F 387
FITTS, Andrew G 358
FITZ, Charles T 357
FITZGERALD, James 330 Owen
343 Wm 397 399
FITZHERBERT, James 132 133-
35 143 176 214 309 316 348
Jonas 235 Samuel 396
FLAGG, Josiah 382

FLANDERS, Reuben 358-59
FLANNERY, John 402 404
Patrick 402 404 T 402 Thomas
402 404
FLEMING, Wm 370
FLETCHER, Amos 34 Asa 33
Captain 34 Nathan C 125 264
Oliver 321
FLEWELLEN, George 318
FLINT, Andrew I 398 James 398
James A 398 Royal 30
FLOYD, Daniel 352 387
FLY, J G 335
FOGG, Greenleaf M 360 John
M 360
Peleg 358 Samuel 315
FOLEY, James 312
FOLSOM, Andrew 364 John
H 387
FORBES, Charles H 361 Wm 385
FORD, John 354 Elijah 322 John
356 John P 371
FORNIER, Joseph 312
FORSYTHE, (Gilbert&) Forsythe
370 John 103, 162 165
FOSS, Alfred 314 Christopher
319 Joseph 311 322 Richard
317
FOSTER, Albert 387 A M 381
Cyrus W 381 David 319 398
Ezekiel 153 218 380-81
Ezekiel Gilbert 382 Foster
(&Norton)380 Francis 397
Jabez W 378 J B 393 Jeremiah
381 Jeremiah Jr 380-81
Marcellus L 397 Merritt C 317
Nancy 397 Robert Jr 378
Stephen C 264
FOUNDS, J 369
FOWLER, Jeremiah 379 Matthew
382 Peter 309 316 349 Samuel
370 Wm 379
FOWLES, Daniel 361

FOX, H S 97 100 102-04 106
117 162 165 218 275 Joseph
317 Fox(& Libby) 402 Michale
330
FOY, John 371
FRANCIS, Joseph 360
FRANKLIN, Benjamin 283 285
292 M 335
FRASER, J 371 James D 371
FRAZIER, Alex 67 Peter 39 91
FREEMAN, Asa 387 David 346
Pliny 391 Wm 383
FREEZE, Retire 384 Samuel 373
FRENCH, Aaron 352 Dr 334 Dr D
E 333 Ebenezer 386 Ezekeil 319
John A 389 Joseph D 352 Lt 335
Matthew H 390 W H 331 332
334 335
FRINK, James 372
FRISBY, Jacob 319 Samuel 319
Timothy 319
FROSHEY, Otis 322
FROST, Aaron 381 Albion 155,
177 183 202-05 216 230 263
Dr 160 Charles 381 Frances
322 Oliver 394 397
FRY, Samuel 372
FULLER, Frederick A 390
Joshua 388
FULLERTON, George W 358
FULTON, Joshua 318
FURBER, Thomas 354
FURBUSH, Noah 318
FURLONG, Samuel 383
FURNAL, Solomon 352
FURZE, Joseph 310 318
GAGNE, Anthony 308
GAGNON, Alexander 400 Antoine
400 Francis M 400 Prudent 400
402 Thomas 400
GALES, Solon 352

GALLAGHER, Cornell 314
Francis 348 John 402 J S 326
Martin 235 Michael 235
GALLANG, Thomas 371
GALLATIN, Albert 22 44 75 190
GALLAUGHN, John 403
GALUSHA, Alexander 336-37
GAMBEEN, Cornelius 39 99 C 403
GAMBLE, Alexander 320
Alexander 2nd 320
GANDREAU, Paschal 400
GARDINER, ___ 348 George 389 John 312 400 Nathan 316 Thomas 92 Wm 127
GARDNER, Bela 309
John 400 Samuel J 382 Wm 399
GARLAND, Benjamin 386 Edward F 397 Elhanan 394 Horatio 315 Samuel 15
GARNIER, Ave 313
GARVEY, John 319
GATES, E C 383 Salmon 378
GAVAH, Augustus 308 John B 308
Battiste 313
GAY, Benjamin 388 Ijay Gay 390
GEARY, Daniel 330
GELBERT, Edward 400
GENTRY, Wm 330
GEORGE, Obadiah 364 Stephen D 364 Timothy 38
GERAL, Daniel 358
GERMAT, ___ 313
GEROW, Abraham 310 318 Isaac 310 Joseph 318
GETCHELL, David 360
GIBBS, Wm 306 Wm H 178
GIBERSON, A 404 Alfred 402 John 372 Julia Ann 402
GIBSON, Nathan 310

419

R 372 T 372 Wm H 319
GILBERT, Gilbert (&Forsythe) 370 Thomas 373
GILKEY, Freeman 319 Samuel B 321 Wm 311 Wm B 319
GILLELAND, George 312
GILLIGAN, Edward 379
GILLSON, Charles 311 Thomas 311
GILMAN, Alvin B 390 John S 396-97 Jesse 312 Joseph 178 Joseph or Jesse 321 Wm A 356
GILMANTON, I P 327
GILMORE, D 372 James H 361
GILMOUR, Gilmour (Rankin&Co) 371
GILPATRICK, Thomas 311 322
GINN, Wm H 357
GIVENEY, T 404 Thomas 402
GIVERSON, Alfred 402
GLASIER, Stephen 371
GLASS, Moses 403
GLEASON, Jesse 379
GLENELG, Lord 100-01 106 220
GLIDDEN, Ephriam 360 John 358 Otis 352
GLORIN, James 313
GODAIN, Daniel 313 Joseph 313
GODDARD, Henry 381 John 392-93
GODFREY, Andrew 384 Mr 43
GODING, Amasa 396-97 Wm 397
GODROW, Newell 313
GOLDEN, ___ 324
GOLDIE, Col 185-86 219-20
GOLDTHRITE, Jacob 52
GOLDTHWAITE, ___ 324
GONYOU, Antoine 313 Bosal 313
GOOCH, Benjamin Jr 378 Samuel 319
GOODALE, Ephriam Jr 386
GOODENOUF, Joseph 308 312 322

GOODENOW, Joseph 312
GOODHUE, Nathaniel 320
GOODNIGHT, Jacob 310 318
GOODRICH, Jesse W 382
GOODWIN, Benaiah 383 Chapman 390 (Jere?) 310 Jeremiah 125 236 Wm 382
GORDING, Wm P 399
GORDON, Ebenezer H 358 Stillman 397 Wm F 400
GORE, Martin 382
GORNIER, Jerome 313
GOSFORD, Lord 118
GOSLAND, Rice 319
GOSS, Cyrus 389 393 John T 397 Mr 85 132 Thomas 309 315 347 Thomas Jr 315 399
GOSSELIN, Anthony 401
GOTERO, John 370
GOULD, Alvin 319 C P 383 Horace I 358 Isaiah 319 Joseph 359 370 Oliver 312 321 Samuel 312 Thomas 360
GOUVAIN, Christopher 313
GOVE, Elijah 322
GOVIN, Joseph 400
GOWEN, Robert 92
GRACE, Cyprian 344
GRAFTON, Henry D 341
GRAGG, John 329
GRAHAM, Andrew 321 James D 267 Major 113 338
GRANDER, Stephen 352
GRAND-PIERRE, 29
GRANGER, Joseph 382
GRANT, Andrew 315 Giles C 363 James 318 Samuel 310 318
GRANTHAM, George 315
GRASS, Moses 402
GRAVES, Thomas 352
GRAY GREY, Ephriam 357 George 383 Hiram 352 Jacob R 371 Justus 316 402 Robert 330 Shadrach 361
GREELY, Anna 99 Council 99 Ebenezer S 97-101 103-106 108-109 Esther (Moore) 99 Lucinda 99 Sarah 99
GREEN GREENE, Abraham 318 Charles F 379 Franklin 383 Franklin Jr 389 George G 149 157 James 335 Joseph 317 John H 319 Roscoe 89 Simon P 387 T 329 331 Tim 332 340 Wm 310 318
GREENELL, Moses S 352
GREENLAW, ___ 323
GREENLEAF, Jonathan 310-11 317 Moses 73
GREENLIEF, Luther H 387
GREENOUGH, John R 388
GREENWOOD, Harrison G O 397
GREER, Seth 391
GRELAND, J H 336
GREW, James 313 400
GRIBBIN, Peter R 358
GRIFFIN, George M 329
GRIFFITH, Edward 329 Rear Adm 14
GRIMES, Hugh 312
GRINDEL, David R W 359 John 361
GROSS, James 98 Christopher? 319
GROVER, Henry 314 Stephen 45 343
GUAY, Frances 397
GUERETTE, Marie A 400
GUIGEY GUIGGEY, Alexander 402 404 Boynard 316 Brinard 402 Edward 401-02 404 James 316 402 404
GUILD, Moses 387
GULLIER, Francis 309
GULLIFER, Thomas 360

GUPPY, Wm P 362
GUPTALL, John P 352
GUTHRIE, Samuel 322
HAFFORD (See Harford)
HACKER, Isaac 396
HAGAN, James 344
HAGGERTY, John 370
HAGGITA, Peter 321
HALE, Albert 317 Dennis 398
403 Dexter A 397 Elias 387
Elisha 403 398 Franklin 343
Joseph H 389
HALES, Wm 389
HALEY, Samuel 387 Wm 398 404
HALL, Daniel B 357 E C 310 318
Ephriam 317 George H 364
James S 383 John F H Josiah
315 357 Luther 381 Silvanus
352 Thomas 311 Tobias 378
381 Tobias A 379 Wentworth
319
HALLETT, Wm 324
HALLOWELL, Abner R 394
HALSEY, Robert 384 Stephen A
391
HAM, Abner 318 Daniel 352
James 318 John 388 Solomon
352
HAMBLET, Capt C R 209
HAMBLETON, Rufus 321
HAMILTON, Alexander, 190 283
Charles 384 James 311 John C
320 Richard 320 Sumner 360
Wm 316
HAMLEN, Cyrus 380
HAMLIN, Elijah 126 128 157
178 226 Elijah L 356 389
Hannibal 125 129 264
HAMMAT, Wm 388
HAMMOND, Abraham 346 Andrew
313 Augustus 352 Charles 402

404 Charles H 388 James 310
318 Lt Gov 81 Joseph S 387
HANCOCK, Lewis 356
HANCOCK GUARDS, 238
HANESY, James 322
HANNING, Joseph 371
HANNINGTON, Daniel 373 Wm Jr 371
HANSCOMB, John 356
HANSON, J 352
HARDEN HARDIN HARDING,
Amaziah 322 David 314 Jared
387 Patrick 310 318 319
HARDIE, James A 337-38
HARDIS, J A 336
HARDISON, Hiram 397 Ivory 399
Oliver A 399
HARDY, Joseph 352
HARFORD HAFFORD HARTFORD
HAYFORD, __ 342-43 __ 355
George 33 John 33 37 86 89
308 343 400 John Jr 313 343
Phineas 33 47 313 343 Randall
91 343
HARIT, Thomas 371
HARLOW, Wm B 394
HARMON, Abial 362 David 317
HARPER, Charles 329
HARRINGTON, J 383 Nathaniel
310 318 Wesley 352
HARRIS, George 380 Hezekiah
322 Jairus 358 John C 399
Peter T 380 Stephen 396 399
HARRISON, Wm H 7 277
HARROW, Jacob 307
HART, George 307 Samuel K 388
HARTGROVE, Charles, 248
HARVEY, Asa 234 Francis 313
John G 327 Lt Col Sir John 6 98
100-04 106-07 117-18 (137)
138-41 143-46 152 154 157
172 185-86 188 194-96 198
210 218-25 235 (250) 251 258

260 266 269-71 368-69 374
Reuben 396
HARVIE, J M 328
HASEY, __ 115 Andrew W 388
John 348 Joseph395 Wm 319
HASKELL, Alonzo 319 Edward
322 John 311 Nathaniel 352
Zelotes 319
HASKINS, J A 331-32 335
Joseph 337 Joseph A 337 J S
333-335
Lt Haskin 338 Romulus 386
HASLETT, George 319
HASSARD, Thomas 390
HASTINGS, James 388 Luke 319
HATCH, Harvey 390 Nathaniel
386 391 Wm P 360
HATFIELD, David 369
HATHAWAY, Calvin 369 J S 333
335 John H 337-38 John S 337
Lt 334-35
HATHORN HATHORNE, Benjamin
352 Russel 352
HATTON, Nathan 355
HAVEN, Joseph B 318
HAWES HAWS, Benjamin 397
Wm B 178 363
HAWKS, James 314
HAWKSHAW, Captain185 W 136
HAYDEN, Aaron 379 Elias 398
Freeman 396 Samuel 398
HAYES, Charles 389 John314
John L 393 Jonathan 312 320
Newton 379 (Trew?) 330
HAYFORD (see Harford Hafford),
HAYNES, Aaron 356 Allen 202
Alvin 356 J C 240-41 Mr 177
Nathaniel 385 Stephen P 361
HAYWARD, George 373
HAYWOOD, Albion P 319 Joseph
383 Joshua 383 Willmoth 361
HAZEN, Moses 28

HEALD, Amos 316 Dennis 316
Isreald 352
HEALEY, Wells 390
HEARD, Henry 316
HEART, James 235
HEATH, Isaac 356 John A 357
HEBERT, Fearmer 67 Leazel 313
Simon 27 62 87 88 126-27 342
372
HENDERSON, Alexander P 371
Edward 311 319 John 313 400
Patrick Jr 371 Sewell 395
HENEY, Archibald 379
HENLEY, Thomas 330
HENNIGAR, John 370
HENRY IV, 25
HERRICK, George S 360
Wentworth 310 318
HERRIN, Appleton 352
HERRINGTON, Charles 319
HERSEY, Elijah 320 Franklin
356 Samuel F 377 394
HERVEY, David 352 Joseph B
389
HESSELTINE, John E 386 Peter H
386
HETZEL, Abner R 326-28
HEWES HEWS, Benjamin 397
Caroline P 397 Garrett 319
Stephen 397 Wm 319
HEWITT, Wm 330
HEYWOOD, Charles349
HICHBORN, Nathan 364
HICKEY, John 315 346-47 396
HICKS, Benjamin 316
HIGGING, John L 404
HIGGINS, Bradford 360 David Jr
352 Dyer 352 John L 402 404
HILFERTY, John 388
HILL, A 372 Aaron 394 Abraham
372 388 Bennett H 330-31 B H
333 D H 335 340 George 372-
72 George A 372 Hill (&Emer-

ton) 372 Horatio N 384 James 327-28 J B 389 John 393 John B 387 393 J M 328 L 372 Lt 332 S 372 Sewall 398 Thomas 202 Thomas A 385-86 388 390 Thomas H 384 (Todd&) Hill 372 Wiggins 385 388 390
HILLMAN, Samuel 359
HILLS, Luther H 384
HILTON, Daniel 318 Silas 321
HINCH, Robert 322
HINCKLEY HINKLEY, Andrew 381 Daniel 393 John 379 Joshua 379 Mary Ann 393 Samuel B 393
HINDS, Wm 311 322
HISCOCK, Elias 319 327
HITCHAMBOW, John 308
HOAR, J 370
HOBART, James S 391 James T 382 Thomas 316 387
HOBBS, George 379 Henry 125 Isaac 379
HODGDON, John 153 202-03 281 386-88 392 Joseph 361 Moses 361 Timothy 352
HODSDON, Charles M 359 Maj Gen Isaac 107 120 147-49 154-57 177 179 185 199 201-05 208-11 213 225-28 230-32 234-41 243 245 252 386-87 John L 171 178 210
HOGAN, John 319
HOLBROOK, Henry J 383 Watson 388
HOLDEN HOLDIN, Amasa 352 Philip B 319 Ralph 310
HOLLAND, Cornelius 78 John 314
HOLMAN, David 329 John 329 Wm 316 Levi 315
HOLMES, Jeremiah 389 390

423

HOLT, Samuel H 358 Stephen D 357
HOLTON HOULTON, Harrison 319 James 307 310 319 Joseph 61 307 310 319 Samuel 307 310
HOLT, Seth 362
HOLWAY, John 380
HOLYOKE, Edward 388 Jacob 360 John 388
HOMAN HOMANS, James S 360 John 320
HOMER, Homer(&Palmer)389
HOOK, Benjamin Jr388 Josiah Jr 384
HOOKER, Joseph 325 331 J 333-34 338
HOOPER, Joshua Jr 388 Mr 85 131 Nathaniel S 316 352 Nehemiah 309 N 347 Story 346
HOOPKING, Stephen 352
HOPE & CO, 283
HOPKINS, Daniel 396 Samuel M 357
HOPKINSON, Jonathan 398
HORN, James 358
HOSKINS, Eli 390
HOUGHTON, Partmon 379
HOUSTON, Samuel 360
HOVEY, Manasseh S 360 Moses 378
HOWARD, Augustus 317 Daniel 322 Daniel H 359 Daniel M 377 Howard (&Brown) 369 James 317 Jesse 320 Leonard 393 Lewis 388 Lydia 317 Willard 318
HOWE HOWES HOW, Benjamin 396 397 Charles H 383 Estes 188 George 312 321 322 397 Simeon 379 Thomas 377 Sylvanus 310 318
HOWLAND, Charles 387

HOYT, Enoch 396 Enoch W 396
Levi 396 Melville C 396 Simeon
398
HUBBARD, Henry 387
HUDLEY, David 396
HUDSON, L 352 Samuel 388
HUGHES, John 400 Lt Gov 81
HULL, Isaac 5 Wm 5
HUMPHREY, Abel 398 403 John
370
HUNNEWELL, __ 342 Barnabas
86 88-92 127 343 Barnabi 313
HUNT, Albert G 359 S L 390
Sanford M 379 Thomas 354 Wm
314
HUNTER, Alfred 111 Francis P
318 George 330
HUNTON, Jonathan G 73-4
HUSKISSON, Wm 75
HUSSEY, Franklin 354
Batchelder 319
HUSTON, Samuel 315
HUTCHINS HUTCHINGS, Cyrus
321 Jesse 361 John 394
HUTCHINSON, Benjamin F 357
Christopher C 318 Ebenezer 395
Isaac L 318 John 318
HURD, Charles C 352 Henry 402
404 330 John 352 Manoah 360
HUXFORD, James 178
HUYLER, Martin 330
HUZZY, Miles 352
HYDE, Henry W 396 397
INGALLS, F P 202 Moses Jr 361
INGERSOL INGERSOLL, Charles J
292 George W 390 Zebulon 263
276 319 327
INGRAHAM, __ 372 John C 318
INGRAM, Robert 321
INMAN, George H 315 Richard 54
IRELAND, Benjamin 359

David G 360 Gen James 38-42
54-5 111 202 Silas 397 Silas
Jr 398
IRISH, Simeon 317
IRONS, John F 341
IRVINE, James 330 James R 330
IRVING IRWIN, I R 331-32 J R
332-35
ISAACS, C E 335 340
JACKINS, John W 318 Samuel E
318
JACKSON, Andrew 9 71 77 80
92 93-4 98 Heman S 390 Henry
30 Isaac 389 Mortimer 381 Sir
Richard Downs 277
JACOBS, Alexander 322
W 333
JAMES, Joseph 362
JAMESON, David 317 John G 356
Rufus 312 Wm 390
JARVIS, Charles 78 137 139
145-47 154-56 175 177 181
206 212 217 225-28 230-36
243 251-55 259-60 262-63
275 353 356 John H 388
Leonard 78 384 Ralph M 369
JAY, __ 292
JEFFERSON, Thomas 96 283
JELLISON, Atwell 317 David C
361
Derry P 358 Josiah 317
Theodore 382 Thomas 322 Wm
322
JENIAN, Joseph 308 Lorent 308
JENKINS, James 391-92 Thomas
360
JENNINGS, Charles 359 Stephen
D 358-59
JERMER, Jeremy 308
JEWELL, Oliver H 317
JEWETT, A G 152 229 Daniel
372 Edward D 393 George 382

George K 393 397G K 77 Luther 382
JOHNS, T 328
JOHNSON, Benjamin 390 Charles 53 132 309 347 386 Daniel 395 Edward 96 Ephriam 360 George 313 Jacob 243 356 James 396 John 31 32 313 Lewis 53 309 323 347 Mr 127 Louis 316 Pascal 313 Philip C 264 278 Robert 359 Sarah 396 Wm 316 361 Wm L 359
JOHNSTON, Daniel 401 Hugh 373-74 Jonathan 316 Lt 113 Wm 313 396
JOLLEY, Richard 319
JONES, __ 372 Amasia 386 Andrew P 321 Archibald 390 Brig Gen R 328-29 Daniel 318 Isaac 48 James 136 John 310 318 320 John H 319 Jones (&Colpitts) 370 Joseph 311 319 Leonard 315 391Richard 330 Samuel 333-35 Stephen 311 358
JORDAN, Abel S 362 Dominicus 278 Elias 314 John 373 Joseph 361 Joseph W 388 Noah 321 Richard 398 404 Sabin P 379 381
JOSIA, Betis 308 Jeremere 308
JOSLIN, T C 372
JUDKINS, __159 Benjamin 361 Jedediah H 352 353 J T 352
JUDSON, Hendrik 319
JUMPER, Charles 358-59 Cyrus 358-59 Wm 359
KARNEY, John 234-35
KAVANAGH, Edward 78 82-85 92 286-87
KEAN KEANE, Anthony 349 402 Michael 402

425

KEATON, John 344
KEEGAN, KEELEY, Michael 127 James 398 403
KEEN, Phillip 319
KEEP, Marcus 397
KEISOR, Francis C 360
KEITH, Isaiah 320
KELLAR, John 380
KELLEY, Albert L 390 Charles 358 Jeremiah 318 John F 364 L 403 Laura 309 Lawrence 316 348 402 Patrick 316 402 403 Thomas 402 Rufus 315 Samuel P 321 Shubael 317 Thomas 403
KELLOCH, Rufus G 97
KELLOGG, Eli 315
KELLY, Albert L 389 Lewis C 390 Webster 390
KELSEY, Joseph 388
KEMPTON, Seth 317
KENDALL, Green 319 John 346 Joshua 310 Joshua G 307 Joseph 310 Samuel 307
KENNEDY, Abiel W 390 Alexander 398 Thomas 313 396
KENNY, Thomas 343
KENT, Gov Edward 108-13 120 124 153 202 264 272 278 285-87 362
KERBA, Marble 313
KER KERR, Ker (&Campbell)372 Robert 310 Robert K 326
KETCH, Thomas 343
KETCHUM, __ 373 Joseph 318 Richard 137 139 R 372
KEY, Francis S 9 Thomas 330
KEYES, Elias 389 Lt 192
KIDDER, Josiah 390 Samuel 310
KILBURN, C L 336 Levi R 362
KILBY, Daniel 378-79 John 378-79 Wm 378

KIMBALL, Charles 321 Edward D
393 John 359 Joseph D 315
Thomas 318
KINEAR, George 370 Wm 374
KING, Gilman D 372 Rufus 21
Samuel T 384 Wm 10 13 15 16
36-8
KINGSBURY, J J B 328
KINGSLEY, Freeman 383
KIRBEY KIRBY, Justus 387 Major
137 146, 150-51 224 Maj R M
328-29 332 Robert 317
KIRSTEAD, Samuel 370
KITTRIDGE, George 387
KNEELAND, Ezra 352 David d361
KNIGHT, Arstron 319 [Austin?]
311 Eben 330 Ephriam 315 G
372 Joel 382
KNOWLAND, John 315 Thomas
399
KNOWLES, Isaac 355 John 309
311 397
KNOWLTON, Gilbert 362
KNOX, Gen Henry 30 Thomas 319
LABEE, Joseph 400
LABEREE, Isaac 352
LABLANCHE, Michael 313
LABLE, Francis 313
LABREE, John 313
LACKEY, Henry S 363
LADD, Alexander H 393 Charles
H 93 George W 393
LAFERRIER, George 400 Joseph
400
LALOUTRE, 27
LAMB, Nathan 320
LAMBERT, Capt 147 James 322
Jesse 364 Samuel 320
LAMORD, Louis 400
LAMPHREY, Gilman 379
LAMPTFORD, John 330
LAMSON, Samuel 397
LANAGAN, James 330 J 333

LANCASTER LANKESTER, David
362 Solomon P 361
LAND, James 359 John W 361
Mathias 361 Moses M 352 Oliver
52 Thomas 318
LANDER LANDERS, Jacob P 178
James 310 Peleg 310 319
Thomas 310 318
LANDRY, ___ 342-43 Auguste
313 Laurence 313 Paul 313
LANE, Benjamin 394 Rufus 378
LANGEVANE, Gregorie
313 Monsieur 269
LAPOINTE, Louis 313
LARASSAUS, Honerd 308
Benjamin 308
LARIBEE, Samuel M 352
LARKIN, Nicholas 314
LASELLE, Wm 362
LATES, John 370
LATHROP, Stephen 310
LAUSHIERE, Harris 308
LAWLER, Martin 314
LAWRENCE, Ambassador 64
Charles 27 Gov 28 Capt James 7
John N 362 Ronald 362
LAWRY, Zenas 388
LAWTON, John 361
LEACH, Isaac 317
LEACHEAD, Matthew 330
LEADBETTER, Samuel 111
LEAVITT LEVETT, Benjamin B
380 D F 356 Dudley 317 Dudley
F 377 394 Eliphalet 361 George
W 317 352 John 359 Joseph
384 Samuel 396 397 Silas 59
Stephen 321 Wm F 77
LEBLANC, Edward 313 Louis 400
LECLERK, Edward 313
LECOMPTE, Peter 313
LEE, Thomas 374 Thomas C 374
Wm 311
LEEBORE, Lewis 308

LEGARNIER, Ballazer 313
LEGASSE, Oliver 313
LEGGE, Lt Gov 81
LEIGHTON, Amos C 352 Capt 229 Mark 381 Seba F 359 Stephen 358
LEONARD, George 385
LEPOINTE, Oliver 401
LESHERE, Gabriel 371
LESLIE, Nathaniel 315
LETES, Wm 370
LEVASSEUR, Jules 401 Julien 401
LEVENSALER, Atwood 278
LEVEQUE, Daniel 313
LEWIS, Almond 315 Isaac 315 Oliver 329 Samuel J 381
LEWSURE, Betis 308
LEYCROFT, Wm 330
LEZERT, Peter 308
LIBBEY, James 321 Charles 357 Frances 380 Richard 321
LIBBY, David 320 John 320 John C 364 Libby and Fox 402 Wm C 352
LINCOLN, Enoch 43 44 48 50 56-9 63 65 71 73 Ephriam 389 390 George 361 John 318 John P 318 Levi 188 Levi Jr 44
LINDSAY LINDSEY, Hezekiah 318 James 318
LINTON, J 372 Thomas 399 400
LITCHFIELD, Wade 320
LITTLE, Henry 388 Henry W 352 Josiah S 389 Mark 264 Nathaniel S 278 Otis 384-85 388 Wm Jr 357
LITTON, Jacob 352
LITTLEFIELD, James 358 Robert 360
LIVINGSTON, Edward 80 90
LIVY, Peter 313
LIZERT, Louis 313 Olwan 313

427

LIZOTTE LISOTTE LEZART, Peter (Pierre) 24 82-3 86-7
LLOYD, James 248 Thomas 318
LOCK, James 315
LOGAN, Charles R 359 George P 359 John 311 320
LOMBARD, ___, 368 Ernest H 368 Wentworth 317
LONG, ___ 372 E R 328 George 313 345 James 371 Jean Baptiste 67 Long (&Gordon) 324 Marmoise 345 Memen 313 Phillip 345 Robert 388
LONGBOY, Michel 313
LONGFELLOW, Jacob 380 Nathan 380
LONGLEY, Asa 358 Edward P 359
LORD, Horace 361 Jacob 317 Jeremiah 178 Joseph 387 Nathaniel 314 389 393
LOTHROP, Stephen 318
LOUCE, Joseph 13
LOUDER, Jonathan 178
LOUGEE, Simeon 321
LOURING, John 320
LOVEJOY, John 330 Wm 315
LOVELAND, Isaac 322
LOVELESS, Wm349
LOVELY, John 316 402 404 Wm 309 316
LOVETT, Alfred S 361
LOVEWAY (Lavoie?), Edward 313 John R 313 Laurence 313
LOVIS, Ambrose 381
LOWDER, Jonathan 360 Samuel 385 Samuel Jr 385 Wm 385
LOW LOWE, Daniel 355 Elijah Jr 160 214 John Jr 389 Joshua A 162 278 Wm G 355
LOWELL, Barnabas T 383 Charles 356 J A 380 Joshua A 380 Levi L 382 Wm 356
LUCAS, Wm K 388

LUMBERT, Enoch R 178
LUNDY, Wm 402 404
LYFORD, Fifield 178
LYLE, John 330
LYMAN, James W 379
LYONS, Alpheus 125 264 Charles 310 318 Jeremiah 310 318 Jul 310 318 Mikiel 322 Timothy 332-33
MACKAY, Mr 127
MACKENZIE, Wm L 117 118 122
MACLAUCHLAN, James A 5 72-3 84 91-2 100 111 132 135-36 144 157 172 174 248 250-51 257-58 260 270
MACNAB Col Alan 119
MACNUTT, W S 366
MCALLEAN, Patrick 330
MCALLESTER, Wm 383 John P 384
MCALLISTER, John Jr 372 John Sr 372 S B 354
MCALMON, D 373
MCBRINE, James 320
MCCANN MCCAN, Robert 348 398
MCCANNERY, Robert 352
McCARON, James 377
MCCARTHY, Michael 332 M M 333
MCCARTY, Mitchell 316
MCCASLIN, Andrew 310 318 Elexander 320
MCCLAIN, Luther 352
MCCLAREN, Adam N 337-38
MCCLUSKY, Charles 320
MCCORMICK, Charles 399
MCCOLLISTER, Abiel 315
MCCOLLUM, Malcolm 318
MCCONDAR, Ephriam 307
MCCONDRAY, Ephriam B 360
MCCORISON, Sylvanus B 355

428

MCCOY, James 235
MCCRATE, Mr 162-63
MCCREA, ___ 313 Wm 53
MCCRILLIS, WM H 178 210 377 393
MCCURDICK, John 317
MCCURE, Peter 308
MCDANIEL, Henry 313 Thomas 315
MCDERMOTT, Michail 330
MCDONALD, Isaac 316 John 393-94 402 404 Thomas 399 Widow 313 Wm 310 318 320
MCDONNOUGH, Com 22
MCDOODLE MCDOUGAL MCDOUGALD, Alex 309 316 349 E 384 Peter 309 349
MCDOWELL, Lt 325 329 Irvine 339 Irwin 332 J 331
MCELTHONE, Felix 330
MCFADDEN, McFadden (&Marten) 370
MCFARLAN MCFARLAND, George 336 George W 358 Samuel 372
MCFARSON, Charles 313
MCGAFFEY, Samuel 390
MCGARY, James 320
MCGAW, Jacob 385 Thornton 386
MCGEE, Wm 330
MCGILVERY, Hugh 397
MCGLAUGHLIN, B 402 Daniel 402 Sarah 402 404 Thomas 399 400
MCGLINCH(Y), James 311
MCGOULICK, James 330
MCGREGOR, Wm 329
MCGROUTY, Wm 320
MCGUIRE, John 345 Solomon 352
MCINESTER, Daniel P 394
MCINTIRE, Rufus B 78 125 130-32 134-38 142-44 150 152 175-77 205-08 211-12 233-34

240 243 247 260-61 264 355
Samuel 316 Theodore B 390
MCINTOSH, __ 356 I M 333 John
310
MCKAY, Edward 343
MCKEA, Jared 315
MCKEEN, John George 391
MCKELPIN, Thomas 320
MCKENNY MCKENNIE, Cyrus 315
Isaiah 360 Isaac 315 Michael
316 Wallis 354
MCKENZIE, Capt 248 Ebenezer
399 G 372 Peter 397
MCKINNEY, Isaac 352 Jonas 320
Michael 402 404
MCKINSEY, John 378
MCKUSICK, Royal 82 Z E 382
MCLAGGEN, (Dock&) McLaggen
371 McLaggen (&MCLean) 372
MCLAIN, Thomas 398
MCLANE, Louis 95
MCLAREN, A N 332-35
MCLAUCHLIN, Bernard 349
Daniel 349
MCLAUGHLIN, Barnard 309
Barney 316 Daniel 309 James
385 Wm 390
MCLEAN, (McLaggen&) McLean
372
MCLEOD, Alex 119 275 John Wm
373 McLeod(&Campbell) 371
MCMAHON, David 330
MCMAHONE, Michael 330
MCMAN, John 314
MCMILIN, James 329
MCMULLEN, Daniel 320
MCNAMARA, John 314 Miss 158
MCNEAL, John 330
MCNEIL, David 317
MCNELLY, James 309
MCPEACE, Daniel 400
MCPHERSON, __ 372 Charles
89 344 James 344

429

MCPHETERS, Josiah 361 Samuel
361
MCRAE, Andrew 347 John 370
Wm 344 347
MCSHEA, Patrick 396
MCTOSH, James G 361 Wm 361
MCVAY, John 370
MCVICAR, John 320
MACHIN, Catherine 320
MACKALL, Wm W 333 339
W W 331-32
MACOMB, Adams 354
MACUMBER, James 352
MADDEN, James 329
MADDOCKS MADDOX MATTOCKS,
Amos 86 89 91 343 Joseph 218
247 356
MADISON, Dolley (Cutts) 123
President James 4 16
MADORE, Augustine 400
Benjamin 401 Francis 401
George 401
MAGRUDER, Lt John B 325 331-
35 337-38
MAHAU, Michael 314
MAHONEY, Margaret 320
MALISEETS, 24
MALONE, James 345
MALLORY, Mary 320
MALY, James 313
MAN MANN, John 320 Michael
308 Thomas 362
MANSER MANCER MANZER,
__ 372 George 309 344 347
Reuben M 320 Rufus 320 403
MARCEAUX, Jere 313 Nicholas
313
MARCH, Leonard 377 389 397
MARKEE MARQUE MARCHEE, Paul
308 Paulite 67 Peter 45 47 53
62
MARLEY, Samuel 322

MARQUIS, Christopher 400 Paul
308 400
MARSHALL, Alfred 278 312 321
MARSTON, George F 394
MARTEN, (McFadden&) Marten
370
MARTIN MARTON, Albert 387
Andrew 308 313 Basil 313
Bazell 308 Belon 308 Billand
313 Charles 308 Chrystatine
308 Cyril 313 Francis 313
Francis Jr 308 Frederick 313
George 398 George W 398 Henry
B 358 Henry E 330 Hiliare
401Jacob 311 320James G 330
332 337 J G 333 335 337 John
313 320 John B 308 313 John
Baptiste 24 Joseph 308 313
Lawrence 313 Lt 334 Michael
3rd 308 Michele 313 Pillaud
313 Patrick 313 R 126 Raphael
87 Raze 313 Simon 308 313
Stephen 318 Thomas 313 Urbain
401 Wm 320
MARTURE, Henry 313 Louis 313
Vatel 313
MASERVE, John L 389
MASHAW, Joseph 308
MASON, Charles P 387 Dr 207
Ethan A 357 I 356 John 380
Moses 162
MASSE, John 400
MATHERSON MATHISON, John
311 315 399
MATHES, Benjamin 81 Benjamin
Jr 380
MATTHEWS, George 369
MAUL, John 330
MAUZEROLE, Joseph 27
MAXFIELD, Eliphalet 178-79
183-84 229-30 Eliphalet L 360
MAXIM, George 360 George W
178 229

MAXWELL, Col 140 151 186-87
218 223 Thomas J 322 Wm 352
MAYBERRY, Charles 330
MAYHEW, Wm 378
MAYNOR, Moses 360
MAYO, John M 387
MEAD, Noah 388
MEGGUIRE, Charles 322
MELVILLET, Melville 369
MEMET, __ Memet372
MENLASON, Pierre 26
MENZIES, Archibald 369
MERCHANT, Wm Y 398
MERCURE MARKURE, Joseph 308
Lewis 308 Louis 24 29 Michael
24 Michael 308
MEREAU, A 313
MERRILL, George W 361 James
317 Joshua 321 Leander A 352
Nathan L 390 Wm B 352 Wm P
352
MERRITHEW, Anthony 235 James
235
MERRITT, Western 379 Weston
381
MERRYFIELD, Alvin 360
MICHAUD, Antoine 401 Battis
51 Benjamin 401 Daniel 99
Ellebert 400 Ettienne 400
Eugene 400 Joseph 308 343
Paschal 400 Raphael 67
MICHEAUX MIJEAUX MIZEAU
MICHEAUX, Andre 313 Cephas
313 Charles 313 Edwin 313
Freeman 313 James 313 Joseph
313 Laurient 313 Marcel 313
Rean 313 Romaine 91 Seriam
313
MIELLE, Miselle 29
MILES, __ 372 Jesse 387 Josiah
361
MILLER, Alexander 322 A Q M
229 Asa 352 Charles W 157

Edward W 50 52 62 89 91
Eliphalet 178 John 352 John E
362 Wm 92
MILLETT, Isaac 352 John 352
Wm 352
MILLIKEN, D 372 Mr 185
Nathaniel 125 Robert 399
MILLS, Thomas 335 Wm H 178
201 209 245
MILTON, Frances 311 321
MIRESHIRE, John 308
MITCHELL, Edward 390 Elijah S
364 John 23 292
MONCTON, Colonel 28
MONROE, Edmund 381 404
Edward 403 Hugh 370 James
21-2 36 John 388
MONTGOMERY, Henry 362
MOODY, Carleton P 361 Rufus
361 Wm B 362
MOOR, Alexander 320 Daniel Jr
322 Jerome 321 Wyman B S 393
MOORE, Benjamin 357 Cyrus
377 David 311 317 G M 388
Isaac W 357 James W 379 383
Levi 352 Robert 355 Samuel
383 Wm 310 311
MOORES, Wm 358
MORE, Jerome 329
MOREAU, Joseph 313 Louis 313
MOREHOUSE, ___ 372 George
46-8 54 62 John 235
MOREY, George 389 Philip 320
Solomon 358
MORGAN, J B 390 John 361 John
S 352
MORIO, Jereman 308 Jarom 308
MORISON, Dorilis 393 Edmund
312 Samuel, 273 Stephen 397
MORRELL, George 320 Ichabod
315 Micajah 307

431
MORRILL, Amos 355 Anson P
395 Frederic 361 Louis 310
318
MORRIS, Abraham 178 Abram
357 Batis 308 Calvin 398
Captain 14 Isaac 316 398
Thompson 326-28
MORRISON, Allen 320 Edmund
321 Isaiah 308 312 321 L E 326
Samuel 308 312 321 Samuel Jr
308 312 321 Sol 334 Stephen
308 312 Wm 321
MORSE, Aaron 388 Lyman 387
Samuel A 380
MORTON, C F 326 Charles F 69
Randal(Moulton?) 364
MORSE, Ezekiel 355
MOSHER, S & P 369
MOSIER, George 398
MOULTON, Daniel 360 Solomon
390
MOWE, Robert 380
MOWRY, Jabez 378 Martin 349
MUDGE, Richard Z 265-66
MUDGET, Simon 355
MULLEN, Edward 330 Wm 313
400
MULLIGAN, Edward 336
MUMFORD, Nehemiah 309 Wm
346
MUNROE, J 372
MUNSEN MUNSON, Joel 397
Rufus 403
MUNY, John 330
MURCH, Benjamin 355
MURPHY MURPHEY, ___ 344
Collingwood 316 402-3 John
398 404 S 384
MURRAY, C 372 Gov 81 Martin
316 396 402 404 Samuel 364
MUSAROD, Frederic 313
MUSSEY, Charles 382
MUZEROLL, Francis 401

MUZZY, Nathaniel 352 Rufus 352
MYRICK, Esia 315 Lendall 355
Nathaniel 358
NADARD, Firmen 308
NADEAU NEDEAU NEDDO, Aime
400 Cafrot 400 David 313
Freeman 313 John 313 Joseph
313 400 Joseph 269 Joseph 2nd
400 Louis 313 401 Oliver 313
Thomas 400 Wezaw 51
NARY, Thomas W 395
NASH, Amaziah 382
NASON, Israel 317 James 379
NAUMAN, George 330-34
NEAL NEIL, Danie 311 317
NEALEY, Daniel D 364
NEDAR, Benjamin 308
NEDOW, Joseph 308
NEECCHOSON [see Nickerson],
Ely 308
NELSON, Admiral 2 Alfred 111
Chaplin 317 402 Dennis 318
Ensign John 178 Joseph 317
360 Orrin 318 352
NEVERS, Alexander 371 George
92 371 John 248 Samuel 346
372
NEWCOMB, Charles 362
NEWELL, John 334
NEWMAN, Samuel 311 322
NICHOLS NICKELS, Amos 60
Asaph R 125 Jere O 381 John
395 James 316 396 Wm 379
383
NICKERSON (see Neechoson),
Free-man 365 Nathaniel 365
Shuber Jr 360 Warren 2nd 386
Wm H 386
NILES, James 321 John 320
NOBLE, Sanford 315 396-97
NOLAND, John 316
NOLEN, James 318

NORCROSS, Charles 321
Nicholas G 387
NORTON, Jabez 381 383
(Foster&) Norton380 M P 74
111 Samuel Jr 361
NOTTAGE, John 143
NOYES, Calvin L 361 J C 110
Joshua A 162 George 357
NUGENT, Thomas 345
NYE, Alvin 154-55 227 231-32
235 251-52 254-58 260-61
David 386 Timothy Jr 354-55
386 Wm 320
O'BRIEN, Henry 330 James 330
335 Michael 310
O'BRINE, Mitchel 320
O'CONNOR, John H 330
O'DONNELL, Hugh 330
O'NEAL, Edward 344-45 John
344
O'ROOKE, James 360
OAKLEY, Thomas J 391
OAKS OAKES, Ebenezer 395
Electus 313 344 George 359
George W 352 Israel 311 320
John 316
ODELL, Wm F 46 374
OLIVER, David 370 Nelson 320
OLUDE, Joseph 313
ORFF, Simon 360
ORCUTT, John G 357
ORN, Rufus 320
ORRACH, James L P 383
OSBORN, Thomas 307 310
OSGOOD, Almon E 355 Alva 362
L H 389
OTIS, John 285-87
OTTY, Allan 369
OUELETTE OUILETTE, Antoine
400 John Baptiste 400-01
Joseph 401 Julien 401 Louis
345 Wm 400

OUTHOUSE, John 310 318
Nicholas 318
OVERLOCK, Christopher 358
Martin 358
OWEN, John 320 Wm Fitz-Wm 373
OWENS, John 309
PACET, Frances 313
PACKARD PACKERD, Andrew K 399 Ansel 399 David 318
Eleazer 308 320 George 399
George W 399 Shepard 399
Thomas P 318
PAGE, David 157 Horatio N 388 Jere 354 Moses S 361 Norman 360
PAINE, Enoch 389 George 330 358 Jonathan 318 Zebulon 379
PALMER, __ 372 Ambrose 399 Courtland 93 Daniel 359 (Homer&) Palmer 389 Jonathan 315 Philip 370 373 Wm H 358
PALMERSTON, Lord 77 107 265-66 283
PAPINEAU, Louis J 117-18 122
PARADIS, Luke 401 Octave 401 Peter 313Remi 401 Vanson 313
PARENT, Solomon 372
PARK PARKS, David 348 David O 402 D O 403 George 320 402 George F 403 Gorham 108 202-03 267 272 312 Hannah 402-03 Jonathan 309 316 402 Joseph 320 348 Roderick R 362 Rufus 386 Thomas 320
PARKER, Christopher 335-36 Edwin 315 Eleazer 310 John349 Mrs 309 Neville 374 Oliver 389 Robert 374
PARLIN, Jonas 278
PARON, John M 313
PARQUEE, Paulet 313
PARR, Lt Gov 81

433

PARRIS, Gov Albion K 39 41-4 61 Virgil D 162 278
PARROTT, __ 354 Wm P 111-12 130 206 233 235 243-44 246-47 259 389 353 356
PARSER, John B 308
PARSON PARSONS PERSON, Budd 384 Charles 352 Job 354 John 360 Moses 320 Solomon 387 389 Wm 20 315 Wm D 377
PARTELOU, Henry A 373 John R 373
PARTRIDGE, Jesse 402-03 John 330
PATTEE, Stephen 395-96
PATTEN, Amos Patten385 389 Charles 362 George W 327-28 Moses 385 Moses Jr 389 Willis 389 390
PATTERSON, George G 360 Isaac 365 Otis 382 Samuel 360
PAULEY, T W 335
PAYSON, John 92
PEABODY, George A 379 Stephen 371
PEARL, John344
PEARLEY, Jacob 315
PEARSON, John 370
PEASE, Elija 352 Warren 352
PEASLEY, Enoch 360
PEAVEY, Charles 379 380 Hiram 358 John J 380 Jonathan 358
PECK, Joseph 370 Elias 370
PEEL, 283
PELCHEY, M Nicholas 308
PELKAY PELKEY, Alexander 313 Augustes 313 Isaac 399 Joseph 308 Ran 308
PELKET, Eluy 313
PELLETIER, Charles 400 Cirville 400 Joseph 400 Marie E 400
PELTIRE, Nicholas 308 Nicholas Jr 308 Peter 308

PENDERGAST, John 345
PENDLETON, James H 365 Nathan 394
PENNIMAN, Jacob 378 Wm F 380
PENNINGTON, James 352
PENROSE, James W 328
PERCE, Martin 352
PERKINS, Charles 382 Gordon 357 Jarvis 22 Robert 388 Stover 361 Thomas 365
PERLEY, Aaron 318 Frederick 311 Moses H 368
PEROT, Lavier 313
PERRINGTON, James 320
PERRY, George 389 Oliver H 7
PERSONS, Elisha 63
PERRY, Isaac 370 John 314
PETERS, Charles 100 374 Edward D 393 James 370 Harry 374 John 384 Marcus 322 Peters (& Wilmot) 342 372 Solicitor General 4 Wm 318 Wm Tyng 374
PETIT, Luke 318
PETTEE, Stephen 320
PHILBRICK, Gilman 318
PHILBROOK, Colonel 228 Jason R 358
PHILLIPS, Alphred 352 Governor 26 Robert 372
PHILPOT, M__ 312
PHINNEY, John 315
PHIPPS, Samuel 383 Stephen E 397 Wm 383 389
PICKARD PICKERD, __ 372 Ames 178 Gilbert 401 Eleazer 307 Jacob 321 Morris 235
PICKERING, Daniel 359
PICKETT, Gould 370
PIERCE, Abraham 308 310 320 Amos 308 Benjamin L 315 B K 331-34 George 384 Heywood 386 389 Leonard 320 378 Lt

Col 333 Parker H 389 Samuel 362 Waldo 390 Waldo T 386 389 390 393
PIKE, Colonel 217 Elijah 157 Freeman 321 James S 382 Robert 378 Sergeant 70 Wm Pike 379 382
PILES (see Pyles)
PILKAY, John 313
PILSBURY, Daniel 384 Edmund 387 J H 134-35 137 John H 377 N O 389 Peter 358
PINE, Pine (& Porter) 372
PINGREE, Asa 393 David 393 Thomas P 393
PINNET, Thomas 400
PIPER, George 352 Stephen 352
PIQUET, Francis 313
PITCHER, Jonathan Jr 359 Lt 245
PLEIDE PLIEDE, Marin 313 Peter 313
PLEURD, Louis 400
PLUE, Peter 313
PLUMMER, Aaron 318 Bidfield 178 363 George 352 Jonathan 18
PLUNKET, Peter 314
POINSETT, Joel R 113-14 191
POITIER, family 27
POLIS, Joseph 111
POLLARD, David 344 Stillman 318 Joseph 315 356 376 Mr 146 Wm 311
POLLOCK, Thomas 345
POMEROY (see Pumroy), Cyrus 395 James 316
POND, Asa A 382 George 312 Sabin 384
POND'S, __ 244-45
POOR, David 311 John A 388 393

POPE, Wm 378 380 381 Wm H 380
PORTER, __ 372 Andrew 320 Benjamin 38 Colonel 353 George M 384 Giles 331 John 384 399 Joseph 177 387 356 359 Luther 31 (Pine&) Porter 372 Robert 399
PORTIS, 29
PORUS, Francis 356
POTTER, Cyril 313 Marstie 352 Oliver 352
POWERS, __ 343 Addison 396 James 309 344 349 Jonathan 355 Levi 399 Patrick 313 399 Sampson S 111 Walter 48 51 82 85 89 91 313 343 344
PRATT, Alexander 352 Benaniah 397 Benjamin 360 Charles R 397 399 David 317 Eben 382 George 360 J 372 John 361 Jonathan Horatio 359 Lawson 321 Lewellyn 399 Samuel 387 Thomas L 322 Wm 398
PRAY, John 358 Sylvester 352
PREBLE, Wm Pitt 67 75 77-8 80 286-87
PRENTISS, Henry E 178 181 183 184 210 394 James H 331 333-38 Wm 44
PRESCOTT, Jeremiah 387 Reuben S 388 R S 356
PREVOST, George 4 6 12
PRICE, Patrick 338
PRIEST, Joseph 362
PRIM, John 357
PRINCE, B K 335 Job 125 129 Lucius 352
PRITCHARD, John 311
PROCTER, Colonel 7
PROSSER, Benjamin 310
PROUTY, Lavinia 322
PUFFER, John 358

PULLEN, Stephen 310 320
PUMROY (see Pomeroy), Francis N 365 James 322
PURDY, Patrick 330
PURINGTON, James 390
PUTNAM, Aaron 159 308 310 320 Amos 308 310 320 Isaac 310 John V 317 Joshua 310 320 Joshua 2nd 310 Josiah 308 Lysander 320 Rolf 383 Romain L 320 Stern 320 Sterritt 310
PYLE PYLES PILES, Solomon 316 Solomon F 398 399 Wm 53 309 316 323 347-48 395
QUALY, Martin 314
QUIMBA, Gilman 352
QUIMBY, Lt John 178
QUIN, Ephriam 355 James M 379
QUINT, Luther 319
QUINTON, Jesse 320
RABETAI, John 313
RACLIFF RATCLIFF, __ 369 Alanson 396-97 Benjamin 321 398 Francis M 397 Joseph 398
RADIKER, John 316
RAFFORD, John 309 316 347-48 395 Thomas W 397
RAMOUX, John 313
RAMSDELL RANSDELL, Charles 386 389 John 399 401 Samuel 386 Wm 360
RAND, James 346
RANDALL, Benjamin 162 Philip 355 Stephen 312 321 Wm 352
RANKIN, Alex 373 (Gilmour,) Rankin & Co 371
RASIN, Peter 313
RAWSON, Ebenezer Gilman 177-78 229 388 E G 377 386-87
RAY, Isaac 379 Robert 370
RAYMOND, Aaron L 378 380 Andrew 410 George L 137 John

401 John E 395 Thomas 362
Washington 371
REA, John Jr 357
READ, Gardiner 319 George
384-85 Henry 352 John 317 M
352
READY, Wm 330
REDIKER, John 396 Thomas 401
REDING, Ebenezer 378
REDINGTON, Alfred
REED, Henry 317 Heywood 311
John 311 317 370 Perrin S 315
Rufus 370 Sanfield 397
Solomon E 315 Wm B 388 390
REEVES, S K 332 Isaac L 339
REINHART, Louis 313
REMICK, F S 356
REMINGTON, D 333
RENWICK, James 267
REY, Herod 313
REYNOLDS, Bela R 378 John 330
RHOADES, Francis W 390
RHODA, Samuel 319
RICE, Aaron 33 Francis 46 51 62 86-7 91 99 126 270 313 320 344 Jonas 378 (Wynn?) 317
RICH, John 311 Nehemiah 390
RICHARDS, Almon S 395 H F 72 Josiah 361 Robert 402 403
RICHARDSON, Alford 381 C&T 370 Henry 390 Joshua 382
RICKER, John 359
RICKETTS, Lt J B 325 331-32 335 James B 339
RIDEOUT, Edward 398
RIDLAND, Silas 353
RIDLON, Benjamin 353
RIEUX?, Jno 309
RIGBY, George 315
RIGGS, Wilmot 360
RILEY, Thomas 398 Wm 398

RINES, __ 354 Allen 360 Amos 356 Stover 130 144 261 273 312 353 356 390
RING, David 384 Elizabeth 327 George 384
RIPLEY, Major 192 Orison 222 269
ROACH ROACHE, John 330 Philip 310
ROBERTS ROBBERTS, Amos 384 Amos M 386 391 Freeman 391 Jesse 353 John 91 Moses 353 Samuel 358
ROBERTSON, John 372 Richard Jr 365
ROBICHAUD, Joseph 400
ROBINS ROBBINS, America 315 Lucinda 315 Walter 380 381 Wm 353
ROBINSON, __ 235 A M 356 Angus 322 Benjamin 388 Beverly 374 Charles 353-54 Charles N B 365 Chase Jr 384 Daniel 374 379 Edward 110 Frederick 374 George 311 James 353 John M 374 Lt Col 225 Oliver 315 P 374 Wm H 374
ROGERS, A 402 Alphonzo 319 398 George 370 402 402 404 J 402 James 316 353 356 John 370 Jonathan P 138 142 150-54 Michael 309 R 402 (Smith&) Rogers370 T 402 Thomas 309 349 Wm G 361 Zebadiah 385
ROI, Benoni 400 John 400
ROLF, Henry 398
ROLLINS, __ 353 Axel E 396 Franklin 356 John 322 321 Joseph 317
ROSE, A H 369 Daniel 44 73
ROUSSEAU, Pattazer 313
ROW, Charles G 353 Solomon 361 W A 353

ROWE, Benjamin 178 Edward 387
ROWELL, Hezekiah 385 H 388
RUGES, David 353
RUGGLES, John 110 162 188-89 202 Oaks 378 Wm H 378
RUSH, John D 314
RUSS, Jesse 360
RUSSEL RUSSELL, Jacob 310 311 Jacob M 317 376 James 311 320 322 J B F 69 310 John 92 271 321 402 404 Jonathan 190 Michael 316 402 Michel 349 Thomas 402 404 Wm 322
RUTH, James 321
RUTLEDGE, John 336-37
RUVIS, J K 331
RYAN, Daniel 310
John 314
ST ARMAND, Louis 401
ST AUBIN, Joseph Louis 29
ST GERMAIN (dit Ecureill), John Baptiste 401
SABINE, Eliphalet Y 379 Lorenzo 379 Wm A 379
SAFFORD, Calvin 358-59 Hiram 358-59 John 59 Simeon Jr 359
SAMPSON, Darius 359
SANBORN, Jacob H 389 James 361 Moses 389 Robert 320
SANDS, John 402 404 Samuel 398 404 Sands & Walton 404
SANFORD SANIFORD, James 330 Thomas 310
SANGLER, Wm 353
SANIOY, John 313
SANSFACON SAUSSFACON, __ 51 Joseph 62 344
SANTON, Gallon 13
SARGEANT SARGENT, John 178 202 Wm 353
SAUNDERS, Capt H 331-34 336 George 331 Henry 330 John 317

437

SAUSIERE SAUCIER, Antoine 400 Bellanne 400 Chement 309
SAVAGE, __ 72 Alexander 388 Daniel 45 48 86 88-9 91-2 313 344 Martin 400 Wesley 313
SAWTELLE, Asa 353
SAWUIRE, Germanis 309
SAWYER, Asa 360 Eliza 396-97 George 315 George W 387 Henry K 59 Isaac 321 James 235 321 M P 391 Nathaniel 178 N 209 Thomas 264 380
SCARLETT, Joseph 315
SCHOEDDER, John 47
SCUDDER, John 47
SCOTT, Aaron 317 Andrew 316 391 396 398 Frances 319 John 361 J W 328 Lewis 398 Moses 322 Robert 396 Wm C 372 Wm 321 Winfield 3 4 6 8 119-20 163 191-96 198-99 221-22 250 258 274 279
SCRIBNER, Simon 311
SCRIVEN, Richard B 326
SEABORN, Robert 330
SEAMAN, Alfred 358
SEARWAY, Francis 313 John 313 John P 314 Samuel 314
SEGEE, George W 365 James 132
SERENE, Michael 308
SERRETT, John 353
SEVERANCE, George 359
SEVEY, John E 381 John S 381
SEWALL, Benjamin 403 404 George P 390 Thomas R 389
SHACKFORD, Jacob 379 Wm 379
SHAOUGENET SARRISIN, 29
SHATTUCK, Benjamin 382
SHAW, Advardes 387 Benjamin 202 387 390 Enoch C 387 Isaac 353 John M 358 359 Joseph 356 Leonard 379 Luther H 359 Neal

D 378 380 382-83 Putnam 310
319
SHEA, James Shea 402 404
SHEAR, Robert 58
SHEET, Samuel 362
SHEIGHEN, Wm 317
SHEPARD, Charles H 320 John
315 Moses 390 Samuel 317
SHEPLEY, Ether 123
SHERBROOK, Lt Gen 14 15
SHERBURN, Wm Jr 360
SHERIDAN, Hugh 322
SHERWOOD, Joseph 369 Joseph S 102
SHIELDS, Ezra 321 John 311 321 Thomas 321 Samuel 311
SHIMON, Clemo 308
SHINING, Francis 310
SHORETTE, Wm 314
SHOREY, David 360 Edmond 321 Edmund 310 Joseph 317
SHUGREN, R 404
SHUGRUE, Dennis 402
SIBLEY, Abram 360 E S 330-32 Ebenezer S 332 336-38 340
SILESTE, Peter 46 62
SILSBEE, Samuel 384
SIMONDS SIMMONDS, Charles 369 373 D A 383 Thomas 383
SIMMONS, Col S S 217 James 356 Luther 321 Wm 335
SIMONTON, (J? S) P 326
SIMPSON, Charles 399 George W 80 Jacob 362
SINCLAIR, Gideon R 356 Jefferson 158 381 390 397 Joseph P 358 J R 53
SIROIS, Maurice 401
SKIDGELL SKIDGELS, Henry 320 Wm 320 398
SKINNER, Elijah 387 Samuel 311
SKILLINGER, Jeremiah 317

SKOFIELD, Thomas 384
SLOAT, James 323
SMALL, James 378
SMART, ___ 323 Charles 45 52 310 319 Charles L 361 Lewis 322 Reuben 63 Reuben S 178 240
SMILEY, John 127
SMITH, Albert, 162 281 Asa 390 Andrew 371 Barney 322 Bartlett 320 Benjamin R 357 Christopher 60 Daniel 310 319 399 David 310 315 319 Dennis 314 343 Edward 389 Ezor 320 Francis 314 Francis O J 110 153 162 202-03 278-80 286 292 George 235 George S 380 382 George W 396-97 Gideon 370 Gilford 322 Hiram T 70 Hugh 311 317 Isaac 310 320 323 381 402 404 Isaac B 398 399 Major James 178 212 230 233 235 James 314 370 John 353 370 Joseph 322 390 Joseph B 357 Joseph L 377 Joseph O 322 J R 326 Leonard 322 Life 378 Mr 177 Nathaniel 322 Paul 312 Rendall 390 Reuben 384 R L 327 Rufus 358 Gov Samuel E 73 76-78 87 89 90 Samuel 397 Smith (&Bull) 372 Smith (&Rogers) 370 Stephen 322 T 370 Thomas 361 Thomas W 168 Walter 387 Wm 335 391 Wm H 377 Wm W 360
SMYTH, G S 35 Robert McNeel 387 391 Wm 387 391
SNOW, Henry 355 Kenny 361 Reuben 322 Warren 324 Wm C 362
SNOWMAN, John 357
SNYDER, Antes 326
SOLEY, Edward 379

SOMES, John 353 Joseph 353
SOMERS SOMMERS, Michael 235
Patrick 402 404
SOMPPHISAW, Joseph 309
Lewis 309
SOPER, Henry R 377
SOUCI, Horace 314 Joseph 314
Joseph Jr 345
SOUCIER, Clement 314 Jere 314
SOUCY, Cylestine 314
SOULE, Solomon 315
SOUTHARD, John Jr 362
SPARKS, Jared 281 285-86
SPAULDING, Alpheus 317 322
Daniel 311 321 Prescott 320
Seth 318
SPENCER, Asa 353 David 353 J
353 Joseph 320 Peleg 16
Samuel 357 362 Stephen 311
SPILLER, Samuel 353
SPOFFORD, John T 315
SPOONER, Asa 358 359
Charles 321 Daniel 394
SPRAGUE, Charles S 358 Henry
A 359 Jeremiah 310 319 Joseph
315 L 328 331 Lawrence 326
328 Peleg 281 Stephen 380
SPRINGER, John 322 George 322
Samuel 322 Studley 322
SPROUL, Amos 389
SQUIRES, Zebedee 345
STACEY, James S 315
STACKPOLE, ___ 320 E G 353
STAFFORD, Edward B 365
STAIRS, Barney 314
STANIFORD, Thomas 68 326-27
STANLEY, George 149 157 217
239 Gould 310 George W 56
STAPLES, John 311 320 Mark
321 Joshua 357 Winslow Jr 353
STARRETT STERRITT, George
388 Wm 319
STAVERS, Charles 358

439

STEARNS STERNS, David Jr 365
Wm 344
STEBBINS, Laura A 403
STEEVES, Andrew 370 Henry
370 James 370 George 370
John 370 M 370
STEINHALL, John W 336
STEPHED, Lewis 309
STEPHEDDO, Phinney 308
STEPHENS, James H 321
STEPHENSON, Isaac 99
STERLING, John 402 404
STERNS, Samuel 388
STETSON, Charles 45 52 157
343 Isaiah 393 George 394
Lemuel 383 Reuben K 390
Simeon 390
STEVENS, Edward 370 Hiram
397-98 Isaac 381 John 311 321
J L 388 Jonathan L 384 Joseph
C 177 236-37 245 388
Nathaniel 381 Peltiah M 319
Samuel 379 Wm 381
STEVENSON, Andrew 102 107
STEWARD STEWART, Charles
397 Frederic 358 Henry L 178
James H 358 John 312 321
Peter 374 Sylvanus 317 Thomas
92
STICKNEY, John 278 384 R C
384
STILES, Abner 321 Asa L 360
Joseph 321 Oliver 370 Stephen
370
STINCHFIELD, Seth 322
STINSON, Albert 384 Horatio N
362 James 323 390 Joseph C
362 Samuel 363 Wm B 365
STITHAM, Andres 320
STOCKING, Samuel 391
STONE, Lewis 310 319 Stilman
320 Wm 319
STONER, Wm 348

STOVER, Wm 315
STRATTON, Wilder 127 396
STRAW, Asa 318 Robert C 357
STREET, Frederick 105 145 J A 373
STRICHMAN, __ 314
STRICKLAND, Hastings 130-33 137-39 146 202 212 356377 391 394 Samuel P 391 393 394 Lysander 394
STRIEBE, Wm 330
STRONG, Caleb 10 16
STUART, John 387
STUBBS, Cyrus 357 James 362 T 365
STUGGS, Ephriam 355
STURTIVANT, Curtis 359 Francis 353
STYMENT, Benjamin 371
SUCIE, Michael 401
SULLIVAN, James 20 Jeremiah 336 Mick 248
SUNDERLAND, G 335 336
SUTHERLAND, Hector 395 Lydia 96
SUTTER, James 321 James A 398 Richard 396 Stephen 396
SUTTON, Capt John 259
SWAN, Caleb 383 Samuel 383
SWEENEY, Edward 314
SWETOR, David 127 James 127
SWETT, Jacob P 362 Winborn A 390
SYDENHAM, Lord 267 269-71
SYLVESTER, David 399 John 312 Samuel 202
SYPHER, David 320
TABOR, Isaac 320 399 J 369
TACHEVAN, __ 115
TAGGERT, Francis 310
TALBOT, John C 380-81 Micah 381 Micah J 264 380 M Jones 380 Peter 380 Peter Jr 380

TALCOTT, Capt A 267
TALLIEUX, Billau 314 Joseph 314 Laurent 314 Rame 314 Raymond 314
TALMADGE, Benjamin 33
TAPLEY, Abner 393 David 371 Timothy C 362
TARBELL, Jesse 316 397 Wm 397
TAREO TARRIO TERRIO, Frederic 308 Lawrance 309 Siomon 308
TARGETT, Francis 320
TAYLOR, Abner 390 Alexander 322 Calvin 397 Elijah 357 George 370 James 308 373 James U 310 319 Jonathan P 248-49 Theodore 387 Thomas 371 Thomas A 393 Wm 370
TECUMSEH, 8
TEILING, Thomas 348
TERRIO, Bellony 45
TEWKSBURY, Parker 322
THACHER, Mary 379
THADDEE, Joseph 314
THATCHER, George Jr 123 Samuel Jr 387
THAXTER, C H 356
THAYER, Solomon 378-79
THEANEY, Samuel 345
THERIAULT, Joseph 27 Remi 401
THIBODEAU THIBODEAUX TIBEDORE, Adolph 314 Alevey 309 Battiste O 314 Betis 309 David 309 314 Fearmer 67 Firman 314 372 Francis 309 314 401 Francois 314 George 309 Greguire 309 Jean Baptiste 27 John 309 314 John B 309 314 John B Jr 309 John B 3rd 309 John Betis 309 John B O 309 Joseph 309 314 Lewis 309

Louis 314 Michael 309 Michel 345 Micheal 314 Registe 401 Simon 314 Susan 309 Oliver 309 Paulet 309
THISSEL, John 390
THOMAS, Isaac 310 316 348 395 James 310 312 John 314 Leonard 398 Prince 356 Stephen 320
THOMPKINS, D D 333-36 Daniel D 337-38
THOMPSON, __ 116 Abner B 102 113 125 149 157 183 186 205 230 237-40 264 E G 387 Daniel 337 James 395 399 James W 356 Jeremiah B 317 John 402 Lewis 378 Nathaniel 317 Tobias 357 Wm 310
THOMS, Harrison G O 359
THOMSON, Charles Poulette 267 George 371-72
THORNCRAFT THORNCROFT, James 321 398
THORNDIKE, Francis 178
THORNER, Norman 336
THURLOW, James C 353
THURSTON, Samuel 388
TIARKS, Dr 75
TIBBETTS, __ 51 __ 350 Asa 387 James 92 Mr 144 249 "Tibbetts" 133 135-36 142 248
TIDD, David 319 John 310 319
TIDSWELL, Richard 310
TIGHE, __ 314 Michael 91 344
TILDEN, Charles K 388
TILLY, Thomas 310
TINGLEY, Daniel Jr 370
TITUS, George N 382 Jonathan 369
TODD, Alfred 310 319 Francis B 389 Israel 398 James 330 Robert 384 R M 372 Todd (&Hill) 372

441

TOLAN, Michael 330
TOMPKINS, __ 350 D D 331-332
TORRANCE, Levi S 360 Samuel S 360
TOSH, James 352 Wm A 361
TOURNEY, John 310
TOWER, Levi Tower362
TOWLE, Elisha 247 356 Francis F 322 George W 353 356 387 John 359 Josiah 87 389 N C 403 Thomas I 360
TOWNE, Ebenezer 310 319 Salem 380
TOWNSEND, Manley B 382
TOZIER, Benjamin F 359 Wm 390
TRACY, Asa 311 317 Israel 361 James 317 Jonathan 311 317
TRAFTON, Eben 399 John 386 John B 396 398 Mark 386 389 Noah 353 Wm B 398
TRASK, Wm 322
TRAVERS, John 317
TREADWELL, Benjamin 320 James 365
TREAT, Joseph 384-86 391 393 Nathaniel 202 Nathaniel G 320
TREVETT, Samuel S 362
TREWORGY, Charles D 359
TRIPP, Thomas 310 319 321
TRIPPLER, C S 327
TRUE, Abner 54 Abraham 394 Jabez 393 Jonathan 397
TRUEWORTHY, Jeremiah 320
TRUNDY, Levi 365
TRYON, Samuel 251 257 374
TUCK, Charles M 353 Andrew 353
TUCKER, Capt 231 Daniel S 381 Isaac 359 James S 381 Joel 316 John 353 Robert Jr 381
TULL, James 320
TURDEY, Henry 309

TURNER, [A?] H 321 Barnard 371
Daniel 402 404 Isaac 370
James F 353 John L 398 Luther
Jr 353 Nymphas 259 354 356
Paul 316 Richard 372 Wm 358
TWITCHELL, Milton 359
TWADDLE, John 316 John 402
TYLER, James 365 W 314 John
277 279 281 284 286 290 292
Lendal 383
TYRELL, Wm 333
ULMER, Martin 390
UPHAM, Edward E 381 George 235
UPTON, James 402 404 Samuel 384 Wm 398 404
VAIL VEAL, Aaron 122 David 321
VALENTINE, Valentine & Collins 289
VAN BUREN, Abraham 326 Martin 70 77 100 102-3 106 109 111 119 122 160-61 163-65 189 265-67 271 (274)
VAN NESS, D 331-32 335 David 276 339
VAN PELT, James 310
VANCE, Wm 378
VANDINE, Ezekiel 320 Wm 320
VANNING (Venning), John 234-35 248-49
VARNEY, Paul 178 Silas 311
VARNUM, Augustus 320
VASSAL, John 314
VASSICUR, Nore 314
VAUGHAN, Charles R 50 60 95-6
VAUGHN, David 369 John 348 Samuel 369
VEASEY, Joshua 382
VEAZIE, Jones P 393 Samuel 153 203 385 393
VERNON, Moses 372 Robert 320

VERRILL, Wm 365
VERSIER, Benjamin 309 Henry 309
VIANCOURT, Phinehas 314
VICKERY, Joel 306
VICTORIA, 23 96 210 223 287
VIOLET VILET, Alexander 309 Augustus 309 Francis 309 Isaac 309 Isaac 3rd 309 John 309 Larison 309 Larrier 314 Razamon 314 Thadee 314
VODGES VOGDES, Israel 330-32 341
VOSE, George 388 Rufus 125
WADE, John317 348 Joseph W 355
WADLEIGH, Azriah 353 Ira 384-86 390-91 394 Jesse 390
WADSWORTH, Samuel B 379
WAGG, James 353
WAGGAMAN WAGGEMAN, George 331-32 G G 336 339
WAITE, Alvin 382 B F 372 C A 327-28 Elbridge W 398
WAKEFIELD, Elbridge G 315
WALKER, Alfred 353 Cushman 319 David 178 209-10 212 Harrison 397 Hazen 399 John 125 387 Joseph 397 Wm B 357 Wm L 387-88
WALLACE, Richard F 338
WALSH, Andrew 316
WALTON, Charles 399 James 398 403 404 Lydia Ann 399 Thomas 402 404
WARD, ___ 404 Catherine C 403 John 330 369 Wm 402 404
WARDLE, James 370
WARDSWORTH, George F 382
WARK (see Werk Work) Samuel 402 403
WARNER, Eben 310 Ebenezer 308 320

WARREN, Henry 178 202 389
Neal 390
WASHBURN, Israel Jr 393-94
WASHINGTON, George 283
WASS, John 378 Wm 378
WATSON, Dr 204 E 404 Edmund
317 Eliphalet 402 Ira 322 John
311 Jonathan 320
WAUGH, George 388
WAYNE, H C 331 333-36 Henry C
337-38
WEAVER, Andrew 398
WEBB, James 320 John 125 264
WEBBER, Ambrose 322 Edmund
308 312 George W 321Isaac
315 Ivory 322 John 73-4
Joseph W
WEBSTER, Augustin 89 91
Augustine 343 Augustus 314
Benjamin 341 Capt 337 Daniel
163 189 190 274 277 279 283-
86 291 292 Ebenezer 132-35
137 142 143 384 393 Ebenezer
Jr 394 John S 383 L B 276 329
332-33 335 338 340 Lucien B.
337-38 Samuel 383
WEDDERBURN, Alexandre 375
WEDDING, Robert 330
WEEKS, Benjamin345 349 396
Hanson 315 Jacob 396 Jacob B
398 John 315
WEIGHTMANS, George 330
WELCH WELSH, Aloniso 311
Alonzo 319 Wm 314
WELDON, John 373
WELLINGTON, Duke of, 16 22
Joel 349
WELLS, Mathias 320 Moses K
308
WENDALL, Wm 330 335
WENTWORTH, John 386 Samuel
353

443
WERKS (see Wark Work Works),
Jacob 353
WESSELS, Henry M 327-28
WESSENGER, John 397
WEST, George 40 62
WESTERVET, Harmon 379
WESTFORD, Wm 315
WESTON, David 321 George M
403 Gershom B 387 John 321 N
53 Nathan 356 Samuel 365
WETMORE, A K 99 Caleb Jr370
Justus S 370 Thomas 37 46-8
WEYLAND, Michael 349
WEYMOUTH, Alexander H 382
WHEATON, C M 369
WHEELER, David E 379 Jacob
321 Horatio G 378 Levi 314
Simon 321 Samuel 378-81
WHEELOCK, ___ 344 Jesse 86
88-9 91-2 314 344 400 Mr 127
WHELAN, Maurice344
WHIDDEN, Benjamin 397 Charles
395 R 372 Randall154 Rendol
380
WHIPPLE, Shilometh S 382
S S 111
WHITAKER, James 330 Thomas
316 Robert 402 Thomas 402
WHITCOMB, Emmons 317
WHITE, ___ 404 Daniel 384-85
393-94 George 402 404
Greenlief 278 H 353Isaac 310
319 320 J 402 Jacob 310 319
James 278 319 Jesse 310 319
John 310 319 Jonathan 319
Luther C 380 Matthew 397
Moses 320 Samuel 384-85
Thomas 319 Thomas 2nd 319
Wm 310 311 319 402 404
WHITEHOUSE, Daniel 315
WHITEKNACT, Jonah 403-04
WHITING, F 331-33 L 334 336-
38 Levi 336-337 338 S 334

S Levi 337
WHITMAN, Ford 386
WHITMORE, Daniel 398
WHITNEY, Benjamin L 383
Ephriam 383 Jonathan 319
Joseph 378-82 Mary 321 Moses
Jr 319 Orris 317 Samuel 319
349 Sumner 396 397 Wm 397
WHITTIER, Sally 320
WHORLEY, Thomas 311 319
WIDGERY, Wm 36
WIGGINS, Mr 325 Benjamin 356
Rufus 319 Samuel 315
WILDER, Bela Wilder 379
Charles 399 Charles W 390 D Jr
383 Ebenezer 378-79 Ebenezer
C Jr 378 Isaac 399 Luke Jr 390
WILDES, Solomon 381
WILDREDGE, E M 389
WILDS, Joseph 346
WILEY, Joseph 89
WILKINS, Almond 311 John 386
WILLET, Alexander 314 Andre
314 Anthony 314 Auguste 314
Battiste 314 Charles 314
George 314 John
WILLEY WILLIE, Hiram 315
WILLIAM, Netherlands 75-7 80
WILLIAM IV, England 96-7
WILLIAMS, Daniel 192 Henry B
379 Hezekiah 388 John 185
391 Jonathan 382 Joseph H 125
Reuel 80 110 160-63 166 168
274-75 278 Seth 337-38
Timothy 383 Wm 308 310 320
327
WILLIAMSON, Christopher 321
Henry 354 356 Wm D 38 44 82-
3 86 385
WILLING, Thomas 283
WILLS, George 384

444

WILMOT, John M 373 L A 373 Lt
Gov 81 Mr 222 Wilmot & Co 349
Wilmot & Peters 72 323-24
WILSEY, Ferdinand S 379
WILSON, Albion P 355 Charles
311 319 Daniel 264 Gowen 264,
278 316 378 396 Harper 370
Henry 353 James 320 John 310
320 330 372 John D 388 John
Jr 387 Jonathan 55 311 Joseph
378 Lewis 382 Martin 387
Matthew 319 Robert 330
Stilman 388 Nathaniel 378 Wm
373
WINCHELL, Wm 399
WINDER, John H 331 340
WING, Aaron A 394 Charles H
178 213 229 236 238 357 Capt
273 277 J C 355 John B 317
Joseph 371
WINN, John 377 394 398
WINSHIP, Benjamin 311 Thomas
311
WINSLOW, Edward 20 H 356
John 27 99 139 John N 399
Nathan 386 390
WITHAM, __ 354 Ward 130 353
356
WITHERLE, Wm 388
WITHERSPOON, Alex W 340
WITHMAN, Jesse 353
WOOBERT, Mr 126
WOOD, Ansel 353 Ansel J 354
Benson D 362 Daniel 178 210
229 Richard 400
WOODBURY, Levi 80 Wm W 381
WOODHEAD, Joseph 330
WOODLOCK, John 314 Thomas
317
WOODMAN, John 378 J M 386
WOODWORTH, T J & J 370
WOOL, John E 113-14 120

WORK WORKS (see Wark Werk),
Jacob 354 Levi 348 S 404
Samuel 316 404 Wm 316
WRIGHT, Alden B 397 Daniel
353 David 372 Fanny 302
George 248 349 James 235
Lewis 308 Mr 188
WULASTEGWIAK, 24
WYLER, Thomas 373
WYMAN, Daniel 320
XAVIER, Chief Francois 29
YARET, Battiste 314
YEARNTON, Isaac 314 346
YERXA, Elias 258
YORK, Daniel B 397
YOU, Conti 314
YOUNG, Alfred 353 Benjamin
355 David 361 Gilbert 55 John
318 370 Lewis 355 Moses H
178

www.ingramcontent.com/pod-product-compliance
Lightning Source LLC
Chambersburg PA
CBHW071222230426
43668CB00011B/1265